IN AND AROUND

HEYBRIDGE

IN THE

NINETEENTH & TWENTIETH CENTURIES

by Beryl Claydon

Best wishes

Beryl Claydon

Foreword

It is always a delight for a local historian to discover that another book on local history has been published. A delight because it ensures that knowledge that might otherwise be lost is retained forever for the local community - And, not just for the present generation but for future generations too.

It is essential in our world in which geographical mobility is commonplace that those who live in an area are able to plug into its past and then in turn ensure that that past is preserved and remembered. One such way of plugging in is to read books such as this one.

Heybridge is so fortunate in having a local historian of great enthusiasm, huge local knowledge, and above all meticulous scholarship. Her name is on the front of this book - Beryl Claydon. Beryl's enthusiasm shines through on every page, her local knowledge has enhanced the book beyond measure, and her scholarship is displayed for all to see. I have only known Beryl for a relatively few years during her retirement but well remember her, on a history walk through Heybridge, pointing out details which others would have missed had it not been for her sharp eye, keen learning, and a true teacher's resolve that we would all look, see, and understand. A reading of this book will also enable every reader to see with fresh eyes and gain greater understanding of the village of Heybridge, and in doing so also gain a greater insight into England's national story.

I look forward to further books and articles drawing upon Beryl's vast encyclopaedic store of knowledge about 'her' village. Finally, I would urge every local resident of Heybridge, as well as those with a Heybridge connection, through family or work ties, and wider still all those with an interest in the history of this county of Essex, to rush out and buy not one copy but multiple copies for friends and family.

William Tyler, MBE, MA(Oxon), MA, MPhil

Times do not change . . . still a status symbol! Left to right:Reg Claydon and Ernie Doe, about 1920

'Annie' leaving Maldon for Osea.
SOURCE Maldon Society

Heybridge Mill 1946.
PHOTO by kind permission of Lloyd Blackburn

Contents

Perambulations and personalities around Heybridge

Introduction

I am grateful to a very long list of people who have helped me in many ways; the bibliography reveals the sources I have used but this book would never have been written without the generous computing help of Mark White and his partner Dawn French of MDW Technology Heybridge, Chris Voisey, and Diane Wintle who helped with proof reading. Thanks to Ellen Hedley who lent many of the illustrations from her collection of historic postcards and to the Maldon Society via John Prime and Lloyd Blackburn, as well as as Lloyd's personal photos.

These notes were initially intended for a leaflet prepared to accompany a walk in Heybridge and to provide material for an exhibition in September 2005 to commemorate the bicentenary of Bentall's factory coming to Heybridge. The exhibition was financed by Heybridge Parish Council and supported by Maldon District Council who provided the design services of Chris Voisey. Visitors to the exhibition were kind enough to say I should write a book lest the fascinating facts I was discovering be lost.

I am most grateful to many people who have known Heybridge a lot longer than I have for their reminiscences and information and have mentioned many of them by name. Thanks go especially to Harold Lewis who has lived the greater part of his life in Heybridge and has answered many of my queries about the history of Heybridge. I have had many conversations; some people would not mind being quoted but others were reluctant. This is the reason why I have not always made direct quotations and have left out references to speakers' origins. When I have learned more than one version of events, I have had to weigh up contributory factors to decide which to use. Joanna Trollope set one of her novels in Bangalore and at a lecture in Colchester Library, I asked if she had been there. She replied that she told readers who remembered the place differently that their memory was at fault! This may apply to some of the entries here. Please let me know the mistakes.

The references and acknowledgements at the end of this history include the sources of information and images featured in the book.

After eight years of research and discovery, the time came to call a halt; such an account is never complete which may mean readers know interesting facts of which the author was unaware.

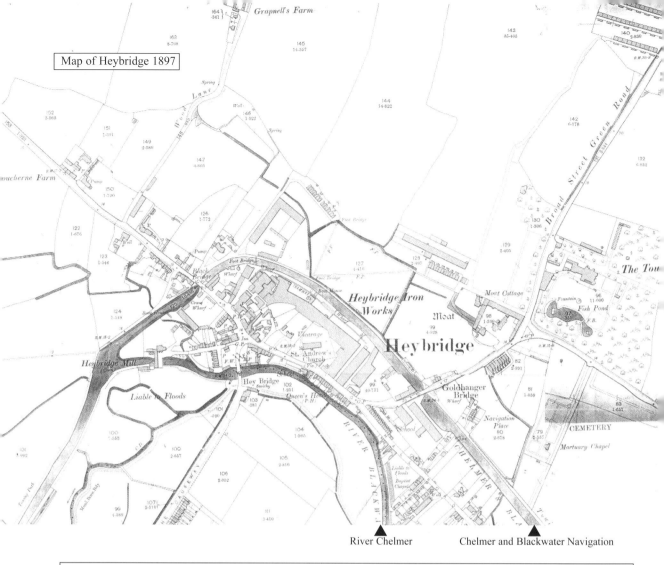

Map of Heybridge 1897

River Chelmer   Chelmer and Blackwater Navigation

Population figures for Heybridge

The population figures for Heybridge show a trend but boundary changes make an accurate comparison impossible:

1801 - 368
1841-   1,117
1881 - 1,677
1901 - 1,623
1931 - 2,061
1951 - 2,253
2001 - 7,627

The population at the 2001 census for Heybridge East, including Heybridge Basin and Osea Island, was 3,882 and of Heybridge West 3,745, with Colchester Road being the boundary between the two. The total of 7,627 will now be greater: houses have been built since then, particularly on Elms Farm. The population is likely to be nearer 10,000.

1.0 History Highlights

1.1 Tidwaldington

Tidwald is the name of Heybridge in the Domesday Survey; it is an Old English place name. An alternative explanation is that Tid lived in a wood (wald) where he had an enclosure (tun). There had been an Iron Age settlement on the north bank of the River Blackwater before the course of the river changed. During the twelfth or thirteen century, the marshland between the Chelmer and Blackwater was embanked and a causeway was built linking Fullbridge Maldon and Highbridge.

In 1276, after a massive bridge with five arches of stone replaced the old medieval one across the River Blackwater, Edward I decreed the place was to be called Highbridge, a Middle English name. This bridge was replaced with the two arched brick bridge in 1870 that has been enlarged since. The bridge between the Causeway and Hunter's Garage has been the parish boundary for centuries. Edward II had this route surveyed in 1324. The causeway is a raised way between Maldon and Heybridge and is the ancient route into Heybridge across Potman Marsh. Heybridge is in the Thurstable Hundred; there were ten farms in Heybridge for at least 800 years; only part of one farm – Canterbury - remains as such today. The historic list of Heybridge farms includes Grapnells, Boucherne, Canterbury, Jacobs, Draper's, Saltcote, Elms, Middle Farm, Glebe Farm and Hobbs and Steele's Farm (now called Home Farm - the site of Bentall's Works' extensions). The only manor was Heybridge Hall. The first recorded chimney in England was at Heybridge about 1271.

Sheep grazing on the Heybridge saltmarshes were an important source of wool for the medieval cloth makers. Before the decline of the industry from 1780 onwards, local women in their own homes would spin wool which was then collected by packhorse to go to the cloth industry centres in Colchester, Braintree, Coggeshall and Witham and wool was exported from Heybridge Creek by ship.

Many hedges and woods were grubbed out early in the eighteenth century to make way for wheat, barley, turnips, and clover.

Heybridge became much larger during the second half of the twentieth century when houses were built on the site of the Towers, in Heywood Way and on the Colne estate, on Jacob's Farm, on May & Butcher's yards and on the former allotments in Heybridge Basin as well as on the timber yard opposite. Further development has taken place in the Crescent Road, next to the canal off Hall Road and on Elms Farm. One hundred and twenty-four houses are due to be built at the end of Hall Road opposite the Maldon Hythe.

2.0 Heybridge Parish Boundary and Local Government

2.1 Heybridge Parish Boundary

On the Ordnance Survey map of 1874, the Heybridge/Maldon parish boundary was a ditch that ran from Hey Bridge, behind the Causeway, to the rear of Maldon Ironworks to the River Chelmer eastward of Tesco's pedestrian bridge. Heybridge had access to the River Chelmer and Maldon Harbour at that point. The last part of this ditch was filled in when the new office block was built between the old Ironworks and the Heybridge Approach roundabout. The Tesco site used to be in Heybridge.

Parts of Heybridge were incorporated into the Borough of Maldon in 1934 when Heybridge Parish Council was abolished. Changes in the Langford/Heybridge boundary have resulted in the boundary being between the railway bridge and the Langford Old Rectory now in the parish of Heybridge. Heybridge no longer has access to the river at Fullbridge

The civil parish of Heybridge used to go as far north as Captain's Wood. The rural parts of Heybridge were transferred to Great Totham when Heybridge became part of the Borough of Maldon in 1937; the civil boundary now crosses Broad Street Green Road making Pleasant Cottage (number 24), Harold Lewis' home, the last house in Heybridge. Great Totham became responsible for burials in this new part of their civil parish but the area remains in the ecclesiastical parish of Heybridge. (Great Totham Parish Council expressed their annoyance at a meeting the author attended). The parish boundary goes south of Barrow Marsh Caravan Park and Vaulty Manor to reach the River Blackwater just north of the Osea causeway. Osea Island is in the parish of Heybridge today. The boundary in 2009 became the old bed of the River Blackwater from Sadd's Dam at the end of Hall Road, behind The Street to the junction with the canal at Heybridge Mill. Visitors leaving Maldon along the Causeway enter Heybridge in the middle of the two arched bridge over the River Blackwater that has been widened since it was built in 1870. Opposite Heybridge Mill, the Chelmer and Blackwater Navigation becomes the present boundary until it reaches the original River Blackwater opposite Maldon Golf Club House which it follows to Langford Road mid-way between the disused railway bridge and Elms Farm roundabout.

2.2 Local Government

In 1896, Heybridge had its first Parish Council which it lost in 1937; its last Parish Council meeting took place in September of that year when the urban part of the village was incorporated into the Maldon Borough. The rural parts of Heybridge were added to Great Totham Parish. Heybridge and Great Totham parishes became part of Maldon Rural District. The Local Government Act of 1974 created Maldon District Council by amalgamating Maldon Borough Council, Maldon Rural District Council and Burnham on Crouch Urban District Councils. While villages outside Maldon and Heybridge had parish councils to decide local issues, Maldon and Heybridge District Councillors became ceremonial Charter Trustees with no powers to levy a precept. Local matters concerning Maldon and Heybridge were decided at Maldon District Council meetings and the primary level of local government was lost. Parish councils look after the immediate interests of their communities and levy precepts to provide money for local facilities. They consider local needs, comment on planning matters and run many village halls, some street lighting and recreational amenities. Heybridge, the largest parish in Maldon District, had no parish council; the four Heybridge District Councillors had to wait for Heybridge matters to come up on the lengthy District Council agendas where fellow District Councillors from all the parishes in Maldon District decided local matters concerning Heybridge and Maldon. Two separate councils were created in 1987; Maldon Town Council and Heybridge Parish Council. Heybridge was one of the largest ratepayers in the district and Heybridge Parish Council was then able to spend the money collected in Heybridge on facilities for Heybridge. The powers and duties of the town and parish councils are the same; the town council has a mayor and a parish council has a chairman, both councils are elected at four yearly intervals.

Heybridge Parish Council 1934: **Back row** (left to right): Ev Last, Arthur Nelson Alexander, 'Padge' Wakelin, Malcolm Willis, William Charlie Last **Front row** (left to right): Mr. Anthony, Clifford Betts, George Free, Mr. Gower, Mr. Weaver. SOURCE Heybridge Parish Council

The bridge boundary between Heybridge and Maldon
SOURCE Ellen Hedley collection

Factors that have influenced the growth and development of Heybridge:

The coming of the Chelmer and Blackwater Navigation
Bentall's move to Heybridge
Flooding risks

3.0 The Chelmer and Blackwater Navigation, and Heybridge Basin

Peter Came's dissertation on the History of the Chelmer and Blackwater Navigation is in the Plume Library. Today, it is the starting point for all serious research on the history of this waterway. Maldon had three churches in the thirteenth century: St Peter's, All Saints and St Mary's. St Peter's and All Saints were combined to form one parish; All Saints. St Peter's church fell into disuse and partially collapsed in the seventeenth century, followed by the collapse of the tower in 1665 which damaged the nave. Doctor Plume, Archdeacon of Rochester Cathedral had been baptised in All Saints Church in 1630 and educated at King Edward VI Grammar School in Chelmsford. He financed the re-building of the tower and the adjoining brick building to house his working library that he bequeathed to his birthplace, the town of Maldon. He left a legacy to support the library and to buy new books. The upper floor housed the library and downstairs was to be used as a free school - the precursor of Maldon Grammar school. The library is well maintained today and welcomes visitors to see the historic collection.

3.1 Origins

The confluence of the rivers Blackwater and Chelmer is nearly opposite to the Hythe Quay, Maldon. The present Heybridge Creek (the River Blackwater) ran behind Hall Road and The Street where wharfs and many small anchorages and landing places were well developed by 1600 along the winding, marshy River Blackwater. Heybridge rivalled Maldon Harbour's trade in importing coal and iron and exporting grain and dairy produce. Goods landed in Maldon had to be taken up the steep hill while Heybridge had flat access to the main roads. The Corporation of Maldon demanded tolls by all users of the Heybridge wharfs from the fourteenth century and in 1618, a chain was fixed across the channel to ensure vessels paid the tolls. In the sixteenth century, it took a slow horse-drawn wagon usually about two days to reach Chelmsford from Maldon over Danbury Hill, the highest point in Essex. The road was a sea of mud in winter and a dust bowl in summer.

The Maldon port had stagnated in the 1790s: the harbour is at the lowest bridging point where fresh and salt water more or less meet and where silt and mud collect. Access to the wharfs at the Hythe and Fullbridge was complicated by the movement of stones and gravel. Hoys, the precursors of barges, that carried coal could only take full loads of 25 chaldrons at the time of spring tides and at other times could carry only half loads (1 chaldron = 1.28 tons). Mill owners along the Navigation at Moulsham, Barnes, Sandford, Johnson's, Paper, Hoe and Beeleigh mills were afraid water from their millponds would be depleted and hinder milling. Only Barnes at Springfield remains intact. Hoe Mill was originally known as Holme Mill; the Saxon word for island is holme. It was sited on the western end of the island formed where the River Chelmer splits in two.

An Act of Parliament in 1766 had failed to obtain permission to canalise the Rivers Chelmer and Blackwater because insufficient money was raised. (An Act of Parliament used to be necessary for each new canal). However, when it was discovered in 1790 that the depth of water at Fullbridge was not enough to take vessels over 50 tons and, since much of the Navigation's traffic was expected to be coal and timber normally carried in vessels of over 200 tons, the Maldon opponents to the canalisation were upset.

Opposition to building a waterway from Heybridge Basin to Chelmsford was led by John Strutt (MP for Maldon 1774-1790) in 1793 when he subscribed £50 to the cause with John Crozier, John Baker, John Sadd and Samuel Bright, all wealthy merchants in Maldon. Water millers were afraid of the loss of water to drive their mills; they and the others feared the loss of income from trade and the revenues from harbour dues if cargoes were transferred from Heybridge Basin to Springfield Basin by water. Indeed, thousands of tons of coal and general goods were shipped annually through Maldon Harbour and taken in wagons to Chelmsford; a slow and expensive method of transport.

When the Navigation was being planned, the Rev. John Priddy, vicar of St Andrew's Church, Heybridge, from 1783 to 1797, noted it would be beneficial for trade in Heybridge and gave it his support. Lord Petre and Thomas Berney Bramston met at the Black Boy in Chelmsford to inaugurate the Company of Proprietors of the Chelmer and Blackwater Navigation that was floated under an Act of Parliament in June 1793. The promoters sought £32,000 in share capital, initially; £23,300 from Essex and £4,100 from Leicestershire in £100 shares. In 1794, a further £8,000 had to be raised. By 1797, Leicestershire investors had bought 157 shares and only 117 shares were retained in Essex because Essex men believed there would be no quick profit but Leicestershire investors had prospered from canals there and in the Midlands. However, by 1850, most of the shares were held by mill owners on the Navigation, principally by Cramphorns and Marriages.

3.2 Route and construction

No time was lost after the passing of the Act of Parliament in June 1793. A committee to manage the affairs of the company was appointed on the 15th July 1793.

John Rennie, the well-known canal architect, was put in charge while his assistant Richard Coates, appointed resident engineer at £420 per annum, actually did the work. In the letter book of the company dated 15th August 1793, there is a letter from John Rennie requesting that Mr. Coates be asked to mark out the line of the new cuts, seek sources of brick earth for the locks, to arrange for stones and coping to be obtained from Dundee and recommending that timber cut to required sizes be acquired. Richard Coates was a Springfield man (1763-1822) who is buried in Springfield Church cemetery. His brother, George, a stonemason, assisted him. Charles Wedge carried out the survey and we know the course of the Navigation from his drawings.

Although called the Chelmer and Blackwater Navigation, the waterway mostly follows the River Chelmer. This waterway is called the Navigation because the greater part is formed from the rivers Chelmer and Blackwater that have been made navigable by straightening and deepening. The source of both rivers is near Saffron Walden. The River Chelmer eventually passes through Chelmsford on its way to Maldon; a total of thirty-five miles. The River Blackwater is known as the River Pant beyond Braintree. It goes through Coggeshall and Kelvedon on its way to Langford where it joins the River Chelmer; a total of thirty-three miles.

Langford Mill's right to water necessitated the use of the former River Blackwater, now named Langford Stream, to flow south to join the River Chelmer at Beeleigh to form the junction with the canalised River Chelmer. Meanwhile, the River Blackwater flowed through Langford Mill and used a ditch flowing southwards to skirt a small island and join the Navigation opposite the Maldon Golf Club House.

In 1792, Nicholas Westcombe, the Langford mill owner, had a survey made which enabled him to cut a channel known as Langford Cut in the following year. This runs parallel to the River Blackwater from his mill to the River Chelmer at Beeleigh. During the construction of the Navigation, the owners of the Navigation paid Mr. Westcombe to deepen the cut to match the depth of the Navigation so that the miller could use the new Navigation. Before the disastrous fire on 25th March 1875, the business man and barge owner Adolphus Piggott was sending out 8,318 sacks of flour annually to London. The third hole of Maldon Golf course is crossed by the disused part of the cut from the Navigation to the River Chelmer. It used to be the depth of the original Langford Cut but later Southend Waterworks carried out work that made it shallower. It still adds interest to the approach to the green. Thereafter, the Navigation followed roughly the original course of the River Blackwater to opposite Heybridge Mill where a new cut, a canal, called the Long Pond, goes under Black Bridge to Wave Bridge where the canal, a mile long, crosses Potton Marsh to the Basin sea lock between the canal and Colliers Reach. The Long Pond skirted Maldon Borough boundary so that vessels using the Navigation avoided paying tolls to Maldon Harbour Board. The Navigation was dug by hand.

Water in ditches from Wickham Bishops and higher ground passes under Langford Road and through the Elms Farm development to join up with the water from the deep ditch along Holloway Road at the bank of the Navigation opposite Heybridge Mill. A chunker or elm 'pipe' was inserted under the Navigation in 1790 to carry this water to the River Blackwater, now Heybridge Creek, at Heybridge Mill. The remnants of this chunker; six lengths measuring 12ft. and 15ft. and one of 4ft. in length, total at least 85ft., were lifted from the bed of the Navigation and taken by lorry to the maintenance depot at Heybridge Basin. The 'pipe' was 29in. across and 16in. in depth. One elderly man told the author he had crawled through the chunker as a child.

The chunker has had to deal with greatly increased volumes of water since the 1990s as impervious houses, driveways and roads on the Elms Farm development have prevented the dispersal of surface water. In 2010, contractors were engaged to renew the chunker. Dams were installed on both sides of the chunker; millions of gallons of water were pumped over the dams to ensure the boats in Heybridge Basin stayed afloat. The new chunker is buried beneath the bed of the canal; it is a large, circular, concrete pipe which takes greater peaks in flow caused by the run off from Elms Farm and reduces the flooding in the area. More than £1 million was spent on repairs and improvements in 2009-2010 including bank repairs at Beeleigh Lock, repainting Wave Bridge, and replacing Hall Bridge while a new crane has been located at Heybridge Basin to help lift out many larger boats for pressure washing and hull blackening.

South of the Langford Road and adjacent to the old railway line in a small field parallel to the Langford/Heybridge Road two depressions with high banks can be seen. They have been created recently to receive water from ditches draining down from Wickham Bishops and to minimise flooding risks on Elms Farm.

There is another deep ditch on the eastern side of Maypole Road which carried flood water from Great Totham via Langford Cross into a wide ditch along Holloway Road. Kathy Lang, who lives in Holloway Road, remembers when a balloon was passed through the Victorian culvert where it had collapsed between Holloway Road and Crescent Road opposite to detect the blockage. This caused Holloway Road to flood causing traffic to be diverted along Crescent Road. Floods are not expected along Holloway Road but in January 2011, after exceptional heavy rain, the entrance to Crescent Road from Holloway Road, near the telephone box, the entrance at the Langford end and Maypole Road were impassable. Another flood closed Holloway Road in the spring of that year.

Heybridge Creek, the original River Blackwater, passes behind The Street from Heybridge Mill to Sadd's Dam (built in 1954). It is no longer tidal since the dam was built to prevent serious flooding in Hall Road. The dam does not allow water to enter the Creek at high tide so that at times of heavy rain water can build up behind the dam. The estuary is known as the River Blackwater from the confluence of the Rivers Chelmer and Blackwater opposite the Hythe until it enters the North Sea.

The Rivers Chelmer and Blackwater drain about two thirds of Essex. Since ditches and streams flowed into the rivers, the Navigation Company was required to build weirs to allow the entry of this water into the waterway and to control the flow where straightening had created a loop. Owing to the slow flowing river, the water over the cills of the locks is only two feet.

The Navigation stretches for 13½ miles and has thirteen locks (locks retain water in the waterway and they enable lighters to go uphill. Springfield Basin is 75ft. higher than Heybridge Basin); this and the towpath were declared a conservation area in 1970. The Navigation was begun in October 1793 at Heybridge Basin and reached Hoe Mill by 1795. The stretch from Beeleigh Weir to Heybridge Basin is the longest section on the waterway without a lock. A new canal was cut from Heybridge Mill to the sea lock at the Basin. It was known as the Long Pond and was outside the borough of Maldon.

The Navigation was 30 feet wide at the surface and 20 feet at the bottom; suitable for 30 ton lighters. A new lock, Maldon By-Pass Gates, was built in the 1990s beside the new bridge over the Chelmer and Blackwater Navigation linking the A414 to Heybridge Approach. Pairs of lock gates last about twenty years and are made by the Navigation Company's staff.

The Act of Parliament authorising the building of the Navigation had granted the Company powers of compulsory purchase and about 63 acres of land were thus obtained for a total of £5,352.2s.0d. The cheapest land on Heybridge Marsh cost just over £32 per acre while Little Baddow Meads land cost £136 and that at Springfield was £279 per acre. The Dean and Chapter of St Paul's Cathedral were the biggest landowners in Heybridge at the time and had to surrender land in the Basin as well as at the Langford end of the village. The blue posts that can be seen along the route of the Navigation are boundary posts defining land acquired by the Company of the Chelmer Navigation. They were necessary then because accurate deeds from maps prepared by surveyors were rare.

About fifty men, who came from Suffolk and who had made the Leicestershire canal, started work at Heybridge Basin in October 1793; they completed the work in June 1797. Digging by hand, they made a navigable waterway by widening, straightening and deepening the two rivers. These navvies (navigators) were paid 15s.0d. a week in cash for a six-day week including nights; a high wage in those days.

Construction of the waterway was difficult because the route is through gravel. Richard Coates overcame this problem by having a wide trench dug and lining the trench with clay. Bricks used in the construction of locks, lock houses and bridges were manufactured locally at Sawpit Field, Ulting and in Boreham. John Haywood, carpenter and timber merchant of Maldon, supplied one hundred and nine loads of faggots and brushwood for firing the brick kilns. Essex is a county with very little good building stone but it has a wide variety of clays and sands that provided the brick, tile and pottery makers with a plentiful supply of their basic materials. Probably about one hundred and sixteen brick making sites were in production between 1837 and 1854. Sixty-seven brickworks are shown on the OS six inch New Series maps revised between 1914 and 1922 but production ceased during W.W.2 because the glow from the kilns would have been navigational aids for enemy aircraft. Only three brickworks remained in Essex around 2000: The Bulmer Brick and Tile Co., W. H. Collier, Marks Tey Brickworks and Hanson Brick, Great Wakering. Locals used to be able to identify where the bricks had been made!

The stretch alongside the Maldon Golf Course is crossed by Chapman's Bridge. This original listed brick bridge was restored in the 1990s. It is interesting to see how original fields were bisected during the construction of the Navigation between Chapman's Bridge and the new Maldon relief road.

Wide-beamed lighters with a shallow draught had plied between Osea and the port of Maldon before the building of the Navigation. They carried heavy loads across the mud flats of the Blackwater on the tide. The channels and locks of the Chelmer and Blackwater Navigation were made shallow enough for this type of craft. They were 17ft. long and 16ft.1in. wide at the gates. So that future generations can see an example of this working vessel, a Trust was formed in 2005 to preserve the Susan, a vessel built in 1950s by Prior's of Burnham on Crouch and moored at Sandford Lock.

The lock between the River Blackwater and the Navigation at Heybridge Basin was completed in 1793; the gates of this lock open toward the Navigation so that the force of the water flowing toward the River Blackwater keeps the gates closed, a pair of gates on the River Blackwater side of this lock open toward the estuary of the lock so that the force of water from the estuary keeps the gates shut. After the great flood of 1953, concrete panels were installed to raise the levels of the sea walls around Heybridge and Mill Beach and a further gate slides across the opening to link the sea wall on either side of the Navigation. The excavated earth and gravel from the sea lock and turning basin was used to make a mound, Lock Hill, for wharves, offices, public houses and workers' cottages.

The Navigation to Little Baddow was completed in 1796 where a coal wharf was built and the first shipment of coal, 150 chaldrons (188 tons) from Sunderland, came into the Basin in the brig Fortune Increase, captained by Robert Parker, then merchants transferred the coal into a lighter called Peace. Colliers' Reach in the estuary is a reminder that ships bringing coal from north east England ports 'laid' in the Reach. Tepin Woodcraft built this first lighter that was towed by horses to Little Baddow where the cargo was put into carts and wagons and taken to Chelmsford. One hundred and fifty sacks of flour from Hoe Mill were carried on the return journey to Heybridge Basin and thence to London.

Under the Parliamentary Act, the Navigation Company was not allowed to own or operate lighters so local men tendered to an agent to shift cargoes. Lighters were not powered; they were towed by horses using the tow path. The Navigation was completed from Heybridge to Springfield Basin in 1797; thirty-nine months' work. The Mildmay entail had prevented development of the whole of Chelmsford until 1839 which is the reason why the wharfs at the head of the Navigation were built in the parish of Springfield as close to the town as possible. Chelmsford town was closely encompassed by entailed land belonging to the Mildmay family, but in that year the entail was broken and about 400 acres of land, adapted for building ground, was sold for about £80,000, in lots to suit purchasers. (Whites Directory 1848).

The population of Springfield grew by 108% in the first thirty years of the nineteenth century while that of Chelmsford increased by 45%; this caused a grave housing shortage in Springfield. "Properties were sub-divided into tenements, rows of terraced cottages were built and old buildings were converted into low rent properties".

Before the building of the Navigation, Colchester and Maldon were the principal towns of the area while Chelmsford was a small market town. The Navigation enhanced Chelmsford's central location in the county; lighters carried greater quantities of cargo more cheaply and quickly, especially fuel and other bulky goods such as timber, stone, manure and lime, that led to the growth of industry and retail trade and resulted in the town becoming the principal trading town of Essex. After the opening of the Navigation in 1797, stone masons, iron works, the gas works, storage for timber, slate and chalk clustered around the Basin. Cargoes, especially coal, were distributed from there to surrounding villages. Villages had wharfs along the Navigation but after 1843 when the railway reached Chelmsford this trade declined.

The Navigation took 30 ton boats up to 16ft. wide with a draught of only 2ft; it is the shallowest waterway in England. Ships as big as brigs could pass through Heybridge lock and lie in the Basin whilst unloading cargo into lighters for the onward journey. Tolls were paid to the Chelmer and Blackwater Navigation Company for passing through the sea lock at Heybridge Basin and the locks on the way to Chelmsford and for docking at Springfield Basin.

3.3 The Basin at Heybridge

This was dug out of Heybridge Marsh in the middle of nowhere and outside the boundaries of Maldon Borough in 1793 from a piece of marshland that had no buildings on it. It could accommodate vessels up to 300 tons. Fullbridge Maldon could accommodate vessels up to only 80 tons. Weather-boarded cottages, numbers 1-7 Lock View, now listed, were built in 1798 to accommodate shipwrights, sail makers and others to work on the ships arriving at this small port which served Chelmsford and the surrounding district. Joseph Sadler was in business as a sail maker and ship chandler in Heybridge Basin until he moved to Maldon about 1870. An employee, Arthur Taylor, bought the business in 1914 and carried on the business as Arthur G. Taylor in the sail loft at Maldon Hythe.

Inside the Basin, it was calm on even the windiest days and Maldon seafarers and shippers could see the ships in the Basin and rued that they were stealing their trade. The port of Maldon's trade declined as trade on the Navigation prospered.

The coming of the canal prompted the Enclosure Act of 1811 which enabled a road to be built to Heybridge Basin and cargoes could be sent to places north of the Navigation such as Witham, Wickham Bishops and Kelvedon. By 1811, the settlement had twelve dwellings, a public house, a foundry, a granary built to store valuable perishable goods and premises for small businesses such as a rope walk, a boat builder and brewery, stables and a shipwright's shop with buildings on the south bank, but there was little development along the rest of the Navigation. The Basin brewery was converted into cottages and a dwelling with four rooms. The land between the Basin and Goldhanger Road was parcelled up into ten lots varying in size from one acre to $3^{1}/_{4}$ acres. Lot 1 was advertised as 'having extensive frontage on the Navigation and was well adapted for a wharf for vessels of large burthen'. The Dean and Chapter of St Paul's Cathedral received £37.13s.4d. for the salt marsh at the Basin in 1796. Perhaps the commercial success of the Navigation may be measured by the rise in the price of land to £91.4s.0d. in 1807.

Opposite, across the lock (now 26ft. wide and 107ft. long) and behind Lock House built in 1842, is a private house which was once the navvies' bothy. South of the entrance to the Navigation on the River Blackwater, the grey painted Defender was berthed for several years. She was built in Lowestoft in the mid-seventies for the Sultan of Oman as a fast attack vessel. Her original name was Al Majiha. She served the Omani navy for nearly twenty years. When Lowestoft celebrated the town's ship building history in 2001, the ship was given back to be part of the display. She has changed hands several times during her time at Heybridge since being gifted back to Lowestoft. A new owner, Royal Navy Lieutenant Chris Enmarsh, moved the ship to Fullbridge, Maldon where she is being prepared to deter Somali pirates from boarding the many ships that pass along the East African coast line. His company is a private protection firm that oil companies hire to protect their oil platforms which are towed close to the coast of East Africa. It is intended that she will be manned by hand picked ex-Royal Marine Commandos and run as a professional naval ship, obeying the rules of engagement. A 40mm cannon has been mounted on her fore deck and a 20mm on her aft deck with two machine guns on each side, giving 360 degree coverage. A Maldon based marine engineering company, run by Jim Dines, has improved the power system and made internal engineering changes to the cabins. This work, including replacing the twin engines, will be trialled in the Blackwater before the Defender returns to Falmouth.

Recently, the picturesque and historic feel of the Basin has been used for film sets including children's films, The Fourth Protocol starring Michael Caine, a Lovejoy production, Changing Rooms, Portrait of a Village and Snow Goose.

3. 4 The inland port of Heybridge

As development took place, the village of Heybridge became an inland port. A number of wharfs were built along the canal: R. and G. Coates, J. Tanner at Black Bridge, Benjamin and Robert Dixon millers from Wickham Bishops and Thomas Maldon of Chignall St James. William Bentall moved his factory to Heybridge in 1805. In 1814 he acquired a site from Matthew B. Harvey called Street House with a malting and a wharf; he added two dwellings, a malting office and kiln, as well as coal, lime and timber yards from Harvey. On the completion of the Navigation, Richard Coates, (who had been the resident engineer and supervised the building of the Navigation) became a very successful businessman with his brother George. They had wharfs and warehouses at Springfield Basin and in Heybridge where they accumulated vast stocks of coal, coke, gravel, timber and lime and owned limekilns. By 1841, they owned thirty-one shares in the Chelmer and Blackwater Navigation and they had interests in ships. On Richard's death, their businesses had a turnover of £10,000 per annum.

Heybridge had been a small port on Heybridge Creek (the River Blackwater) where it joins the River Chelmer opposite Maldon Hythe; merchants had to pay tolls to Maldon Borough. The Navigation had been built outside the boundary of the Borough of Maldon. Development had been expected in Heybridge Basin but wharfs were built in Heybridge where Maldon Borough could not levy tolls. Continued evidence of these wharfs is shown on the 1897 Ordnance Survey map where wharfs are shown along the banks of the Navigation on the north and south banks through Heybridge. It would seem that goods were loaded and unloaded into small workshops and stores built on narrow plots with a cottage. Mr. and Mrs. Len Chaney opened ladies' and gentlemen's hairdressers in the late 1930s in a wooden building on the site of a wharf. The shop was demolished in 1960 and Wave Bridge Court, a development of flats, has been built on the site.

As the twentieth century unfolded, Heybridge was no longer considered to be an inland port and became a market village focused on local trade.

3.5 The history of Moulsham Mill and nineteenth century trade on the Navigation

3.5a Moulsham Mill

The history of Moulsham Mill is not untypical of other mills along the Navigation and shows how they have been modernised to keep up with innovations:

Saxon Times - mill owned by the Abbot and Monastery of St Peter's Westminster.

1531 Henry VIII confiscated the mill on the Dissolution of the Monasteries.

1534 the mill leased to John Longe.

1667 The Strutt family ran it and they rebuilt it in 1712.

1780 white weather boarded water mill built.

The Bullens followed the Strutts; they demolished the wind mill.

William and Henry Marriage, twins, were the tenants in 1840 when they installed steam power in a new brick built mill to supplement the water mill. They owned various mills along the River Chelmer. The Marriages were French Huguenots who had come to Essex around 1640. They settled in Stebbing. In 1647 the religious denomination then known as Quakers came into being; Francis Marriage became the first person to be known as a Friend (it was his great great grandson, Edward Marriage, who bought East Mill Colchester in 1840).

1891 Marriages renovated Moulsham Mill and converted it to roller milling which produced up to sixteen times more per day than traditional wind or water mills. This caused wind and water mills to go out of business. Marriages introduced electricity to drive a pair of stones to grind wholemeal flour, although stone ground flour continued to be produced by the undershot water wheel until 1958. Marriages operated other mills.

1917 The Mildmays sold the mill and Marriages sold the trade machinery.

Moulsham millers constructed a wharf beside the mill on the Chelmer and Blackwater Navigation to receive wheat and coal and export flour. Farmers brought wheat to the mill and returned home with coal that was used in the new steam powered agricultural machinery. In 1840 Marriages installed steam power requiring coal in the mill so they no longer faced the problem of slow flowing river water in times of drought to drive the mill machinery. The mills along the Navigation exported flour to London.

3.5b Nineteenth century trade on the Navigation

Sea going vessels entered the Basin at Heybridge via the sea lock and unloaded directly into the Chelmer lighters which carried coal for domestic use to Springfield Basin and to flour mills between Heybridge and the Springfield Basin when the mills were converted to steam later in the nineteenth century.

In 1842, 60,000 tons of traffic passed through Heybridge Basin. One horse could pull 30 tons of cargo. The Basin was enlarged and improved in 1843. The Lock House, the lock keeper's cottage, was built in 1842. Ships of 300 tons could be accommodated in the Basin but ships of that size could not navigate the silted channel to Maldon Harbour. Small sea going ships could even reach Heybridge which was nearly a mile closer to Witham, Braintree and Kelvedon. Kelvedon flour was loaded onto ships at Goldhanger Bridge (Wave Bridge). Mr. Dixon of Wickham Bishops urged that the Heybridge Hall Bridge be kept high enough for sea-going ships. This bridge was re-built in 2010 but not as high; passengers in leisure boats on trips from the Basin to Tesco's have to keep their heads down when passing under the bridge.

It was not until 1811 that the Chelmer and Blackwater Navigation Company's income was appreciably above its expenditure and a dividend was paid to shareholders. Between 1811 and 1845, the company enjoyed prosperity; greater cargoes were carried more cheaply and the company had the monopoly to carry bulky goods. In 1831, coal represented 73.3% of all goods carried. After 1811, William Bentall and later his son, E. H. Bentall, imported coal, pig iron and timber for their foundry in Heybridge and took out the finished agricultural machinery all around Britain and worldwide. Bentall was also a wholesale iron and timber merchant. 1,890 tons of foreign wheat came through the sea lock at the Basin for mills along the Navigation that was milled with 1,069 tons from central Essex to produce 2,960 tons for export by the Navigation. Other freight was lime and timber.

The Basin spread along Borough Marsh Road (Basin Road) by 1840; The Jolly Sailor, The Chelmer Brig, a chapel, a shop and numerous buildings and wharfs serviced the shipping and barge traffic. By 1840, twenty to twenty-four barges a day were passing through the locks at Heybridge Basin and there was a time when men unloading barges received tokens for one pint of beer at the Jolly Sailor. Coal came from the North East and timber from the Baltic States. The return cargoes were flour from mills sited along the Navigation. In 1848, the Basin could accommodate vessels of 200 tons.

The price of coal was reduced because transport costs of bringing coal to merchants at Baddow Lock were so much lower. Cargoes of coal, limestone, cement and timber were carried from the seaport created at Heybridge Basin in lighters 60ft. long and 16ft. of beam that had a draught of 2ft. The locks of the canal had been constructed to take these horse drawn lighters that could carry up to 30 tons.

In 1846, the Navigation carried a record tonnage but it was largely made up of construction material for the Eastern Counties Railway. The Navigation Company feared the competition and reduced their tolls in 1846. 50,000 tons of cargo was carried annually until the mid 1860s when the rail network became national and henceforth trade through the Navigation declined seriously.

From 1846 to 1865 the Chelmer and Blackwater Navigation Company prospered: revenue from tolls averaged £2,000 per year in spite of rail competition after 1848. Huge quantities of sea borne coal from wharfs in Heybridge were delivered up to 25 miles away to Braintree, Witham and Maldon and agricultural products - wheat, other grain, chalk and lime made up other cargoes. Piggots Mill at Langford received 1,994 quarters of wheat and exported flour. The company was selling land annually as well as willows, pollards, poles and gravel. Heybridge Basin was again enlarged to take five or six more ships.

Bentall continued to import his raw materials via the Navigation. In 1865, he received 2,000 tons of iron, 400 tons of coke, 1,100 tons of coal chalk for his blast furnaces and 31 tons of bricks by boat. Sea going ships could deliver their cargoes to the works while rail deliveries would have necessitated transport from the Maldon Railway terminus. Merchants in Heybridge and Springfield Basin had existing wharfs that had been established before the coming of the railway.

3.6 Springfield Basin: the terminus of the Navigation for Chelmsford

The wharfs here received huge quantities of grain, coal, timber, slate, chalk, lime and stone in open lighters with a capacity of 25 tons that were towed by a single horse; also a wide range of manufactured goods.

The lay-out of the Springfield Basin changed over the years. Horse Pond Bridge used to be over the River Chelmer but the area was redesigned to achieve flood limitation; in 1943 the bridge disappeared to be remembered by a road named High Bridge Road. It was in that year that bombs destroyed the Roseberry Temperance Hotel and a parade of shops. Dora Ratcliff's antique shop overlooked the river; she put up a bell from which hung a rope that the swans learned to pull when they wanted food. A swan sat majestically on eggs visible to the traffic on the road every year.

3.6a Chelmsford Gas Works

Chelmsford Gas Works was formed in 1819. It was the first inland gas works in Britain which became possible because the Navigation could carry huge amounts coal and did so until 1927. Brigs, two masted larger vessels square rigged on both fore and aft masts with crews of four to six men, carried coal from the North East into Heybridge Basin. Their cargoes were transferred into lighters to take coal to Chelmsford Gas Company. Two crews from Chelmsford and two crews from Heybridge Basin worked the Navigation. They both had a bunk house or bothy at Paper Mill that was halfway between Springfield and the Basin. Horses had to haul 20 tons of cargo for eight hours a day against the stream from the Basin to Chelmsford and slowed up as the day wore on. They had ten minute breaks to crop grass.

Two bargemen, a horse leader and a steersman, left Heybridge Basin with a loaded barge early in the morning and reached Chelmsford where they waited for the barge to be unloaded or they would take an empty barge to Paper Mill Lock, sleep in the bothy and stable the horses ready to leave for Heybridge next morning to pick up another barge to travel to Chelmsford that day.

3.6b Brown and Son Timber Merchants of Chelmsford

Richard Coates settled in Chelmsford when the Navigation was finished and became a major carrier. He and his brother, George, carried on the timber importing business of George Clift.

Their nephew Brown and his son took over the business on Richard's death and traded as Brown and Son which they developed into a large general builders' merchants. They continued to bring in all their supplies of soft wood by water until 1972. Travis Perkins are now the owners of the firm in the twenty first century.

In the beginning, Brown and Son used the canal to carry coal for general sale and for heating their furnaces. Over the years, they changed to importing only sawn foreign timber and buying trees locally. After the sea lock was enlarged, small coastal vessels up to 300 tons could be accommodated; sailing barges with a skipper, a man and a boy could pass into Heybridge Basin. Early in the twentieth century, Browns bought timber from the Baltic States in larger steam powered vessels that had to anchor near Osea Island in Stansgate Hole; a deep salt water depression over 20ft. deep in the river where ships always stayed afloat and were anchored. They were unable to enter the sea lock and a string of dismasted Thames barges collected the timber which was towed into Heybridge Basin - the author saw this in the 1930s. A barge named Alice, known as Black Alice, was converted with bunks to house the men employed to transfer the timber from the sea-going ships to the barges to save them going home. Latterly, one or two ships a month in summer carrying 500 to 1,000 standards of timber came to Stansgate Hole. Browns picked Darby, the river pilot, up in Heybridge Square at 4am and then collected Maldon fishermen and drove to them to Maylandsea; they were then rowed out to the Baltic ships. Every sawn plank had to be man-handled from the hold over to the lighters. Ships' derricks swung panels of wood up and over the ships' sides. Workers had half an hour for breakfast and one hour for dinner and finished work at 4.30pm. The work was hard but well paid.

There were water mills at intervals along the Navigation. They ground corn into flour while Little Baddow Mill produced paper. Water was impounded at each mill by a weir to provide a good head of water to turn the mill wheels.

Horse drawn wooden barges and lighters were replaced by motor driven vessels in the 1950s, while in the 1960s all horse drawn lighters were replaced. The last horse man was Fred Hoy. Steel barges came in; their steel corners were cut off each side to get through the locks, later they were welded back on. They were driven by giant, noisy Harbourmaster outboard motors; one benefit was that they kept the Navigation clear of weed. Finally diesel powered units were used for the journey from Heybridge Basin to Springfield Basin. These vessels had no tiller; the diesel unit was manoeuvred to steer them. Timber for Browns was carried along the canal until 1972 when containerisation of timber, improved roads and port links made the trade uneconomical. Browns black tarred timber storage shed and other buildings near Lock House have been demolished.

3.7 1880s' changes in management style

A committee of upper class landed gentry had run the Navigation until the 1880s. They were replaced by local middle class professional and businessmen, among them Frederick, Reginald and Henry Marriage, T. J. D. Cramphorn and three solicitors. As the tolls had fallen, money from the sale of assets was invested: buildings were refurbished and buildings were bought, generating increased income from rents and leases. The small company was efficiently managed because these local businessmen had good knowledge of local conditions and were aware of national trends. This guaranteed the survival of the company for a longer time.

The Navigation sought to attract trade by reducing tolls from time to time. Expenses exceeded income by £5,944 annually on average. In 1867, more coal was carried by rail than on the Navigation; 62% of coal was carried on trains by 1880. The 1894 Railways and Canal Traffic Act limited the railways' ability to raise charges and enabled the canals to be competitive until 1914. A building boom in Chelmsford benefited Brown and Sons because of increased timber imports from the Baltic. Bentall could import iron and steel by rail to Chelmsford and by canal barge to the Heybridge works or by ship to the Basin and barge to the works. Increased road building after 1875 caused stone and crushed granite to be carried along the Navigation to Springfield wharfs. Essex County Council, established in 1888, imported granite via the Navigation after 1892. A large wooden shed on the north side near the Ship Inn was used to store perishable cargoes.

3.8 River pilots

Pilots came into being to guide ships through a safe passage into harbours and through dangerous waters. The Stebbens were very skilled boatmen who, after years of experience, knew the estuary's tides and weather conditions. They guided boats of all kinds, from London and ports along the East Coast, through the Blackwater estuary - Heybridge is seventeen miles from the open sea.

Around 1900, Charlie Stebbens used to row to Bench Head, which is beyond Mersea Island (Britain's most easterly populated island), and Bradwell on Sea in all weathers to meet ships coming up river. These sailing ships could be delayed 12 hours and even 24 hours. With cold tea and cheese sandwiches, Charlie Stebbens had to wait for them - his dinghy buffeted by wind and waves. He brought the vessels to Colliers Reach where the cargoes were transferred to lighters journeying through Heybridge Basin, along the Navigation to Springfield Basin.

Charlie Stebbens gave up being the Trinity House pilot when he took over the licence of the Old Ship public house. His son, Cecil, became the Trinity House River Blackwater pilot and carried out the duties for forty five years. He became lock keeper as well when John Ellis slipped on ice and drowned in the lock in 1942; he combined the two roles until 1945. His son, Ivan David, known as Darby, carried out the duties of lock keeper during his father's piloting absences. Darby ferried his father in the little dinghy, Seagull, to the large timber coasters at the mouth of the estuary. There were often long waits; ships were delayed or diverted to other ports. Darby used to draw the dinghy alongside the tall ships for his father to catch a 30ft. rope ladder to climb up the ships' sides even in darkness and with a huge swell. The ships were piloted up the river to Stansgate Hole off Osea Island. When the ships left the estuary, Cecil often disembarked off Harwich where Darby would pick him up. Darby told Dudley Courtman that on one occasion, in the days before mobile telephones, he remembered the ship dropped Cecil off unexpectedly at Southend and he had to drive from Harwich to Southend to collect him. During the depression years of the 1930s, he would have passed the merchant ships that were out of service moored in the estuary off Bradwell on Sea.

Darby Stebbens piloted the last eel ship, the Solglimpt, into the Basin in 1968. Three generations of the Stebbens family, Charlie, Cecil and Darby, were River Blackwater Trinity House pilots until the 1960s.

3.9 Navigation bridges and locks

3.9a Bridges

The Navigation Company was required under the Act of Parliament 1793 to be responsible for bridges over the Navigation: to build them, maintain them and to build bridges where fields had been severed - John Rennie designed all the bridges. They had clap gates; two gates that were hung on a central post. Horses could push one to go through and over the bridge and the other one could be pushed to allow the horse to leave the bridge. The clap gates prevented field animals from straying.

1. Chapman's Bridge was built in 1796 as a swing bridge which pivoted at one end like a gate. The bridge crossed the Navigation to allow farm implements and people to cross the water. When the bridge was against the canal bank, lighters could pass along the open waterway. Later, this wooden bridge was replaced by a brick bridge that was restored around 2000. It is here that the towpath changes from the north bank to the south bank while a footpath continues under the new bypass road and leaves the Navigation to reach the tidal River Chelmer and Maldon. The rather uneven towpath from Chapman's Bridge to Heybridge Basin is classified as a bridleway rather than a footpath. Cycling is allowed on a bridleway but it is unlawful on a footpath; bicycles may not be ridden on the rest of the towpath to Chelmsford.

2. Black Bridge is one of the four built of timber and brick. This was a cheaper method of construction and, initially, the company was anxious to save money and calculated repairs would not be too expensive. After 1881, the Navigation Company had to spend more on maintaining and repairing ageing bridges and locks than the tolls they were receiving. Over time, the bridges were replaced with brick, steel and concrete structures. Repairs to Black Bridge cost £120 in 1884; the Navigation Company rebuilt the bridge in 1891 for £75 while more repairs cost £40 in 1911. This bridge has always carried a highway. When the weight of steam and other powered vehicles increased at the end of the nineteenth century and the beginning of the twentieth century, it was realised that the Navigation Company could not be expected to provide suitably strong bridges and the Black Bridge was taken over by Essex County Council c.1920. Some say a timber whim damaged the Black Bridge. Work to build the present stone faced bridge began in 1924.

Until well into the twentieth century, Isaac Belsham and Sons, maltsters, coal and coke merchants had wharfs on both sides of Black Bridge.

Black Bridge appears on the 1777 Chapman and André map but Essex County Highways Department would not allow Heybridge Parish Council to name the bridge on maps recently.

3. Wave Bridge - The Chelmer and Blackwater Navigation Company formally handed the Wave Bridge to Essex County Council in 1910. They rebuilt it in 1910 at a cost of £1,624. The ornamental palisading on both sides of the bridge and the Essex Coat of Arms were manufactured in Maldon Ironworks. Wave Bridge was mined in 1940 in case of invasion; the charge holes can be seen today. In 2010 the bridge was re-painted smartly.

4. Heybridge Hall Bridge - The original swing bridge was built in 1787. It was redesigned by John Clark in 1808 and rebuilt by Charles Moss, a bricklayer, and John Johnson, a carpenter, of Little Baddow, for £268.4s.6d. It was rebuilt again in 1877 for £164. The main beams were replaced by steel girders in 1895. This bridge rose high over the Navigation to allow sea going ships to reach the inland port of Heybridge. In 2009, the Inland Waterways Association took away the badly eroded old deck; much of the work was carried out by volunteers. The design of the original timber bridge was carefully followed but the new timber bridge is lower since there are no wharfs between the Black Bridge and the end of Hall Road and Heybridge is no longer an inland port needing the high bridge over the Navigation. Canal users, horse riders, cyclists and walkers benefit from the improved access to the towpath and the Navigation but boat users have to duck their heads when passing under the bridge now. This new timber deck is approached on either side by a track edged with handsome brick parapets. Essex County Council contributed £35,000, Maldon District Council helped with the funding and Essex Waterways and its partners found the rest.

Heybridge Hall and Chapman's bridges were built to enable farmers to access their fields severed by the waterway.

The banks of the Navigation between Heybridge Basin and Hall Bridge have had to be raised since the waterway is higher than Potman Marsh. At the beginning of the twenty first century the grass beside the canal is very green during summer droughts. Is there a problem?

3.9b Locks

The Navigation has eleven pound locks and one sea lock at Heybridge Basin to cope with the 76ft. 11in. drop from Springfield Basin to the Heybridge Sea Lock. The locks are Heybridge Sea Lock, Beeleigh Lock, Ricketts Lock, Hoe Mill Lock, Rushes Lock, Paper Mill Lock, Baddow Mill Lock, Stoneham Lock, Cuton Lock, Sandford Mill Lock, Barnes Mill Lock and Springfield Lock. The locks hold water in the Navigation that would otherwise flow into the Blackwater estuary. The two pairs of gates of each pound lock open toward Chelmsford so that the pressure of the water flowing down toward the estuary holds them tight together.

After the 1953 floods, the sea walls were raised. In 1963, a new sea lock was installed between the River Blackwater and the Navigation at Heybridge Basin to be the same height as the raised sea walls on either side. It is designed to hold back exceptionally high tides from entering the canal and to hold back water in the lock against low tides. The sea lock is 55 metres long by 7.5 metres wide; it is fitted with two upper gates that resemble pound lock gates but are very much larger and with a much more robust hinge assembly. The lower gate is a steel sliding caisson type. The gates are operated by an electric motor. The latest 1965 extension enables vessels of 130 feet in length and 24 feet beam to enter the Navigation. There are three sets of gates which mean there are three lengths of lock that are operational, they are the long lock at 55 metres, a medium size lock at 33 metres and a short lock at 17 metres. The locks allowed coasters to enter Heybridge Basin where timber was transferred into barges from which the sails and tackle had been removed. Browns owned thirteen such barges that were towed by the tug George Ray, captained by Dilbury Clark, two at a time, to the enlarged Basin. A tug had been specially designed at a cost of £7,000 to pass through the enlarged sea lock.

3.10 The history of Southend Waterworks

In 1924, the Southend Waterworks Company obtained an Act of Parliament allowing them to take water from the Rivers Chelmer and Blackwater in Langford for treatment and distribution. Stan Jarvis wrote "Langford Mill was bought by the company in 1924; all the original machinery was removed and a pump installed to extract water from the River Blackwater. The millpond acts as a reservoir and the weir allows excess water to return to the main stream of the River Blackwater". The mill now stands empty.

In 1925, a huge reservoir was excavated at Langford by an army of manual labourers assisted by steam cranes. The site for the waterworks was acquired from Lord Byron who decreed that the works should be screened by trees. The beautiful grounds used to be tended by a team that was also ready to go to any pipe line breakdown in the days before mechanical equipment was available to do the work.

In 1927, the company built the pumping station in Langford to supply Southend-on-Sea. Water was extracted from the Rivers Chelmer and Blackwater and held in two thirty million gallon reservoirs before being treated and pumped to Prittlewell, about 14 miles away. The pumping station buildings of stock bricks with concrete block dressings in some ways resemble a chapel. There were three engines that were larger than a double decker bus, two were always running whilst the third was maintained or repaired. Barring accident or breakdowns, the engines would run for about nine months before being stopped for inspections. The reservoirs received water from the River Chelmer at Rushes Lock from where it gravitated to the treatment plant a distance of 2½ miles and the intake of water from the River Blackwater at Langford Mill. Basically, it went from the reservoirs to the purification works. After treatment, it passed into a 500,000 gallon covered reservoir before being pumped to Southend in the east and to Canvey Island, Benfleet, Pitsea and Laindon in the west where it supplied 96 per cent of Southend area needs. After 1945, water from Langford was also pumped to Oakwood Service Reservoir in London for distribution.

There were two reasons for shutting down the steam boilers in 1963: increasing demand meant more power was needed than could be provided by steam; and the Maldon/Witham railway line was closed so that coal could not be transported by rail. A new all electric pumping station took over. The tall elegant 150ft. hexagonal chimney was felled; the timing was unfortunate because that week the author had used it as a landmark to guide the visiting Clacton-on-Sea ladies' golf team on their way to play a match against Maldon.

The original pumping station works was shut down in 1963 and abandoned in 1970. The building and engine were scheduled as an Ancient Monument in 1986 which safeguards its future. The pump house now houses the Museum of Power which is set in 7 acres of grounds and is run by volunteers. Examples of power sources of all types and the major roles that they have played in history are in the exhibition.

One of the three engines and a pump set named Marshall was rescued. It had been installed by the Lilleshall Company in Shropshire in 1931 and is believed to be the last steam engine built by them. Restoration and conversion to oil was completed by April 2011 and it can now be seen working. Exhibits are preserved in immaculate condition, characteristic of the work of engineers of that era. The enthusiastic, hard working volunteers organise events and exhibitions throughout the year. For example: steam rallies, classic vehicles, heavy horse shows, motor cycle and classic American car rallies to raise funds and stimulate interest. There is a tea room and a miniature railway which takes passengers on a ride around the grounds.

The extensive treatment plant buildings to the west have been completely demolished; there is no trace of them. Oval Park CML Microcircuits concerned with electronic design and manufacture has been built on the site.

In 1970 a new complex was built next to the storage reservoirs which can process 12 million gallons of water daily.

3.11 Company of Proprietors of the Chelmer and Blackwater Navigation becomes a limited company

Acts of Parliament defined the business a company could carry out precisely and in detail. In 1908, Parliament legislated to allow the establishment of limited liability companies. This not only avoids the cumbersome and expensive process of making Acts of Parliament necessary for each new company but it allows companies to be formed with wide objectives: the broader clauses allow companies to develop as business opportunities arise. The Company of Proprietors of the Chelmer and Blackwater were the second Essex Company to change to this status, the Essex Chronicle had been the first.

3.12 Jottings about the Navigation

The salt water of the River Chelmer from Beeleigh to the Hythe froze in 1895; a cricket match took place on the frozen river and people skated.

Willows used to make cricket bats are grown as a cash crop and are an important source of revenue for the company.

After W.W.1, yacht moorings were introduced on the Navigation as well as houseboats; the fees and charges became a useful source of income. A few people lived on the houseboats and did not leave the Navigation; they rowed to the Basin for their water. Later, when people acquired bigger boats and had more navigational knowledge, they ventured into the River Blackwater.

The last cargoes of coal were carried around 1914, thereafter only timber was carried.

Jimmy Woodcraft and his partner Sam Clark, Basin men, owned the barge Diligent; one of the last two barges that used tiller steering.

The author was driving across Beeleigh Bridge early in the 1960s when she saw Mr. Walker, the Witham veterinary surgeon, wearing a blue hunting coat on the bank of the Navigation taking part in an otter hunt. At that time otters were common but they became an endangered species by the 1980s because chlorinated pesticides contaminated the water resulting in loss of habitat and water pollution. Otters are now recovering strongly aided by the UK Biodiversity Action Plan. It is hoped they will be re-established in all rivers that they used to inhabit in the 1960s. While coypu have been eliminated, voles are menaced by mink and surveys are currently being undertaken.

A few fresh water fish pass through the lock gates into salt water where they die. On one occasion when Dennis Hicks was visiting Heybridge Basin, he saw hundreds of dead fish, including a carp in the mud at low tide.

The last ship to unload in the Basin was the Danish coaster Conland, she left through the locks on 2nd January 1972 and Tulip Clark took her cargo to Chelmsford. The large black tarred shed used by Browns for storing timber near the sea lock has been demolished.

Humphrey Spender, the artist and photographer, lived in Ulting from 1949 until 2005. He became vice-chairman of the Chelmer Valley Association that was formed to protect the water meadows of the valley between Maldon and Chelmsford from gravel digging. He scrutinised every planning application relevant to the Chelmer Valley. The Association secured a ban on jet skis and power boats on the fishing lakes.

There were approximately one hundred and forty moorings in Heybridge Basin in 1989; two thirds were leisure boats and some were fishing boats. In that year, the charge for the storage of boats in winter was one of the lowest rent/tolls in the country.

David Patient recalls that the police divers used to train in the sea lock. They retrieved an amazing assortment of articles but never the tools the workmen had dropped!

Visitors will be able to visit the Susan, the last surviving wooden canal lighter on the Chelmer and Blackwater Navigation when she has been fully restored under the auspices of the Chelmer Lighter Preservation Society led by John Marriage. She was built in Prior's yard in Burnham on Crouch in 1953 and was the first lighter on the Navigation to be fitted with an engine.

The Navigation is now a Conservation Area.

3.13 Post W.W.2 and the Inland Waterways Association

Railway companies bought many inland waterways in the nineteenth century during the huge railway building era but not the Chelmer and Blackwater Navigation. This meant that the Chelmer and Blackwater Navigation was not nationalised by the Labour Government when the railways were in 1947.

The Company of Proprietors of The Chelmer and Blackwater Navigation Ltd had to go into administration in 2004 because of accumulated heavy losses. The judge granted the administrator nine months to disentangle the problems. Failure to devise a scheme for the continued operation of the business would have resulted in liquidation; land acquired by compulsory purchase through the 1793 Act of Parliament would have to be returned to its former owners - a frightening prospect. The administrator's duty was to dispose of assets for the benefit of the creditors. This has meant the sale of the tearooms at Paper Mill Lock, The Old Ship Public House at Heybridge, the barge Victoria that offers excursions and the lock cottages at Paper Mill Lock, Hoe Mill Lock and Sandford Lock as well as surplus land.

The Inland Waterways Association (IWA) was founded in 1946. It is a registered charity. It "advocates the conservation, use, maintenance, restoration, and development" of the Navigation for public benefit.

The Inland Waterways Association's subsidiary company, Essex Waterways Ltd, undertook to operate the Chelmer and Blackwater Navigation on 14th November 2005 and the company came out of administration. Essex Waterways Ltd is a registered charity and is able to secure funding from sources denied to the Navigation Company. The Proprietors of the Chelmer and Blackwater Navigation remain the owners but the Inland Waterways Association has undertaken the responsibility for the day-to-day running of the canal and for the income and expenditure relating to it. Letters of Comfort were received from Essex County Council, Chelmsford Borough Council, Maldon District Council and Essex and Suffolk Water Company from whom it was to receive financial help.

Initially, Essex Waterways Ltd appointed Colin Edmund as general manager; their only employee - other employees had to be made redundant. Today, volunteers carry out much of the work.

The Navigation has been plagued by pennywort, a weed from America which spreads at an alarming rate. Volunteers have hand weeded and cleared the waterway but the battle must continue. Grants have been received and some heavy machinery can be used but even small pieces of the weed will take root so continuous vigilance is necessary.

The IWA seeks to continue and expand business activities and opportunities. The income received is reinvested and used to maintain and improve the Navigation. Income is generated from licensing boats using the Navigation, for mooring boats, houseboats and acting as a haven for boats sheltering from the tidal Blackwater estuary, the sale of fishing rights, for operating the sea lock at Heybridge Basin and associated services. Income also comes from the growth and harvesting of willow trees along the Navigation that takes around twenty-five years from planting to harvesting; the bark is stripped with an axe. The trees are felled, the trunks are chopped into sections about 4ft. tall which are split down the natural lines of the wood into a further ten slices. One tree makes between thirty to forty cricket bats.

The four directors of the Inland Waterways Association are unpaid. Over the years, they have co-ordinated large programmes of improvements and secured grants from various bodies to carry out the work. Over £1 million was spent in 2009. Their leadership has attracted many volunteers who carry out much of the maintenance and improvement work. Work parties meet regularly, weekly and at weekends throughout the year under the auspices of The Chelmer Canal Trust. These volunteers refurbished Springfield Basin in twelve days. The national volunteer group, the Waterways Recovery Group, enjoys visits to the Chelmer and Blackwater Navigation. Their February camp in 2011 took out the old Hall Bridge prior to contractors installing new timber deck beams and re-building the brick parapets.

Essex Waterways is responsible for the water supplies, waterside furniture, the operating mechanisms, Lock House at Heybridge Basin, the small office at Paper Mill, facilities for boaters at Springfield, Paper Mill Lock and Heybridge Basin and the maintenance of vessels, motor vehicles, plant and equipment. This huge undertaking by a voluntary association is unprecedented and courageous.

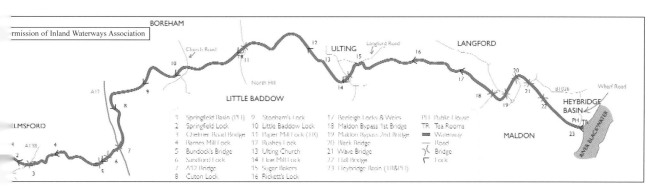

Bridge across the Navigation SOURCE Lloyd Blackburn, Maldon Society
This bridge was demolished to be replaced by By-pass Gates bridge.

The author and her mother among the passengers aboard the barge Julie in 1971

Black Bridge - Essex County Council built this stone faced bridge in 1924 to replace the original black timber and brick bridge

Wave Bridge - The holes beneath the bridge were made ready during WW2 to take explosives should the need arise to blow the bridge

The old chunker coming out SOURCE Maldon District Council

The replacement being installed SOURCE Maldon District Council

4.0 Bentall family, the history of the family and the company

William Bentall's move from Cobb's Farm, Goldhanger to Heybridge began the transformation of Heybridge. William's son, Edward Hammond Bentall, and his son, Edward Ernest Bentall, with their engineering skills, their inventiveness and business acumen changed Heybridge from being an agricultural village with ten farms to a 'factory' town manufacturing agricultural machinery of national and international fame.

4.1 Early history of the family

The land on which William Bentall built Benthall Hall in Bosely in Shropshire in 1535 had belonged to the Benthall family since before the Norman Conquest. William died in 1572. His grandson, Lawrence, completed the house in 1583. The house is now owned by the National Trust and is the home of Edward and Sally Bentall. National Trust Handbook: 'Handsome 16th century house situated on a plateau above the gorge of the River Severn, this fine stone house has mullioned and transomed windows and a stunning interior with carved oak staircase, decorated plaster ceilings and oak panelling'.

The 'far flung' descendants

There are, or have been, branches of the family in Heybridge and Maldon, widely in Essex, in Kingston upon Thames, in Devon, Worthing and Vancouver.

In a directory of 1839, Josiah Bentall is listed as a linen draper, probably at 56 High Street, Maldon. Anthony Bentall came from Missenden into this drapery business in 1848. The firm traded as Anthony and Son from 1866 to 1890 and after that as Bentall and Son.

Anthony Bentall's son, Frank Bentall 1843-1902, married Laura and started a haberdashery store in Clarence Street, Kingston upon Thames in 1867 to impress his father-in-law in premises 24ft by 40ft. This grew to become the flagship of eight department stores throughout the country that were sold to Fenwicks for £71 million in 2001. L. Edward Bentall of Kingston upon Thames owns one of the two original Bentall cars today. Anthony's son, Charles, born 1852, moved to Worthing where he started a drapery business that was later bought by the Kingston on Thames firm.

The success of the Maldon firm is reflected in their expansion. Initially they traded from number 56 High Street, acquired number 58, and in 1882 they added number 50. Numbers 56 and 58 were sold in 1902 and Bentall's retained number 50 until 1910.

The 1861 census records Anthony as having six sons by his first marriage to Emma and living in Church House (famous for being the home of Edward Bright, the fat man of Maldon). In 1891 he is described as a retired draper.

Anthony's son Leonard worked with his father in the Maldon businesses. A description of the firm 1888-1890 says that the drapery shop was conducted on three floors; the outfitters had four floors with the windows tastefully arranged with the newest and most fashionable goods. There was a millinery and mantle making workroom and the firm made a special feature of supplying funeral furnishing and undertaking. In 1891, it is recorded that Leonard and his wife Susannah lived over the shop with ten shop assistants, two servants and three sons.

Leonard Bentall, 1841-1911, was Mayor of the Borough of Maldon in 1890, 1895 and 1905 and it was he who urged the council to build the Marine Lake. He was a Magistrate, a Deacon of the Congregational Church and held many other public offices as well as being a member of the Liberal Party. When he was riding home from Hatfield Peverel around 1899, his horse was frightened by the noise of a motor car and he was thrown to the ground and fractured his skull. He was unconscious for several weeks, indeed he never recovered fully from this accident.

The Devon family and the Vancouver families descended from Anthony Bentall, a yeoman farmer from Halstead who died in 1661. Joyce Woodhouse, whose mother was a Bentall, lived in Felsted. She told me that her mother's brother, Charles, had emigrated to Canada around 1912 after working in construction at Compton Parkinson's in Chelmsford. He had worked his way across the country to Vancouver and eventually founded a famous, most successful, big construction business that traded as Dominion. There is a four block mixed development in Vancouver called 'The Bentall Centre' with Charles' statue in it. He became internationally famous for his charitable work in developing countries to which he gave his money, his time and expertise.

The Heybridge Bentall family tree

The family descended from the Benthall family who lived in Bosely in Shropshire before the Norman Conquest.

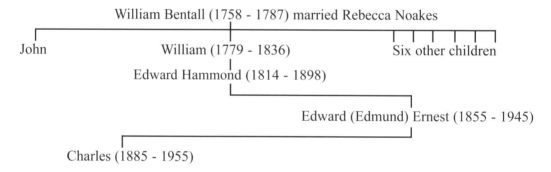

4.2 William Bentall 1779-1836

This yeoman farmer invented the cast iron Goldhanger plough for use on Cobb's Farm in Goldhanger he had taken over from his father around 1790. The plough was made of cast iron, bolted on to a wooden frame. It ploughed more deeply, turned the heavy soils of Essex over more effectively, and proved to be durable and easy to use which resulted in other farmers asking him to manufacture ploughs for them. In 1797, he built a small foundry, a smithy and a joinery shop on land opposite his farmhouse and employed seven men to make the Goldhanger plough. It is thought that this was in the field named Foundry Field in Goldhanger. William pondered whether he should be a farmer or a manufacturer; it was his wife who encouraged him to be a manufacturer and he ceased farming in1795 to manufacture agricultural machinery.

His inventive genius caused his mind to buzz with ideas and he succeeded because he was a brilliant inventor and engineer. Two copies of the plough have surfaced, both manufactured before a patent was taken out; one at Purleigh Hall and the other at Mangapps Railway at Burnham on Crouch. Both have "Warren Maldon Ironworks" in their castings. Joseph Warren originally came from Broad Street Green and later moved to Maldon Ironworks, the site of the present Tesco store; he was not alone in copying this design. Bentall's Goldhanger plough was the first to be manufactured under a brand name on a commercial basis.

William Bentall moved three miles to Heybridge in 1805 to build heavy farm machinery on the former Hobbs and Steele's farm, next to the Navigation. He bought the site from Matthew B. Harvey and the firm was known as Heybridge Iron Works.

The raw materials he needed included coke, which he bought from Daniel Belsham, a Heybridge coal merchant, who coked coal in his coal yard at his wharf in Hall Road, Heybridge where he had a cinder oven with limehouse and kiln nearby. This coke oven, cinder ground and coal yard were still working beside the Hoy Inn in 1828. (Hunter's Garage was built on the site of the Hoy Inn). Later, Bentall imported coke himself. He bought pig iron initially from Robert Greenwood, the Maldon ironmonger, until he imported pig iron direct from the North of England. He also needed timber and limestone.

William Bentall chose to come to Heybridge because these bulky raw materials could be brought in along the Navigation and the finished agricultural machinery to be exported was sent out along the Navigation. Bentall's products were sold through agents to farmers in neighbouring counties. This expansion took place during the Napoleonic Wars when importing wheat from Poland became difficult and vast acreages of land in England were broken up. By the 1830s, William Bentall was producing several thousand ploughs each year and he had added England's first steam-driven threshing machines to his range in 1807. William Bentall invented seed drills, horse drawn rakes and roller crushers but did not take out patents. He made a chest for Goldhanger Church in 1815 and, in 1822, cast over a ton of guttering and down pipes for Southminster Church.

We know that William married Mary Hammond as his third wife. His son James Bentall was a draper in Rayleigh when he married Sarah Belsham on 5th July 1842 in Goldhanger Church and his father was described as a farmer.

4.3 Edward Hammond Bentall 1814-1898

Edward's mother was determined that he should enter the business and arranged that Old Martin, an old experienced workman, should teach her son. Edward Hammond was shown how to make a plough share by Old Martin and Mrs. Bentall rewarded him with a new velveteen suit. Edward Hammond worked alongside men in the workshops to learn the trade. He took over the management of the firm at the age of 22 when his father died in 1836. Like his father, he was a brilliant engineer and an acute man of business. Richard Poole, printer of Maldon, described E. H. Bentall as "a gentleman of fine physique and manly bearing, of keen forethought and highly intellectual and inventive genius". Richard Poole remembers that an iron column was cast and installed by Bentall as a gesture of friendship in the printing works when E. H. Bentall observed that they were in a dangerous condition. Edward Hammond Bentall began trading as E. H. Bentall and Co in 1839. The 'and Co' was fictitious because Edward was still the sole proprietor and it was a private firm until 1946.

4.3a The plough

In 2005, Maldon Museum sought a Goldhanger plough for an exhibition. Fortunately, Paddy Lacey remembered that Norman Wasteney, a Chignall Smealey farmer, was researching Bentall's history. He owned a genuine improved Goldhanger plough that had been patented in 1841. This plough now stands in the courtyard outside Maldon Museum.

E. H. Bentall patented the Goldhanger Plough in 1841 to prevent further copying. Maldon Iron Works' advertisement for iron implements is still on the blacksmith's premises in Bradwell-on-Sea. The firm manufactured Goldhanger ploughs before the design was patented. The plough sold for £3.6s.0d. in 1845 with a 7s.0d. (35p) discount for prompt payment. Fourteen thousand of these Broadshare ploughs were sold between 1846 and 1854. E/ H. Bentall invented the Bentall Patent Broadshare cultivator in 1842. This was the turning point of the firm when 14,000 were sold in the first eight years. Later, he replaced the wooden frame of the plough with rolled angle iron which was stronger and lighter. This was the time when a wide range of farm implements began to be manufactured from iron. Maldon Ironworks' plaque is still on the dilapidated smithy in Bradwell on Sea village advertising iron farm implements. The firm won a gold medal at the Great Exhibition in 1851, which made them famous nationally. They won first prize, £5, at the Royal Agricultural Show in 1854. By 1861, Edward Bentall employed one hundred and forty-five men and forty-five boys. Two thousand cake breakers were made each year and by 1870 twenty thousand pulpers, chaff cutters and oil cake-breakers were produced annually. General castings as well as agricultural implements were in steady demand: grates, range backs, doorscrapers, barge wheels and 'smoking trays' and any parts for other tradesmen which he was commissioned to manufacture. A new gate for the Goldhanger Church yard was made in 1839. Even a lawn mower was manufactured that sold in large numbers.

4.3b Expansion

The success necessitated an extensive building programme: a new factory and buildings that filled in the site between the Navigation and Heybridge Street and a large increase in staff. The well in Well Yard beside the church supplied the factory and Bentall houses, including Woodfield Cottages, with water. This expansion coincided with a run down in shipping. Many Heybridge men went to work at Bentall's, initially as labourers, but later in more skilled jobs and clerical posts. Edward continued to market implements under a brand name on a commercial basis. He relied on mass production, regional distribution and the innovative idea of appointing agents nationally, and later internationally, rather than direct selling to customers. The Bradwell on Sea blacksmith and Doe's advertised their Bentall's agency and the signs were seen until recently. John Wright of Chipping Ongar was an accredited Bentall agent who was struck off the list for selling plough irons made by another firm and this was reported in Circular 23 (Bentall's newsletter).

The agents' customers were encouraged to write complimentary letters, praising the quality of goods, which were to be used for advertising purposes. E. H. Bentall received over 1,000 in one year. Agents exhibited plaques advertising that they were agents for Bentall's.

The Ordnance Survey map of 1874 showed the works to have spread round three sides of St Andrew's Churchyard, hemming it in against The Street while the works fronted the Navigation from Black Bridge to Wave Bridge, covering more than thirteen acres. In 1881, E. H. Bentall employed two hundred and eighty-seven men and fifty-two boys.

Bentall realised that nuts and bolts were costing the firm too much so he invented a semi-automatic machine to manufacture nuts and bolts at a rate of 32 per minute. Bentall Brothers erected a brick building near Fullbridge in 1878 as a nuts and bolts factory. They became a healthy selling product at a fraction of the previous cost. Large quantities in brass were sold to the Admiralty. Victor Moore made taps and dies for the production of nuts and bolts. It would seem the circumstances must have changed, because Peter Belsham's research says that in 1891 Oliver Belsham converted the unsuccessful nuts and bolts factory into a roller flour mill, three floors in height with five pairs of rollers that were steam driven. It was Oliver Belsham who built Fullbridge House, a fine Georgian style house, at right angles to the road that was last lived in by Weston Eve and his sister before being converted into offices. E. T. Baker was running this as a corn rolling mill by 1898; he introduced electricity generated by dynamos to power the machinery and illuminate the premises. Fullbridge had been built originally in 1825, and an iron tank bridge was erected in 1877 which became unsafe during W.W.2 and a temporary bridge was built alongside it and used until 1960 when the present bridge was installed.

During the nineteenth century the Bentall works coked its own coal. Bentall invented turnip cutters, root-pulpers, chaff cutters, oilcake breakers etc. The high quality and range of machinery and the quantities sold brought great prosperity to the firm. In 1871, a German firm from Augsburg ordered 5,000 chaff cutters. This sparked off markets in Germany, Austria, Hungary, Poland and Russia as well as in the Colonies. Records show that whole trainloads of chaff cutters went by rail from Maldon to Warsaw in the late nineteenth century. The business expanded by providing a hiring service for threshing machines that were used only seasonally.

Cast iron grave markers showing the deceased's name and date of death were manufactured at the Heybridge Works and can be seen in local cemeteries.

Edward Hammond Bentall expected his workers to put in long hours for comparatively meagre wages. He visited workshops two or three times a day and slackers felt the weight of his walking stick across their backs. This was a time when many workers walked to the factory. Colin Barbrook's grandfather lived in Heybridge Basin and set off at 6.30am to walk along the Navigation. Although a hard taskmaster, E. H. Bentall looked after men who were sick or who had an accident. He reckoned a bottle of port was the best medicine in the world while Mrs. Bentall gave soup, jellies and warm clothing to families of sick workmen. Long serving, old workers were given a few shillings a week when they became too old to work. When he saw Old Martin still working, he awarded him 12 shillings a week for life. Old Martin stopped work two weeks later but he lived for only four more days.

E. H. Bentall was a keen yachtsman and designed his yawl, Jullanar. His revolutionary idea was to eliminate all unnecessary fore and aft deadwood; this improvement was not generally adopted until the 1890s. The Judging Committee of the Shipwrights' Exhibition 1875 ruled the design was not fit for cruising or racing. The next year, 'The Field' prophesied "she would be a torment to everything afloat". Bentall said his intention was to build "the longest water-line, the smallest frictional surface, and the shortest keel". One of his best known sayings was "If I can put a plough through the earth, I will build a boat to go through water". E. H. Bentall's ideas were realised by the famous yacht designer, John Harvey of Wivenhoe, who applied scientific reasoning and mathematical principles of naval architecture to the design which was, in many ways, ahead of its time. In 1955, a roll of old drawings, revealing the original plans for this yacht, was discovered in a disused room of what became the Benbridge Hotel. They were presented to the Science Museum in London.

One account says that the boat was started at the Bentall factory with direct labour probably with some shipwrights from the Wivenhoe yard until construction reached just above the waterline. E. A. Fitch wrote "It was taken to a field behind what is now the clubhouse of the Blackwater Sailing Club near where the piece of wall of the salt works stands".

The boat was towed to Wivenhoe to be decked, rigged and fitted out as a yawl and was named Jullanar after the Princess of the Sea in the Arabian Nights. Bentall had no opportunities to race her against famous racing boats but she was fast and the boat became known as "an absolute wonder in a hard wind". She cruised to the Mediterranean and proved to be an excellent sea boat but not very suitable for sailing in the shallow Blackwater estuary. In 1877, the Jullanar was sold to Mr. McCleary who had phenomenal success racing her, winning £1,065 prize money in one year. She was popularly known as Bentall's Plough and was broken up soon after 1900.

The crew of the Jullanar was ferried from Osea to Heybridge by the Spray, a flat-bottomed boat designed by E. H. Bentall. E. H. Bentall's son, E. E. Bentall, with his brother, William Rufus Bentall cruised locally in the Spray.

John Harvey emigrated to the USA in 1881 where he flourished as a yacht designer. E. H. Bentall died in 1898 a few months before the founding of the Blackwater Sailing Club.

E. H. Bentall was a member of the Maldon Company of Volunteers in its early days. He raised the 1st Essex Volunteer Engineering Corps in Heybridge in 1865, largely for Bentall employees - it was a breakaway group from the Maldon Rifle Volunteers. E. H. Bentall commanded one company since he had once been an officer in the 23rd Rifle Volunteers, while his son, E. E. Bentall, commanded the second company. E. H. Bentall built the Drill Hall which became known as the Heybridge Headquarters and it seems likely that there was a rifle range on E. H. Bentall's land used for the Blackwater Sailing Club premises since a fragment of one wall, inside one of the existing club buildings, can be seen to bear the marks of bullets. The Volunteers Companies came to an end in 1876. The Maldon Rifle Volunteers, raised in 1860, were absorbed into the 2nd Volunteer Battalion Essex Regiment in 1863. They wore a rifle green uniform from 1883 until 1908. In that year, this battalion was converted to become the 5th Battalion Essex Regiment (Territorial Force) and the scarlet uniform of the regular parent regiment was adopted.

Stuart Joslin knew that his grandfather, James Edward Joslin, was born in 1852 in Heybridge and worked all his life at Bentalls during E. H. Bentall's reign. In 1871, he was a painter living in Hall Road Terrace with his wife and four children. He was still living in Hall Road with his wife and nine children in 1891 but by 1901 he had become a foreman painter and was living in The Street. He moved to 32 Well Terrace, the end house next to the school, in the 1900s to live in housing provided for the foreman grade of workers.

James Joslin joined the 1st Essex Volunteer Engineering Corps in 1875 at the age of 23. The oval medal with a picture of Queen Victoria is a long service medal awarded to him in January 1895 for at least twenty years' service in the 2nd Volunteer Battalion. He became Colour Sergeant, the most senior solder of the 5th Battalion Territorial Force from 1908 to 1914 and is photographed wearing their scarlet tunic. He died in 1944 aged 92.

Many social events were held in the Headquarters until it was demolished in recent times. E. H. Bentall was MP for Maldon from 1868 to 1874 - one term. He did not stand again.

4.3c News

On Tuesday 23rd April 1889 Anne Lewis, aged 28, was walking along Goldhanger Road when Frederick Ford, aged 15, offered her a lift. Mrs. Lewis had a baby daughter in her arms and her toddler son with her. Ford was delivering coal and other goods from E. H. Bentall to poor people in Heybridge. He stopped to unload a bag of coal and left the reins on the side of the cart, returning to find the horse had trotted off through the gates to The Towers. The cart overturned, pinning Mrs. Lewis' legs and leaving her unconscious. She died shortly afterwards. Her husband, Rowland, was a machinist in Bentall's nut and bolt factory and lived at 103 Woodfield Cottages. He later became a lay preacher at the chapel in Broad Street Green.

E. H. Bentall built a large house in Great Totham (the site was then in Heybridge Parish) for his son that was later bought by Sir Claude Champion de Crespigny and renamed Champion Lodge. It has been a residential care home named Totham Lodge for over forty years. "Sir Claude filled it from floor to ceiling with big game trophies; lion, tiger, stag, buck, antelope, warthog, wild boar and every conceivable form of shootable fauna leapt at one from the walls or glowered from glass cases. Even the dining room chairs and the fire side settee were upholstered in zebra skin" (Wentworth Day).

His third son, Frederick Arthur Bentall, was in business with his brother, Edmund, under the name of 'Bentall Brothers, Drill Makers, Fullbridge'. Edmund forsook this business to be a barge-owner and hay merchant at Fullbridge. He became famous as a fine yachtsman and John Howard, the Maldon boat builder, built one of his yachts, Box Iron, as well as the barge Hyacinth for E. H. Bentall in 1889.

E. H. Bentall built The Towers in 1873 (see 5.1). He was a JP, a Non-Conformist and he founded the Reform Club at 52 High Street Maldon in 1874 which recruited 200 members. The premises had reading and conversation rooms, library and billiard rooms and, at the rear, quoits grounds, skittle alleys and pleasure grounds where garden parties were held occasionally. The club moved to no. 52 Silver Street in 1900 and became known as the Constitutional Club.

E. H. Bentall died in August 1898, aged 84. His coffin was driven in a glass carriage through a crowded, silent Heybridge to the Maldon Railway Station for the journey to Boxted for burial in the family vault.

James Wentworth Day did not like Edward Hammond Bentall although he acknowledged his inventive genius. He describes him as a man who thundered out passages from the Bible to his family and his work people and ruled his wife and children with a rod of iron. E. H. Bentall was a man who surrounded his house with enormously high, strong, concrete walls because he feared he might be besieged and beaten up one dark night by a mob of dissatisfied work people. The pretty French governess of his children, who had been dismissed on the grounds that she was pert, answered him back, and was a bad influence on the children, was the mother of a brood of his illegitimate children who were hidden away in France. This did not become known until after his death but explains his many business visits to France where he had set up an agricultural machinery factory to support his second family.

4.4 Edward (Edmund) Ernest Bentall 1855-1945

The management of E. H. Bentall and Co. was undertaken by E. E. Bentall who was married to Maud Miller, in 1885.

The Pictorial Record of Witham and District described Heybridge Works around 1880. This is an edited extract:

"Bentall's was one of the chief firms in the country concerned with the revolution of farming methods by the introduction of machinery. Much of the machinery employed was invented and improved by them and they made and repaired it all on the premises. Their reputation for high quality led to the utmost confidence in their products. Their reputation went back to the invention of the Goldhanger plough. These ploughs were turned out in large numbers also lever, double tom, mangel and potato ploughs chiefly made to be drawn by two horses. The Goldhanger plough was widely used by most of the farmers in this area when ploughing with horses until the 1930s.

The main entrance was in Heybridge Road where a large pair of gates opened on to the main yard. To the left was the enquiry office, and on the right the private and clerical offices which were connected to every part of the works by telephone while a tramway intersected the premises giving every facility for the transit of goods from one part to another".

The magazine described the various departments including the moulding shop and foundry which were the basis of the works 400ft. long by 50ft. wide containing three fine cupolas, constructed according to Mr. E. H. Bentall's own ideas. The furnace was fitted with a Baker's Pattern Blower, driven by a 10hp beam engine and there were also core drying ovens, black sand beds and other necessaries for casting purposes. Castings up to 10 tons were made. A small brass foundry was also attached.

"Next the smithy, where implement parts such as plough beams, spindles, tines, bracings, etc, were prepared, from the large stores of iron being on hand. The turnery was housed in a building 200ft. by 50ft. A photograph shows lines of machinery powered by belts suspended from overhead power to lathes, drills, shaping and planing machines etc. Adjoining the fitting shop, the iron and wood parts were put together and the machines built up ready for painting. This was done on the floor of a large two-storied warehouse, 300ft. long by 60ft. wide, where the larger implements, such as mowers were stored. The upper storeys contained stocks of grist mills, food preparers and smaller machines generally, which were constantly being depleted by the execution of orders. The woodworking departments included a wheelwright's shop, where felloes, shafts, spokes, etc., are prepared from roughly shaped timber; a wood turning shop fitted with four large lathes, the saw mills and carpenter's shop. These were fitted with circular and band saws, boring, tenoning, morticing and planing machines etc., of a most improved character; close at hand was a large store filled with shaped timber in the rough, in addition to which large stocks of wood in plank and baulk were on hand, seasoning for future use."

Ev Last was a Bentall's pattern maker in the days before drawings for steel components. The patterns were painted red and hung in the store to be collected by factory workers when needed. Peter Gladwell was a pattern maker who was appointed foreman of the wood shop where wooden components for elevators, conveyors, and replacement parts for old ploughs and disc harrows were made. The beechwood was soaked in oil which made the wood very hard.

Products were moved around the works on rails through big double doors. The nut and bolt factory presented a very busy scene where some hundreds of machines were employed on various stages of the manufacture. There were numerous stores throughout the works. The Navigation ran alongside, on the banks of which were wharfs for storing iron; about 1,000 tons of pig iron was stored.

The firm had its own diesel electric generators in a building running parallel to the canal. The engine produced DC current. At times when the outside AC supply was cut, switches had to be thrown and belts changed to obtain power from the firm's generators to keep production going. Jim Mudd looked after this operation and sounded the works' siren.

E. E. Bentall and his works manager invented a safety mechanism on the Bentall chaff cutter. The feed rollers stopped automatically if an arm or hand went too near the knives. This invention resulted in increases in sales because they were the finest in the world.

Realising the importance of the internal combustion engine as a source of power for agricultural machinery, E. E. Bentall designed and built a petrol engine to power a wide range of agricultural machinery in 1900. His design concentrated on two things, economy of operation and strength of construction. Pistons and cylinders were made of especially hard metal to reduce friction to a minimum and a cleverly designed and patented diaphragm pump was proof against all leakage. The components were standardised so that repairs could be carried out by farmers with Bentall spare parts.

The Bentall engine was a slow running machine with extremely low petrol consumption, and so easy of access that any farmer could himself replace a defective part. "They were the lowest priced petrol engines on the market" (Peter Kemp). They could be used to drive chaff cutters, crushers, pumps and even milking machines. Thousands were sold. E. E. Bentall was awarded gold medals at the Exhibition in Turin for the chaff cutter and the petrol engine, and awards elsewhere.

At the same time as E. E. Bentall was designing a petrol engine for farm use, he had the idea of adapting it for use in one of his many hobbies. E. E. Bentall was the first man to own and drive a car in Maldon in 1900. It was a twin cylinder Georges Richard. He replaced this with a four cylinder Richard Brasier two years later. E. E. Bentall engaged Ernie Linnett as his chauffeur; he had been articled to the company at the age of thirteen. He was to go on to become the chief engineer of the Bentall car department.

4.4a The Bentall car

E. E. Bentall set about designing a car. At the time, petrol engines for cars were made with separate cylinders and he adopted this principle. In 1905, the company invested £60,000 for serious car manufacture using Bentall's foundry to manufacture the majority of the components and a chassis of Bentall's design. These vehicles had the fuel tank under the front seat and a distinctive round radiator in the beginning, manufactured in France by Molineaux. Teams of skilled workmen built one vehicle at a time and Ernest Linnett was the foreman of the car building shop. In Peter Kemp's opinion, there was no better English car of its date and price class; he lists ten of its virtues including the excellence of its gear changing.

Originally, four models were made; a 2 cylinder 8hp car, only two of which were produced, and three larger cars rated as of 11, 16 and 16-20hp. The 11 hp two seater car cost £220, the 16hp car cost £278 and the 16-20hp Landaulette, built in 1908 with standard side entrance was marketed at £420. Later, the 8hp chassis could be bought as a van or commercial traveller's brougham. There was only one local agent, Glovers of Witham, who ran a whole fleet. London sales were handled by Acre Autocar Co. of 117 Long Acre Street and sales depended on personal recommendation. Locally, the Rev. Eyre, Rector of Great Totham from 1877 to1918, a noted motoring enthusiast, sent his 16 year old groom to learn how to drive. Sir Fortescue Flannery, Maldon's MP, bought one of the last 1912 16/20 cabriolets finished in dark green and black striped livery. (A lorry was first used at the factory on 6th November 1905 and it was still in use in 1927.)

Up until 1912, about one hundred cars were manufactured. Customers could specify which car bodies they wanted and were offered a choice between Thomas of Islington, Munnions of Chelmsford, Adams of Colchester or a coach builder the buyer selected.

Ernest Linnett retired in 1951. He had driven Bentall's customers and had accompanied a Great Totham doctor to Scotland in a car he had built. On that journey, they achieved 45 mph and did 18 miles to the gallon. In those days, motorists wore goggles, deerstalkers and waterproof driving capes.

Munnion's of Chelmsford, coachbuilders, finished one car with an ash frame, green baize hide seats and hand-turned bright brass mirror. The car had been sold to a civil servant in Sri Lanka. It returned to England in 1951 where it was used as a tractor for four years on a Devon farm before being restored. When Bentall's advertised for a Bentall car to celebrate their one hundred and fiftieth anniversary, the farmer was persuaded to part with the car. Ernest Linnett came out of retirement and rebuilt the engine from memory and supervised the first restoration which took two years. The four/five seater open tourer body was crafted by Munnion's as their last coachwork job. After Bentall's Heybridge liquidation, the car was bought by Mr. L. Edwards Bentall of Bentall's PLC, then the owner of the department store in Kingston upon Thames, for whom Richard Peskett of Hindhead carried out a fine restoration. The car had been built some months before it was registered on 28th April 1909 with the number F3243. It had four cylinders, 16-20 horse power, 2418cc and reached a top speed of 28mph, standard side entrance and the market price was £327.10s.0d. The car has made visits to Maldon, Heybridge and Langford Museum of Power.

Charles Bentall, E. E. Bentall's son, had one of the 16-20 models and drove it over 50,000 miles before handing it over to George Bacon, one of the first commercial travellers to use a car for his job. He used the car for many years and covered a huge mileage in it.

Just as the Bentall car was to go into production with all the necessary tools and jigs made and purchased, two blows made the car unattractive proposition for buyers. Firstly, the monobloc came into fashion and secondly, the introduction of a horsepower tax based on cylinder diameter. The Bentall 'square' engine with diameter and stroke nearly equal attracted a higher road fund tax. Other, later manufacturers were able to switch their engine designs to ones that attracted a lower rate of tax. It was too late for Bentall's, even though their cars were of good design, sound and easy to drive in comparison with other current models.

The cars were built in the building running parallel to the road on the way to Springfield

Cottages from Black Bridge where Alan Collins now has a garage. Even in 1907 the firm was exporting cars; a photograph in a Queensland Australia motor magazine shows Mr. Tremearne and Captain Woodger standing next to a Bentall's car beside the Cutty Sark in that year.

John Parker has researched the history of the Bentall car and discovered that there is a second car in Australia owned by Mr. Rod Banks-Smith of North Dandenong Victoria. This car appears to be a pre-production prototype made in 1904, one of two runabouts to test their viability before manufacture began in 1905. They were never offered for sale but we may assume that the Bentall family used it as runabout and gave it to their friend, Noble Pennall, who took it to Australia. About 1955, Rod Banks-Smith, a keen pre-First World War motoring enthusiast, discovered this wreck of a car and was able to acquire it. He was a qualified mechanical engineer and painstakingly restored this two-seater, 2 cylinder and 8hp runabout. Because the prototypes proved to be under powered, production models had four cylinders and 16-20hp.

E. E. Bentall hosted a meeting of the Essex Automobile Association in the spring of 1906 when Wolseys, Fiats, Mercedes, Darracqs, Humbers and a massive 70 horsepower de Dion drove up the drive to the Towers.

The venture into car manufacturing was a costly failure; the tooling up and production planning had cost £60,000. However, the designing experience of developing the petrol engine was not wasted because the knowledge was used to develop and manufacture petrol and paraffin engines for farm use. They produced the first horizontal engines in Britain and sold thousands of them.

1907 Victoria County History lists Bentall's products as: ploughs, horse gears, chaff cutters, mowers, root pulpers, nuts and bolts, harrows, root cutters, horseshoes and grist mills.

By 1897, pig iron came directly from the north of England by sea and the Navigation until 1984; at least 1,000 tons were held in stock at any time.

From 1904, Bentall's manufactured valves for internal combustion engines for W. G. James Ltd in Osnaburgh Street in London. Mr. James' father had been station master at Maldon East Station. Precision engineering was needed for the manufacture of valves; Bentall's were contracted to W. G. James to supply valves to Dennis, the maker of fire engines, Listers of Dursley, manufacturers of stationary engines, Fords, JAP General Motors and the general motor trade. Bentall's were producing a million valves a year by 1955. Ray Burns joined Bentall's in 1953 and became foreman of the stores until Acrow closed the valve shop to transfer the manufacturing to another company in their conglomerate, then Ray Burns became a progress chaser until Acrow closed the works in 1984.

Bill Oliver, who researches the service personnel killed during W.W.1 and 2, notes that Bentall's factory was on a three day week when W.W.1 was declared. By 1914, around six to seven hundred workers were employed and the works covered 14 acres. The factory produced over 14 million shell cases as well as their traditional agricultural products during the war. The demand for agricultural machinery increased as serious food shortages led to increased home food production. Bentall's had their own electricity generating station to avoid production stoppages expected during the war.

Bentall's must have been one of the first firms to employ women in the foundry at the beginning of W.W.1; pneumatic hoists were installed to help women lift heavy weights. Alfred

Moody was employed as a shorthand typist around 1920 but after a short time decided he preferred an outdoor life. It is interesting that a man had learned this skill then because it became a woman's skill soon after. Mrs. Dowsett, whose husband became Mayor of Maldon much later, taught shorthand and typing in Miss Cottee's school in Chelmsford in the early 1920s where she taught the author's mother. Peggy Dibley left Maldon Grammar School early in the 1930s as her grandparents thought she would do better to learn office skills rather than stay on at school. Her parents were fined because they had signed an agreement for her not to leave before she was 16. Peggy Chapman, nee Bright, left Witham Senior School after one year to go to Miss Isted's in Hatfield Peverel to learn shorthand and typing. She left two years later in 1942 at the age of 14 to work at W. A. Claydon's where the two men clerks had been 'called up'. She worked there for 40 years.

On a cloudless night, Friday 16th April 1915, a German Zeppelin Airship raided Maldon and Heybridge at 12.15am. Jim Clark, who worked at Bentall's and lived in the Roothings, picked up an unexploded bomb at Heybridge Hall that was slightly larger than a miner's lamp and looked like a bees' nest.

Leaving off time was fixed at 5.30pm in April 1916, a time clock for recording the time employees worked was introduced on 16th September 1916 and the 47 hour week began on 1st January 1919 when work started at 8am.

Alan Bingham, a clever engineer, was works manager from the early 1900s to around 1920. He developed the No.7 mower and invented the chicken plucker. He had to leave Bentall's on 17th April 1928 to carry on his own business with his sons at the Friary, Maldon, where he had a small iron foundry. Mr. Powell succeeded him at Bentall's.

On Tuesday 2nd May 1922, there was an engineers' lockout at Bentall's, leaving the men unpaid until 12th June when the gates were unlocked. Betty Feeney was the daughter of Evelyn Wood Last, known as Ev, a staunch socialist who worked as a tool maker at Bentall's. He is remembered for the public service he gave to the village. Betty said her father told her about Sam Ruggles from Springfield Cottages and seven other men who wanted to start a union during W.W.1. They were called in and sacked and told to join the army since there was no other work in Heybridge. Fortunately, all survived the war.

At the end of W.W.1, E. E. Bentall joined an association of engineering firms under the name of Agricultural and General Engineers Ltd (AGE Ltd). The share capital of the company was turned over to the new group. Although they were the largest firm in the consortium, they had only one vote.

The firm prospered in the boom years that followed the war but the AGE group could not weather the economic slump that followed and went bankrupt. Many lost their jobs at Bentall's. Crittalls were expanding their Witham factory and provided a special coach to transport their workers. Peter Newton's father, a carpenter, found a job at Crittall's; he cycled there from Heybridge to work a 12 hour day shift one week and a 12 hour night shift alternate weeks for 49s.0d. a week. He bought two of his six sons and himself new boots at the end of the first week. Peter Newton's father continued to work at Crittalls until he retired. The family moved from Boulton Cottages near Mill Beach to a council house, 3 Colchester Road, around 1931. Other Heybridge men went to work at Crittall's. This was a time when unemployed people had to appear before a magistrate who had to certify that they had actively sought work - if they did not, they had their benefit cut by a copper or two.

The inter-war years were lean times; during the Depression of the late 1920s and early 1930s, most Heybridge men were unemployed as Bentall's was suffering from the economic downturn when new farm machinery was not being bought. Fred Mott records that in 1928 Bentall's workers were on short time; 7th January a five day week, 8th February a three day week and on 12th August a five day week. This was at a time when there was Saturday work. Sidney King, Sheila Bremner's grandfather, was head carpenter at Bentall's in the 1930s and trained apprentices. Before W.W.2, Alf Bacon drove the old flat bed open lorry to Maldon East Station daily around 4pm with heavy machinery. Peter Gladwell was foreman of the wood shop in the 1950s and 60s which was located in the former motor shop and supervised the manufacture of wooden grain conveyors, crates for the despatch of goods and various wooden goods used throughout the factory. In 1935, Bentall's sold tractor disc harrows for £34 and a tractor plough for £14.7s.0d.

E. E. Bentall, with help from his friends, bought back the ordinary shares of his own company from the Receiver in 1933 and began the uphill task of restoring the company's fortunes. Hard work and sacrifices by staff and directors resulted in the debts being cleared and the borrowed capital repaid. The accounts showed a small profit in 1938.

E. E. Bentall was chairman of Heybridge Parish Council and a District Councillor with O. D. Belsham in 1898 at which date Heybridge was an electoral division of Essex County Council. Miss Miller, Mrs. Bentall's sister, lived on Cromwell Hill in a house that is set back next to the Masonic Hall, she taught June Carpenter at St Andrew's Sunday School. Mrs. Bentall went to live in Bell House next to Wickham Bishops Church. E. E. Bentall sold The Towers in August 1925.

Shortly before W.W.2, Bentall's was contracted to Handley Page Ltd, aircraft manufacturers, of Cricklewood, North London to manufacture parts and assemblies. They became the firm's main sub contractor. They produced the front floor (bomb floor), front and rear gun turret decking, undercarriage assemblies, tail fins, control cables and many other small parts for Handley Page 'Halifax' bombers and parts for Horsa gliders that carried troops to the Continent on D. Day. Bentall's sub-contracted the work to a number of large and small firms in the area as far out as Clacton on Sea and Southend, including John Sadd and Crittalls. E. G. Claydon, the garage proprietor in Hatfield Peverel, stood and worked alone machining components to very exact dimensions daily in his garage premises.

Mr. Harry R. Chick was a clever engineer, a good organiser and a successful businessman; he was works manager of Bentall's before and during the W.W.2. His day began with a tour of the works and little escaped his notice. He made known his displeasure of mistakes and poor workmanship but bore no grudges and never referred to the matter again. He called the men 'son' when speaking to them. He was totally committed to the firm; he stayed on when workers were on overtime and even had his hair cut in his office. He was also a talented artist. In addition to manufacturing war supplies Mr. Chick expanded the firm and continued to manufacture agricultural machinery, increasing production to cope with the revival of agriculture; the output of agricultural machinery was doubled. One thousand men and women were employed. He had to leave when Bentall's became a public company and the structure of the company changed.

Betty Feeney was born in 1916 and died 2008; she left school at 13 to be apprenticed to an upholsterer in Witham. Charlie Belsham sold her a bicycle for £5 and she cycled to work. In bad weather, she used the train from Maldon East Railway Station. The fare was 6d. each way; finding the fare was difficult on her wages of 5s.0d. a week. She married and had two sons and a daughter. When the marriage failed she earned money by repairing and altering clothes at home. During W.W.2 Betty worked at Bentall's making bomb floors for Handley Page Halifax bombers. One girl had to hold the heavy parts in place sitting on a stool while another girl riveted them. Mr. Chick ordered that all stools should be removed. She was sacked when she went to object and immediately went to Crittall's and got a job as a welder. Crittall's said, "Not another one". As a socialist, she was pleased to find the firm had a closed shop policy and joined a union. In the late 1960s and 70s, Mrs. Feeney was a popular teacher of soft furnishing at Friary evening classes after gaining qualifications at Chelmsford Technical College. She was a passionate member of CND and went on many marches in the 1960s.

She did not lose interest in politics in her old age. The home-made poster in her living room proclaimed:

> "Tony Blair,
> the bastard,
> I did not vote for him"

Joan Fenn told the author she spent her childhood in King's Lynn. She enrolled in the Women's Technical Service Register and attended a course in London followed by work at de Havilland's Mosquito factory at Hatfield. After a further course, she worked at Marshalls' Flying School where aircraft were repaired. She was then assigned to Bentall's as an inspector for the Aeronautical Inspection Directorate checking Halifax bomber parts. At first, she lodged with Mrs. Reed in Boulton Cottages, and later with Mrs. Playle in Hall Road before marrying Dennis Fenn, the Heybridge man who became a teacher.

4.5 Charles Bentall 1885-1955

Charles Bentall lived at Five Corners, Wickham Bishops, a house that was built by the Bentall family to their own design in three phases beginning in 1880 and completed in 1905. He then moved to Bridge End House next to what became the Benbridge Hotel and lived there during W.W.2. He joined the local Home Guard and chose to be an ordinary soldier not an officer. Peggy Dibley remembered taking notes from Charles Bentall in Bridge House for a book about how to run a company. Acrow converted the house into offices for the management team when they took over the company. For a brief time it was a students' hostel.

Five Corners was sold to the Prances in 1927, when the two brothers (one was a priest) and their sister returned from South Africa. In 1940, Miss Prance was living there alone and feared the house would be commandeered by the army so she arranged for Dr. Barnardo's Homes to rent it. Miss Prance moved into a cottage in the grounds and bequeathed a parcel of land on the site to the Scouts which they use as a camp site. In 1945, Lister Bass bought the house and it has been the Bass family home since. Henry Bass and his family and Rodney Bass were living there in 2010.

Bentall's remained a private company until 1946 when it became a public company with Charles Bentall as chairman and David P. Ransome became managing director the next year. He had been with Ransome, Sims and Jefferies and brought managerial staff with him; F. W. Curle as works manager, A. Clark as fitting department superintendent, L. Hipkin as foundry superintendent, B. Jacobs as buyer and E. Jolly as head of drawing office and Mr. Chick had to leave. The flotation was necessary since private family companies could not finance large scale industrial re-equipment after the enormous increases in personal taxation. The firm's flotation as a public company meant there was money to re-equip and expand. David P. Ransome introduced new products including ally trailers, muck spreaders, potato spinners, weighing machines, elevators and Powling Processors. The manufacture of ploughs was discontinued.

In 1949, Bentall's bought Tamkin Bros. of Chelmsford who manufactured a wide range of machinery. They were famous for their steel tractor wheels which were of a single plate with unique curved lugs bolted on each side; they manufactured one-man operated two-row sugar beet lifters, the tamkin-rafo hay sweep, machinery for harvesting potatoes - a potato spinner, tamkin-bird road bands and the tamkin darby combined mole drainer pipe and cable layer. This production was transferred from their Chelmsford works to Heybridge.

During W.W.2, Bentall's worldwide sale of coffee processing machinery fell but after the flotation there was money to expand this side of the business. There were only two companies specialising in this machinery in the country. Bentall's trade recovered and sales rose six fold, their technicians travelled the world advising growers on mechanised coffee processing and their coffee crushers were used throughout Africa. A Bentall company was set up in Zimbabwe in the early 1950s.

After W.W.1, Bentall's bought a huge aircraft hangar and erected it on the north of the canal. It stood empty until 1949 when a new foundry was built within it. The building was lit by natural light and had open air space. The facilities for the men included showers, footbaths, wash basins and lockers. One night, a laminated wooden strut caught fire. Prompt action by a security man and Tom Jarvis saved the building. Wood and metal patterns were made in the new pattern shop next to the foundry. Pattern making is the most skilled job in a works and demands absolute accuracy.

The letter Charles Bentall wrote to Frank Andrews in 1945 thanking him for 53 years' service reflects the loyalty of many workers to the Bentall firm. The firm's existence for one hundred and fifty years was celebrated in 1955 when there were five hundred employees.

In the 1940s, the office and works staff began work at 9am, lunch hour was from 12.30pm to 2pm and leaving off time was 5.30pm. After W.W.2, the works staff began at 8am. A tidal flow of workers on foot and bicycle traversed the Causeway in the morning and evening and the long lunch break enabled workers to go home to eat; it was the custom for many to do so.

Another tradition was the widespread use of nicknames in all walks of life. Here are a few: Padge Wakelin, Lofty Gooch, Tubby Wager, Quaff Gill, Chink Gill, Dicky Taylor, Shaver Gill, Kipper Blighton, and Long Tom Hawkins. Denys Harrison in his book The Story of a Waterside Community lists fifty used in the Basin and Shirley Burns (nee Boutwell) had seven brothers who were all known by their nicknames.

Tom Jarvis organised the Quality Control Department. The firm had set up a training department in the 1960s and when the director of training left, Tom was asked to supervise the five year apprenticeship programme part-time. The apprentices respected Tom Jarvis; they appreciated his wise leadership and the quality of the courses he devised. Apprentices followed a full time mechanical engineering course in their first year and then went to college one day a week while they gained six weeks' experience in each department of the works to enable them to decide which specialism to follow. Braintree College was chosen because their courses were geared to the needs of Lake and Elliotts', Bradbury's and the Rayne Foundries, which suited the requirements of the Bentall's works. Apprentices went on to take City and Guilds examinations, Higher National Diplomas and Certificates while some studied further to gain degrees This was the era of Training Boards that were an incentive to firms to participate in apprenticeship schemes. Bentall's trained forty boys at a time. In total, one hundred and twenty-eight apprentices started these courses. Many continued employment at Bentall's while others were assured of posts elsewhere because of the high reputation of Bentall's training scheme. Martin Shaw completed a mechanical engineering apprenticeship and won the best apprentice of the year award. He was one of the technicians who visited Venezuela and Tanzania to demonstrate mechanised coffee processing. Julian Lewis chose electrical engineering. Steven Nicholls became a self employed technical author and his brother, David Nicholls, went on to be in charge of the computers used in the manufacture of the Triple 8 Tourist Class racing cars. A gauge of the success of the scheme is illustrated by the efforts boys from a wide area made to gain one of the limited number of places.

Harold Lewis started work in the turnery at Bentall's in 1940 at the age of 14. He worked on lathes for about a year but he persuaded his father to ask the management if he could transfer to the drawing office where he joined John Playle. David Ransome placed his men in supervisory roles when he became managing director in 1947. This caused Harold Lewis to seek a job at Maldon Ironworks. Sadd's took over Maldon Ironworks and when they realised they had no drawings of their products, they asked Harold Lewis to work in Sadd's offices to produce them. The job did not work out so he went to work for a firm of consultant engineers in Colchester. The firm was asked by the National Coal Board to design a coal plough. When Harold Lewis' connection with Bentall's and ploughs was remembered, he was asked to be responsible for the design. He worked with National Coal Board staff as consultant and his design of a percussive coal plough to work at the coal face was accepted. The contract for manufacturing the coal plough was placed with Bentall's and Harold Lewis was brought in to supervise the production. He was promoted to be Bentall's chief draughtsman. Harold Lewis was the research and development manager when Acrow failed in 1984.

Managing director, Jeff Roberts, succeeded David Ransome in the early 1950s. In the mid-1950s, he combined Bentall's with J. Woolley of Tamworth who manufactured food mixers for animal feed and this resulted in a further advance into the grain storage and drying businesses by Bentall's. Stanley Cutler, Woolley's works manager, came to Heybridge and later became managing director of E. H. Bentall's where he developed the grain handling activity. The Bentall factory workshops were confined to the south of the canal, other than the generating station, the motor shop and the foundry, until Acrow's extension in 1974. North of the canal, the Moat (known locally as a pond) covered the present car park adjacent to St Clare's Hospice. This was fed by a stream that wended its way from south of the Roothings gardens through what became Bentall's Sports Field, to Colchester Road, between Well Terrace and the school, to Hall Road. This ditch was piped but in 2008 heavy lorries broke the pipes and caused flooding at various points; they have had to be renewed. Older Heybridge residents, including Jill Babbage and

Chris Wareham, remember climbing over the fence from Stock Terrace to collect frogs' spawn and watch sticklebacks in the streams that ran through this field.

4.6 Acrow 1961

Bentall's became part of the Acrow Group. They bought Bentall's in a deal with S. Josephs and to gain a source of labour for producing scaffolding to meet the demands of the building trade boom.

William A de Vigier, a Swiss refugee, had arrived in London in 1935 with £50. He invented steel props which were adjustable for length by means of a robust screw thread. This was to revolutionise scaffolding. He called them Acrow props. He had named his company after his solicitor, Arthur Crowe. His first works, the Coronation Works, were in Saffron Walden. By 1939, 40,000 Acrow props were in use in England.

During W.W.2, de Vigier's factories manufactured bomb trolleys, parts for tanks, engine frames for Mosquito aircraft and forms for the concrete Mulberry Harbour. He introduced equal pay for women welders because they made fewer errors than their male counterparts.

After W.W.2, William de Vigier expanded in Britain and worldwide as a public company. The Bentall site saw the development of a giant complex covering 150,000sq.ft. and costing £2million. The plant was heated by direct-fired natural gas. The administrative office block was built in 1974 on Bentall's Sports Club site and is now the site of Bentall's Complex (see section 11.2). The executives' offices became a student hostel temporarily; later it became the Benbridge Hotel. Mr. de Vigier, Acrow chairman, said at the opening ceremony on 4th October 1962 that Acrow bought Bentall's because the firm had failed to progress with the times and that he would make Bentall's the brightest jewel in the Acrow crown.

Acrow promised there would be no redundancies when they took over. Harold Lewis' father, Albert, had served Bentall's since 1919 but six months after Acrow took over in 1961 when he had six months to serve before he retired, he received his redundancy notice. Albert Lewis' pension was 10s.0d. for every year he had served after 1919. Sixty-five other employees including John Nicholls after forty-five years' service, and Jack Newton were made redundant. In 1981, twenty-four of the three hundred and seventy-two employees were made redundant.

Acrow ceased to make traditional agricultural products in Heybridge and branched out into products to meet the changing needs of agriculture. With the coming of combine harvesters, farmers were faced with post-harvest problems of storage and the need for grain dryers. Simplex of Cambridge had been formed in 1936; De Vigier bought the company and transferred production to Heybridge early in the 1980s. This firm and the various firms operating on the Heybridge site were henceforth part of Bentall Simplex. This included a production line for corrugated sheets with shallower corrugations that allowed the free movement of grain when the silos were being emptied. The panels could be rolled to match the various diameters of the silos being produced. Another production line manufactured steel sheets, vitreous enamelled, used for green forage silos and manure. In the early 1970s, Goldhanger silos were developed for the drying and storage of granular products. The design for the arrangement of bins/silos was adapted to suit the available farm building space; the largest single unit could store 100 tonnes of wheat. Bentall's new products were innovative bulk storage systems, machinery for slurry conservation and horticultural equipment. Bentall Simplex elevators and conveyors were matched with their seed cleaning machines and circular grain silos named Big M. An advisory service was also formed. Bentall's grain drying plants were selling well to North America, Australia, Africa, (Ivory Coast, Zambia), Europe, (France, Spain, Switzerland), and South America (Venezuela, Nicaragua).

The firm had many agents in the world, especially in the coffee growing areas adjacent to the equator, that passed requests to home based Bentall representatives who travelled the globe. All aspects of business within French speaking African countries were considered so vital that Bentall's had two established agents in France. The United Kingdom and Ireland was covered by area representatives. When technical problems arose, a Bentall service engineer was sent immediately, anywhere in the world. This happened around 1968 in Eire when harvested wheat contained a large amount of dust. The wheat was being dried at a low temperature for biscuit making and the dust slowed the throughput. Six technical staff were sent from Heybridge to sort out the problem. Messrs. W. Powling, H. Lewis, G. Dalton, S. Oxley, P. Tatlow, R. Birdsell and staff from the agent went; this slowed down manufacturing in Heybridge.

Harold Lewis, as research and development manager, remembers visiting clients from 1960 onwards. He went to Hungary five times (he did not like drinking their coffee but Hungarians liked his tea), to Italy twice to inspect machinery Bentall's had installed to dry rice, to Canada three times for grain drying machinery, to Portugal twice about rice drying machinery, to Sweden for 800 tons of hard board for the manufacture of bins, to France three times, Holland three times, and to Iraq when Saddam Hussein was in power in 1980, where he had designed machinery to deluge sheep by spraying them. He made day visits to Ireland, driving to Heathrow, catching a plane to Dublin and returning the same day.

Harold Lewis supervised the installation of a grain drying plant at the co-operative farm at Paks near Sezekszard in Hungary. The plant had been ordered very late. The maize harvest was being collected when heavy rain for several days delayed the operation of the plant that had been officially opened in October 1972. The president of the Dunamenti Egyesules set the farm members two tasks; one, to assemble a building over the plant so that the plant could be operated in all weathers which was accomplished in five to six days; and two, to use a bulldozer to dig trenches to be lined with polythene and into which the undried maize could be deposited and then when the clamps were opened in February, the maize was dried and came out in fine condition. Previously, maize was cob dried maturely in wire net cages with a loss of 59% of the crop.

Bentall's employees in the drawing office were amused by one project. A prototype of a nuclear shelter was manufactured in Sawston before the factory closed and installed on the Heybridge factory site. It had vitreous enamel panels and was stocked with items needed to survive the days after a nuclear bomb attack. The man in charge of marketing had brochures printed but no shelters were sold.

Most of the components, such as the saw chain, electric motors and the petrol engine (which came from Aspera in Italy), were bought in and assembled in Heybridge. The managing director of this part of the Acrow Group and the production was transferred to Heybridge.

Coffee machinery such as hullers and pulpers and whole coffee processing installations were sold to Africa (Zaire Ivory Coast, Somalia, Dahomey), and South America (Venezuela, Peru, Chile). Farmers in developing countries sought Bentall's hand operated machinery.

Harold Lewis went to Venezuela with Mr. Taylor to erect and assess a pilot plant that had been designed to clean water used to convey the coffee cherry through the pulping machines so reducing the pollution from the pulp when the water was discharged into streams or rivers. 5,000 gallons of water was used to wash one ton of coffee beans. The water became red and polluted rivers and soil. The machinery aimed to make the re-use of water possible but proved to be suitable only for small areas. The trial plant was at Aroa, 60 miles from the factory at Borquisimeto where they were based and from which they were taken by road daily. Aroa was a tiny village with one shop. Andrew Springett was another Bentall's apprentice who worked abroad selling, setting up machinery and servicing plant in countries including Arabia, Venezuela, Iran and Nigeria.

Bentall's ball bearing company products were in demand worldwide; indeed Bentall's were selling to more than sixty countries.

Christiane Lancaster's parents were Indo Chinese (now Vietnam) who left their country when they feared accelerating civil war. Christiane was educated in French universities and had degrees in French and Spanish and was qualified as a teacher in France. She met her husband when teaching in England. They were both teaching after their marriage when they decided to leave teaching in April 1975. They agreed to take any job, Christiane saw a job advertised at Bentall's in the accounts department, and she applied for it and was accepted. Her manager thought she was over qualified for the post but the firm had unknowingly acquired an essential member of staff. She was able to translate all enquiries from French and Spanish speaking clients; deal with quotations, prepare leaflets and brochures for printing and proof read the work produced by agencies. She helped to prepare the leaflet on ball bearings that had a photo of her right hand displaying bearings and her, on the cover, on her bicycle by the Navigation.

Mrs. Lancaster accompanied foreign customers to act as interpreter on their visits to the Heybridge factory and sites in Essex and Suffolk where Bentall's equipment existed and was in operation. In the office, she was a credit controller corresponding with problem foreign clients, translating letters of credit and invoices issued by the Export Department.

There were spin offs to this work; she accompanied wives of important Venezuelans shopping at Libertys and met the 'Number 2' of Zaire who invited her to visit his country before their civil war. She attended the Acrow conventions under the auspices of the Swiss chairman, Mr. de Vigier.

The journeys by Bentall's staff and the work of Mrs. Lancaster illustrate the global nature of Bentall's business in the twentieth century. The firm was carrying on foreign trading begun by E. H. Bentall over a century earlier.

Initially, trade unions were not encouraged and clandestine meetings took place in workers' homes. Eventually, George Wager started a branch of the Transport and General Workers' Union and became the secretary. Bernard Towson was responsible for founding the branch of the Amalgamated Engineering Union. Others followed and shop stewards were appointed. There was one strike that Mr. de Vigier settled personally; he called the leaders into his office and sacked them all.

Doris Chapman grew up in Sunningdale until she went into service in Kensington aged 15. She started as a scullery maid, and then worked as kitchen maid before becoming cook. She married

Percy who was estate carpenter for Peter Jones at his farms in Goldhanger, Peldon and then Latchingdon. She cooked meals at the Latchingdon Primary School for ten years before she moved to Bentall's to run the factory canteen in the old kitchen at the Headquarters. All the food at Latchingdon Primary School and in Bentall's and Acrow's canteens was prepared with fresh ingredients. The kitchen was dark and difficult to keep clean and even had dog hairs from the dog training sessions. Acrow built modern canteen premises on the former office block site behind the Benbridge Hotel. All the equipment was new but the roof leaked and Mrs. Chapman mopped up puddles on arrival in the mornings. The staff ate downstairs and workmen upstairs. Mrs. Chapman used to get a lift to Heybridge with a Bentall's workman; they left home at 7.30am; she travelled by bus when he lost his car. The factory employees had a choice of two main courses and two puddings. She cooked roasts, meat puddings and shepherd's pies and sometimes chipped potatoes. The second courses included rice puddings, spotted dicks, fruit pies and custard. Gladys Wire prepared the vegetables. Apprentices paid only 9d. for the meal. All workers' meals were subsidised. Mid-morning and in the afternoon, trolleys with tea and coffee and titbits - bread pudding was a favourite - were wheeled across The Street from the Headquarters into the workshops and offices. On her first day, when the afternoon tea trolley came round Christiane was surprised to find out that staff always brought cakes in on their birthdays. It was a tradition and typical of the friendly family atmosphere in the works. She found it a contrast from teaching when there is often no time for a break. Many people who have worked at Bentall's have stressed how happy they were working there.

Acrow Heybridge was a division of a very large and profitable organisation with full order books. Although other companies in the conglomerate had gone into administration, the employees were shocked when, in August 1984, receivers came into the Heybridge Works to value the assets. Bentall's Heybridge works were closed down and most of the Heybridge workers were made redundant. Some continued to be employed until February 1985. Mrs. Lancaster worked for the receivers until March. Bentall's workers who lost their jobs received no compensation and lost some of their pension rights.

A two day auction sale of Bentall's machinery was held in April 1985 and details were given on the sale notice; over one thousand lots went under the hammer. The factory buildings erected in 1869, which fronted The Street opposite the Heybridge Inn, were demolished in 1987. The few factory buildings that have not been demolished within the site have been converted to other uses. Behind the 2 metre high brick wall stretching from Going's Wharf to the churchyard, instead of shops and offices, many businesses operate on the site today. The largest firm is Wyndeham Heron Print Works who use the huge modern factory building erected by de Vigier on the Bentall's Sports Ground. The administrative block has been converted into a shopping centre, offices, veterinary and pediatrists' surgeries (see section 11.2).

The Bentall Car 2 seater model SOURCE The Bentall Story by Lt.Commander P.K.Kemp FRHist.S., RN

The Goldhanger Plough SOURCE The Bentall Story by Lt.Commander P.K.Kemp FRHist.S., RN

Colour Sgt
James Edward Joslin
By kind permission of
Susan Watkins

Wash Day at The Towers by J Playle

5.0 The Towers and The Lodge

5.1 Acquiring the site for the mansion

Edward Hammond Bentall decided to build himself a mansion. First he had to obtain the site. Deeds show that Oliver Herring rented Heybridge Hall from the Dean and Chapter of St Paul's Cathedral. On 9th June 1848, Edward Hammond Bentall purchased four acres of Heybridge Hall land including land south of Goldhanger Road on which were located Well House, yards and gardens, appurtenances, one little meadow and a croft. At the same time, he bought land north of Goldhanger Road up to Beckingham Road. He paid £325 to the Dean and Chapter of St Paul's Cathedral for the two pieces of land. Since Oliver Herring had entered into a lease for twenty-one years on the land south of Goldhanger Road on 24th June 1844, Bentall had to pay Herring £275.15s.6d. for the loss of the land in that lease agreement.

A map of 1874 shows E. H. Bentall personally owning The Towers on 12 acres of land; Hobbs and Steele Farm House, now called Home Farm, with the Plantation, now King George V Playing Field, as well as the land south of Goldhanger Road which became the vegetable garden.

5.2 The Lodge

E. H. Bentall built the Lodge before embarking on The Towers in order to test the feasibility of a pioneering form of construction using concrete blocks cast on the site in variously shaped moulds. It was the first time concrete was used as building material in this country. The Lodge was built in 1870 on the land north of Goldhanger Road bordered by what was then Broad Street Green Road.

The Lodge, a listed building on Colchester Road, is now painted pink and is all that remains of the original prestigious estate. The listed building is described: the building is constructed with an early, and stylistically elaborate, use of concrete as a building material. It has a central stack with 4 pots with Greek key design in Classical style. The side elevation has a Doric column, pier with 2 pilasters, circa 1870. Attached to the right side is a pedestrian gate, flanked by pilasters with cornice over and two large square concrete carriage gate piers, incised to represent masonry with stylised Greek-key design above heavy wooden gates with elaborate iron grilles at top.

Joy Price (nee Wire) remembers playing with Marjorie Butcher, the daughter of the gardener, who lived in the Lodge in the early 1940s and Betty Chittenden went to Marjorie's birthday party there during the W.W.2.

After The Towers was dynamited, the Lodge was left standing. Henry Jackson, a Londoner, was looking at the derelict building when the site foreman jokingly said 'You would not want to buy it'. Henry did and paid £1,000 for it in 1960 and lived there for about thirty years until he went to live in Boucherne Residential Care Home. The present owner enjoys living in the Lodge with its pretty little garden.

5.3 Building The Towers

In 1873 E. H. Bentall chose Charles Pertwee, a little known architect, to design the mansion, The Towers, to incorporate his innovative ideas. The cast blocks were decorated by Italians and it is probable that concrete was used for economy reasons since aggregate could be obtained locally and Portland cement could be brought round cheaply by water from the works at Dartford.

Also, chalk was turned into lime that could be used to make cement for the concrete buildings. Mr. Bentall worked closely with the architect on the shape and layout of the house so that he could indulge in his hobbies of astronomy, natural history, botany, and fruit culture and provide secret rooms and passages for his cult of spiritualism (a popular Victorian pastime) in the forty nine rooms. The house was two storeys high but the tower to the main house was three storeys high giving views over the Blackwater estuary and the surrounding land. There were no fireplaces in the original building; heating under floor was by ducted hot air to all rooms. All the windows were double glazed to ensure an even temperature all over the house. The mansion was sumptuously decorated. The building cost £65,000.

His passion for Italy was reflected by the classic Italian statuary, and the many good pictures including some first class reproductions of the Renaissance painters. Several Roman stone coffins were found on the site during the building.   Ten feet high stone dashed walls enclosed The Towers; remnants of these walls can be seen today.   Italianate landscaped grounds surrounded the ten acre site and included a lake where swans were kept. Two towers (one was a water tower and the other a bird tower with many slits in the walls for birds to enter for nesting) and an impressive cylindrical aviary set amongst fir trees and hot houses for his grapes and fruit were built.

5.4 Concrete walls

Not only was The Towers and its grounds surrounded by high, stone dashed concrete walls but remnants of this type of wall can be seen in many places in Heybridge which signifies that the land and the then property on it were previously owned by Bentall's.

5.5 Later history of The Towers

John Playle: "I well remember as a boy scaling the walls near the Cedars c.1930 to scrump delicious William pears that were grown espalier fashion in the kitchen garden on a south facing boundary wall. Afterwards we would creep stealthily through the undergrowth stepping lightly on a bed of pine needles and make our way to the Bird Tower to glimpse perhaps a new migrant or a green woodpecker. The route through the glade, beneath the trees was unforgettable; the smell of the pines, the wonderful sight of blue cedars interspersed with cypress, juniper and yew. But most of all, I suppose, was the feeling of danger that trespass gives you and the breathlessness that sends the pulses racing."

Susannah Wright (known as Sarah) was a cook for the Bentalls at The Towers. Mr. E. H. Bentall wanted her to go to London for cookery lessons when he moved into The Towers so that she could cater in a style appropriate to his new grand house. She told him she was unwilling since she intended to marry Jim Hinton. Bentall said he would sack him if they married. They married, he sacked him and they had to move to Sunderland to get work. Jean Styles, nee McLauchlan, who has researched the McLauchlan family history, says that as this was a time of agricultural depression in Essex when many farm labourers were unemployed, northern coal mine owners advertised for workers especially in County Durham and some of her relations had to go north. The Hintons eventually moved back to Heybridge and lived in Hall Terrace. Their daughter, Lydia Hinton, married Fred (erick) Mott who kept a diary from 1895 to 1930. It paints an impersonal glimpse of Heybridge and provides interesting details of Bentall's, where he was a wheelwright. He records in his diary that his rent was raised from 2s.4d. to 2s.7d. in 1909.

The 1881 census records the set-up in The Towers: Edward Bentall, his wife, her companion (Georgina Baker), a butler, cook, kitchen maid, scullery maid, needlewoman, parlour maid, and two maids were living in the house. It would seem that while Ernest Linnett acted as Mr. Bentall's chauffeur at a time when few knew how to drive a car, he was also foreman of the factory maintenance section. He lived in a cottage in Holloway Road near Langford Cross. His sister, Mrs. Dick Houlding, Min or Minnie, founded the Triangle Garage with her husband, Dick Houlding on land that was formerly The Towers' vegetable garden. A photograph shows an early Bentall car in front of a line of garages at The Towers with Charlie Burns, the chauffeur, standing beside the car. There was living accommodation above the garages.

The 1901 census records that Edward Bentall and his wife Maud were in residence at The Towers, plus three daughters, a son, a governess and nine servants. The Towers was the home of three generations of the Bentall family. According to Fred Mott's diary, The Towers was sold in August 1925. Mrs. Bentall went to live in the Bell House in Wickham Bishops; her chauffeur lived in a cottage in the grounds of the former rectory.

"The Towers was owned by the Loyal Order of the Good Shepherd from 1930 to 1940. It became a convalescent home. The Order of the Good Shepherd was a society for promoting health and help, very much like insurance societies or BUPA in modern times." (G. W. Gifford) The society covered most of the United Kingdom with the head office in Ely, Cambridgeshire. They had many homes but The Towers was the largest.

William Gifford was the superintendent and his wife the matron. Their son and only child, G. W. Gifford, paints a picture of luxury. There were twelve maids, including a chef or cook (the cook in the 1930s was Olive Hutley), an assistant maid and other domestic help. Three gardeners attended to 12 acres of gardens, kept animals and cultivated a large vegetable garden. The superintendent even generated the electricity. There were twelve bedrooms, four were dormitories containing nineteen beds. Patients from Lincoln and Norfolk came to convalesce and stayed for an average of two weeks. They enjoyed four meals a day and the matron ensured diets were followed and doctors visited. Evening entertainment was provided in the large lounge by talented local performers and on other evenings other forms of entertainment were mounted including whist drives. Radio programmes were piped into the lounge; a surprising innovation since broadcasting was in its infancy.

Ruby McColm went to work as maid to the matron and she remembers there were lots of bedrooms and a huge wide marble staircase which the servants had to run up and down continually. She recalls cleaning the billiard room. It was hard work and she had late duties, often until 11pm.

At the beginning of W.W.2, soldiers from 28th Company Royal Army Service Corps were billeted in the Towers and the ARP made it a prepared base for the treatment of air raid or invasion casualties. Later, it was a POW camp for Italian soldiers in their grey and yellow uniforms. They seemed to come and go as they pleased and worked at various farms to which they had been allocated by Rena Burrell from Cumberland, a member of the Land Army. After W.W.2, Rena Burrell helped to run the Jolly Sailor in Heybridge Basin with Jane Clark and later her daughter, Mona. Jill Babbage remembers the POWs played football with children on the 'Planny'. Once, when she was about six, she stayed too long and was late back for afternoon school. The prisoners repaired the sea wall between Saltcote Mill and Osea Road and laid a rail track to carry materials. Jack Rayner remembers the tasty half a loaf of bread filled with onion and sausage meat that the kind prisoners used to give him and his sister. The Towers was used as temporary housing for returning servicemen while some POWs continued to be in residence. It was converted into sixteen flats in 1950. The house deteriorated and was acquired by developers who found that the only way to demolish it was with dynamite in 1960. The rubble was used for foundations of Bradwell Power Station. The houses lining Cedar Chase and Fir Tree Walk were built on the site of The Towers.

5.6 The Towers fruit and vegetable garden and orchard

Across Goldhanger Road, the fruit and vegetable garden and orchard were surrounded by brick cavity walls 8ft. high surmounted by 17½ in. square paving stone stones. The wall went along Goldhanger Road, formed the cemetery boundary and is the rear garden boundary of numbers 9 to 21 Goldhanger Road where it returns to Goldhanger Road. The wall from number 9 Goldhanger Road to Well Terrace was pierced in two places by tall wooden gates through which children peered in during the 1920s.

Part of this frontage was sold to Dick Houlding and his wife, Min, where they started the Triangle Garage. Initially, they lived in the bungalow behind the original garage premises that were not demolished until 2008. Later, the Houldings purchased the Home Farm house and farmyard where modern garage repair workshops and office accommodation were built, while on the opposite side of the road, the original garage site was used for petrol pumps, a shop selling a wide range of merchandise including newspapers, sweets, soft drinks and some groceries. The original garage site was cleared in 2008 for redevelopment.

The Lodge, entrance to The Towers
SOURCE
Ellen Hedley collection

Annie Buckley worked as a kitchen maid at The Towers in 1910

6.0 Bentall's Workers' Houses

Bentall built houses for his workers surprisingly early and some have been listed and are on the Essex Heritage Conservation Record.

6.1 The Square

The earliest Bentall's workers' houses were built in 1815. They are the four brick built terraced cottages in The Square; numbers 7, 9, 11 and 13. They face the former Half Moon public house. The plaque within the filled-in central window shows 1827 and GB but it is thought to be the date of kitchen extensions at the back and GB may have been the builder. There used to be shops in the front rooms of each of these cottages in the late nineteenth century. The end house facing the Benbridge, number 13, has a double front and was known as the Breakfast Rooms or at another time 'The Men's Room' where Bentall's white-collar employees had their breakfasts at trestle tables sitting on benches. A shoe repairer lived in number 11; it is double fronted and Eileen Cannom believes two families lived there at one time. There was a sweet shop and number 7 was a greengrocer; brickwork on number 7 shows where a metal advertising sign used to be fixed to the wall.

Charles Wakefield was the tenant of number 13. He had started work at Bentall's in 1884 and became gatekeeper in 1901 when his duties included locking up the works at night. Charles had followed his father who worked at Bentall's until he retired in 1893. Charles Wakefield had seven children packed into this house with two bedrooms and a third above the lean-to kitchen.

Joshua Freeman bought numbers 7, 9, 11 and 13 in March 1919 from Wells and Perry, the Chelmsford Brewers. A cheque for £372 for the balance of the purchase price exists. Joshua Freeman ran the Half Moon public house opposite from 1894 to1917. He gave the four cottages to his son Harold when he married in 1933 and Harold lived in number 11 until 1966. Mr. Wakefield died in 1957 and Harold Freeman gave number 13 to his daughter, June, on her marriage to Bruce Holland. They lived in a caravan on the site of the demolished Black Huts until they had finished renovating the house. There is a W.W.2 air raid shelter connected with number 11 at the rear of the house; these air raid shelters are very difficult to demolish.

Harold Freeman had been apprenticed as a carpenter. He joined the Fire Service in 1939 and rose to be sub-officer. The pay of a retained fireman was low so he supplemented it by other work; making coffins for Arthur Smith, the Maldon undertaker, and wooden toys at Christmas

---

FOOTNOTE: In 1938 Maldon Fire Station was in London Road where a cottage next to the entrance that housed Maldon Museum had to be demolished to allow the new larger appliances to come and go. Maldon Museum was displaced; their artefacts were put in store in various places in the town. Cath Backhouse led a group to campaign for the re-opening of the museum, their efforts resulted in the Museum being located upstairs in a room above James and Geo. Matthews, seed merchants (now Prezzo), and then into The Spindles on the path leading to the Maldon Vicarage and finally to the former park keeper's cottage, by the main iron gated entrance into the Promenade Park. Maldon District Council owns the building. Skilled volunteers access and conserve artefacts following national procedures while others clean, steward and mount displays for the yearly themes. Some displays are permanent.

time. After W.W.2, he worked for Mr. Mott, the builder, before branching out on his own as a general builder and carpenter while he continued to be a retained sub-officer in the fire service in Maldon until his retirement.

6.2 Woodfield Cottages

These concrete cottages were built in 1873 with flat roofs; older Heybridge residents still call them the Flat Tops. The forty single storey cottages were built in three parallel terraces. The low iron pump between numbers 146 and 154 and the cast iron lamp standards between numbers 134 and 135 are listed. Each semi-detached washhouse contained a copper mounted on bricks, a large sink and an earth closet bucket with a wooden seat above a galvanised bucket. Squares of newspaper hung on a string from a nail. Water was carried from communal taps in the yard. The original flat concrete roofs leaked and were replaced in 1918 with slate covered gabled roofs and ridgeline stacks.

The cottages were sold by auction in 1930 for under £100: tenants bought some and others were bought by landlords as investments. Ray Burns, who was able to buy his later, converted the wash house into a modern bathroom. Some houses have had the small walk in larder converted into a shower room. Ray worked at Bentall's and Acrow until the bankruptcy when he found a job at ICS. All his working life he came home for his mid-day meal.

Ray Burns' father worked as a gardener at the Towers and later at Home Farm to look after the horses when Mr. Lotts lived there. The family lived in 121 Woodfield Cottages. His mother came from Bradwell on Sea to be a domestic servant at Home Farm and married Mr. Burns as his second wife after his first wife's death and she continued to live there for the rest of her life. Ray was born a fortnight before his father died, aged 72, in 1933 and has lived there all his life, even after his marriage to Shirley.

The houses are listed today because of their innovative concrete construction. Some modifications, including modern attic conversions, had been carried out before the importance of the listing was appreciated. Planning permission ensures that repairs are undertaken with original building materials and the alterations do not ruin the symmetry of the terraces. The 1922 OS map shows a path from Barnfield Cottages to Woodfield Cottages.

6.3 The Roothings

The Rev. John Wade reported that on Friday 16th April 1915 Jim Clark, who lived in the Roothings, picked up an unexploded bomb at Heybridge Hall. It had been dropped from a German Zeppelin during a raid at 12.15am on that day on Maldon and Heybridge .

These two terraces of eight in line, two up two down style cottages were basic workers' accommodation. They were built in the mid-nineteenth century. They were sold for £50 in the 1930s. Standing at a distance from the cottages and their gardens, it is noticeable that the ground lies low compared with the land around it. The reason for this is that Bentall dug gravel from there as well as near Barnfield Cottages to make concrete.

The gardens are separated from the cottages by a path and are entered through gates. All but one garden is opposite their front doors. Just one lies at right angles to these gardens and across the bottom of them. Many residents plant these quite large gardens as 'rooms'. They are full of surprises with attractive planting.

Number 15 was unimproved until very recently. It was owned by a Romford man and rented to a long-standing tenant who died in the 1990s. It had the only pair of brick built privies across the back yard that used to house earth closets that were demolished during refurbishment. The privies were built against the boundary wall. The spoil from the Colne Estate houses was heaped up against this wall on the estate side to be level with the wall and grassed over. It forms a small amenity area maintained by the Heybridge Parish Council. Many of the cottages have been enlarged with extensions to the front and, more commonly, to the rear.

Mr. Treadwell was an engineer at the Acrow Saffron Walden factory when he was offered a post in Heybridge and the tenancy of number 3 the Roothings, just before he was to be married in 1962. Later, he bought the house through Crick and Freeman, the Maldon solicitors.

There is a footpath from Springfield Cottages along the front of the Roothings to where there used to be a footbridge next to number 1 and across the ditch to another path to the present St Clare's Hospice Day Centre. Bentall's workers from Springfield Cottages and the Roothings could walk through a meadow, across a footbridge and over the canal to the works on the south side of the Navigation. There were no factory premises on the north side of the Navigation until after W.W.2.

Unfortunately, the footbridge next to Number 1 the Roothings was removed when Colne Estate was being developed in the 1970s. A new path was made along the side of Number 1 to connect with new paths from the Colne Estate to provide a pedestrian route in front of the Roothings and the lane along the Bentall's concrete wall to Black Bridge. Instead of a few Bentall's employees using the path between the cottages and their gardens, the route is used by many people from the Colne Estate causing Roothings' residents to suffer from vandalism and anti-social behaviour at all times of the day and night.

6.4 Well Terrace

A terrace of eight two-storey brick built cottages was erected mid nineteenth century for supervisor level employees. The architectural detailing and the better quality of the bricks reflect the higher status of the employees; the detailing of the brickwork is especially interesting. Few original windows remain but the surviving examples have vertical sliding sashes with fine glazing bars. Each cottage had a plot of land at the rear and a small front garden. Some still have the original Bentall concrete boundary walls and gateposts. To the rear, all the cottages have retained their brick-built back-to-back outhouses.

Adam Garwood, Historic Buildings Record Officer, Essex County Council, described the terrace as a fine, rare example of nineteenth century industrial housing which merited preservation. Unfortunately, the delay in achieving listing has meant that owners have modernised the windows and front doors and which makes listing unlikely.

Tenants have included The Towers' head gardener, Mr. Crouch, in the first house (number 25), Mr Weaver, Fred. Bacon (Alf's brother), Sid Fenton, foreman blacksmith who lived at number 32, and Mr. Frederick Mott, a wheelwright, who moved to number 30 on 19th May 1927 where he paid 2s.7d. rent per week. At the Bentall house where he had lived in 1909, he had paid 2s.4d. a week and James Edward Joslin, foreman painter at Bentall's and Colour Sergeant in the 1st Essex Volunteer Engineering Corps after 1865 until 1876, was another tenant.

Well Terrace was built on part of Well Farm which E. H. Bentall had bought to create the vegetable garden and orchard for The Towers.

6.5 Stock Terrace

Stock Chase runs from the Triangle to Stock Terrace. Originally there was a gated entrance to Barnfield Cottages and Stock Terrace from Stock Chase. Outside the gate, there were two superior, detached houses; Moat Cottage (Lodge) and Chase Cottage built in 1856 which were occupied by relatives of the Bentall family who worked in the firm. Mr. Wyatt, sometime company secretary, lived in Moat Lodge with his sister, Maisie. Peter Newton was pleased to have a part-time job at Moat Lodge. He earned 1s.6d. a week getting in coal and wood for half an hour after school and on Saturday mornings for three hours by chopping kindling, doing errands, buying cracked eggs from Mays, collecting meat from the butchers and cleaning table knives before the days of stainless steel or EPNS. At 11am, he went to the kitchen with the servant for tea and one of Miss Wyatt's rock cakes.

Miss Wyatt visited the sick and took them honeycomb moulds. Jill Babbage remembers her coming to see her grandmother. Jill and a friend used to take Miss Wyatt's dog for a walk in Stoney Meadows; they were frightened when Lappage's cows chased them. After the death of Mr. Wyatt, his sister had a series of lodgers including Miss Hepburn who ran the Bentall's canteen. She went to Bentall's dances in a kilt and later began and owned the Kiltie Cake shop in Tiptree. Natalie Wakelin lived with Miss Wyatt after the death of Padge Wakelin but later divided her time between her two daughters.

The pump was turned on daily to provide water for those living in Stock Terrace, Barnfield Cottages, Woodfield Cottages and Boulton Cottages who received their water from the well in Well Yard. The water tower behind Stock Terrace has been demolished.

Stock Terrace is a row of twelve three-storey town house style dwellings built for Bentall's workers with large families during the second half of the nineteenth century. Accommodation is on three levels providing greater living space. The main elevations are enhanced by fine brickwork and windows with vertical sashes with narrow side lights to the façade that faced Bentall's factory while the rear windows were plainer four light sash windows. Projecting to the rear and straddling the property boundaries are single-storey gable ended utility/toilet ranges. Some have been converted to other uses. It is an impressive range of purpose built housing. Adam Garwood, the Essex Historic Buildings Records officer, thinks the insertion of modern double glazed windows in three of the properties impacted on the integrity of the terrace.

One or two of the houses were used to accommodate young, single employees who were supervised by a landlady. Maggie Lloyd was the sixth child in her family, when she was three in 1925, they moved into Stock Terrace. The house had two large bedrooms on the first and second floors connected by staircases with the living room, front room and kitchen on the ground floor. Maggie remembers very happy times when the back door was always left open to welcome friendly neighbours. Two families shared a back yard.

Jill Babbage's mother was born in Woodfield Cottages. Her grandfather, William James Livermore, worked in the Bentall foundry and died early so Jill's parents, Mr. and Mrs. Alf Payne, and her grandmother moved into Stock Terrace in the 1920s. Mr. Nash from London bought some of the houses in Stock Terrace in the 1930s and Alf Payne collected the rents.

June Carpenter's maternal grandfather, Frederick Wager, worked on a farm and lived at Hill Farm Cottages in Tolleshunt D'Arcy. He started work at Bentall's when he had two children. He was granted a house in Stock Terrace where ten more children were born. When his family left home, he moved to Boulton Cottages. Frederick and Annie's (nee Wager) eldest child, Annie (June's mother) was 25 when the youngest, Cicely, was born. Annie went to work for the Eves at Fullbridge House when she was 13 where she always felt hungry. (This was at a time when one in three working class women under 20 worked as a cook, cleaner or nanny; there were 1.3 million domestic servants in Britain. W.W.1 opened up opportunities for women to do men's jobs and escape from domestic work. Flora Thompson in Lark Rise noted that when the girls left home for domestic service it made room in the cramped houses for younger children and the boys who worked on local farms). Annie did not stay long at the Eves, she went to Kingston on Thames during W.W.1 to help her sister, Florence, run a dairy business. They collected churns from the station and carried out milk rounds. The younger sister, Cicely, remembered, with gratitude, the money Florence sent home for her. After the war Annie returned to Heybridge where she met and married June's father, William (Billie) Hinton. They lived in Hall Terrace next to the Co-op while Billie Hinton's father, James, lived at the other end of Hall Terrace. This was the James that E. H. Bentall sacked when he married his cook and had to move to Sunderland for work. June's mother, Mrs. Hinton, did Mrs. Houlding's washing for 2s.6d. a week, she also did housework. Mr. Houlding started off repairing and selling bicycles and, at one time, June got a bicycle in lieu of wages for the work her mother had done.

6.6 Barnfield Cottages

This row of eight single-storey cottages was built for Bentall's workers in the early twentieth century. They were built on the field named Barnfield on Timothy Skynner's map of 1754. The cottages are of similar design to Woodfield Cottages except that the roof coverings are red Courtrai tiles, probably because the walls were designed to carry the heavier roof load. Slate had been used on Woodfield Cottages when the pitched roofs replaced the flat roofs because the walls had not been designed to bear the greater weight. The cottages were of the most basic level of worker accommodation with two small rooms with high ceilings for living and sleeping. Each unit was originally lit by vertical sliding sash windows. Each house had a detached washhouse across a path from their front door. There is a capped off communal tap that used to serve the cottages.

These houses were not listed so it was possible to make changes early in the twenty-first century. Number 8 had a two storey extension which is hidden by a tree. Numbers 3, 4, 5 and 6 were bought by a builder who demolished their wash houses and built three bungalows on the site. The ceilings in the houses were dropped, two storeys were created and the upper floors are lit with Velux roof lights so that the external appearance is unchanged. The internal arrangements of the rooms in each dwelling have been changed and they vary slightly.

Peter Newton's brother was an apprentice at Bates Motors in Spital Road, Maldon, c.1930. He remembers that he and his brother collected old tyres in a handcart for a Guy Fawkes' Night bonfire near Barnfield Cottages. Coming down Market Hill, they held the cart back with a rope.

6.7 Boulton Cottages

Four pairs of semi-detached two-storey managerial cottages were built in 1908; two of the four front onto Stock Chase and the other two pairs are set back. Land allocated to the tenants for gardening was not adjacent to their houses and tenants had to cross neighbours' land to reach their own. Number 1's garden ran along Stock Chase to Stock Terrace. Leonard Marshall lived in Butt Lane, Maldon and walked to Bentall's to work as a toolmaker. He was a sidesman at Maldon Congregational Church where he met Lily Robinson who came from Suffolk to work for Mrs. Bert Sadd. They were married in 1928 and bought number 3 Boulton Cottages that had previously been rented by the Gills and their large family. This was a time when Bentall's workmen's houses were being sold. Mr. Marshall died in 1946; his widow lived there until she was 93. Basil Frost moved from one of Sisson's cottages in Hall Road to Boulton Cottages. He had worked in the Co-op butchers in The Street until it closed down. He worked part-time at Buntings in Maldon High Street until he was well into his nineties and died in 2004.

Earlier, between Stock Terrace and Boulton Cottages, the building of a nut and bolt factory was started and never completed. In W.W.2, a trench 3 - 4ft. deep shored up by concrete walls was used as an air raid shelter by the Wareham family and others. A bed made from planks was used by the two Wareham children. A bungalow has since been built there, next to Stock Terrace.

6.8 Saltcote Hall and Cottages

A. Bentall built Saltcote Hall in the 1860s. The original house was Georgian in style but a double storey extension was added to one side which was subsequently reduced to a single storey. Francis May lived at the Friary until he moved to Saltcote Court in 1881. (Saltcote Hall has been variously known as Saltcote Court, Saltcote Hall or Saltcote House). Francis May owned the farm in the twentieth century. He was famous as a breeder of British Friesian cattle and for the breeding of 'May's Saltcote 2-Rowed Winter Barley' seed. Frederick Chaney's daughter, Mrs. Twin, remembers her father told her that his first job as a boy was to clean shoes at Saltcote Hall for the May family. Francis' son, Donald, took over the house in the 1960s and made changes in a contemporary style. When Donald decided to retire around 1970, the farm was offered for sale in three lots by Kemsleys; the arable land behind the Hall was sold off for sand and gravel extraction, the marsh field was bought by Blackwater Sailing Club to be made into a sail training lake but Saltcote Hall failed to sell. Dennis (Tubby) Wager bought the hall in 1976 with two adjacent fields and one on the opposite side of the road along Basin Road where horses graze.

Mr. Wager had been a farm worker at Saltcote Farm when he became a bricklayer. Later, he was a successful builder and married Pamela Woodcraft. They had two children; Andrew and Susan. Andrew has five Suffolk Punch horses which he shows at agricultural shows in Eastern England including the Suffolk Show where he won a first and two thirds in 2007. Preparing the horses for showing is time consuming; manes are braided up, harnesses are polished and the horses carefully groomed and each owner has his own colours. Horses are led before the judges at walking pace and trotting. Andrew is helped by his sister, Susan.

Originally, three pairs of cottages were built back from the road near the sea wall by Bentall's as management level accommodation in 1910. They were of the same design as Boulton Cottages in Stock Chase and appear under that name on the 3rd edition (1920) of the OS map before they were renamed Saltcote Cottages. Number 1 was built nearest Basin Road where

Peter Newton was born in 1921. It used to be lived in by Mr. and Mrs. Hillier who ran a little sweet and general shop in a wooden building close to the road and their neighbours, in number 2, were the Braybrooks. Mr. Wager converted numbers 5 and 6 into one house for Mr. and Mrs. Donald May when they left Saltcote Hall. The conversion was renamed Saltcote Lodge in 1987. Now, numbers 1 and 2 have been made into one house. When numbers 3 and 4 were burned down, they were re-built to front Goldhanger Road forward from 1 and 2 and 5 and 6. Robert Barnard, who was killed in a car accident in October 2011 near Godlhanger, inherited number 3 from his father and Wyn Wright bought number 4 before 1957; they are two separate houses.

6.9 Springfield Cottages

This group of twenty semi-detached dwellings were built in 1912 in mews style on land purchased by Bentall's from Sir Claude de Crespigny in 1903 on a field named Springfield (the field had a spring) on Timothy Skynner's map of 1754. The higher standards of building reveal that they were meant for managerial staff at Bentall's. The development was awarded a prize for design at White City in 1911, hence their nickname White City. The Arts and Crafts influence in the design resembles similar houses in Hampstead Garden Suburb and in Letchworth. Each one and a half storey cottage provided three up and three down levels of accommodation.

Two rows of semi-detached houses face each other across a private, unmade lane. The lane is made up of strips of land in front of each house that each householder owns; originally they were called allotments on a map.

John Edward Nicholls bought number 17 in March 1965 for £1,000 where his widow, Dot Nicholls, has lived for over fifty years. They lived in Cold Norton when they married in 1952. She and her husband used to cycle to work in Heybridge, Dot at the laundry and John at Bentall's. They were able to rent 36 Hall Road Terrace in 1954 but when number 17 Springfield Cottages became vacant they were granted the tenancy because John Nicholls was an inspector of castings at the foundry. He walked along the Roothings footpath to work at Bentall's. The house had a living room which they used as sitting room with a coal fired range, above which was a 5ft. high mantle shelf. The adjoining kitchen had another small range, a butler sink mounted on piles of bricks, a tiny pantry and a concrete copper. The Nicholls family ate their meals around a table in the front room. Originally, an earth closet was outside and there were three bedrooms (one is now usually turned into a bathroom). There were no washhouses. The gardens at the back were enclosed by iron rail fences. Residents have altered the houses internally and the Nicholls have doubled the size of the living room.

Number 12 was purchased by Annie Miller in 1931; it was the only privately owned house in 1960. Clifford Pratt says it is believed she may have been Bentall's company nurse.

Clifford Pratt is the last surviving Bentall's foreman to live in Springfield Cottages. He had been apprenticed for five years to Ken Cockell as a tool maker while Ken Cockell had been apprenticed to Evelyn Wood Last. Following Cliff's National Service, he returned to Bentall's and eventually became foreman of the tool room as a well as maintenance foreman. Cliff's dance band, the Cliff Cannal Band, (Cannal was his mother's maiden name) played for dances in halls around the district in the 1950s and 60s. He played the trumpet and tenor saxophone, Peter Jarvis and Charlie Tait the guitar, Norman Robbins the double bass, Len Woods the drums and Gordon Crabbe the keyboard. Peter Jarvis left to run his own band. This is not the first time Heybridge people made music. In his article about Broad Street Green around 1879, Evelyn Last mentions Harry Busson, an engineer at Bentall's, a leading light in Heybridge Brass.

Clifford Pratt rented number 11 from Bentall's in 1960 and later from Acrow. Mr. Pratt was able to buy the house in 1965.

Dennis Fenn was born in Wantz Road, Maldon. The family moved to Barnfield Cottages for a short time before going to number 8 Springfield Cottages. Dennis's grandfather worked in Bentall's paint shop while his father was in the valve shop. The family had an air raid shelter in the garden that later tenants found very difficult to demolish. There were fifty-seven consecutive nights of air raids after the Battle of Britain. Dennis Fenn attended Maldon Grammar School, walking home to Heybridge for lunch. He trained to be a teacher before W.W.2 then served in the RAF, and taught at Heybridge School after the war; his next post was at the Templars' Primary School in Witham to which he cycled daily for seven years. His bicycle was a Rayleigh that cost £6.19s 6d, it had Sturmy Archer gears, cable brakes and sporty up-turned handlebars.

Mr. and Mrs. Evelyn Wood Last, who were the parents of Betty Feeney, lived at number 14 Springfield Cottages. Harold Lewis remembers that when he first knew Ev, as he was known, he was working in a section of the lath shop or turnery. He made patterns of production machine parts used in the manufacture of Bentall's products, for example, drilling jigs for components. Ev Last was a traditional Bentall employee; loyal, hard working, experienced and he had a wide knowledge of Bentall products and their manufacture. He had a great sense of humour and was much liked.

Keith Searle played with Ev's grandsons when he visited his grandfather who lived opposite Ev in Springfield Cottages. He recalls that Ev had a very active retirement. In the shed in his garden he sharpened lawn mowers, chopped scraps of wood he acquired from Sadd's and sold bundles for fire lighting; he built a tree house for his grandchildren to play in and he built many sheds and outhouses around Heybridge. He pushed an old perambulator which acted as a barrow for his jobs around Heybridge. He was a keen supporter of the Swifts and printed match 'programmes' and a book about the Swifts' achievements. Even in his later years, he was one of the first to skate on the Navigation when it froze over.

June Carpenter's grandparents, Octavius (William) and Elizabeth Hinton and their twelve children lived in number 1 Springfield Cottages.

On Friday 13th July 1962 over a dozen pensioners who were tenants in the Roothings and Springfield Cottages received one month's notice to quit their homes which had to be vacated by 17th August. The notice stated "As a natural consequence of the reorganisation and expansion of our company's activities, it is urgently required that we transfer skilled men from other factories and to this end we must obtain housing for them and their families. Previous to this move, we wish to modernise the cottages that we own, and within the next few weeks we intend to put this rebuilding into operation."

Among the retired Bentall workers in Springfield Cottages who received notices to quit were:

Mr. and Mrs. Evelyn Wood Last, Ev had worked at Bentall's for fifty-two years and moved into Springfield Cottages fifty years previously when it was new. He paid 6s.6d. a week rent then and £1.2s.6d. in 1962.

Mr. and Mrs. Ruggles, aged 78. It was thought that the shock of the move contributed to the death of Mrs. Ruggles six months later.

Mr. and Mrs. Tom Gill who were both 78,

Miss Clara Hinton,

Mr. Arthur Whittaker,

Mr. Arthur Lewis,

Mr. and Mrs. Rosamund,

Mrs. Fenn,

Mrs. Hinton (no relation to Clara) who had lived in number 2 Stock Terrace in Heybridge all her life was re-housed by Maldon Borough Council in a bungalow in Saxon Way Maldon.

Mr. and Mrs. Alf Livermore.

Deeds lent to the author show that Miss Clara Hinton bought number 1 on 19th March 1965 where she had brought up her siblings after the death of her parents. Kenneth Henry Jamieson bought number 10 on 1st March 1965.

As soon as the cottages were vacated, they were put up for sale.

6.10 The end of houses for Bentall's workers

Bentall's had provided accommodation for all grades of employees from 1815 for about one hundred and five years; this system ended in 1930 when Ernest Bentall died. Woodfield Cottages were auctioned off and could be bought for less than £100. It would seem that when David Ransome became managing director in 1947, some tenants of Bentall houses received notice to quit. When Mr. and Mrs. Alf Livermore were given notice to leave Springfield Cottages, they moved to a pre-fabricated house in Spital Road. Claude Cowell and another estate agent put sale notices on properties that were to be sold off. Some residents bought their own houses while investors bought others. Acrow gave tenants, who were not employed in their works, notice to quit when they took over Bentall's. There is a suggestion that Acrow did not know they had bought the houses.

June Carpenter with her grandparents at Springfield Cottages

7.0 Flooding

Hilda Grieve in The Great Tide describes Essex thus: "The county of Essex is a walled fortress; it has more than three hundred miles of man-made defences that barricade its flat marshland borders against the thrusting tide outside." The coastline stretches from the head of the Stour Estuary to the Port of London. The Blackwater Estuary forms a considerable part of that coastline. For eight hundred years, man has fought to keep the sea out of Essex while the mean sea level relative to the land rose progressively and ever higher tides have been recorded. The highest tides occur between about 21st March and 23rd September, at the equinoxes, especially when gales heap them up and drive them with greater fury against defences built up to keep the sea at bay. It has been catastrophic when this coincides with a surge from the Atlantic Ocean into the North Sea and low pressure causes the sea levels to rise.

The past, present and future of Heybridge is affected by flooding.

Dengie is mentioned as early as 1355 when the area suffered several breaches in the sea walls. Floods have been recorded in 1380 and, around 1450, flooding caused the foundations of St Andrew's Church tower to be undermined. This resulted in the tower collapsing into the nave leaving only the chancel.

In 1532 the Statute of Sewers authorised the appointment of Commissioners charged with the drainage of low lying land liable to flooding but the bodies to enforce the building of sea defences took centuries to evolve. The King appointed Marsh Bailiffs to these Commissions later known as Court of Sewers, who were to be responsible for seeing that owners and occupiers should share the responsibility for the upkeep of sea defences of their lands in proportion to the quantity of land they held and that defaulters should have to pay for the work others had to do. The north shore of the Blackwater did not come under the regular jurisdiction of the Court of Sewers for centuries. What was done depended on the judgement and available money of the landowner or his tenants. Floods were recorded in 1550, 1707 and 1736.

In 1844, the Ordnance Survey adopted a system of heights in relation to an assumed mean sea level at Liverpool. Ordnance Datum Liverpool became the standard for measuring heights of sea walls and tides.

From about 1847 sailing ships bringing coal from Newcastle-upon-Tyne began to make a habit of lying against the sea wall after discharging their cargo at Maldon so they could use clay dug from the meadow behind the sea wall as ballast for the return journey. Their efforts weakened the sea wall so much that it collapsed during one of the great tides, probably in 1856, creating what is known as the Ballast Hole.

On 20th March, 1874, an extraordinary high tide inundated Heybridge Hall Farm. The tenant, Edward Faux, liaised with John Oxley Parker, the then land agent for the Milbanke estate. A bundle of letters in the Essex Record Office records the extensive damage. The letters between them are written on small sheets of notepaper, one letter writer used thin paper that resembled tissue paper. They record the extensive damage caused by the over topping of the sea wall: crop losses valued at £55.6s.0d., the loss of recently repaired fences, hedges that had been washed away, dykes and ditches that had to be cleared again, fallow fields that had been contaminated by sea water and the hay and straw lost from them causing sheep deterioration. This was especially serious for Edward Faux who, in the short time he had been a tenant, had spent money to improve the farm by draining, cleansing and deepening dykes and manuring the land. John Oxley Parker negotiated with Edward Faux and proposed that to compensate him he should receive an allowance off his rent of £200 at Lady Day and Michaelmas 1874 and Lady Day 1875, £100 in the five following years, that the roof of Heybridge Hall should be repaired forthwith and the barn roof by July 1875 (it would seem that these repairs were overdue). E. William Milbanke wrote in September 1874 that it grieved him that John Oxley Parker had let Faux off rents listed earlier since he had to pay for the raising of the sea wall as well. Indeed, he feared he could be called on again to raise the sea wall; this had reduced his income so much that he feared he would have to borrow to meet his outgoings. John Oxley Parker was so annoyed at the delay in settling this matter that he threatened to quit as agent. It would seem the matter was resolved since the terms were agreed on 18th September 1874 and the hall roof was repaired by the landlord while it was agreed that the barn repairs could be deferred until July 1875.

There was a disastrous flood in Essex on 29th November 1897 when between 30,000 and 35,000 acres of land went under water. Dengie had Commissioners whose appointed engineer reported that the height of the tide was unprecedented and, combined with the stormy weather, had caused the tide to over top the sea walls. The top of the walls were cracked and porous because the summer lack of rain and the long period of dry weather into November meant that water had entered the top of the walls, penetrated cracks and passed downwards and through outlets at lower levels carrying with it part of the earthworks. The back part of the earthworks was loosened, gave way and weakened the front part which collapsed causing breaches. Two hundred and fifty men, including soldiers, were engaged to make first aid repairs along a twenty five mile stretch along the south bank of the Blackwater in the Dengie peninsular. The soldiers were withdrawn by March 1898; the repairs were almost complete and reckoned to be sufficient to withstand any ordinary tide. Eventually, the Marsh Bailiff and the consultant engineer persuaded the Commissioners that the walls should to be a standard level of 16ft. Ordnance Datum: Owners had to raise their walls 12-18 inches, the base of the walls had to be widened so that the crest could be 4ft. and the wall became about 18 inches above the 1897 tide level. The Dengie Commissioners strictly supervised this work; landowners had to finance it under threat of penalties of double the cost of the work. Indeed, it was reported that Dengie Commissioners had carried out repairs effectually and at once.

Hilda Grieve recounts that one Tollesbury Farmer said that where there were no Commissioners, "Every owner did or failed to do what was right in his own eyes" and many could not face the cost of recovery. Northey Island had twelve breaches in its sea walls and rapidly reverted to saltings. It was not cleared for over a year. Land flooded by salt water takes years to be fit for cultivation: the salt not only injures plant growth, but spoils the condition of the soil, worms are killed and it is not until they became abundant again that the texture of the soil improves.

Exceptional tides caused by violent gales brought flooding to the Blackwater Estuary in the new year of 1905. Benjamin Turnage Handley, a local character, owned the Bath Wall; a spur of mud bank that extended from the Hythe about 200 yards downstream. He had an open air bathing place hiring out bathing machines for river bathing and rowing boats and ran a ferry service across the river to the Heybridge bank. Maldon Corporation constructed the Marine Lake by damming the creek that ran behind the Bath Wall creating a 200ft. wide by 700ft. long lake which was embanked at a cost £525. 8,000 tonnes of earth were removed by thirty-five unemployed men supervised by Mr. T. R. Swale, the borough engineer. The lake was opened in 1905.

The flood of 1910 resulted from an exceptionally high tide which swept over wharfs at Fullbridge and flooded Sadd's works to a depth of four feet. Peter Kemp, an historian, wrote "tree trunks, stacked on either side of the works road, floated away, to come to rest at random, in some cases more than a mile from the original stack." The tree trunks had to be collected up and restacked. The large stock of building material and planed timber suffered loss or damage.

Heybridge and Heybridge Basin suffered from severe flooding in 1928, twenty-three Basin houses were affected and the Blackwater Sailing Club gave 5cwt of coal to each house to help them dry out their homes. The tide of 6th/7th January 1928 was described by the Essex Chronicle as "the highest flood tide within living memory". Nearly every house in Hall Road flooded, some to a depth of 5ft.; Bentall's timber store under the paint shop was flooded to a depth of 2ft.; the church vicarage and school flooded. The sea wall broke opposite the Promenade and the sea water contaminated the fresh water. Trees near Sadd's entrance gate floated up Station Road. At Maldon, the tide was 9 inches higher than in 1897 and the dry High Street was flooded to 5ft. deep in 20 minutes. In Heybridge, a lime kiln had blown up. The tide was 2ft. higher than what was to occur in 1953.

In Hall Road, Mrs. Hinton was in labour with June and could not rescue any belongings from the ground floor rooms. Walter Wiseman told of the bread bin floating up to the ceiling. Mrs. Mynard lived with her daughter and son-in-law, Bobby Payne, who sat on the windowsill and played his ukulele while people trundled their belongings in dustbins up the road. A local Basin character, Aunt Dinah, was found floating on a mattress.

When the 1861 Act was passed well over half of the tidal defences were not even under commission. This Act allowed the setting up of elective drainage boards on application by a proportion of the land owners affected. At the root of the problem was who should pay for the drainage work and tidal defences. The water from the unrated upland areas made its way to the sea through the much smaller low-lying rated districts which meant that the areas liable to pay were small. In Essex the tidal defences were not even under commission and the elective drainage boards were not set up until well into the twentieth century. The Chelmer and Blackwater Drainage Board was set up in 1921 and the one for Maldon in 1922 but there was no one in charge of main rivers.

The Land Drainage Act of 1930 resulted from the Bledisloe Commission's report which swept away all previous Acts and established land drainage on a broader basis. Essex Rivers Catchment Board was constituted in 1931 and embraced a number of small watershed areas and main rivers with outfalls between Dovercourt and Barking Creek including Holland Brook, the rivers Colne, Blackwater, Chelmer, Crouch and Roach and three tributaries of the Thames - the Beam, Ingrebourne and Mar Dyke.

In April 1932 all the Essex coastline between Harwich and Barking was surveyed; of 321 miles of tidal defences 200 were in a very dilapidated condition, parts of the walls originally stone pitched to a proper slope had become 'sadly neglected' and liable to become exceedingly dangerous at any time unless £176,000 be spent immediately to put them in a proper state. The upper reaches of the Blackwater and their tributaries were in a deplorable condition. The Board had to struggle to find ways of financing this essential work.

Essex has the longest coastline of any county in England. The lengthy coastline around the Blackwater estuary is protected by sea walls that are built out over the saltings. The foundations of the sea wall were made by digging a trench, removing the soft mud and replacing it with marsh clay, dug from fleets or borrow pits in the saltings, along the inside of the wall and about 20ft. from it. The clay was stiffened with brushwood while the wall was built up with clay, chalk and stakes. Sea walls were faced with bound bundles of brushwood to protect them from high water wave action in earlier times. Firm, solid walls were created by skilled workmen with Kentish ragstone from Medway quarries brought to Essex estuaries by barge. Cheaper concrete facing blocks are used nowadays. Sea walls are usually about 8ft. above the salt marsh and 3ft. wide at the top which becomes a footpath.

Sea walls have always been threatened by high winds and freak tides necessitating expensive maintenance and repairs. Global warming threatens to cause significant rises in water levels around the Essex coastline. Will the heavy capital investment required to protect the Essex coastline be made?

In 1934 a momentous decision was made by the Essex Rivers Catchment Board to purchase a Priestman dragline excavator. In 1932, the Board's first chief engineer calculated a dragline excavator would carry out the work "ten times better at half the cost and in a quarter of the time compared with hand labour". The machine cost £1,050 and the drudgery of spade, plank and barrow was on the way out.

A revolutionary development took place in 1938 when Heybridge Hall marsh wall was reconstructed. Instead of expensive ragstone, 5 inch thick hexagonal concrete blocks were cast and matured and laid on a bed of clay and grouted in bitumen. This saved £1,375. Later, 15 inch square blocks 5 inches thick were used. They formed a waterproof facing to the walls, flexible to swelling and shrinkage of the clay body of the bank and the beat of the sea upon its face.

On the night of 12th/13th February 1938 a south-west gale veered to the north-west and blew continuously throughout the Saturday night and finally veered to the north-east. A surge of water travelling down the North Sea heaped up by the gale resulted in heavy wave action on the Essex coast. Both sides of the Blackwater suffered as water flowed over long lengths of wall, washing out the back in places, breaching in others or washing the top off and making short work of weak and unimproved patches. The Board's works committee reported that had the surge come three or four days later a tide of two feet higher would have resulted and the Board would have been unable to cope. They referred to the risk in Heybridge where industrial concerns, Bentall's and Crittalls, and large residential areas were sited on land liable to flood if the sea breached or overflowed the sea defences.

A sub-committee decided that the standard for estuary walls should be fixed on the basis of 1ft. to 2ft. freeboard above the highest recorded level, the amount of freeboard varying above the exposure and aspect of the walls and the importance of the area to be protected, with still higher freeboard where necessary on the open coast. These plans were stalled by W.W.2. In 1943, floods swept away a rustic structure crossing the Beeleigh Weir which accommodated horses pulling barges.

There was a tide in 1944 that was nearly as high as that of 1938. The Catchment Board carried out extensive improvement schemes from 1946 to catch up on the neglect of the war years so that when the floods struck on 1st March 1949 there was no wholesale collapse along the Essex coastline, but Old Hall, Tollesbury and land on the south of the Blackwater were flooded because the walls were very dry and the crust of clay cracked up to 2ft. deep. Nine thousand acres were flooded and the land is sinking all the time.

Flooding used to occur regularly in the vicinity of Heybridge Triangle. Children needed wellington boots to get to Heybridge Primary School. Hall Road suffered severe flooding before Sadd's Dam was built in 1954; Crittall factory workers were known to put their fingers in gaps of the walls to hold back water during floods. At that time, workers went home to have their dinner in the middle of the day. They needed to watch the level of the floods to see if it was possible to get through on their bicycles.

The author noted that there was a terrific gale blowing during the afternoon of Saturday 31st January 1953. Indeed the gale was greater than had ever been recorded. The Victoria, a British Rail steamer, sunk in the Irish Sea with the loss of one hundred and twenty-eight lives. The North Sea tides come from the Atlantic Ocean as a wave some hundreds of miles long, it enters the North Sea twice a day through a channel between north of Scotland and Norway. The gale force winds forced 15 billion cubic feet of water into the North Sea and raised the sea levels an extra 2ft. The tide was higher than previously known. This wave moves from north to south along the east coast of Britain. At Costa Hill in the Orkneys, a mean wind speed of 90mph with several gusts exceeding 121mph, the highest reaching the unprecedented 125mph was recorded; this is classed as a hurricane. 100mph west nor' westerly winds forced water from the North Atlantic down into the North Sea and coincided with a full moon and low pressure that results in high tides. "The catastrophe was unexpected; there was a complete lack of real-time information. No regular updates of news, no mobile phones, no internet. Landlines linked only via local exchanges constrained by the need for human operators and few families with phones at all." (Jules Pretty) However, it was acknowledged later that nothing could have been done even if warnings had been given. In Essex social events carried on during the evening. Sea washed over Harwich Quay at 10.15pm on three sides and water surged through the little harbour town that was under 3ft. of water within minutes. The waves were built up by the action of the gale on the tidal surge causing solid walls of sea to pour over the sea and river defences. This happened at the time of low barometric pressure and high spring tides.

No ebb had occurred that Saturday afternoon. The wind seemed to be holding up the water. There was an extraordinary high tide. By 10'clock in the evening, the sea had completely covered the saltings and was working away at sea walls widening cracks in the clay and undermining the foundations. By midnight, so much water had piled up in the North Sea that sea walls had been over topped, breached and beaten in a few short hours on the East Coast.

At 10.20pm, a man watched the Marine Lake in Maldon fill to its 2.5 million gallon capacity in twelve minutes but very few people were aware that the Blackwater had burst its banks. A group of Maldon fishermen had decided to sleep on their boats; their colleagues who tried to reach theirs half an hour later were unable to do so. The sea wall near St Peter's Chapel at Bradwell on Sea was breached and the sea surged through a hole in the wall bringing a wave several feet high. At Canney Farm near Steeple seventeen prize winning Friesian cows were drowned.

That evening, the author and a friend, Betty, from Maldon, had been to a dance at Crittall Social Centre in Braintree where Alf Wood and his Legionnaires had played. Driving home, they were unable to get into Maldon because the Square, Heybridge, the Causeway and Foundry Terrace were flooded. They were able to reach the author's parents' home and tried to telephone Betty's mother but the telephone was out of order. They did wake the next door neighbour who got up and told Betty's mother, who thought it sounded fishy.

At this time, the tidal River Blackwater flowed from the confluence with the River Chelmer along behind Hall Road, parallel to The Street, under Heybridge Bridge to Heybridge Mill. Properties fronting this river were accustomed to regular flooding from the Blackwater at the rear of their premises and from The Street at the front. This time, about two feet of water flowed into houses along Hall Road and the Square and straight out again. Next day, the Fire Brigade pumped out the cellars of the Queen's Head after the first tide ebbed, and then they pumped out the Anchor at 3pm.

Spring Lane ran from Hall Road to the wall on the River Blackwater. There were nine cottages in the lane rented by tenants. On the corner was Mr. Sisson's bakery and further down the former Baptist Bethel Chapel. The Cannom family lived in a house at the bottom of the lane next to the sea wall. On the Saturday night, the sea wall was breached and water rushed along Spring Lane. When Mr. Cannom tried to enter the house, the door had to be pushed hard because the water had reached the top of the dining room table on which the dog was cowering and shivering with cold. All the Cannoms' belongings and furniture were lost except those in the bedrooms. They did not receive any compensation since flooding was regarded as an Act of God. Subsequently the cottages were condemned and the tenants, except the Cannom family who owned their house, were re-housed in council houses. Spring Lane no longer exists. The lane can be seen on the east of Eltime premises. From 2010, factory premises on the east side of the former lane were vacant and the Crittall's / Ever Ready / ICS factory premises on the west side were vacant.

June Holland remembers that water came into the lean-to kitchens of The Square terrace but not into the living rooms or front rooms because they were two steps up from the kitchens.

About 2ft. of water went into houses and their basements on the Causeway and Fullbridge and it flowed straight out again as the tide ebbed but those near Fullbridge and in Station Road had to be pumped out by firemen. Local people were accustomed to seeing cows huddled on the slope to the five barred gate next to the present Mobility Shop after rain flooded the field which factories now cover.

At 12.50am the level at Heybridge was seen to drop. Afterwards, local opinion believed that this was due to the pressure on Heybridge being reduced by the breach in the sea wall beyond Decoy Point since the Old Fort sluice blew about that time. This caused the water to tear through and to run like a river straight down Goldhanger Road towards Heybridge. Hilda Grieve describes how thirteen pedigree Friesian heifers took refuge on the mound of the duck decoy. A farmer and his wife took no notice of their dog's barking not realising that the sea was over their front lawn and onto the flower beds. A couple returning from a dance drove straight into the advancing stream, the engine stalled but they managed to drive on the starter motor onto slightly higher ground. They removed the car seats and put them on the roof of the car and sat on them while they waited until the water fell.

At the mouth of the Blackwater, the water began to pour in through breaches in the sea walls at Bradwell Waterside while the tide at St Peter's Church had receded after the first surge forward before midnight. Then in a rush the water swept over the walls into the fields. The third surge caused it to pour down steadily into the marshland and flow across the fields as far as the River Board man could see as he watched from the higher ground at his cottage. The sea walls at Eastlands let go and water burst through many gaps.

Between 1am and 2am, the water flowing down Goldhanger Road spread out into the caravan parks at Osea Road and Mill Beach. Caravans were toppled over and shifted around; one was even washed onto the top of the sea wall. The manager of Osea Road glanced out of his window and thought he saw frost until his dustbin hit the side of the bungalow. He drove his car to higher ground and carried his wife and two children to it through the water that was waist deep on the last journey. Crossing Goldhanger Road, by

Caravans in the 1953 floods

now a foot deep, he went to Vaulty Manor to rouse Mr. Seabrook, the owner of the farm and caravan park so that the farm workers living in low-lying cottages and cattle on the marshes could be contacted.

On Goldhanger Road, near the entry to Basin Road, Pat Yates saw a woman wearing a fur coat get out of a car. Instead of shallow water, she stepped into a ditch and the water came up to her chest. The Yates continued on their way to the family's chalet which was 2ft. above ground on piers. They found the chalet was flooded half way up the walls and that all the furniture was piled up behind the door making entry difficult. Their two gas cylinders had gone but her father found some in a heap of debris by the sea wall.

The caretaker of Mill Beach camp and his wife were awakened by the movement of their caravan which was rocking in 2ft. of rapidly flowing water. They waded through to dry ground to the home of friends. The next day the sight of three hundred and fifty damaged caravans that had been tossed here and there was such that Dan Kingston thought it was the end of the venture. Actually, business boomed in August of that year. Permanent occupation of caravans in caravan parks situated in the Flood Risk zone is not allowed from 1st March to 31st October because of the higher risk of flooding at that time of the year.

Heybridge Hall Farm was flooded. The residue of salt on the arable land rendered it uncultivatable for six years.

The Chelmer and Blackwater Navigation and the River Chelmer brimmed over and united between 1am and 2am obliterating much of the Maldon Golf course.

At Beeleigh, water reached almost unprecedented height causing extensive damage to the weir and its adjacent bank. A sailing barge was floated from the sea up the tideway and put into position across the breach where it was filled with concrete and sunk. It has made an effective foundation for the necessary repairs and is 12ft. down below the level of the ground beyond the concrete tow path. There used to be a spectacular waterfall of 13ft. where the River Chelmer rushed into the River Blackwater until the River Authority changed the lay-out at Beeleigh in the 1960s to prevent flooding. Self acting weirs now control the flow.

On the Sunday, Christine Wareham left her home in Stock Chase Heybridge to walk to Maldon to meet her friend. When she reached Foundry Terrace, a row of houses for foundry workers north of Mill Lane, she had to walk on planks put down over the flood waters to reach Fullbridge.

On the same day, the author went along Goldhanger Road to view the floods that stretched from Spickets Brook to Osea Road where the sea wall had been breached for thirty feet. On Mersea Island, there were lots of breaches in the sea wall and boats were scattered higgledy-piggledy, beach huts smashed and houses flooded.

On the Monday after school, the author took Glynis Davies, Hazel Easter, Doris Overall and Brenda Moore, pupils from Maldon Girls' Secondary Modern School, to Burnham on Crouch where they saw breaches in the sea wall, Wallasea flooded and Burnham on Crouch streets awash.

Services could not take place in St George's Church in Heybridge Basin in January.

A tall dam, known locally as Sadd's Dam, was built between Heybridge Hall and Potman Marsh across the channel as part of the programme of flood defence improvements in 1954. Water is held behind the dam at high tide but at other times passes through into what is now known as the Heybridge Creek which flows into the River Blackwater near the confluence with the River Chelmer.

There had been eight hundred and thirty-nine breaches of Essex sea walls. The next spring tide was due two weeks later. The catchment control office asked for volunteers to fill sandbags to fill the breaches and raise the sea walls. They had only 54,000 in stock. One thousand people went from Colchester to Shrub End, Rowhedge and Ardleigh to fill 90,000 sandbags a day by the Tuesday. Volunteers loaded them onto lorries, railways and cars. By the next weekend, eight thousand civilian and servicemen were working on sea walls and over the next fortnight eight million sandbags were filled and laid. Two to three feet were added to the sea walls, the bases were widened and broader terraces created.

Heybridge suffers from tide locking when high tide levels prevent the river from flowing away. Towards the end of the twentieth century, Peter Nickolls, sometime Mayor of Maldon, remembered seeing water within 2in. from the top of the sea wall around Heybridge Hall from his home in Maldon.

Denys Harrison describes the flooding in Heybridge Basin since 1785 in his book "Heybridge Basin The story of a waterside community 1796-2002".

During the sixteenth century, the aim was to prevent the sea from breaking in while in the twentieth century the aim was to get the land waters out. This is the reason for concrete barriers atop the sea walls at Mill Beach, the Basin and along great lengths of the Blackwater estuary.

8.0 Farming in Mid Essex

Farming has always been a cyclical industry. This chapter seeks to give a glimpse of conditions on Essex farms since 1800 during the times of prosperity and of hardship.

8.1 The history of the growth of the Petre land holding In Essex

The Petre family was numerous in Devon in the sixteenth century where John Peter was a rich farmer and a wealthy tanner. His son, William, later Sir William, was educated at Exeter College, Oxford where he achieved degrees in Canon and Civil Law. As a lawyer and protégé of Thomas Cromwell, he became Principal Secretary of State to Henry VIII and was responsible for the dissolution, confiscation and closing of monasteries. One of Sir William's tasks was the negotiation of the closure of Barking Abbey. He secured for the abbess the highest pension ever granted and was able to rent Ingatestone Hall, a Barking Abbey nuns' manor, in 1539 from King Henry VIII and later to purchase it by hire purchase. He was knighted in 1543 and changed his surname to Petre.

Sir William held the post of Secretary of State through the reigns of Edward VI, Mary and Elizabeth while unwaveringly adhering to the Roman Catholic faith.

Sir William Petre's only son, John, was raised to the peerage in 1603 as Baron Petre of Writtle. The family supported the Anglicans in their villages and successive Lord Petres acquired many estates in Essex over the years after the Reformation. While Roman Catholics were debarred from holding civic office in the country until 1829, the Lords Petre concentrated on managing their estates well and became one of the biggest landowners in Essex.

In 1842, Lord Petre bargained with the great Eastern Railway Company and received a huge sum of money for allowing the railway to cross his land. He used this money to buy many manors in the Dengie Hundred. Even in 2000 it is recorded that the present Lord Petre owns 3,000 acres of Essex; some farmed in house and the rest leased out.

8.2 The Strutts of Terling and their influence

Sir William Gavin writes in his book 'Ninety Years of Family Farming': "the Strutt family emerged from the ranks of small yeoman farmers early in the seventeenth century by operating water-mills on Essex rivers around Chelmsford and Maldon. The money the mills made always went into the purchase of land which they chose wisely and managed well." In 1720, John Strutt handed over the water mills to his sons. He bought four farms in Terling (it is confusing that the eldest Strutt son was always christened John). The next Strutt bought five more farms in Terling. Colonel Joseph Strutt succeeded his bachelor brother and died in 1845 having bought 2,330 acres and been MP for Maldon for thirty years. He had married the daughter of the Duke of Leinster. When he was offered a peerage in 1821, he asked that it be conferred on his wife so that he could stay in the House of Commons; she became the first Baroness Rayleigh and, henceforth, the title passed to eldest male heir.

The third Lord Rayleigh (1842-1919) inherited from his father, the second baron, 7,000 acres in Essex in 1873. A physicist, he followed a distinguished academic career in Cambridge University as a research scientist. He was one of the twelve original members of the Order of

Merit and won the Nobel Prize for Physics in 1904 jointly with William Ramsey for their discovery of argon.

The third Lord Rayleigh left his brother; Edward (1859-1930), to manage the farms. He said, 'Edward earns me my pocket money'. His son, the fourth Lord Rayleigh, was also a distinguished scientist who continued to leave Edward Strutt to manage the farms. Edward had assumed complete responsibility for the farms at 22 years of age in 1876 and provided the leadership until March 1930. He inaugurated a system of accounting that is revered today but was considered extraordinary then. The accounts are famous for their detailed costings; the wages paid on each farm every week, the cost of feeding animals, the daily milk etc. These statistics formed the basis of the farms' management. Another clue to Edward's farming success was his encouraging attitude to his farm bailiffs; they respected him as the master craftsman who had detailed knowledge and wise judgement. Another characteristic was his marked aversion to spending money; he neglected building maintenance. He practised 'making do' throughout his life; this was necessary when the great depression hit farming in the 1880s. He was able, with his brother's financial support, to back tenancies and farmed derelict land himself. He took over 854 acres in 1876, 2,344 acres by 1882, 3,596 acres by 1882 and by 1896 he farmed 4,315 acres. During the years of the depression, it became clear that intensive milk production for London would be profitable.

During W.W.1, Edward Strutt became the chief agricultural advisor to the Ministry of Agriculture. Edward Strutt regarded the farms as business which was a completely new concept at the time. He set an example of good husbandry and was an agricultural innovator whose farming methods were admired and copied. The obituary in the Times compared his pioneering role in British agriculture with that of Jethro Tull, Bakewell and Coke.

8.3 The ups and downs of farming in the nineteenth century

The Napoleonic Wars were raging at the beginning of the nineteenth century. Wheat had been 43 shillings a quarter in 1792; the price had risen to 126 shillings a quarter in 1812. This caused real hardship to agricultural workers but protected farmers and landowners by keeping up the price. The Corn Laws had banned imports of grain until domestically produced grain reached a certain price. The Corn Laws were repealed in 1846 enabling the importation of cheap wheat from North America; fewer farm workers were needed and many emigrated either to the industrial towns whose manufactured products paid for the imported foods or to the Colonies. However, the 1850s and 1860s saw Victorian agriculture enjoy something of a golden age. There was a period of high returns with the introduction of improved breeds and crops, fertilisers and the replacement of wood by iron in the manufacture of many agricultural implements. There was a greater use of scientific methods and steam power was used for ploughing, threshing and winnowing.

The long slump - the Great Depresstion - began with six years of bad weather from 1875 to 1882 that caused poor harvests and other agricultural calamaties, flooding devastated arable farming and outbreaks of foot and mouth disease occurred between 1881 and 1883. Then as now, wheat was an important farm crop in Essex. Cheap grain from the Prairies could be sent to ports quickly and cheaply by rail and crossed the Atlantic in steamships that lowered the costs. Grain came into the Basin for mills along the Navigation and into Maldon Harbour. Britain was importing 65% of its needs.

Andrew Marr writes that British agriculture endured a long slump from the 1870s until 1940 but W.W.1 did lift farm prices.

Bentall's, the major employer in Heybridge, benefited from the expansion of the prairies of North America. This was made possible by easier, faster and cheaper transport of grain and meat to Europe in steam ships, by refrigeration and the growth of the railway networks and by the use of barbed wire to extend farms in Canada and New Zealand. Bentall's exported agricultural machinery to the developing farms in Africa.

A glimpse of the state of farming in the nineteenth and twentieth centuries in Great Britain follows. It is the background to farming in Essex. Rider Haggard, writing about conditions mid-nineteenth century, recalls a visit he made to John Lapwood, a retired farm worker, with Charles Strutt. Lapwood had worked on farms around Witham for over fifty years.

"John Lapwood, by the help of some kind friends, was spending his last days in a little cottage with his wife and we found him - an aged and withered but still apple-cheeked individual - seated upon a bank enjoying sweet air although a bit draughty. Wages in his young days for a horseman were 9s.0d. a week and 8s.0d. for daymen when weather allowed them to be earned. During the Crimea War (1853-56) bread cost him 1s.0d. a loaf with most food proportionately high. For months at a time, he had existed on nothing but bread and onions, washed down when he was lucky with a small beer. They had no tea but his wife made a substitute with burnt crusts soaked in water. There was generally a little cheese and butter for the children of whom there were eight, but he could not put it in his own stomach when they were hungry and cried for food. "Things is better now" he added. The continuous diet of onion often blistered the roof of his mouth, and when this happened the onions had to be soaked first in salt water to "draw the 'virtue' out of them". Rider Haggard commented that his condition was that of ten thousand others, his 9s.0d.a week had to feed, clothe and house ten souls while bread stood at 1s.0d. a loaf

John Joseph Mechi was a genius who analysed practical farming problems logically and scientifically and made farming experiments in Tiptree. He had been born in 1802 to an Italian father and a German mother and became an astute business man who made his fortune from the "Magic Razor Strop" which he patented. Although he kept his many business interests in London, he immersed himself studying farming and bought, initially, 128 acres of poor marshy clay soil in Tiptree. William White in his History Gazetteer and Directory of the County of Essex 1848 described it then as one of the worst farms in county; he purchased it for £3,250; "but he has since expended upwards of £7,000, in draining and improving the land, and in the erection of a handsome residence, (Tiptree Hall) and extensive and well arranged farm buildings, of brick, iron, and slate; with an efficient threshing machine, including machinery for shaking the straw, dressing the corn, cutting chaff, bruising oats and etc." It became a profitable model farm where experiments were carried out. Cattle were kept on slatted floors, manure was collected in a vast reservoir, liquefied and distributed by steam engine through subterranean pipes over all parts of the farm which it irrigated and fertilised at the same time.

It is recorded that Warren manufactured Mechi's trench plough in 1845. We may assume this was not their only transaction. E. H. Bentall got Mechi to pre-view his inventions.

Mechi had an annual agricultural show in July attended by agriculturalists from Essex and neighbouring counties where new machinery farming methods (including the use of steam power) and ideas were demonstrated although in the beginning his ideas had been ridiculed. By 1856 he was entertaining some six hundred people annually. He wrote three books; 'Letters on agricultural improvement' 1845, 'Experience in drainage' 1847 and 'How to farm profitably' 1853.

In the year 2010, he was remembered for active support for the inauguration of the Agricultural Benevolent Institution in 1860. Wilkin and Sons commissioned Ann Courtney to write a play 'The Magic Box' based on Mechi's life to commemorate Mechi founding the Agricultural Benevolent Institution in 1860. The first of a series performance by the Mad Dogs and Englishmen Theatre Company took place in the Mulberry Orchard behind the Wilkins' jam factory in Tiptree in July 2010 sponsored by Wilkins. It was a riveting story and a spell binding production.

Mechi died in poverty in 1880 after the Unity Joint Stock Bank, of which he was a governor, failed and he had an unfortunate connection with the Unity Fire and General Life Assurance Office. He was too ill to deal with the situation and forfeited the opportunity to be Lord Mayor of London. The land he farmed is now used by Wilkins for growing fruit for their jams.

The national agricultural depression began in 1875. An investigator, reporting to the Richmond Commission in 1880, said that it had affected Essex. The situation worsened by 1881. A very large number of farms were in landlords' hands and were hardly cultivated, or were farmed by landlords. For example, the state of agriculture was deplorable between Chelmsford and Maldon; land was derelict, full of weeds and natural rough grasses on which a few cattle were picking up a bare living, farmhouses were empty or used by caretakers who were often the men who had failed on the same farms.

In 1875, wheat was sold for 55 shillings a quarter and farm workers wages were 10 to 12 shillings per week. In 1894, wheat was sold for 23 shillings per quarter. Bad harvests, imported cheap wheat and fodder from the New World caused 38,000 acres of land in Central Essex to go out of cultivation in 1885. The situation was exacerbated in the 1890s when frozen meat from Australia, New Zealand and South America came into Great Britain. This was a time when farm workers left the land to work in Bentall's factory. At first, they walked in from the villages; later the workers were given Bentall houses.

Farmers from distant parts of Great Britain were tempted to migrate to Essex because of the nearness to London making it possible for produce to be transported economically to the metropolis by water and rail. Landowners in Essex were desperate for tenants; they offered incentives to the incomers and advertised attractive leases. This, plus the fertile land of Essex and the favourable climate, resulted in waves of immigrants to the county.

Wilkins owned Trewlands and farms in Tollesbury and Tolleshunt Knights from 1711; they began making jam in 1885, today it is called conserve. At first, the company was called Brittania but became Wilkin and Son Ltd in 1905. Wilkins bought Tiptree Hall, the farm and farm buildings in 1913 where Mechi had conducted his experiments. From the first, it was stipulated that their jam should be free of glucose, colouring and preservatives. The firm exports savoury sauces, jellies, honey, teas, cakes and Christmas puddings to seventy countries. The company received its first Royal warrant in 1911 and today the warrant covers all Tiptree products. The Queen visited the company to mark the firm's 125th anniversary. Peter Wilkin, the chairman of the company which is renowned for its benevolent treatment to its employees and their families, has made over shares in the company to employees to prevent the take over by big firms.

8.4 Scottish farmers came to Essex at the end of the nineteenth century

The weather in Scotland in 1879 was very bad; snow, gales, frost and gale force winds lasted for five months, animals died of disease and whole herds succumbed. When farming thrived again, Scottish lairds wanted bigger rents; Ayrshire rents rose steeply and leases contained restrictive clauses forbidding tenants to sell hay and straw and compelled them to follow strict crop rotations.

A few Scottish farmers came to Essex between 1880 and 1883 when Essex landlords were finding it difficult to find tenants. The Scots were energetic, intelligent and financially sound and created such a good impression that Lord Petre and estate agents began to advertise Essex farms in the leading Scottish newspapers, including the Kilmarnock Standard, which attracted a cluster of farmers to Essex from around Kilmarnock, among them the Hunters. "Essex farms within 25 miles of London at low rents and with freedom of cultivation." One night in June 1885, sixteen Scots slept at Ongar Park; Hugh Craig took Parsloes Hall the next day and the rest eventually took farms in Essex.

Lord Petre was friendly with a Glaswegian solicitor who arranged for Robert Hunter to become a tenant of Lord Petre. The Hunters kept cows; Mrs. Hunter made cheese that had to be turned daily while it was maturing. She had nearly drowned when she fell into the curds at the age of two. The fields were fertilised with seaweed, sheep were kept on the hills. In summer, the Scottish farmhouse was let while the family lived in out buildings and slept in the attic. Robert was a scratch golfer and had a golf course on the farm.

Another member of the Hunter family came to Essex in 1933. Their cattle from the Kilmarnock area were driven to Glasgow. Their goods and chattels, stock and some farm workers were loaded onto a special train. There were stops on the way to milk the cows and feed the animals and, on arrival at Ingatestone Railway Station, everything had to be transported the two miles to the Forest Lodge. Robert Hunter retired in 1961. His son, Alan, farmed Beckenham Farm in Tolleshunt Major that still belongs to the New England Company, a society established for propagating the gospel in New England. Doctor David Williams became a very rich man who bequeathed money and property to many charities engaged in missionary work. The society owned a farm in Rettenden and property in London - the income from the rent still finances missionary work worldwide today.

Dairy farmers from Renfrew, Ayrshire and Wigtown (south west Scotland) were attracted to Essex. The list of farmers who came to Essex in the late 1800s is a roll of success; as an example Jean Styles, great granddaughter of Robert, relates the McLauchlan history. Robert Spier McLauchlan and his wife Barbara Dale Dickie came to Middleton Hall in Norfolk between 1881 and 1890 from Caddell Farm in Ardrossan where the family had farmed for three generations. From there they moved to Old Hall Blythborough, to Marvels Garden in Pebmarsh and then to Albert's Farm in Felsted and on retirement to Shalford. They had seven children. One died at 20 years of age in Pebmarsh, one emigrated to New Zealand and another to Australia. Jean Styles has discovered that members of her Essex family were recruited by men who came down from the North and County Durham to attract unemployed farm workers for the coal mines during this time. John, Robert's son and Jean Styles' grandfather, farmed in leased farms in Danbury, Braxted and Bures before buying Rivals Farm in Tolleshunt Major in 1920. The farm is now owned by John's grandson, Ivan. Colin McLauchlan described the move from Bures on Michaelmas 29th September 1920 when he, at the age of 9, walked most of the way with the men and the cattle. The journey began at 8am and continued until 5.30pm. Their goods came in a furniture lorry.

Over thirty million of the population of Ireland were totally dependent on potatoes for food when late blight struck between 1845 and 1852. Potatoes became a slimy decaying blackened mass a few days after lifting. They were the main crop since an acre of land supported a whole family for a year; three times the yield of grain. 750,000 Irish people died during the famine and two million left their homeland. James Macmorland left Ireland because of the potato famine and farmed at Old Dailly on the coast near Girvan where he grew potatoes and did open cast mining. During visits, the present David Macmorland's father remembers seeing his relations working at night using hurricane lamps. James Macmorland eventually farmed at Maxwellton. He was attracted by Lord Petre's advertisements and took the tenancies of Lord Petre's farms in Essex in 1899 and passed them to his four sons. One of the sons, Francis Kennedy Macmorland born in 1872, took Reeds Farm in Writtle about 1905. He had five children, one of whom, Francis John Macmorland, married George Free's daughter Laura, known as Peggy, in 1936 and moved to Elms Farm, Woodham Mortimer as tenant of Colonel Grimwood's entailed estate. This may have been connected with the fact that George Free had been a tenant of the Grimwood estate in Heybridge from 1914 until he was able to buy Jacobs and Canterbury Farms in 1938 when the entail was legally broken. Francis John Macmorland formed a partnership with his son, David, and they were joined by David's younger brother Andrew, who had worked for Deals, the seed merchant from Feering. David recalls that he built up his pedigree Friesian herd from his father-in-law's dams and fresh Terling bulls but these have been sold. By 2008, this farming business ran the contracting and the grassland side of the farm while the arable land was let to a neighbouring farmer. David's son, James, works for Billericay Farms Services as a spraying operator. This illustrates the ways farming has changed, reflecting the complexities of farming: the scientific considerations, the huge investment in machinery used for short seasons and the small number of full-time workers.

The following examples of families who came to Essex illustrate a phase of the history of Essex farming during the farming depression of the 1880s and the breaking up of the big estates early in the twentieth century:

Robert Hodge rented Cowbridge Grange Manor at Michaelmas 1893.

The Macauleys came from East Kilbride, in the 1880s.

Robert Hendry came from Falkirk to South House Farm and owned Northey Island. Later, he bought Round Bush Farm in Purleigh.

The Flemings (Anne Hunter's grandfather) came to Springfield Hall Chelmsford from Ayrshire c.1900. Later, they moved to Springfield Barns when there were no houses between the farmhouse and Chelmsford gaol. This forbidding building was erected between 1822 and 1828; it was surrounded by a stark 20ft. high wall 42 ft. long. Anne's mother came south to marry in 1929. Her father began milk rounds in Chelmsford in the 1930s and, enterprisingly, had a horse drawn ice cream float in Chelmsford.

The Gemmills came to near Harlow around 1900.

The Montgomerys travelled from Falkirk and used their horses to carry their belongings to Mountnessing Hall.

Robert Craig came to Crondon Park.

The Browns came south and finally farmed at Maldon Hall. Duncan Brown says that his father, William, was 3 years old when they left Ayrshire in 1901 to come to Ongar. William always remembered that horses in the next railway wagon had greasy feet. The grease irritated their feet and they stamped on the floor all night. Two farming families shared the train carrying all their worldly goods, farming paraphernalia, cattle and horses. Their train stopped at Crewe, as was the custom of Scottish trains, for the cows to be milked. On the Ongar farm, cows were fed and the milk put on trains by 7am to be delivered in London before 10am. Duncan Brown's father told him that all members of Scottish dairy farming families worked - young and old, boys and girls - unlike the families of Essex arable farmers. Today, Duncan farms at Maltings Farm at Little Horkesley. He remembers that George Mitchell came down from Scotland in the 1880s. When his move was a success, he persuaded many Scots farmers to come to the Tendring Hundred. James Brown, William's other son, took on Maldon Hall in the 1930s, first as a tenant and later as owner. Tony and John Brown, James' sons, carried on the farm for some time after their father's death until they sold it to John Speakman.

Mr. T. T. Matthews' family has farmed around Good Easter since 1600. His wife's family, the Kerrs, came from Dunlop in Ayrshire to North Weald in 1889. Mrs. Matthews' grandfather brought the farm lock stock and barrel and travelled by train to Blake Hall Station. The train had stopped at intervals during the journey for the cows to be milked. Mr. Kerr had three sons and two daughters; the youngest son was only six weeks old when they came south. The family lived at Wardens. Their landlord granted them the farm rent-free for two or three years as an inducement. The Kerrs moved to Park Farm Ongar in 1918.

And so the list goes on.

The Scots joined the Congregational Church, the closest to the Scottish Presbyterian Church. They had large families (the Gemmils had ten boys and four girls) and socialised together, meeting at Chelmsford Market on Fridays and the wives lunching together. They played curling at Blunts Farm, Billericay and Crondon Park.

8.5 Lancashire farmers settle in Essex

The Dengie Hundred attracted farmers from Lancashire. Rodney Bass writes that his great-grandfather, Thomas Fisher, came to Andrews Farm, Althorne from the vicinity of Goosnargh in Lancashire. In January 1893 he rented from St Bartholomew's Hospital. They were joined by the Calderbanks and Lofthouse families. Their furniture, luggage, provender, chests, 'piggins' and troughs filled fourteen wagons. The specially chartered train left Preston Railway Station with twenty-six vehicles; cattle and horses occupied nine trucks and the families used two carriages with the guard's van. The farm workers sat at the front, cows were in the next rail truck and then furniture and agricultural chattels. They set out in the evening and the journey took two days. The train stopped so that the cows could be milked.

Thomas Fisher was successful and St Bartholomew's offered him the neighbouring Althorne Hall from 15th February 1897. This farm has remained in the family ever since. Dairy farmers employed fewer workers than arable farmers and Scottish family members carried out a lot of the work on farms. At the beginning of the nineteenth century, the Fishers milked cows early in the morning and rushed the milk in churns to London from Althorne station. It was around this time that the Cowells and Proctors came down to the Dengie Hundred from the same vicinity in Lancashire. Thomas was able to buy Althorne Hall for his daughter's husband, John Butt, for £4,250 and Andrews Farm for his son William for £3,250 in 1920. After W.W.2, John Butt was joined by his son George at Bohuns Farm in Tollesbury which the family still farm. David Fisher, grandson of Thomas, farms at Southminster. Joyce Dicker, grand daughter of Thomas and Mary Fisher, owns Landwick Farm Dengie. Indeed, the Fisher farming family are spread throughout Essex. Rodney Bass, his father and grandfather are part of the Fisher family but worked in Midland Bank.

The wider Fisher family has served Essex and their local communities in many ways.

8.6 The effect of death duties from 1894

Death duties were introduced in 1894 and this resulted in very large landowners having to sell land to pay the tax. Notable sufferers in Essex were Lord Petre, the Round family from Birch and the Capel Cures. Lloyd George's increases in the People's Budget of 1909 meant more landowners had to sell their land, houses and art to pay this tax which effectively broke up many large estates in the twentieth century. Previously, many farms had been rented but the need to raise cash to settle death duties necessitated the sale of farms from big estates and gave working farmers a chance to buy.

8.7 Changes brought about by the incomers

Other incomers to Essex in the 1880s and 1890s have included The Padfields from Somerset, the Coopers from Cheshire and the Wheatons from Devon. Essex arable farmers concentrated on wheat growing in the nineteenth century; their barns and granaries were well maintained but cattle-sheds and stock-houses were neglected. The changes in farming introduced by the incomers can be gauged by reports that around Maldon cows in milk and calf were more numerous by 52% in 1892 than in 1882.

Edward Strutt entered the London Milk Market in 1900; the wholesale side of milk distribution. When a Bloomsbury retailer of milk went bankrupt, Edward Strutt bought the rounds and entered the retail side of dairying. Lord Rayleigh Dairies sold the business, sixteen shops premises and depot, to the Express Dairy Company in 1929 but continued to supply them with milk. Edward's youngest son, known as Ned, became responsible for the dairy side of Lord Rayleigh's at that time. He decided to buy retail firms outside London as another outlet for the milk produced on the farms. The first purchase was Stetchworth Dairies for their distribution networks in Cambridge in 1933. By 1948, another five businesses along the Essex coast, as well as small milk rounds in Essex villages, were added. Around 1950, the new central depot adjacent to Hatfield Peverel railway station was extended and re-equipped to pasteurise and bottle milk for the rounds. Milk for the Express Dairies went to London by tanker. Charles Strutt was the first in England to collect milk in tankers from farms in 1954.

Gerald Strutt, Edward's eldest son, played a leading part in the development of British Friesians from 1905. Milk recording had started in 1896 on the Rayleigh farms and there were between forty to sixty cows on each. From these records and careful observation, the breed was improved and standardised, leading to the British Holstein-Friesian Cattle Society that became the British Friesian Society in 1918. The famous Terling and Lavenham herds were created during fifty years of careful breeding by Mr. and Mrs. Gerald Strutt. In 1913, seventeen cows, forty-four heifers and three bulls were sold at Langford Hall Farm from the Lavenham herd for £28 which was considered satisfactory. It was fortunate that they were able to continue to maintain and improve the herds during the Depression of the 1920s and 30s when many herds were dispersed at disastrously low prices.

One of the attractions of farming in Essex was its nearness to London. Incoming farmers grew crops new to Essex for the London markets: potatoes, vegetables, flower seeds, strawberries and raspberries, others changed from arable crops, especially wheat, to dairy cattle and livestock on pastures and poultry rearing. Poultry rearing flourished when careful breeding produced fine strains that were fed more scientifically and the diet included second rate corn.

Fitch, a Maldon farmer, records that "It may be interesting to mention the large trade which has grown up around Maldon, of producing green peas for London and the other markets. At the end of June and during July, the exceptional deliveries to the two Maldon stations are noticeable by all. The total despatched from here during one season for the London markets has amounted to over 8,000 tons. As instance of the way in which enormous consignments of so perishable an article are dealt with by the Railway Company, we may here remark that green peas received at Bishops Gate on 11th July 1891 weighed 925 tons and filled 313 trucks. The entire consignment was distributed throughout the metropolis before nine o'clock on the same morning". Forty pound Hessian sacks of peas were taken from the fields in lorries after 1920 and driven to the London markets overnight.

Artist's impression of a threshing machine typical of late 1890s

8.8 The story of Brazils Farm, Woodham Ferrers

David Cooper's maternal grandfather came to Essex from Scotland in the late 1920s. His father came from an Essex blacksmithing family, who married the only daughter of the son of the Scottish incomers, and acquired Brazils Farm in Woodham Ferrers. Their son, Gavin, was born in 1947 followed by David who came to realise that he is related to a network of Scottish families who have settled in Essex.

David reminisced about farming in the 1950s and 60s: the farm's case tractor from the USA that had a metal seat that caused the driver to be bounced up and down, the hoods the farm workers made out of sacks to keep themselves dry, and how his father borrowed a black carthorse and tumbrel to collect kale for the cows when the tractor could not get into the field. The last stack of sheaves was threshed around 1950. The Coopers had one of the first combine harvesters; hedges had to be taken out to make fields large enough to manoeuvre this and the new larger farm machinery. They used to have thirty-two fields on 250 acres but now there are only twelve large fields. The 1947 Agricultural Act paid subsidies to farmers to keep food cheap and increase production.

David Cooper recalls that a V2 fell on the farm in 1945 and killed the cowman and all the stock, including the herd of Shorthorns, and destroyed the farm buildings. His father was able to buy the basis of a Friesian herd from Lord Rayleigh Farms. Cows were milked in the dairy and the milk poured into pipes over which water cascaded to cool it before it was put into churns that stood on platforms in the sun until tankers collected it. After 1945, Canadian Holsteins were imported to improve the Friesian breed and the milk yield increased. Brazils Farm milking parlour was built in 1968; milk from the cows went through pipes to refrigerated tanks and brought the temperature down to 3 degrees C. Their herd originally had twenty cows, then one hundred and forty, and finally one hundred and twenty. The cows were fed on kale, sugar beet, brewers' grains, hay and silage and grazed on pastures. There used to be fifteen to twenty dairy herds in the locality but Coopers' herd was the last herd to be sold in the autumn of 2007. Pre-W.W.2, the farm employed twelve men on 260 acres. Now Gavin and David Cooper manage the work on the farm and contractors with their big machines cultivate the fields. The dairy has been converted into livery stables where people keep their horses and look after them while affluent clients pay extra for the full service. Ponds on the farm have been expanded and stocked with coarse fish for anglers.

8.9 Doe's of Ulting

In March 1893, Ulting blacksmith George Wood of Grays Farm, Hatfield Peverel, had a new apprentice, Ernest Doe, from Terling. When Ernest completed his apprenticeship in 1898, George Wood retired and Ernest bravely leased the smithy for £8 per annum. This was the beginning of the firm that was to serve farmers of Essex, later south east England, Europe and then the world. Russia imported two triple D tractors from Doe's. Alan Doe aptly entitled his book "A Century of Service". He recalls that in early days, a queue of a dozen horses usually formed up outside the smithy at 6am and they had to be shod before breakfast. Work continued until 5pm with half an hour for lunch. In the first month, Lord Rayleigh Farms bought one shoe for 6d. The author has seen a photograph dated 1908 of Ernest Doe outside the smithy, showing the Bentall agency sign, with L. Atkins and J. Whybrew who served the firm for fifty years. Ernest's son, Ernest Charles was born in 1904. He and the author's father walked to Ulting

School until the school closed in 1910 when they walked to Hatfield Peverel School, just under two miles along the twisty road. They spoke respectfully of Mr. Billie Bennett, the Hatfield Peverel school headmaster.

By 1910, Ernest Doe had purchased the blacksmith's premises, built Hill View next to the smithy, bought the neighbouring farm, Smiths and Cubitts, and had three sons; Ernest Charles, Hugh and Herbert Walter.

The tractor business started in 1920 when Ernest Charles (I will now call him Ernie) persuaded his father to buy some second-hand F. Fordson tractors from the Ministry of Munitions. Six thousand had been sent from the USA during the war to help the war effort. This is an early example of Ernie's foresight; the clue to the success of the firm. Ernie was a wise man who chose able men for managerial roles and inspired loyalty, which is evident from the long service of many employees.

Doe's became Fordson Tractor Dealers in 1930 and were able to buy tractors direct from Dagenham. Doe's were appointed Case agents for Essex: Alan regarded two models of Case tractors as the best in the world between 1930 and 1940. Further agencies followed, including Allis-Chalmers. It was not until 1936 that the firm generated its own electricity supply by a diesel engine which supplied power to the workshops and the offices.

Doe's were Bentall's agents from around 1900. Alan Doe gave the author a copy of a page from a ledger detailing goods Doe's bought from E. H. Bentall and Co. Ltd in July 1937: wheels, latches and axle Lord Rayleigh's £1.5s.11d, shares A. Ratcliff £1.14s.8d., shoes F. Johnston £3.4s.2d., spade lugs Stock £13.16s.0d., 7ft.6in. disc harrows £30.0s.10d. and much more. Farmers bought a wide range of Bentall's goods from Doe's.

When Ernest Doe Senior became ill in 1936, the firm was managed by Ernie and Herbert (Bert) Doe. By 1939, Ernie ran the agricultural side of the firm, Bert ran the industrial contracting side and Hugh became a full-time farmer.

Historically, corn exchanges were places where corn was bought and sold after the morning's cattle market. In the 1930s, Ernest Doe, and after his illness, Hugh, Ernie and later his grandson, Alan, attended Chelmsford on Fridays and Colchester on Saturdays where they sold tractors, machinery and spare parts, settled customers' accounts and took orders. The firm was represented in the corn exchanges at Braintree, Sudbury and Epping. Corn exchanges played an important role in farming in the county before W.W.2. The buildings were tall and glass roofed for good day lighting so that the quality of malting barley, corn and seeds could be correctly assessed by the corn merchant before he offered a price. Hay and straw buyers, representatives from seed firms, maltsters, seed potato merchants, and sellers of rope, sacks, oil, and even insurers met in corn exchanges. Samples were displayed in stiff brown paper bags, a small linen sack or a canvas bag according to the content. The merchant would assess the sample of malting barley or bread wheat and decide whether it was only fit for livestock feed. Many merchants hired stands from which to transact business. Corn exchanges became out dated when telephones enabled orders and enquiries to be made, combine harvesters threshed wheat in four to six weeks instead of being spread over much of the year and laboratory testing determined the quality of samples, not the corn merchants' teeth.

Colchester Corn Exchange opened in 1884 and closed in 1967, Chelmsford Corn Exchange was built in 1857 designed by Frederick Chancellor and pulled down in 1969 as was the old coaching inn and all the buildings on that side of Tindal Street when the site became part of the High Chelmer Shopping Precinct (1972). Sudbury Corn Exchange was saved from demolition in 1968 and converted into a library that won a design award; Saffron Walden Exchange is now a library as is Halstead Corn Exchange.

Chelmsford Corn Exchange had many diverse uses from dances to dog shows and music festivals. It was used by Chelmsford Girls' High School for the annual Speech Day in the late 1930s. The author remembers pupils were seated in tiers at the back of the stage while parents and guests sat in the body of the hall.

Doe's has 18 branches in the south and east of England in 2011.

Doe's part in W.W.2 is in section 8.12.

8.10 W.W.1 Farming

The collapse and depression of the 1880s still cast a cloud over British agriculture while national policy continued to encourage the importation of cheap food, especially wheat. Four million acres of arable land had been put down to grass since 1875 and many farmers had been saved by dairy cows, cattle and sheep.

Bill Oliver, who researches W.W.1 casualties, says that many middle class men volunteered for the forces immediately W.W.1 was declared but ordinary workers had to work out their notice.

England was importing food for 125 days out of 365 while 80% of our grain was exported to pay for European manufactured goods. Food supplies were dependent on the protection of ships by the Royal Navy. By 1916, the supply of food was precarious because ships were carrying military supplies, industry was concentrating on munitions with a depleted work force and had fewer goods to sell to pay for food, shipbuilding could not keep pace with losses, wheat harvests were down in the Americas and Europe and the potato crop had nearly failed. So many men had left the land to join the forces that much land had gone out of production. Despite opposition to a careful report on the need for drastic action in 1915, the seriousness of the situation did not become obvious until December 1916 when War Agricultural Committees were set up with sweeping powers to increase food production. Edward Strutt played a prominent part in the success of the implementation of this policy despite problems. Malnutrition was widespread; on a personal level, the author remembers a colleague who had endured such a serious lack of food as a child at this time in the West Country that her feet and legs were deformed.

8.11 The interwar years; more incomers

Farmers endured harsh conditions between the two World Wars. Duncan Brown's father recalled that the land between Colchester and Clacton on Sea was uncultivated before W.W.2. The author remembers the uncultivated farms in the Dengie Hundred in the 1930s. The countryside around Heybridge and the Dengie Hundred was in a sorry state; arable land reverted to grass, and buildings, hedges and ditches were neglected.

Scottish farmers moved into Essex in the 1920s and 1930s and Essex welcomed another wave of incoming farmers. Jean Style's grandfather, John, moved from Bures to Revells Farm, Tolleshunt Major that he was able to buy in 1920, the McColms came to Little Totham and

Barbara McColm remembers them as diligent, hard workers who brought many new farming techniques and the skills to make the special Scottish wagons and carts, the Hunters came down from Argylshire c.1930 and Tom Howie came down from Scotland to Little Totham. Mr. W. J. Matthams recalled that when he married in 1930 he was paid £1.10s.0d. for a 50 hour working week (150 pence today). The Rowsells came from Somerset in the 1930s to Mundon Hall, a farm of 1,500 acres which they were able to buy cheaply because it was in a very bad state. They worked very hard to restore it but during the war the Essex War Agricultural Executive Committee was of the opinion that they were unsatisfactory farmers and took steps to evict them. As a result of a campaign organised by James Wentworth Day, supported by the Daily Mail and the Beaverbrook press and the lobbying of MPs, Land Tribunals were set up as a Court of Appeal.

James Barr came from outside Glasgow in 1923 to near Harlow and rented a farm from Mr. Arkwright. He raised chickens and had a dairy herd. He bought Sandon Hall in 1929 with enough buildings to store the feed and farming equipment and house the chickens and dairy herd that he raised on 100 acres of land. He employed sixteen men before W.W.2. Andie Barr, who farms Downhouse Farm, Sandon, emphasised that the descendants of the Scots who came to Essex between 1880s and 1920s are closely linked socially and through marriage.

The Stevensons came from Goosnargh in 1933 to farm at Joyce's Farm, Upper Mayland. Dan Kingston found he could buy a farm as cheaply as a house in 1938. He bought Honeypot Farm in Weeley when farms were being advertised for £5 an acre. Landlords were keen to get tenants, for example, the first year's rent was waived when Charlie Speakman leased Woodham Lodge in 1930 to enable him to build up his herd since he had only six cows.

Edward Strutt, backed by the financial strength of the Rayleigh businesses, continued to grow corn with increased mechanisation and extended the cultivation of high value crops, such as potatoes and sugar beet, and increased milk production.

In 1929 glass bottles were introduced for retail milk sales and during W.W.2 milk ceased to be measured in metal measures from a pail into the housewife's jug and, instead, had to be put in bottles. Many small dairy rounds men could not afford the machinery to put the milk in bottles and the author saw a village milkman pour milk from a jug into bottles, sealing the bottle with a cardboard disc popped in by hand into the groove on the inside of the top of the bottle.

The farming depression lasted until 1937 when the menace from the Nazis caused the government to boost food production.

8.12 W.W.2

During W.W.2, every possible acre of land was cultivated which kept Doe's very busy. They were supplying new tractors including Dagenham built Fordsons as well as tractors coming from the USA. Machine tools were installed to make replacement parts at the Ulting works when a shortage of spare parts became apparent. The first combine harvesters did not impress Ernie Doe but when he saw the Massey Harris Model 21 he knew it had a future; another example of his foresight. The firm became known as combine specialists. They sold new models as they became available. It was a blow in 1957 when they felt obliged to become Ford Tractor main agents and had to relinquish the Massey Harris Combine Harvester sales. Ernie's ability to recognise winners shows when Mr. George Pryor, a client, showed Ernie his experiments with joining two tractors together to create much greater power. Doe's carried out the development work which resulted in the Triple D tractor. Later versions were sold worldwide between 1958 and 1968. Ernie Doe's ability to recruit able employees led to the firm's success and his OBE was well deserved. The present managing director, Colin, is the grandson of Ernie and son of Alan. The firm serves not only Essex Farmers but much further afield today.

The Ministry of Agriculture had ordered three thousand Fordson tractors in 1939 in case war came. By February 1940, 40,000 tractors and 11,000 tractor ploughs had been placed on farms. County War Agricultural Committees were established early, composed of leading farmers who served voluntarily assisted by qualified agriculturalists; best practice was combined with scientific knowledge and experience of local conditions. The committees had great powers to direct individual farmers to plough up grassland, to grow specified crops, to apply fertilisers, to increase or decrease the number of cattle, clean out ditches, and much more. If persuasion failed, they could ultimately take possession of the land. Farm prices were allowed to rise in the first two years of the war which enabled farmers to invest and increase food production after the devastating years of the depression.

There was a shift from animal husbandry to arable farming. Every available piece of land that could be cultivated, and some that could not, was ploughed up. Subsidies made it possible to drain marginal land for food production. Food production doubled in five years. Andrew Marr writes that U-boats in W.W.1 and W.W.2 nearly succeeded in starving Britain into submission. Lessons were learned from the malnutrition in W.W.1. Nutritional needs of various sections of the population were borne in mind when rationing was devised to ensure imports were confined to nutritionally valuable items and shipping space was not wasted on luxury foods. Concentrated orange juice, dried milk and dried eggs took up less space on ships. A fair system of rationing ensured a balanced diet. Various groups were targeted for extra food: factory canteens for workers, school meals for children and British restaurants for others. Canteens had to be provided when two hundred and fifty workers or more were employed.

Bread rationing was imposed in 1947 after a severe winter caused the loss of crops and the country had no dollars to buy wheat; the war had almost bankrupted the country. Meat was rationed until 1954 when, in 2000 terms, the ration was two small lamb chops per week and a small amount of corned beef. Offal was not rationed.

8.13 Jack Cohen and Tesco

During the war, agricultural wages were fixed by the government and the author remembers as a student, cycling from Doe's Corner to an Ulting fruit farm where she picked James Grieve apples; a tricky task because they bruise very easily. Since she was under 18, her wages were two and a half old pennies (1p) an hour. She kept pace with her adult partner who received the adult women's rate. In Great Braxted in 1942, the author received 15s.2d. (75p) for four days' work. £1.0s.5d. for five days' work and another week £1.0s.0½d. for five days' work.

Heybridge women picked fruit for Jack Cohen's canning factory at Hill Farm, Tolleshunt Major. Jack's father was a Jewish tailor who fled from Poland in the 1880s to work in London's East End as a travelling tailor. Jack joined the Royal Flying Corps in 1917 and after the war he became a street trader. In 1924, Cohen met T. E. Stockwell, a partner in the tea importing and blending business of Torring and Stockwell. This led to a deal under which Cohen bought tea at 9d. a pound and sold it in half pound packets at 6d. from a barrow. Cohen and Stockwell needed a brand name and, finally decided on Tesco, incorporating Stockwell's initials and the first two letters of Cohen's name. The deal was an instant success; within weeks housewives were clamouring for the brand. On one day, Cohen sold almost 450lb. of Tesco tea from his barrows. This entailed working up to 15 hours a day, five days a week in various London markets. He was helped in peddling the stock and managing the warehouse by two nephews and his brother-in-law.

In 1944, Jack Cohen bought Little London Farm in Little Totham - a 30 acre fruit farm at the same time as he bought Hill Farm plus Little Renters Farm and traded under the name Goldhanger Fruit Farms. He began canning peas. Growers were contracted to supply washed, cleaned and shelled peas within four hours of vining in the field; this ended pea picking by hand for local women, itinerant gypsies and travellers.

The factory operated nearly 24 hours a day and a succession of lorries carted the peas to Goldhanger. It was a hectic six week season. Housewives liked canned peas because they did not have to be shelled and could be obtained throughout the year. Cohen grew strawberries, blackcurrants and loganberries. He converted Hill Farm into a cold store and the cow shed became a jam boiling plant which was very primitive at the beginning, and other buildings were used for canning. Farmers, including the McLauchlans of Rivals Farm, Tolleshunt Major, grew soft fruit under contract for the factory. The factory canned for Woolworths at the beginning but later to a higher specification for other retailers as the canning business expanded and fine premises were built. The canteen was a vast hall where the author organised a dance for the Thurstable School PTA and lost her way driving home to Heybridge with all the takings in the car.

Six hundred people, including students, worked in the factory in summer during peak times. Three hundred, mainly women, were employed in the winter. The Goldhanger factory closed after two changes of ownership (one was Cadbury Schweppes). The site became Beckingham Business Park and the base of a busy transport firm. Unfortunately, the country roads are not really suitable for the size of the vehicles that come and go.

Maldon Tesco was the first Tesco supermarket. Seats were removed from the old Hippodrome cinema in the High Street and little else was done. The cinema had lain empty and unused since 1936 after Shipman and King built the Embassy. It was the time when Cohen said "Pile 'em high and sell them cheap".

8.14 The end of traditional farming and women's field work

In the 1930s, 40s and 50s, Heybridge women went to work in the fields. In the seasons they picked peas, beans, soft fruit, and apples. Mrs. Marg Frost was one of eleven children and she remembers arriving in the pea field at 3am and having to pick a bag of peas with her sister before breakfast. When she was grown up, she could pick four to five bags a day and remembers picking peas grown by Padge Wakelin on Glebe field in Heybridge. She lived in a council house built around 1950 on that field in Glebe Road for over 50 years.

Ploughing divided fields by stetches, a means of draining them. The 'ditch' created between every six or so furrows would be changed each year. Pea pickers claimed a stetch, pulled up the pea rice, tore off the peas into a bucket, and full buckets of peas were poured into a sack. The foreman weighed the sacks that had to hold 40lbs and tied them up with string. Denis Fenn earned 1s.9d. which was later reduced to 9d. for a sack of peas early in the war. Mrs. Wareham remembers going to Totham as a child on a bicycle with her mother when pickers were paid 5s.0d. a bag of peas just after the war. Judy Betteridge nee Wright, remembers her father organising her and her mother on pea picking forays. Mr. Wright was a licensed fisherman; fishing did not take place at pea picking time. The 'grapevine' revealed where picking was taking place, they left home on their bicycles as early as 3am; the best stetches were weed free in the middle of the field. They started picking around 4 - 4.30am. In the early 1950s, 7s.6d. was paid for a bag. Experienced pickers were very dexterous and were able to pick several sacks in a day. However, the scientific testing of peas for ripeness and the coming of mechanical viners that harvested and processed peas at the optimum time, meant that pea picking by hand ceased. Judy Betteridge earned 1s.6d. picking blackberries in a field adjoining Boucherne in the early 1950s.

Mrs. Wareham went by bus in the 1950s to Great Totham to pick apples at Mr. Smith's farm. She enjoyed the camaraderie and fun; mothers brought their young children who played in the fields. Mrs. Frost remembers going on a friend's trailer behind his car to Woodham Walter to pick apples. Kathy Lang remembers apple picking in Tiptree with a group of friends who did not like climbing a ladder for the top fruit, which she did. This was a bit awkward in the year when she was heavily pregnant. It is sad to realise that three quarters of our orchards have been grubbed out since 1950.

Potato picking was a hard and dirty job for women in the autumn. A plough turned up the potatoes and pickers collected them in buckets. Mrs. Frost, Mrs. Lang and Mrs. Wareham, all Heybridge residents, remember happy times in the fields. The income from field work was a valuable addition to the family finances.

Another useful extra was the Co-op dividend that was credited on every purchase; the amount was written on a 'check' with the customer's Co-op number (which many filed) and the dividend could be drawn annually. These monies paid for household sheets and pillowcases, children's clothes and other home replacements.

George Free had about 350 acres after W.W.2 having bought land over the years. He farmed Jacob's Farm, Middle Farm and Canterbury Farm in Goldhanger Road Heybridge. He had declined to buy Heybridge Hall Farm fearing the expense of repairing the sea wall.

The Rev. John Wade, a United Reformed minister, has written articles about Heybridge and the story of farming from 1910 to 1965. Extracts from his account of Mr. Free's farming year have been used here to illustrate the changes since W.W.2 together with contributions from **Gordon Digby**. Mr. Digby worked on a fruit farm in Woodham Walter for five years until he decided he was interested in the mechanical side of farming. After two years at Doe's, he joined J. Brittain Pash in Chelmsford whose triangular shaped premises faced the old cattle market across Market Road. He became service manager, a sales representative and later their workshop manager. Brittain Pash's ceased trading because their premises were demolished for the County Hall extensions. Mr. Flower started Eastern Tractors and Mr. Digby became general manager of their Chelmsford operation.

"During the late spring and summer, the fields overlooking Goldhanger Road were a hive of activity. From 6am, you could hear the humming of local women talking and gathering in the crops of potatoes, peas or runner beans. The women worked in the fields until 4pm when what they had picked would be weighed and recorded in a book. The produce was put in special sacks or boxes that were stencilled with the name Ellis. The produce would be taken to the goods' yard at Maldon West Station by horse and cart and then transported by rail to Covent Garden in London. Early the following morning, the produce would be sold to shops and markets across the country."

George Free had three regular part-time working women on the farm and women from the nearby council houses were employed when more help was needed. Five men were employed full-time and there were local part-time men at the busy time of harvest and for other seasonal work such as potato picking. George Wade worked for Mr. Free for his entire working life, a total of fifty-four years and he received a long service medal from the Essex Agricultural Society which was presented to him by the Queen Mother. Today, his son, The Rev. Wade, is the proud owner of that medal. There were four working horses on the farm before 1960; two were Suffolk Punches, named Smart and Blossom, and two lighter horses, named Daisy and Vixen. George Free also kept a pony named Toby for his light two-wheeled cart. Horses were still the main working animals: they still did some ploughing and they were used for carting hay in the spring and corn at harvest time, to carry manure for muck spreading from the two wheeled tumbrel, and to pull the seed drill and harrow (for breaking up the clods of soil). Stockmen had to feed their horses twice on Sundays. George Free bought a second Fordson tractor in the late 1940s or early 1950s when the last of the three pairs of heavy horses went and used the remainder of the stables to expand his herd.

There was a herd of pedigree Friesian cows of Terling and Lavenham blood. The herd was regarded as one of the best milking herds in Heybridge and the revenue from the milk paid the annual wage bill for all Mr. Free's workers. The Jacobs Farm herd was fed in the meadow in the winter and grazed on the northern Scraley Road in summer. When grass became short, young stock went to Elms Farm, Woodham Mortimer to feed on grass grown on the heavy land. During the early 1960s, Mr. Free sold his herd of sixteen milch cows. The milking shed is now a successful farm shop.

Miss G. M. Baker of Margaretting records that binders were horse drawn before the use of tractors and they cut the corn and tied corn in sheaves. The sheaves were stood up in traves or stooks so that wind could blow through the centre to dry the corn and any green stuff would shrivel and die. The number of sheaves in a stook varied; short straw sheaves had fewer than longer straw. The stooks were left in the field up to eight weeks. Boys often followed the binder with sticks to chase rabbits as they fled out of the corn. Usually they were allowed to keep those they killed. After the corn had been carted into the stack yard, the women were allowed to glean. They collected corn, some fed it to their chickens while others threshed out the grain with a flail and took it to the miller to be ground.

Corn stacks occupied George Free's two stack yards. A thatcher would visit the farm in late September to thatch the stacks. There was great excitement when George Witney from Little Totham arrived with his steam engine during the damp month of November. The steam engine powered the belt that drove the threshing tackle. Barn work would then begin: a worker would untie the sheaves and toss them into the threshing machine that separated the straw that then was transported by elevator to the new stack being built to be used as litter for the farm animals during the winter. The chaff, husks of the grain and the grains of wheat, barley or oats would descend into separate sacks. Mr. Digby called the sacks that held 2¼ cwt of grain 'killers' because the men had to carry these heavy loads to the carts to be taken to Hasler's Mill at Fullbridge. The oats were used as cattle food in the winter. The winter tasks were hedging and ditching.

Combine harvesters came to England from Canada early in the 1940s. The first made cuts 8ft. wide. Massey Harris set up a factory in Kilmarnock to manufacture machines that cut 8ft.6ins. Gordon Digby drove these very large machines, too large to go on a lorry, from Chelmsford Railway Station to the buyer's farm. Later, when the combines were more compact, they could be transported on a lorry. Today's combines do a 30ft. cut.

Peter Wormell writing in a local newspaper pointed out that the countryside in 1900 looked as it had done for hundreds of years: small fields and hedges, hay and corn stacks in the stack yard next to the farmsteads and barns. There was a school in nearly every village. Villages had shops, often in the front room of a cottage. The fields were hoed by men and women, the harvest carried by wagons to the stack yard and the whole village helped to get the harvest in. The village fed itself; everything that was eaten and drunk was village grown.

In the early 1960s cattle, sheep and pigs were still being driven to Chelmsford Market on the roads. Drovers were accustomed to walk many miles to and from the markets. The author watched cattle being driven down Baddow Road, Chelmsford in the early 1930s. Animals from the other side of Chelmsford passed Hoffman's and Marconi's and through Tindal Square to the market. During W.W.2, sheep grazed on the Warren Golf Course when only a few holes were allowed to be in play. These sheep were driven to market through Danbury, Great Baddow, along Baddow Road to Chelmsford High Street, through Tindal Square along Market Road (now Victoria Road South) to the market. The pens for cattle, sheep and pigs were on the south side of Market Road while all the little animals and birds, such as rabbits, ducks, chickens and guinea pigs, were in hutches on the other side of the road. Farm implements of all descriptions were displayed in front of the old fire station and stalls were in Threadneedle Street. Kathy Lang and her friends truanted from secondary school on the day of the monthly horse market at Chelmsford and rode horses with no tack, bare back and no reins, to show them for the auctioneers - at the same time keeping an eye up for the school attendance officer. Perhaps this gave Kathy her enthusiasm for her adventurous riding holidays to Mongolia, China, Spain, Turkey, and Romania.

Mrs. B. M. Seabrook said cattle were driven on the hoof from a farm near Colchester to their farm, Pond Farm, Tolleshunt D'Arcy for the winter. When they were ready for market, they were driven to Colchester on the hoof.

Goose Cottages in Battlesbridge are a reminder of the time geese were assembled there and the birds waded through warm tar so that the tar 'shoes' protected their feet when on the long walk to the market because birds with damaged feet fetched less money. I am told that turkeys went through the same process on their way to market.

In Langford Road (Holloway Road) the Cock Inn was a meeting place for drovers for many years. Between W.W.1 and W.W.2, farm labourers were working a six day week; the day began at 6am and ended at 5pm with an hour off for breakfast and an hour off for dinner – a total of 54 hours. Most tied cottages had large gardens and there were various allotments in Heybridge but growing food after the long hours of work was a burden; the extra food grown was very important as wages were very low. Men were known to work by moonlight or a hurricane lamp after dark.

For eight hundred years there were ten farms in Heybridge. Now only part of Mr. Free's Canterbury Farm exists as a farm with some of the land of Jacobs and Middle Farm farmed by George Free's grandson, Duncan.

8.15 Farming in the second half of the twentieth century

The emphasis on improving crop yields and farming prosperity continued until the 1950s. Farmers were encouraged to increase food production by the payment of government subsidies to grow crops. As machinery was increasingly used on farms, fewer workers were needed and those who were employed had to be capable of doing some of the servicing, repair and maintenance of complicated and expensive machinery. School leavers complained to the author that they could not find jobs on farms as employment opportunities in the countryside declined. The author has seen a photograph of a Harvest Supper in a village hall (the author cannot remember where) showing numerous employees on a farm, between Tolleshunt D'Arcy and Tollesbury, before the war that contrasts with small numbers working on farms today. The combine harvester replaced men. It carried out all the work of the binder; "the travers' carters, stackers, thatchers and threshing gangs in one operation and the hydraulic tipping grain trailers carried the grain to the new grain barn". Tractor drivers had more than quadrupled their output. Tied houses were no longer needed for farm workers: their location in pleasant rural sites makes them saleable but retired farm workers and their widows still occupy some of them. Time will sort this out. Since W.W.2, there has been a trend for workers to live in council houses in villages rather than isolated farm cottages.

A law was enacted in 1959 that decreed all tractors had to have a safety roll bar to protect the driver if the tractor turned over. Later, tractors had to have a cab. Those doing specialised tasks were exempt, as were those that went into a building.

When it was forbidden to burn straw, machinery was fixed on the back of combines to chop it up so that it could be ploughed in. A factory in Norfolk makes straw building blocks. A lot of straw is collected into huge rolls, wrapped in black polythene and made into huge stacks.

Today, huge machines can be seen traversing big fields with the drivers in their enclosed, air-conditioned cabs, with mobile phones and radios and computer screens that are controlled by global positioning systems. The operations are connected to the farm base stations and progress recorded on digital maps of the fields. The tractor, combine harvester or sprayer will not allow variations of the course set by the computer programmes, as a farmer from Southminster found out when he tried to change direction. The computer can record the most fertile parts of a field so that extra fertilisers can be applied elsewhere. It can assess the soil conditions, minimising the need for farming skills. These machines are accurate to within two centimetres. It is not an uncommon sight to see tractors ablaze with headlights going up and down large fields around Heybridge late at night. This contrasts with pre W.W.2 when a single furrow plough, drawn by a horse, ploughed an acre a day so that a 30 acre field would occupy a ploughman all through January. By 2008, Andrew English described a Case 1H STX with ten furrow plough, twenty five cultivators and myriad rollers that can plough such a field by lunchtime; the machine cost £245,000, used ten litres of fuel an acre and travelled at 7.8mph. The machine cannot drive unless the driving seat is occupied although a driver is not necessary. This seems to suggest that unmanned machines will be developed when the law allows. At the last Royal Show at Stoneleigh in 2009, Robin Page reported seeing "an American Case III (International Harvester) with a 35-feet cutter, combining 80 tons of wheat an hour and costing a mere £270,000" and covering 50 acres in a day.

Years ago, hedges were grubbed out to create the large fields needed to operate modern machinery. Now fields surrounded by hedges are cut by machines that can do a good job in the hands of a skilled driver. Today, ditches are cleared by mechanical diggers that used to be a winter job for farm workers.

There was bad weather worldwide in 2007; early heavy rain in Britain caused crop failures, in Australia catastrophic drought caused the failure of the grain harvest and death of livestock, and there were problems in India and China. The global shortages of key crops such as potatoes, peas, eggs, oranges and meat, meant that British farmers have been allowed to cultivate set aside which was the EU policy of paying farmers for not cultivating 10% of their land to limit out put. Supposedly, this policy was suspended for one year. Shall we ever see again the sad, uncultivated fields that resulted while now increased food production is needed to meet the needs of the expanding world population and wealthy Chinese change their diets by eating more grain and meat? Attempts to grow and use biofuels have been largely abandoned because it caused a rise in world food prices and deforestation.

The Milk Marketing Board was established in 1933 and began operations in 1934. Almost every farm in Essex used to have a small herd of dairy cows and dairy farmers had to sell their milk to the Milk Marketing Board who sold it on to dairies for bottling for home deliveries or to creameries for cheese and butter production. The government's aim for the organisation was to supply affordable milk to the consumer and for the producers to receive a fair price and regular payments to give stability to the milk marketing. The Board was funded by deductions from farmers' milk payments, making them independent of government control. Farmers welcomed a regular cash flow that was unusual in this cyclical industry.

Pasteurisation was invented by Louis Pasteur who first carried out the process on 2nd April 1862. The heat process makes food spoil less easily. However, the ability of the process to kill off the bacteria common in milk that causes human tuberculosis, split the scientists. The first commercial equipment was manufactured in Germany in 1880 and by 1885, milk was regularly pasteurised in Copenhagen and Stockholm. Only 1.5% of Britain's milk supply was pasteurised by 1926. The majority of retail milk was still raw in 1939 but public acceptance came when the technology was perfected after W.W.2 although many small towns and rural areas still drank unpasteurised until well into the 1950s.

Ten gallon churns were collected daily from the farms that were placed on wooden platforms at the farm gate. In this locality, the Board decided which dairies should receive the milk. The choice made by the Board was between Lord Rayleigh's, Chelmsford or Colchester Co-op, or Magness and Usher. Around 1966, the Board pressed farmers to invest in cooling vats and bulk handling equipment. By the 1970s most milk was collected from farms in road tankers. The last churns were collected in 1979.

Milk bottles came in during the 1930s. Some village roundsmen continued to pour milk into bottles from a jug and seal them with a cardboard disc. Later, foil caps came in. Early bottles came in ½ pint, 1 pint, 1½ pint and 2 pint sizes but, by the 1950s, only 1 pint bottles were used. Lord Rayleigh's dairies were the first producers to abandon glass bottles in 1960 when they adopted triangular-shaped tetrapak cartons at their Hatfield Peverel bottling plant. They were mainly sold in shops and supermarkets. Lord Rayleigh's reverted to returnable glass bottles fifteen years later.

There were many changes in the dairy industry in the middle of the twentieth century. From 1950, sophisticated milking machinery led to the concentration of dairying to large units while silage was used for feed in the winter, not hay.

The Milk Marketing Boards ceased operations in 1994 because politicians had to bring the UK into line with other European Union countries. Also, it was believed that competition would create a market that would benefit the consumer. However, producers lost a guaranteed outlet for their milk. Legislators had failed to foresee the buying power of supermarket chains and that some supermarkets would view milk as a loss leader. Subsequently, farmers struggled with returns below the cost of milk production and many went out of dairying while supermarkets imported cheap milk. The EEC Dairy Herds Conversion Scheme 1972 encouraged farmers to abandon milk production voluntarily and keep beef cattle; the quota system was imposed in 1984 under which farmers were paid to give up milk production. At first, there was a market in the sale of quotas because farmers were anxious to get rid of cows when the money they received for milk was below the cost of production. Home deliveries became rarer when supermarkets sold milk cheaply and customers could store bulk purchases in their refrigerators. By 2007, six thousand dairy farmers in England had left the industry and there are very few dairy farmers left in Essex. Lord Rayleigh Farms have adopted the intensive method of dairying; around five hundred milch cows are kept in open sided barns and only 'dry' cows go out onto pastures, cows are milked three times a day and the cows are fed on concentrates. Fishers in Southminster tried the method but discontinued it.

Essex is the driest English county. Droughts during 1975-6 caused farmers to install irrigation systems, create reservoirs and mount huge sprayers to water such crops as potatoes. Fields are covered with polythene tunnels being watered with trickle water hoses around Heybridge. Potatoes have become a useful farm crop in Essex now that the cultivation is wholly mechanised. The planting, harvesting, washing and packing takes place on the farm and the crop is sold to the retail trade, manufacturers and caterers.

Essex has always been the leading cereal producing county of England. At the end of the twentieth century, cereal's reputation as a dirty crop had been eliminated by the use of selective herbicides. Fertilisers restore soils after the impoverishment of cereal crops and wheat has been bred with short stalks that stand up and can be cut be with combine harvesters. Straw is cut up enabling it to be incorporated in the soil since stubble burning is now forbidden. This means wheat can be grown year after year and yields have increased phenomenally. Since the money received by farmers has risen, acreages have expanded and farmers have been able to invest in improvements to their farms. Farms have built their own grain store with conveyors, elevators, a reception pit and a grain dryer because all the grain is brought in within a few weeks. Bentall's produced wooden conveyors and other equipment and several models of grain dryers in the 1970s for these changes. Threshing used to be spread over the winter months and cereal samples were taken to the corn exchanges during the winter. The failure of the wheat crop in 2007 resulted in soaring feed costs for egg producers and pig rearers so that manufactured food products and large scale catering costs increased. In desperation, pig farmers sent breeding sows to slaughter early which affected long term outcomes. The world food shortages brought about by bad weather and the increasing prosperity in developing countries with their demands for food imports may result in the encouragement of agricultural production in Britain and lead to more realistic farm prices. A proper return could see farmers return to prosperity; agriculture has always been cyclical.

Soft fruit has been grown around Heybridge for many years but as more women worked full-time, pickers were hard to get, resulting in farmers developing "pick-your-own" fruit. Many bought freezers to store the fruit through the winter but the cultivation requires careful, labour intensive work. When it proved to be less profitable than expected, farmers ploughed in the plants. The McLauchlans had "pick your own" at one time and were contracted to supply large quantities of soft fruit to Goldhanger Fruit Farms. The Manns at Little Mountains Farm have continued to be successful. As the season progresses, they offer gooseberries, raspberries, loganberries and black currants. Their other speciality is the rearing of turkeys. Because turkeys can die as a result of being in heavy rain, they are kept under large umbrella type buildings with wire netting sides to give them ample air. They sell fresh meat products and frozen soft fruit all year round from their purpose built brick shop.

We are seeing farms around Heybridge cultivated by contractors since farm machinery has become very expensive and used only for short periods each year. Some farmers buy the seeds and fertilisers or, where contractors make the purchase, they cultivate the land and the profit or loss is shared. Other landowners around Heybridge are leasing out farms and fields, often to neighbouring farmers, under agricultural tenancies. Since farmers may not wish the public to know that their farms are cultivated by contractors they are not named here.

Edward Strutt would probably have approved of the planning, recording and statistics produced on computers by farmers today, while farmers bewail the complicated returns required by Department for the Environment Food and Rural Affairs: (DEFRA). Nowadays, some farmers employ secretaries who visit farms, usually on a part-time basis, to keep the records.

8.16 Farming diversification

Diversification is not new:

Mr. and Mrs. Speakman established a camp site in 1933 and supplied campers with farm produce; over the years, it has expanded and become Osea Leisure Park.

A caravan park with about thirty pitches was established at Bradwell Waterside in the 1930s on a field owned by Clement Parker. When the landlord of the Green Man public house owned the site, he sold six plots to members of his family.

The power station was built on Down Hall, the site of pleasant holiday chalets in the 1930s.

Dan Kingston acquired Mill Beach Caravan Park in 1947 and catered for rising numbers of visitors when Mill Beach was a popular resort for caravaners and day visitors before the coming of cheap package holidays to Spain.

Houldings bought Home Farm on the opposite side of the road when Padge Wakelin died in 1953. They built car servicing facilities and office accommodation on the site.

George Free's daughter, Joan, married Norman McCready, Maldon National Provincial bank manager, and their two sons, Simon and Duncan, inherited Jacob's Farm where they run a farm shop in the former dairy. Star, Simon's daughter, offers a wide range of fruit and vegetables from the farm and local suppliers. Shoppers and catering establishments appreciate the range of potatoes. Apples come from Simon and Duncan's sister's fruit farm: Star says there are around forty-five unusual breed of chickens and ducks running about the old farm buildings that are much appreciated by young visitors.

Furzelands Farm, Maypole Road formerly in Heybridge: Maldon Fruit, a wholesaler of fruit and vegetables to shops, restaurants and schools operates from a large warehouse in the farmyard.

Howells Farm, Maypole Road formerly in Heybridge: three farm buildings have been converted into six units. They are rented by Jag Security Ltd, Cary and Company Certified Practising Accountants, Blackwater Osteopathic Clinic with five partners and the Apollo Group.

Mitchell's Farm Barn, Langford Road, Heybridge has been converted into a private house.

Chigborough Farm and Loft's Farm: former gravel pits have been stocked with fish for anglers. Extensions at Chigborough Farm have been turned into a restaurant while other farm premises are used to smoke various delicacies.

David Cooper and his brother at Brazil's Farm, Woodham Ferrers sold their dairy herd in the autumn of 2007.

Hall Farm Woodham Mortimer has created five smart office units, Monument Offices, in former farm buildings.

Pear Tree Farm, Spring Lane, Hatfield Peverel has a restaurant for lunches and teas in a former apple orchard's buildings where cakes and baked goods can be bought and shops are supplied. Among the retail units there are a furniture and gifts showroom, a plumbing and heating engineer and a gourmet foods retailer. There are pitches for five touring caravans with link up to electricity supply and a tipping point for sewage.

Peter Richardson changed Birkett Hall into livery stables in 1988 where between seventy to eighty horses are accommodated for owners who arrange their feeding, grooming and exercising. Rayleigh Angling Society fishes in three lakes on the former farm. Another small pond has ducks and moorhens while 50,000 deciduous trees, including oak and ash, have been planted for which a maintenance allowance is paid for five years that includes coppicing.

Lofts Farm in Great Totham has fishing lakes.

Derek Kelly successfully launched Kelly's turkeys in 1965 at Springate Farm, Danbury, with a new breed that has become nationally known. Derek and Molly Kelly began breeding free range, black feathered turkeys from Oregon stock in 1972 at Springate Farm. Their Kelly Bronze turkeys are reared in family farms around Danbury and noted for their flavour: they are sold nationally and have won many awards - in 2009 they won the Poultry Producer of the Year award.

Mr. Douglas Smith inherited Burnham Wick Farm from his father and spent forty years land draining it. His son, Martin, has blocked the drains on a ten hectare field to create an environmentally friendly habitat for wildlife and received government grants to do so. This was also connected with the national policy of discouraging food production. His farm is a Caravan Certificated Location for five caravans or motor homes.

9.0 Shipping along the Blackwater Estuary

9.1 History

Denys Harrison tells how Captain Robert Parker brought the brig 'Fortunes Increase' from Sunderland with 150 chaldrons (188 tons) of coal on 23rd April 1796 to Heybridge Basin. (It would be interesting to know if Captain Robert Parker was related to the Bradwell family and the author's paternal grandparents). The cargo was taken to Little Baddow in a lighter called Peace, built by Tepin Woodcraft at Heybridge Basin where the Navigation ended at that time. This was the forerunner of the main cargoes between Chelmsford and the port of Heybridge Basin; coal and timber brought in brigs, brigantines and schooners as well as coasting ships including hoys and sailing barges. Much of the coal was brought in little brigs called 'Billy Boys'. Timber came from Scandinavia. Hoys were small to medium coastal vessels with a single mast that had a fore and aft rig with a square topsail.

Barry Pearce's description of a spritsail barge:
On a spritsail barge, the sprit swings so the loose-footed mainsail takes up a similar position on either tack, the top of the sprit held in position as required by wire vangs (guy ropes).

The sheets of the mainsail and foresail are secured to permanent wooden or steel 'horses', fastened athwart the deck. The foresail sheet usually remains in the same tension but the mainsail sheet is held by a double-sheave wooden block to a steel ring (traveller) that transverses the main horse. The tackle can be eased or heaved tight as required by the skipper - or let free when the mainsail is brailed up to the mast - by the mate using a winch.

The topsail is set or stowed from the deck and stays aloft, making it possible for the barge to be crewed by a man and a boy since all the heavy tackle is permanently in place. Coasting barges and 'stack barges carried a skipper, mate and a boy, the boy, perhaps eventually becoming a barge mate and future skipper.

photo of a Spritsail barge by Barry Pearce

In the early 1800s, Thames Barges were built to transfer cargo to and from the bigger ships that could not anchor close enough to the shallow shoreline of the Thames ports of Essex and Kent. Flat-bottomed sailing barges evolved to bring cargoes to and from London; some had a draught of only 2ft. and they were crewed by the skipper and a mate who was often a young boy. The major cargoes outward were wheat and flour to London. From 1870 onwards, cheaper grain was imported from North America to London where it was collected and brought out from London on barges for milling. Barges brought coal, cement, bricks and beer to Heybridge and Maldon. By 1880-1890, barges had developed their present style; the hull defines it - they were a flat bottomed box, a shape that held the most cargo. Later, they were adapted to make journeys of their own; they were fitted with spritsail rigs, a wooden spar (the sprit) supporting fore and aft sail. The sprit was always in place making it possible for the vessel to be handled by a skipper and a mate. Wooden lee boards, measuring 2½ ft. dropped down at the sides of the vessel to provide lateral resistance and to keep the barge down in the water. The expected life of barges and stackies was thirty to forty years but the life was extended by frequent lengthening and re-building, usually after they were damaged. The remains of many sailing barges and smacks lie along the shores of the Blackwater and along the creeks: "By the late nineteenth century, barges had grown in size and could carry loads of up to 60 tons. The tiller had been replaced with a ship's wheel for better handling and the design evolved into an even shallower vessel. They carried 5 tons of sail, rigging and mast" (P. L. Harris).

In the mid-1800s, cargo came from all over the Empire to London where coastal barges delivered it along the Essex coast. The hey-day of Thames Barges came in the 1890s when they voyaged to Holland, Germany, Belgium and France. The coastal barge trade continued into the 1920s and 1930s when auxiliary motors began to be fitted into barges to supplement the sails and diesel engines were fitted in lorries; causing a decline in barge traffic.

New barges were often named after wives or daughters of the Navigation men or barge owners, or after an event in their lives.

9.2 Stackies

These vessels were owned by Maldon hay and straw merchants and farmers including Harry Stevens of Purleigh Hall, James Cardenall of St Lawrence, Richard Seabrook of Tolleshunt D'Arcy and Bradwell on Sea farmers; William Hatch, T. Goymer of Wick Farm and the Parkers. Occasionally, Tollesbury farmers participated in the trade.

John Howard built his first barge Surprise in 1879. His stackies were distinctly shapely, handy and fast. As well as building new barges, John Howard repaired them; refits of stackies usually took place during the harvest season.

Stackies were specially designed barges to carry cargoes of hay and straw from waterside berths on lonely creeks, the foreshore, or in outfalls leading from the hinterland, to go to London and return with manure. Hay and straw from farms along the estuary were loaded and built into stacks by the crew. Two men were expected to build a stack in a day. John Leather describes how hay and straw was made into trusses by hand lever presses. The barge crew built the stack and started by loading the hold with tightly packed trusses and then built the stack 10 - 12ft. high or more above the deck. The stack projected outboard 1ft. from the rail on each side and might weigh 40 tons and reach 12ft. high. The stack was held in place by the stability of its construction and its weight. The top was covered with two layers of straw trusses and covered with three securely fixed stack cloths to prevent the rain from penetrating. During the voyage, this provided a firm foothold for the mate or boy perched on top of the stack who would direct the skipper at the helm, the skipper having no forward sight. The danger during the voyage was from fire.

Vast quantities of hay and straw were needed in the metropolis; merchants dealt in feed and bedding stuff for the horses pulling carriages, drays and omnibuses. On their return, the stackies carried manure and street sweepings to be laid on the land to improve the fields of the local farms. This was inconvenient in the growing season when twenty cart loads from one barge had to be driven up lanes until they found a grass verge to dump it on or until it could be used. The trade route along the Blackwater and 'the London River' became known locally as the 'hay up, dung down'. Stephen Nunn writes that "if the destination was above the Pool of London, the mast and rigging were lowered into the stack by removing some of the hay. This allowed the stacky to pass under the bridges - London Bridge or 'The Tower' perhaps with the help of a 'huffler' (or pilot)".

Stackies were crewed by the skipper and a boy. Most skippers had no paper qualifications but they were excellent practical seamen in their own type of vessel and in waters they knew. There were no formal apprenticeships or qualifications. The large sea going barges had two, three or four crewmen. Few skippers owned the barges they sailed although they often had shares in them. Sometimes they sailed in other owners' barges.

Stackies carried an average of forty wagon loads of hay, barge owners received 7s.0d. for each wagon load; a total of £14. The owner received half this, and the crew £7 from which the boy was paid 3s.0d. a week plus his food, he had 12s.0d. extra when the barge was huffling up narrow, difficult creeks or negotiating through bridges on the Thames. The skipper had two thirds of this and the mate one third. This was fine in good weather but they suffered hardship when the wind was blowing a gale, there was fog in the River Thames, or they were waiting for a cargo; there was no waiting time money. Sometimes mates had to buy their food.

Thomas Kirby from Bradwell on Sea had five sons who were bargemen, skippers and owners. The Directory of Owners records thirteen Parkers between 1825 and 1930; nine men and four women. William Parker (the author's great grandfather) was engaged in the trade in 1850. The Parker family had assembled a fleet of twenty fast barges including stackies by 1900. The author's grandparents lived at Bradwell House on the Waterside where her grandmother owned a parrot. Barges were loaded on to wagons at the quay and barge skippers used to send a message saying 'cover the b….. bird' because the parrot would shout 'whoa' just as the horses got going up the slope from the quay. At the top of this slope, the 'hill', the sails were spread on a small meadow where they were renovated and often recut by the owner's sail maker, 'Yankee' Bill Phillips, before being dressed with the usual preservative mixture of oil and ochre to give the rich, supple tan colour to the flax canvas, as the author found out when she spent summer holidays in a cottage at the Waterside before W.W.2. Houses were built on this site around 2000.

Typically, the Bradwell barges brought general supplies to the hinterland. The local expression was that supplies were 'swum in' and the author remembers watching the unloading of the wagons at the quay in the 1930s. The straw trade had started to tail off from 1912 when horse buses began to be replaced by motor vehicles, and ended in the 1950s.

The tarred wooden workshops adjoining Adolphus Parker's house had been used before 1910 in connection with the barge trade. Adolphus Parker had been apprenticed to Howard, the famous ship builder in Maldon from 1880 to 1888. His indenture is in Maldon Museum. Today, these workshops are used by Essex County Council for Bradwell Outdoor Education Centre where people of all ages take part in sailing, canoeing, archery, high ropes and mountain bicycle events.

9.3 Barges and coasters registered in the inland port of Heybridge and Heybridge Basin in the Maldon Port list:

Ship owners listed (Barges and Coasters) at the Port of Maldon compiled by Richard Hugh Perks names 319 owners. It includes fifty-four owners from the inland port of Heybridge and Heybridge Basin between 1786 and 1935.

William Aldham, Sloop owner and miller of Heybridge 1809-1812

Samuel….Ship owner, sail maker, Heybridge Basin 1810-14

Isaac Belsham, Ship owner, maltster and coal merchant, Heybridge Basin 1838-67

William Bentall Barge owner, iron founder, coal merchant, Heybridge 1827-42

Bentall and Co, Barge owner, iron founders, Heybridge 1889

James Blatch, Ship owner, Heybridge 1843-4

Brown and Co, Lighter owners, timber merchants Heybridge Basin and Chelmsford 1930s

Arthur Butcher and Co, Barge owners, timber merchants, Heybridge Basin 1911-16

William Carter, Ship owner, Heybridge Basin 1861-1870s

Charles Carter, Ship owner, Heybridge Basin 1894-1900s

Carter and Clark, Ship owners, Heybridge Basin 1880s-1900s

John Chaney, Ship owner, Heybridge Basin 1831-1855

John Clark, Ship owner, Heybridge Basin 1878-1890

G Clark, Ship owner Heybridge Basin 1860-2

J T Clark, Ship owner, Heybridge Basin 1894

George Coates, Barge Owner, coal merchant, Heybridge and Chelmsford

Alfred Cross, Barge Owner, Heybridge Basin 1860s

Stephen Cross, Barge Owner victualler, Heybridge Basin 1838-1854

Stephen Cross, Barge Owner, Heybridge Basin 1871-1887

Andrew Douglas, Ship owner, Heybridge Basin 1832-1835

Daniel Eavery, Ship owner, Heybridge Basin 1837-1867

Daniel Eavery, Ship owner, Heybridge Basin 1862-1879

Reuben Farrow, Barge owner, Heybridge Basin 1864-5

John Charles, Float Ship owner, 1864-5

J C Float, Ship and barge owner, Heybridge Basin 1880-1898

George Going, Ship owner, Heybridge Basin 1850s

Octavius Going, Ship owner, Heybridge Basin 1865-1872

Phillip Going, Ship owner, Heybridge Basin 1846-1857

Jeremiah Holloway, Barge owner, wharfinger, Heybridge 1794-1811

Jeremiah Baker, Holloway Barge owner, Heybridge 1853

William Huby, Ship owner, Heybridge Basin 1841-61

John Jeffrey, Barge owner, Heybridge 1852-1862

Henry Joslin, Ship owner, Maldon Fullbridge and Heybridge 1840-1869

Henry Lockwood, Ship owner, Heybridge 1843-4

May and Co Barge, owner, timber merchant, Heybridge Basin 1911

Henry May, Ship owner, Heybridge Basin 1837-1867

John Parke, Ship owner, Heybridge Basin 1843-1853

Robert Parke, Ship owner, Heybridge 1809

Robert Parke, Barge owner, ship builder Heybridge Hall 1810-1935

Thomas Parke, Ship owner, Heybridge Basin 1858-1860

John Perring, Barge owner, Heybridge 1794-1811

Samuel Playle, Ship owner, Heybridge Basin 1845-1860

Richard Raven, Ship owner, Heybridge 1825-1837

Heyward Rush, Barge owner, maltster, Heybridge 1843-1855

Thomas Russell, Ship owner, Heybridge Basin 1849-60

George Smee, Ship owner, Heybridge Basin 1878-1890

William Smee, Ship and Barge owner, victualler, Maldon and Heybridge 1847-1866

Edward Tovee Snr, Ship owner, Heybridge Basin 1861-1870s

Edward Tovee Jnr, Ship owner, Heybridge Basin 1872-1881

Joseph Ward, Barge owner, Wharfinger, Heybridge 1794-1811

Zachariah Webb, Ship owner, miller, Heybridge 1825-1830

William Wood, Ship owner, Heybridge 1825-9

James Woodcraft, Barge and lighter owner, Heybridge Basin 1935

Thomas Worraker, Ship owner, salt mfg. Heybridge 1861-1870s

The importance of coastal trade can be gauged from this list and the ownership along the Blackwater Estuary. Salcott and Virley recorded eight between 1791 and 1872, Tollesbury fourteen between 1787 and 1912, Tolleshunt D'Arcy two between 1803 and 1916 and Bradwell thirty two between 1787 and 1930 including the author's grandfather, Adolphus Parker, barge owner, 1893-1930.

9.4 The Maldon Port List includes barges and coasters outside, but using, the port of Heybridge via the Chelmer and Blackwater Navigation as well as Maldon

The list included coal merchants, corn merchants, timber merchants, hay and straw traders, millers, victuallers, grocers, maltsters, brewers, farmers and a stone mason whose businesses relied on water transport especially in the early and mid nineteenth century before the coming of the railways.

Great Totham 4

Chelmsford 13

Springfield 6

Braintree 2

Hythe Quay 1

Ramsdon 1

Writtle 1

A stackie barge
drawing by Barry Pearce

Wickham Bishops 5

Langford 2

Beeleigh 6

Little Baddow 2

Danbury 1

Great Braxted 1

Woodham Walter

Felstead

9.5 Smuggling

Vessels belonging to some of the most respectable people were seized and condemned for smuggling. These vessels were sold at auction and the money went to the Exchequer. Robert Adams in the Excise Cutter Wasp seized the Endeavour for smuggling; it was condemned and sold at auction at Bradwell on 19th December 1791.

Smugglers from Goldhanger floated rafts of tubs down the River Blackwater and landed them at Mill Beach. It was not until 1822 that enforcement against smuggling was properly co-ordinated when the Preventative Water Guard was formed under the command of HM Coastguard. This unit organised proper boat and foot patrols and set up coastguard stations.

Maldon lost the right to dues and customs in 1838 when the privilege was granted to Colchester.

9.6 Redundant merchant ships in the Blackwater Estuary

During the depression and shipping slump in the 1930s, a line of cargo ships was anchored in the Blackwater Estuary off Tollesbury; on 23rd July 1931 there were forty-three passenger and cargo ships. They were charged a farthing a ton per month, that is around £90, for ships to moor; an attractive low rate. The ships were lit up at night and each had a night watchman aboard.

Over the years, various ships have been moored there during shipping down turns - as containerisation makes traditional ships obsolete, or while waiting for a cargo of seasonable, perishable goods.

Redundant merchant ships off Tollesbury Pier SOURCE Lloyd Blackburn Maldon Society

Perambulations and Personalities around Heybridge

10.0 Langford Road, Holloway Road, Crescent Road & Elms Farm

10.1 Heybridge village houses pre-Bentall and in the nineteenth century

Much of pre-eighteenth century Heybridge developed around the Square and westwards from Black Bridge. At various times, the boundaries of Heybridge have changed. Today, we know the road from Black Bridge to Langford Cross as Holloway Road; it was named after Jeremiah Holloway when this part of Langford was transferred to the parish of Heybridge. The road was not macadamised until the mid-1920s.

It was not until the coming of the Navigation after 1797 that the centre of Heybridge moved and buildings were erected around the church. Jeremiah Holloway lived in Bridge House and owned cottages opposite that are original Heybridge village houses built before the Chelmer and Blackwater Navigation was constructed.

Jeremiah Holloway's mother, who had remarried and become Mrs. Elizabeth Digby, lived in Grove Park, Chiswick and owned land and premises in Wood Lane which she leased to Hagwood Henry Rush of Messing. There was a granary, maltings, a pump house, stables, cart shed and a cottage. He had another malting in Messing. He carried on the business from 1859 until 1892.

Villeins is a listed cottage behind Holloway House. The cottage is one of the original village houses built before the coming of Bentall's. Mrs. Miller, who was a very great friend of the Bentall family, lived at Holloway House. She died on 25th June 1925 at the age of 99 years.

The Cutts Bakery, run by the father and his son, George, was behind Bridge House. Their bread was delivered daily in Heybridge and Rosie Cutts, the daughter, sold bread from their shop in The Street where Betty Chittendon remembers buying sweets.

Major Williams lived in Holloway Road. It was he who met the trains at Maldon East station and took day visitors to Mill Beach; he collected newspapers from the station and delivered them in his two wheeled cart pulled by a donkey.

Woodlands Farm is situated in Holloway Road. Charles (Charlie) Lappage and his wife, Aggie, came from Robin Hood Bay Yorkshire to Layer Marney and then to Elms Farm in Heybridge. Charlie had two daughters and four sons. Two sons, Roy and Arthur, worked on the farm; Jim went to Hereford as a gamekeeper and Fred, the eldest, remained in Yorkshire. The daughters married locally: Norah married Henry Brown, the butcher, on Market Hill, Maldon, and Elsie came south with her brother at the age of three and lived with him in Layer Marney after her parents died until she married Walter Ernest Springett who was a wheelwright. His business was on the Causeway next to Mr. Cooper, the blacksmith. Metal wheels were replacing wooden ones by 1922 and the gypsies, for whom Walter Springett did work, were bad payers so he went to Sadd's where his skills were still needed.

Charlie Lappage ran a dairy at Woodlands from the mid 1800s during the time when Bentall's was expanding. Later, his sons, Arthur and Roy, delivered milk from smart horse drawn carts to Bentall's expanding work force housed in the firm's houses in Heybridge.

Charlie rented Stoney Meadows until he was able to buy it from Arthur Butcher, who had bought it in the Milbanke sale. He also rented land in Wood Lane from the Belshams. In 1940 he bought stables there from Arthur Butcher.

The Lappage dairy herd grazed on Stoney Meadows. Twice a day the cows crossed Holloway Road from the lane beside Chelmer Terrace to the dairy on the opposite side of the road. Mr. Roy Arthur Lappage stood on the crest of Black Bridge and waved a red flag to warn traffic from Maldon to stop. The cows knew their way to and from the pastures without guidance; buses and other traffic were held up. (It was doubly inconvenient if the railway crossing gates were shut following a delay in Holloway Road). Before regulations requiring milk to be sold in bottles in the 1940s the milkman used a measuring jug hanging from the handle on the side of the churn to ladle milk into householders' jugs. Arthur Lappage did a round in Goldhanger Road and to Bentall's workers' houses while Charlie did Holloway Road and Crescent Road from horse drawn carts. After his father's death, Roy undertook his round.

When Gordon Digby was a representative for Brittain Pash, he remembers arriving at Stoney Field when Roy Lappage was trying to plough a field suffering from the water grass plague that grows on low lying fields. Roy's tractor plough would not move through the matted weed. Gordon promised to come the next day with a tractor and plough that turned 16in. furrows over and buried the water grass and all the rubbish. Immediately, Roy part-exchanged his tractor and plough for one of these machines.

Arthur was widowed early and married for a second time to a land girl; they had two children, Margaret and David, while Roy married Joan Butcher, Arthur Butcher's daughter, and they had a daughter, Lyndal, who married Tony Pitt and had two sons. Elsie and Ernest Walter Springett had identical twin sons; Harold and Eric, who became middle managers at Sadd's.

10.2 Heybridge from the History, Gazetteer and Directory of the County of Essex 1848

Barry Pearce lent this book that gives a glimpse Heybridge in 1848. There were two large iron foundries and agricultural implement manufactories, several malt houses, granaries. There was an ancient bridge of five arches. Only one small salt works remains of the formerly extensive ones. The village had 1,177 inhabitants and 2,226 acres of land. Oliver Herring was the lessee of lands and tithes belonging to St Paul's Cathedral while parts of the parish belonged to many smaller owners, mostly copyholders. (Copyholding was an old form of land holding whereby the copyholders were responsible for the repair and maintenance of the property while having the freedom to sell it). See Section 10.6

10.3 Heybridge people listed in the 1848 Directory

In the Maldon trade directory William White combines the entries for Heybridge and Maldon for 1848. This is a list of Heybridge entries: it is likely that entries had to be paid for so this is not a full list

Miscellany

Arthy Mrs.

Bartlem, Thos. Supt of Chelmer and Blackwater Navigation

Boyton, Mr. Thomas

Brooke, James Moffat Esq. Hall Farm

Crane, Rev. Rt. Prentice A M, vicar of Heybridge and Tolleshunt Major Heybridge

Murrells, Edw. hawker

Waring, Mr. Walker

Academies

Hurring, Mary

Wrake, Sarah

Bakers

Cross, Stephen

Worraker, Charles

Yell, Charles

Boot and Shoe Makers

Crumpen, Joseph

Everrett, Thomas

Ramplee, Thomas

Waring, Henry

Worraker, John Basin Heybridge

Brick Layer & Builder

Edwards, John

Butcher

Wood, Wm

Worraker, Charles

Yell, Charles

Carpenters and Builders

Bickmore, Stephen

Hayward Thomas

Montague, Daniel Heybridge Basin

China Glass &c Dealers

Buckley, Wm.

Coal Merchants

Belsham, Danl. and Son (Isc)

Bright, Edward and Son

Coates, George

Going Joseph, Basin

Holloway, Joseph

Keys, Wm.

Corn Merchants

Keys, Wm.

Sadd, Daniel

Corn Millers

Ward, Gepp

Farmers

Parke Robert, Heybridge Hall

Wakelin Wm., Jacob's Farm

Grocers and Tea Dealers

Cross, Stephen

Inns and Taverns

Anchor, Jas. Francis

Carpenters' Arms, Danl. Montague Heybridge Basin

Chelmer Inn, Jph. Going, Basin Heybridge

Crown, HY. Whitmore, Broad Street Green

Half Moon, Robt. Sadler, Jolly Sailor, Edw. Tovee. Basin,

Queen's Head, Edw. Harvey, Heybridge

Victoria, Wm.Keyes

Beer Houses

Joslin Ann, Basin

Smee Wm., (Old Star)

Worraker, Thomas

Iron Founders

Bentall Edw. Hammond, (& patent plough, threshing machine, and agl. implement manfr.)

Warren Jph. Saml. (and agri. implement manfr.) Broad St Green,

Linen Drapers, &c.

Cross, Stephen

Maltsters

Belsham, Daniel and Son

Holloway, Josh. Barker

Keys, Wm.

Rush, Hayward Hy. and Son

Marine Store Dealers

Going Joseph, Basin Heybridge

Mayn., Thomas

Salt Merchants

Worraker, (manfr.)

Ship Agents

Going, Jsh. (& sail mkr.) Basin H

Ship Owners

Bartlem, Thomas Chaney John Basin Heybridge

Chaney, John Basin Heybridge

Going, Joseph, Basin Heybridge

Holloway, Joseph,

Parke, Robert, Heybridge Hall

Sadd, Daniel

Shop Keepers

Banham, Alfred

Garland, Susan

Huby, Wm. Basin Heybridge

Knight, Wm.

Skinner, Sarah,

Waring, Henry

Smiths and Farriers

Collis, James

Mott, William

Warren, Jph. Broad St Green H

Straw Hat Makers

Boyton, Heather

Lewis, Ann

Tring, Elizabeth

Timber Merchants

Belsham, D. and Son,

Coates, George

Sadd, Daniel

Wheelwrights

Stephen, Bickmore

10.4 Jeremiah Baker Holloway

One of the principal landowners in Heybridge in 1815 was Jeremiah Holloway who was a farmer and maltster. He owned Honeywood Cottage and lived in Bridge House c.1847 on the north side of Langford (Holloway) Road. The cottages on the south side are now listed; number 7 Bramley Cottage seems to be two houses knocked into one, number 11 Fox Cottage, and its semi-detached neighbour number 12, number 13 Black Bridge Cottage, number 15 Booth Cottage sometime known as Rooster Cottage, and number 17 Carters. He bought Carters, an inn that was next to the present Jehovah's Witnesses Kingdom Hall, from Robert and Joseph Seaman. He reopened it as the Cock Inn. The Cock Inn was next to the road, with its malting house between two cottages. In a photograph of c.1910 drovers called at the inn on their way to Maldon market with their sheep, cows, or other farm animals. While the drovers refreshed themselves, the animals used to stand in groups in the road. Mr. Holloway was the licensee of the Anchor public house in The Square from 1782 to 1827. White lists him as owner of a barge and wharfinger between 1794 and 1811 and his son, Jeremiah, was co-owner with Charles Murrell Handley of the barge Citizen in 1853.

An example of changes in farming is apparent when Jeremiah Holloway insured a farmer's portable threshing machine and horse powered Smyth drill in 1857 to a farmer who was hiring out agricultural machinery.

When the boundary between Heybridge and Langford was changed, the road between Black Bridge and Langford Cross was re-named Holloway Road.

Steps up and down on the Black Bridge and the houses which formed the original village.

10.5 Chelmer House

Chelmer House is reached from Black Bridge. John Playle lived there until 1927/8 when he was 4½. At one time, Mulley carried on a butcher's business in the annexe at the side of the house. Later, Captain Blood, who was the commanding officer of Heybridge Home Guard in W.W.2, owned the house. He worked in the city and travelled to London by train. He owned the large orchard adjacent to the house and his sister sold apples from an extension on the west side of house. The orchard is still there.

10.6 Boucherne

This house is mentioned in the 1171 Charter of Maldon. Edward I granted it to William de Mandeville, Earl of Essex in 1290. There are no further references until c.1830 when the Belsham family acquired Boucherne Farm. It seems the old farm house was changed; the front wall was extended upwards to make a parapet, the present Georgian windows were installed and the front door was moved to the right, forming a new entrance hall. Probably the impressive curved staircase was inserted then and the main reception room was panelled.

10.6a The Belsham Family

The Belsham family had originated in Wickham Bishops, moved to Goldhanger until Daniel Belsham acquired Boucherne in 1830. The family lived in Boucherne for three generations from 1830 until 1935.

Daniel Belsham 1786-1848 was a coal merchant as well as a corn, malt and oil cake merchant with wharfs on the Navigation in the inland port of Heybridge where he coked coal and owned various properties in and around Heybridge. William Bentall decided to locate his new factory in Heybridge because Belsham's cinder oven with lime house and kiln beside the Hoy Inn (later the site of Hunter's Garage) could supply his works with coke.

Isaac Belsham 1813-1899, Daniel's son, traded as Isaac Belsham and Sons, maltsters, coal and coke. The firm had wharfs near Black Bridge on the Chelmer and Blackwater Navigation until well into the twentieth century where they produced pale malt. They also processed barley by the riverside at Heybridge and at premises in Wood Lane. Isaac Belsham lived in Bridge Cottage with his wife, three daughters and four sons until he died. The large Georgian style brick built house was next to the main entrance of Bentall's works and the front was covered with wisteria.

He owned brick and black weather boarded cottages on the south side of Black Bridge. The entrances to these cottages were reached by steps. Joyce Wisbey remembered climbing up the steps on one side, rushing across the platform and down the other side on her way to school. The original bridge was a black tarred, wooden structure hence its name. This is the name given on the 1777 Andre and Chapman map but Essex County Council Highways Department will not allow that name on maps today.

Oliver Daniel Belsham 1846 - 1924, Isaac's son, inherited Boucherne and took over the well known business of I. Belsham, maltsters, coal and oilcake merchants. Oliver Daniel Belsham gave great service to the district in his long life; he was a JP and vice-chairman of the Board of Guardians, county councillor and alderman of Maldon and a devout member of the Congregational Church and their organist for over fifty years, and much else. When Maldon Rural District Council was inaugurated in 1895, he became their first chairman, his leadership led to the implementation of important schemes such as the waterworks' undertaking.

Daniel's wife maintained the Black Bridge Church, an off shoot of the Maldon Congregational Church and lived in Boucherne for fifty-two years. They had no children.

Three generations of the family had been successful maltsters, oil cake merchants, as well as coal factors and had owned various properties in and around Heybridge. They owned, south of the bridge, wharfs on both sides of the Black Bridge. The wharf and yard was known as Crane Wharf.

Lewis Belsham 1851-1932, another of Isaac's sons, was a bachelor who lived all his life in Boucherne. As a corn merchant, he attended Colchester and Mark Lane markets regularly as well as other markets. He was a senior deacon of the Congregational Church and a noted bee keeper.

Oliver Daniel Belsham and his brother Lewis traded as flour millers and corn merchants in Goldhanger. It was around this time that mill stones were being replaced with steel rollers imported from Germany and France which produced sixteen times more per day than traditional grinding methods; they increased productivity and cut costs at a stroke. They were the death knell of traditional wind and water mills. Meanwhile, mill streams were drying up and the demand for water in the urban area was growing. Oliver and Lewis Belsham converted Bentall's nuts and bolt factory at Fullbridge into a steam roller flour mill in 1891.

Fullbridge House was built at right angles to The Street with a seventeenth century core or earlier timber-framed core next door to Fullbridge Mill. It was largely re-built in 1827 and lived in by the miller Oliver Belsham when he came to Fullbridge Mill.

In 1900, it was recorded that Messrs. I. Belsham and Sons' ledgers went back to 1814 when their principal business was transporting coal to Chelmsford on the Navigation. In 1863, the Belshams received 7,000 tons of coal at their wharf in Heybridge.

It is sad that after three generations in Boucherne this prominent family ceased to exist in Heybridge. On 24th July 1935, all the household furniture was sold at auction.

The Diamond family acquired Boucherne in 1935. In addition to the house and the present garden, which is partially walled, there were orchards that extended to Wood Lane, a rear soft fruit garden and paddocks in front on the opposite side of the road and on the west side of the house. Mrs. Diamond was the daughter of Roger Fry, artist and art critic, who advised on the art collection in the Courtauld Institute Galleries and was connected with the group of writers and artists that became known as the Bloomsbury Set. Mrs. Diamond had studied art in Paris. She married Mr. Diamond, a French man, who pioneered the manufacture of waxed paper for sliced bread wrappers in the Diamond Waxed Paper Works in premises next to the house. It is rumoured that the patent for his invention was not tight enough and denied him a fortune. The Diamonds had two daughters and a son. Mrs. Diamond decorated the walls, doors, cupboards etc. of Boucherne with murals.

The house was sold in 1980 in a derelict state and then sold again to Mr. and Mrs. Harvey who began renovating the house. Mrs. Diamond's paintings and murals were removed to reveal pine panelling. Mrs. Harvey ran a play school in the old bakery.

10.6b Tibballs' Residential Care Home - Boucherne

Carol and Chris Tibballs restored and adapted the oak framed timber structure into a residential care home for twelve residents on 29th September 1988. Mr. Tibballs built an attractive extension to accommodate twelve more residents in 1999. The author has long connections with the home; her mother lived there happily for nine years and, later, she benefited from a two month stay recuperating after an operation. A happy team of local staff, including some who have worked there from the opening, celebrated the twentieth birthday anniversary in 2008. Chris Tibballs tells newcomers that people come there to live, not to die, and residents' happiness and comfort is the home's prime objective, it is an aim that is realised.

10.7 The telephone box opposite Crescent Road

Red telephone boxes became a familiar sight in towns and the countryside between W.W.1 and W.W.2. Few homes had their own telephones before W.W.2. The author remembers her father, a building contractor, refused to have one since he did not want business calls out of business hours. In an emergency, the owners of private phones would allow their phone to be used. The candlestick phones of the times had a tall stand incorporating the speaker and a separate earpiece was held in a clip.

Sir Giles Gilbert Scot won the competition to design telephone kiosks which were introduced in London in 1927. By 1928, 23,998 had been installed throughout Great Britain. His 1936 version commemorated the Silver Jubilee of King George V and 8,000 were installed since every town and village that had a Post Office had one. The design had buttons A and B. Callers put the right amount into the box, operators connected the caller and the money was accepted when button A was pressed. If no connection had been made, button B was pressed and the money returned. In addition to outgoing calls made from kiosks, incoming calls could be received when a rendezvous had been arranged.

Maldon had a telephone exchange but in Kelvedon, Hatfield Peverel and Great Braxted for example, an operator connected callers from a room behind the Post Office. Callers gave the operator the number they wanted and the operator worked out the route and did the necessary plugging in. Peter Thorpe remembers that if the call was far off, the operator would ring the caller back when she had worked out the route. In rural areas, the system had advantages; messages could be left and callers could chat with the rural operators who were often well known to each other. Today's privacy was unknown but it was possible to leave messages. By 1958, subscriber trunk dialling was being introduced enabling long distance callers to make trunk calls automatically without the aid of the operator.

At that time, the General Post Office ran the national telephone service to which you were permitted to become a subscriber when space could be found for you. Around the 1960s, there was a surge in the demand for home telephones and new subscribers had to be willing to have a shared line; this happened to the author in 1965. A knob was pressed when requesting the use of your phone. If a sharer was making a call when their partner picked up the phone; it was courteous to replace the receiver.

In 1959, lightweight plastic phones became available in six colours signalling the end of black phones. The author visited Canada in 1988 and used a handset with press buttons in various colours. She liked it so much that she asked about them in England but phones could not be bought and were only available at an increased rental from BT. Today's young people would be amazed at how relatively infrequently phones were used as a means of communication before the 1980s.

The box in Holloway Road used to be a busy one; lorries bringing loads in the area used this phone to get travel directions to their customers, people used it for social and business calls and others arranged to be at the box at a set time to receive a calls. In 1985 a programme began to replace the red phone boxes and to install pay on answer mechanisms. Holloway Road was not forgotten. Today, few people, young and old, are without a mobile phone and can freely switch between suppliers. How much longer will we keep the Holloway Road phone box?

10.8 Villas come to Holloway Road and Crescent Road in 1900

Villas were built along Holloway Road around 1900. Mr. Lewis had numbers 63 and 65 Holloway Road built by Shirlings, the Maldon builders, on land purchased from the Belsham family of Boucherne. Shirlings' carpenter was Mr. F. Gibson who named the houses Lewis Villa and St Mary's villa after himself and his wife. George Boutwell (Rip) who was John Playle's maternal grandparent lived in Lewis Villa; Rip worked at Bentall's as a turner on a lathe until he retired. John Playle (1865-1945) bought land on Holloway Road in 1904 on which to build a house when his timber haulage business flourished. The area was advertised in newspapers as a desirable residential location. John Playle named his house (number 69) Myrtle Villa, after his daughter who had died in infancy. These six superior villas were built from the junction with Crescent Road along Holloway Road. After 1927, water was laid on to these houses and to those in Crescent Road from the Southend Waterworks but the sewer was not available until late in the 1950s. Waste water was disposed of in soak aways and clothes were not washed as frequently as today. Tin baths were brought into the kitchen on Friday nights and bath water heated in the copper; more than one person used the bath water.

Building along the frontage of Holloway Road must have been speedy because Mr. and Mrs. Bernard Hall's house, 125 Holloway Road, was built in 1903 and houses reached Langford

Cottages by 1904.

Older Heybridge residents call Maypole Road, the road to Wickham Bishops from Langford Cross, The Shoulder of Mutton Road. There was a public house in what is now Gun Hill Farm from 1773 to 1932. It was originally known as the Maypole but later became the Shoulder of Mutton. The road was a favourite walk for Heybridge residents on Saturday evenings until the inn closed in 1932.

Arthur Kemp Tebby RA lived and worked in London in his early life and exhibited at the Royal Academy and the Royal Society of British Artists in the last decade of the nineteenth century. There is a long gap before he exhibited 'A Flower Piece', in London, in 1928. He moved to Heybridge and rented rooms with John Playle's grandmother, Mrs. Boutwell, in Holloway Road before renting 113 Holloway Road. He taught art at Maldon Grammar School and John Playle remembers watching him sketch the Black Bridge and boats at Heybridge Basin.

During W.W.1, Walter and Elsie Springett had identical twins, Harold and Eric. Harold began work in Sadd's in 1929 at the age of 14. He assembled orders at 6am for delivery, cycled home for breakfast at 7.30am and returned at 8am. He came home for one hour for a cooked dinner at mid-day and left work at 5pm. At 16, he went to work in the offices until he became yard foreman at Southend on Sea. He was recalled to Maldon as yard foreman on the day W.W.2 broke out. He had women using tools on the benches as men were called up. German prisoners of war came from Colchester for day work.

Harold Springett bought 113 Holloway Road in 1948 when Kemp Tebby was the sitting tenant; he could not secure possession because of the security of tenure afforded by Act of Parliament and had to live in rooms for the first two years of his marriage. He was not able to live in 113 until Kemp Tebby's death in 1958 at the age of 94. He bought 139 Holloway Road with a mortgage when he had two children. Harold Springett moved into a modern bungalow, 125 Holloway Road, built by Harold Gill, in the last years of his life.

Houses began to be built on the south side of Crescent Road in 1906 with the building of a new police house; number 1 Crescent Road. Ron Harvey remembered PC Scott who lived there. He was a large man; well over 6ft. tall and broad shouldered whose nickname was Tiny. He was a typical old fashioned policeman, able to handle himself in a crisis and was well respected by the one hundred Irishmen who were building the Southend Waterworks early in the 1920s. (They were called navvies because they dug Navigations). They slept rough anywhere in Langford; many of them 'dossed down' in Langford Mill.

The navvies had to walk to the Flying Tinker sited on the present car park of Doe's showroom. This was a beer house licensed to sell beer off the premises; the licence cost £2. Customers knocked on the top half of the door, ordered ale and waited under the small lean-to. The landlord would bring out a jug of ale and a glass, take the money and leave the customer to drink his ale in the narrow garden that ran parallel to the busy road. The last landlord was George William Hymas in 1938. It then remained as a private house until the late 1950s when it was demolished to make a car park for Doe's customers. On their way back to Langford, after visiting the Flying Tinker or one of the public houses in Heybridge, navvies were sometimes found sleeping in ditches. They were also known to fight amongst themselves - PC Scott used to remove his coat and 'persuade' them, in no uncertain manner, to stop fighting and go away quietly.

It was after W.W.2 that a police house was built in Colchester Road. The house is now privately owned since policemen are no longer required to live on their patch. Until the 1960s, policemen had to live in police houses; they were moved regularly to prevent them becoming too involved with villagers. The frequent moves disrupted their families and their children's education and thwarted the hopes of those who wanted to be buying their homes ready for when they left the force. However, a single stable address would mean policemen driving to their place of duty for the shift and returning to their home that may be far away; losing out on opportunities to gain local knowledge in the old fashioned way of policing.

Pairs of villas were built in the early 1900s along Crescent Road. It was the custom then to build a pair; to live in one while the rents from the second helped to pay the mortgage. Plaques on the houses reveal their history: Jasmine Cottages 1908, Eastwood Cottages 1909, Clenthorne Cottages 1909, Wellington Cottages 1910, Fairview 1912 and Eleanor Cottages 1913. Harold Springett and his identical twin brother, Eric, were born at number 29 Crescent Road in 1915. The Springett family rented the house and they had to move out around 1921 when the house was sold to Fred Raymond. They bought 95 Holloway Road. The author has seen a photograph of Fred Raymond in the front garden of number 29 Crescent Road, the last house in that road in the 1920s, looking across a field at a solitary oak tree still standing in the garden of number 57.

Between the wars, five very narrow houses, one room wide, were built in Crescent Road, beyond Number 29. One owner said, "I beat 'em" because rateable value of properties used to be assessed on the width of the frontage.

Number 55 was the nurse's bungalow. She acted as district nurse and mid-wife and many an anxious father raced there. Medical equipment could be borrowed for use in the home. The Parish Council provided a bicycle for the district nurse in September 1916. The back of a horse drawn wooden bus was found in the garden. The seats were like park benches, attempts were made to find a museum that would like it but it eventually rotted away. The nurse's bungalow was the last dwelling to be built in Crescent Road until around 1960 when the road was made up to join Langford Road. Houses were built on the frontage of Crescent Road on land previously owned by A. N. Alexander who sold it when he emigrated to Australia to live with his son after his wife's death. Later, Beeches Road branched off Crescent Road.

The architect designed the lay out of forty-three houses; three bedroom semi-detached and four bedroom detached houses have a uniform style that seems to create a harmonious feeling of community that is now enhanced by mature trees and shrubs. Critics say the style is 1960s dated. Certainly, Crescent Road houses contrast with houses built on the adjoining Elms Farm early in the 2000s where individuality demands a mixture of styles and finishes; where mock Tudor, mock sheets of flint and plaster of various colours sit side by side.

On the north side of Crescent Road, there was a small field near where Mr. Moore, who lived at number 13 Eastwod Cottages, kept cows, with a dairy in the corner. Harold Springett and Mr. Moore's son, Dennis, were soundly admonished by Mr. Moore when he caught them sliding down a small haystack in this field. Cows were taken to his wife's field adjoining Langford Cross when this pasture was exhausted. Later, Mr. Moore bottled milk in rooms he built onto the back of his house, number 13, Crescent Road. A pair of bungalows with very steep roofs was built by the Weavers brothers after W.W 2 on this field next to a wooden house, Crescent House, owned by Mr. Peck, the window cleaner. A large wooden shed nearby was rented by Roy Gilbert in the

1950s as a workshop and garage for the historic cars he renovated. He participated in various rallies including the London to Brighton run in a de Dion and taught metal work at Maldon Secondary Boys' School. The house and shed were demolished around 1970 and new houses built on the site.

Heybridge Laundry was accessed by a narrow drive from Holloway Road and the site extended through to Crescent Road. The laundry was bought by Mr. Wally Sadler from Mr. Rose. During Mr. Rose's ownership, the laundry had been managed by Stan Betts who lived in a laundry house, number 101, at the end of drive onto Holloway Road by which the site was entered. Mr. Sadler's grandmother, who lived in Leonard Road, Colchester near Paxmans, answered the army's appeal to launder for the army when the number of soldiers stationed in the garrison increased during W.W.1. Mrs. Sadler, Wally's first wife's mother, and a neighbour undertook the task in their backyards. After W.W.1, Mrs. Sadler started a laundry in Colchester. Did this spark off Mr. Sadler's interest in running a laundry business? After the death of his first wife, Wally married his secretary who was very business-like and worked hard to make the firm a success. They had a son, Benjamin.

After Stan Betts moved out of number 101, Mr. Leeks, a van driver, lived there and then Mr. Cakes and his son who lit the boilers very early in the morning using hods to carry the fuel. Mrs. Babbage, Jill's mother, worked in the laundry before she married in the early 1900s. A group picture of the staff reflects the feeling of those who worked there that it was a happy place. There was a wooden hut opposite the laundry where employees went for tea and coffee breaks. Harold Springett remembers washing being hung out on lines by girls who had to rush to bring them in when it rained. Mrs. Nicholls worked in the Co-operative shirt factory in Upminster when she left school, she joined Heybridge Laundry as a finisher when she married a Bentall's employee. She pressed shirts, pressed and ironed collars and cuffs and packed them.

This was a time when there was no main drainage in Heybridge; water from the laundry flowed into a clinker beds on the site which acted as soak away, then the overflow was carried into a ditch behind Beeches Road, through the present Elms Farm estate and into the chunker under the Navigation into the River Blackwater at Heybridge Mill. Three bungalows and a house (numbers 26-32) were built on the site of the clinker beds fronting onto Crescent Road in the late 1960s.

William Moore overheard washerwomen at Moore's Temperance Hotel in Kelvedon grumbling about the difficulty of drying household linen in poor weather and persistent rain. He told his son, Eric, who was courting Doris Croyden. The outcome of this was that Eric and his mother Roseanne, and Doris and her mother, contributed £100 each and started a laundry in a former school in East Street Coggeshall in about 1920. This building became the headquarters of the Eastern County Laundries Ltd. The firm expanded in 1936 and developed the County Laundry with premises in Springfield Road, Chelmsford. Dudley Moore, the founder's son, succeeded his father and bought Heybridge Laundry at an inopportune time. Laundering in the home had ceased to be the arduous chore of the past with home washing machines, plentiful supplies of hot water and non-iron fabrics. Heybridge Laundry was closed but the Heybridge rounds continued and the washing was taken to Chelmsford and all the Heybridge staff transferred to Chelmsford. The Heybridge premises were split into units and let; parts were used as a storage depot. It is rumoured that drums of dangerous chemicals caused an explosion that started a disastrous fire in 1987. Number 26 Crescent Road, one of the new properties on the rear of the site fronting

Crescent Road, was seriously scorched and tiles melted. Subsequently, the Heybridge Laundry site was sold for housing and seventeen bungalows that are linked to a call centre for people over 55 were built in the 1980s.

The Chelmsford laundry premises in Springfield Road have been sold and houses built on the site. The firm moved to Widford Industrial site in 2005 and installed the most modern equipment to process 34,000 pieces of laundry a week on contract; bed linen and towels from hotels and tablecloths from restaurants as far afield as Luton, Brighton, London, Buckinghamshire, Cambridgeshire, Norfolk, Suffolk. At Clacton on Sea, three sites have been joined up to create a laundry that processes twice as much as the present Chelmsford works and the two branches trade as Eastern Counties Laundries Ltd. Domestic laundry forms a very small part of the business today; the company hires out and launders sheets and other fabric articles to hotels and restaurants. The author visited the Chelmsford laundry and wished she could get her linen as white and ironed and starched as beautifully.

Three bungalows were built back from Crescent Road in 1957 next door to the laundry site. Mr. Yuill demolished Bentall's factory chimney and used the rubble to make the drive for number 38 that he had hoped to build for himself.

In the early 1960s, Crescent Road was extended to reach Langford Road. Gradually houses were built on both sides. Beeches Road leads off from the south side over a field that had been used by Mr. Alexander, the butcher, to 'finish off' animals before slaughter and Les Wright, the Maldon fishmonger, broke in horses until the field, which had been bought by Claydon's the building contractors, was needed for building houses. Mr. Alexander emigrated to join his son in Australia. The houses at the end of the cul-de-sac that branches off Crescent Road on the north side were built on allotments owned by Mr. Free.

10.9 Langford Cross Enclosure Act 1815

The Commissioners, Messrs. Watford and Mason, appointed to carry out the Enclosure Act of 1815, instructed the proprietors of this end of Heybridge to meet and the majority decided that "sufficient waste land should be sold to pay the costs, charges and expenses of implementing the provisions of this Inclosure Act". There are details of one allocation culled from the deeds of Langford Cross by kind permission of Dr. Waseem Ahmed: The Langford Cross 'indenture' shows that John Wood, farmer of Langford, was granted one plot or parcel of land near the crofts containing 21 poles bounded on the northeast by the road leading from Heybridge to Witham, north west leading from Heybridge to Langford and south west by an old enclosure belonging to Charles Wood. "Hedges, ditches and fences of which said allotment next the said roads shall be made and forever be maintained and kept in repair by John Wood and owners of the same allotment for the time being for the sum of £7.0s.0d.". The Ecclesiastical Commissioners of England and the Lords of the Manor of Heybridge reserved the mineral rights reflecting that the Dean and Chapter of St Paul's had been the original owners for eight hundred years. There were other plots or parcels of land allocated in this award from the Waste Land.

In March of 1823, Thomas Baldwin, house steward and butler to the Rev. William Westcombe of the nearby Langford Rectory, paid John Wood five shillings for a one year lease for two newly erected cottages or tenements on land John Wood had purchased in 1815 with a view to arrangements for longer possession being negotiated. Indeed, the two cottages were bought outright in March 1823 for £145. Langford Rectory was opposite Langford Cross at that time and the road was the boundary between the parishes of Langford and Heybridge. After boundary changes, the former Langford Rectory came within the parish of Heybridge. There were three freehold cottages on this plot according to an indenture of 1864 when Edward Smith, gentleman of Witham, died. His will charged his executors, his wife and son Frederick, to keep them in good repair and insured against loss and damage by fire until Frederick's death when the properties were to be sold. Charles Chaplin, gardener of North Fambridge, became the legal owner of the three cottages after a tangle of unrecorded sales. It would seem that the two cottages had been converted into three and this may account for number 163 having a bedroom over the kitchen of number 161 (known as a flying lease). One tenant put covers over his kitchen and swept his bedroom chimney; the consequences were awkward since his bedroom was above his neighbour's kitchen.

In 1904, a substantial piece of land behind the cottages on what is now Holloway Road was purchased from Thomas William Float by Frank Wilding, a builder from Market Hill, Maldon, together with the three cottages to which he added a single storey tin roofed extension. Numbers 159 and 161 have recently been improved; an extension doubles their size and matches the first half. The lower parts of the exteriors are brick clad with new white weatherboarding above. Number 163 is original and has the earlier extended kitchen with a tin roof. A fourth cottage built at right angles to number 163 was added later.

In 1911, A. N. Alexander is recorded as owning land south of Langford Rectory and later Langford Cross estate. No dwelling has been mentioned on the Langford Cross plot until in 1922 when a diagram shows Arthur Edward May, timber merchant, living in Warren Bungalow. Later, Mrs. Jean Wright owned Warren Bungalow and renamed it Langford Cross. Previously, Langford Cross had referred to the two, later three and then four cottages fronting Holloway Road.

Edward Lee Baker and his family lived in Langford Mill House when he first came from Suffolk to run the mill. He died in 1892 aged 42. His widow, Susannah, continued to live in Mill House until 1905 when, at the junction of Crescent Road and Langford Road, she built Langford Mead, a replica of a house in Collingwood Road, Witham. Edward Lee and Susanna Baker had five daughters; Natalie, Daisy, Ethel, Mary, Jeanne and a son, Edward. Natalie married Padge Wakelin, Daisy married Mr. Dowse and lived in Maldon, Ethel married Mr. Rawlinson and adopted Olive Berridge, and Mary married Sydney Graham Pye late and lived in Langford Lee while Natalie lived with her mother. On the death of their mother in 1914, the five daughters inherited Langford Meads which they left in 1919. Captain Matthew and Mrs. Crystal Ffinch, who had married in 1901, moved into Langford Meads in 1920. They became active in Langford village and church life. Mrs. Crystal Ffinch was the daughter of Sir Claude de Crespigny. Dan Kingston, who owned Mill Beach Caravan Park, bought Langford Meads in 1964. The house was demolished in 2007 and five large detached houses have been crammed into the site.

South of the Warren Bungalow a plot of one acre and three roods was owned by Henry Isaac Belsham, Oliver Daniel Belsham and Lewis Belsham with Henry Noel Belsham and Edward Williams in January 1900. Emily Minter bought a small field from Emily Harriet Wren in February 1913 and in August of that year she married Mr. Moore. Mr. Moore used this field as pasture for his cows. The deeds of this transaction show that the right of way for a path to the eastern end of the field was to be retained for Warren Bungalow (Langford Cross).

Horwood House Industrial School in Witham, a Montessori School, was started in 1917 in 59 Newland Street, Witham for eight small poor children from London by locally eminent trustees: Miss Katherine Hunt, daughter of the vicar of Feering, the Rev. Canon Galpin of Faulkbourne, Mr. A. G. Ionides, engineer from Doncaster, Mrs. N. le Grand Hill of Berwicks, Hatfield Peverel, Miss Edith Luard, Ivy Chimneys, Witham and Miss E. M. Packe, Langford Place. It was certified in 1918 for ten girls. This Montessori school was re-certified in 1923 for ten boys and girls under 8 years on admission. The Witham building had been part of the George Inn before 1807; it was briefly an iron foundry in 1870 and later renamed Horwood House. The present Witham Barclay's Bank was erected on the site in 1939. A helper, Vera G. Wright, wrote a book entitled The Unrelated Family (c.1920). She called it "an old fashioned-house in an old fashioned town". As a trained teacher, Miss Wright volunteered temporary help because of her interest in Montessori methods of child rearing. It would seem from documents held by Dr. Ahmed, the then owner of Langford Cross, and from a sentence in Vera Wright's book, that the superintendent was Miss Katherine Hunt, a trained teacher who had studied the upbringing of young children following the Montessori methods and was pioneering this experiment. Subscriptions were collected and this home started.

On Vera Wright's arrival, she encountered a small group of children who were there for various reasons; the police had referred them, they had been neglected, ill-treated or deserted, their mothers were ill or could not afford to keep them, or their surroundings were bad. Dr. Maria Montessori (1870-1952) believed that working with children older than 3 years was too late for the most beneficial results. This explains the ages of children in the Witham home who were mostly under 4 years old. Their speech on arrival was limited and ungrammatical. The physical needs of this small group were lovingly catered for in pleasant surroundings. Dr. Montessori recommended a sparse environment of carefully chosen materials to enable the child to work, concentrate and enjoy. Their education was based on Church of England religion with daily Bible stories and prayers which were given priority over other subjects. Sundays were a special glorious day, smart clothes were worn, favourite food served, and there were no lessons. There was a prayer room in the house where children went to say private prayers at any time of the day as well as a place for collective worship. Children had their own possessions and duties but shared a common life. Providing clothes was a problem since money was short.

Montessori play apparatus based on the interests, needs and developing abilities of the children was available. Dr. Montessori's methods were followed in Witham aiming to "develop creativity, problem solving, social and time management skills, to contribute to society and environment, to become fulfilled persons in their particular time and place on earth". The children did not wear uniforms and had the run of the house and garden and could get dirty and often looked scruffy. From an early age, they learned by doing; they acquired the ability to do everything for themselves in the course of time and to help each other. There were few rules and "the reasons for courses of action were explained to them leading to good tempers and cheerfulness". Children performed regular chores suitable to their age, even going on errands in the town in pairs. There were no grades and ordinary prizes and punishments were discarded. This was a family and the children regarded themselves as brothers and sisters. The Montessori organisation in London has no record of this venture but promised to refer to it in their international magazine since they believed it must be one of the earliest Montessori homes in England.

The trustees of the Witham home bought Warren Bungalow, (Langford Cross), in Heybridge from Edward Arthur May, journalist and timber merchant and the May of May and Butcher's, in December 1926. Horwood House School moved there and the same committee catered for eleven boys and girls under 8 on entry, the same principles were followed with Miss Katherine Hunt as superintendent. It would seem the two storey extension was attached to the rear of Warren Bungalow at this time. Mrs. Wright, a later owner, said there were three upstairs rooms and a box room but no plumbing while downstairs there were two bathrooms and the sitting room and dining room. The school closed in December 1933. Miss Hunt became choir mistress of the St Giles Church, Langford's Choir; Albert Chaplin was chorister and remembers she had a beautiful voice.

Miss Frances Gray, High Mistress of St Paul's Girls' School located in Kensington in London visited Stepney a year after her appointment. She was shocked and bewildered by the crowded tenements, pawnshops and wan-faced children in filthy clothes. She was so horrified by this situation that, in 1912, she decided to concentrate the school's charitable efforts in Stepney. St Paul's School Union for Social Work rented a couple of rooms in Rectory Square where boys and girls were looked after; in 1918 Dame Colet House in Mile End Road was set up and named after the mother of John Colet, priest in St Dunstan's Stepney before he became Dean of St Paul's in the sixteenth century. Stepney was one of the richest parishes in England at that time. It was John Colet who used his fortune to set up St Paul's Boys' School in 1509 and money from the John Colet Foundation was used by the Mercers to create St Paul's Girls' School in1904. Dame Colet Cottage was established in a disused public house, concentrating on medical services, dental care and baby clinics. In 1923, the services are listed as Infant Welfare Clinic, Care Committee, Minor Ailment and Dental Clinic, Wolf Cubs, Girl Guides and Girls' Club. The list in 1937 was even longer and included free legal advice. We are concerned with their purchase of Warren Bungalow in June 1937, "a cottage in Heybridge, to serve as a (cheap) holiday home for the people of Stepney, young and old - The Frances Gray Holiday Home". In practice, this was for mothers and their children. It would seem that the 'cottage' included land formerly owned by the Belshams in 1900 as well as the Langford Cross plot of the original enclosure allocation. A large wooden shed from May and Butcher's, visible from the road on the Langford side of the frontage, sheltered the children in bad weather. Mrs. Wright (nee Jean Reid-Scott), who had renamed Warren Bungalow, Langford Cross, used this shed to store boats and built an international Cadet dinghy in it. Now, a substantial detached house (169 Holloway Road) has been built on the site; it fronts the road on the Langford side of Langford Cross. The home was managed by Miss Katherine Hunt who had previously been one of the trustees and superintendent of Horwood House, the Montessori Home in Witham.

Miss Hunt built a wooden building beyond Mrs. Moore's field as a schoolroom, later the exterior was plastered. Behind it was a shed where children played in wet weather. The children who lived in and used the path through the field, passed the allotments owned by A. N. Alexander, to get to the schoolroom. Harold Springett's daughter had a small child's painted chair from the school when it closed and the chair is now used by his son's daughter. Later, the school was converted into a bungalow, known as Bon Chance, which has been lived in by various owners; unfortunately one of them surrounded the site with cupressocyparis leylandii which were never pruned. The conifers became virtually the height of the neighbouring semi-detached houses and their roots extended far into their neighbours' gardens preventing plants from being grown. The wet weather shed near the school had been used as a stable but the last owners converted it into a games room with a snooker table. Bon Chance was demolished in 2007 and three large, detached houses have been built on the site with a gated entrance. The cupressocyparis have been trimmed a bit.

Albert Chaplin, who worked at Southend Waterworks, remembered Robin Moore, killed in the RAF in the war, coming from London to visit the cottage. He also knew Nellie Jones, another visitor to the cottage who became housekeeper to Mr. Pelly, chief chemist, at the Waterworks after he was widowed. When Southend Waterworks reservoirs and treatment plant were being developed in Langford, Langford Mill was acquired by the company and converted to an abstraction point during 1924. The Mill House had been split into two flats; the ground floor was occupied by Mr. Pelly and Mr. Goulding, resident engineer, lived in the flat above. The Waterworks' official opening was in 1929. John Playle shows in a sketch how large machinery was taken by road to Southend Waterworks at Langford from Maldon East Station by his father in 1927 - along the Causeway, over Black Bridge, along Holloway Road and to Langford. Two lengths of rail were used. One length was laid and a locomotive pulled the wagons carrying the machinery along the track, while the used track was lifted and laid in front of the loco. It must have been a slow process.

The 'cottage' (Langford Cross - Francis Gray Holiday Home) was sold in 1951 because that type of charity was beginning to seem inappropriate in the age of the welfare state. The proceeds were used to fund a third Dame Colet House in Stepney. Langford Cross has been owned by a series of private owners since the closure of "Langford Cross Children's Home" and land surrounding Langford Cross has been sold. Norman Mott, a local builder, bought Mrs. Moore's field and the allotments owned by Mr. Free where, around 1970, he built houses on both sides of a road that joins Crescent Road on the north side. Eileen Ponder and Ivan Brand, whose houses were built on the allotments, benefit from the greater fertility of the soil.

10.10 Elms Farm

Part of Elms Farm development was pasture for centuries and included Stoney Meadow, Canal Pasture and Middle Meadow that were sold by Lord Lambourne and Mark Richard Milbanke, trustees of Sir John Peniston Charles Milbanke Bart, on 30th May 1919 to May and Butcher for £875 when the Milbanke entail was broken. At the same Milbanke sale, Long Common and Cow Shed Meadow including five hundred thriving willow trees were sold for £1,350 to Arthur Butcher who leased this land to the Lappages who were able to buy it later.

Before the development of the Elms Farm was allowed, English Heritage gave a grant of £1 million for one hundred archaeologists to uncover five hundred years of British history; from Late Iron Age, say 100BC, through the Roman occupation AD43 to 410, to Early Saxon c.AD600 when the site was abandoned, possibly due to flooding. The archaeologists worked from September 1993 to April 1995. They excavated a section of a Roman road and a round temple. While agriculture was important, there was evidence of sea borne coastal trade and imports from France and Rome. Artefacts revealed that Heybridge is an older settlement than Maldon. The finds were taken to Colchester Castle Museum for evaluation. It is hoped that money for the report on this internationally famous dig will be found.

The development of Elms Farm estate was begun in 1995 and since then around six hundred houses have been built.

Roy Lappage on one of Lappage's milk delivery carts

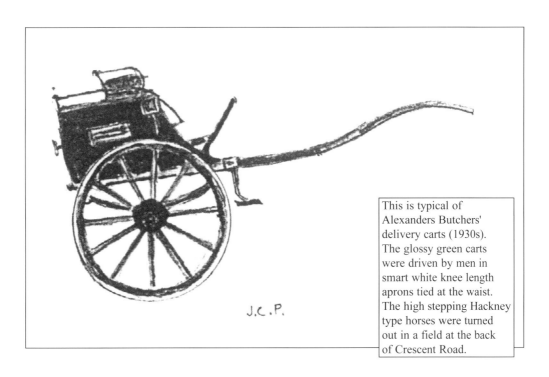

J.C.P.

This is typical of Alexanders Butchers' delivery carts (1930s). The glossy green carts were driven by men in smart white knee length aprons tied at the waist. The high stepping Hackney type horses were turned out in a field at the back of Crescent Road.

Four cottages built in 1815 - the first Bentall's workers' cottages opposite E. H. Bentall's home (later Benbridge Hotel) before he built The Towers. SOURCE Ellen Hedley collection

The original vicarage built in the seventeenth century and demolished 1906 so that a three storey house could be built on the site. SOURCE Ellen Hedley collection

11.0 The Square and the Street

11.1 The Square

11.1a Bentall's main gate, Benbridge Hotel, Half Moon, Hills and other shops

There used to be a square of turf at the junction of The Causeway, The Street and the road to Langford that is the site of the present mini-roundabout. Older residents remember Mrs. Foad ringing in the New Year with a hand-bell in the Square to summon patrons of the two public houses and nearby residents to celebrate and enjoy her scrumptious mince pies. This practice has been revived in recent times. It was in 1975 that the mini-roundabout was constructed at a cost of £100,000 to sort out the traffic problems at this busy junction.

Isaac Belsham lived in the red brick, Georgian-style, Bridge Cottage. This wisteria covered house was built directly onto the footpath and was surrounded on the south side of the Navigation by Isaac Belsham and Sons' wharfs and coal yard on both sides of Wave Bridge. The house was bought by Bentall's and lived in by Charles Bentall while the adjoining site was used as a store for out of date Bentall's machinery. A Bentall car was housed in a garage there: Peter Foad as a teenager polished the car weekly on Saturdays. Later, Ken Baker, a director of Bentall's lived in the house that was demolished in the 1950s. Ken Baker worked for the National Coal Board in the Central Engineering Establishment at Bretby before he came to Bentall's.

Last's bought the wharf and coal yard on south side of the Square which became their builders' merchants. On the north side Moat Housing built their modern headquarters over looking the Navigation on what had been Isaac Belsham and Sons' wharfs. Moat Housing has expanded to provide and administer social housing in places far away from Maldon District including Birmingham, causing them to move their headquarters to Dartford in Kent. Maldon District tenants feel they miss the local connection. Moat now shares the Heybridge building with the Prison Fellowship and has further space to let. The older SVT building next to Moat's office block was used, according to an employee, for recording TV programmes before home recorders. It is now split into six office suites.

After the failure of Acrow, most of the original Bentall's factory premises were demolished in 1975 and some new units constructed. This is seen at various times around the present Benbridge Hotel where Gratech services Land Rovers, Range Rovers and Discovery vehicles, Maldon Shot Blasting and Powder Coating operates, Air Domestique who undertake steel fabrications and welding, Jig Saw supplies fire appliances and Interior Brands are a showroom exhibiting well known High Street brands.

The manned main gate of the Heybridge Ironworks, Bentall's, was between Isaac Belsham's house and the present Benbridge Hotel. Mr. Alf Hobden, the last gatekeeper, who had only one arm, looked smart in his navy blue uniform in the 1940s and 50s. He sounded the hooter, known locally as the Bull, as a warning at 7.40am and at 8am. Dennis Fenn lived at 8 Springfield Cottages and he recalls the slow, steady tread of punctual men passing his home on their way to work and Sam Ruggles running to be on time. Workers clocking in after 8am were docked a quarter of an hour's pay. The dinner hooter went at 12.30pm, the warning at 1.20pm and the clocking in deadline at 1.30pm. The knocking off time hooter went at 5.30pm. Work finished earlier during the depression in the 1930s. It must be remembered that few homes had clocks and the hooters marked the times of day for many people. The hooter was used as the air raid siren during the war.

Various industrial buildings and offices are located in and around the former Bentall's offices.

11.1b Benbridge Hotel

The Benbridge Hotel was William Bentall's home, Bridge End House, when he moved to Heybridge; it is a listed building. The shape suggests it is a heavily disguised medieval timber framed building with half hipped roof common in Essex. The dormer windows and brick frontage are likely to have been added in the eighteenth century. The house became the Bentall's company boardroom and offices for the senior management when Edward Hammond Bentall built The Towers in 1873. Later, a general office block, now demolished, was built onto the rear of the house where Miss Clements was the housekeeper before W.W.1 and lived in a single storey, red bricked, slate roofed annexe that still exists at the Half Moon end of the Benbridge. She entertained John Wade's mother, Lena Wakefield, there and taught her shorthand and typing. Lena lived at number 13 Bridge Terrace opposite and liked sleeping in Miss Clements' home - probably because she had six brothers and sisters.

Miss Clements looked after the house and office block for many years. Office staff foregathered in a room downstairs for morning coffee and afternoon tea but all went home for lunch. Miss Clements provided refreshments for staff when they worked overtime or did fire watching in W.W.2. She was a Sunday school teacher. Latterly, she sat by the fire while Mrs. Hovell made the beverages. When Mr. Chick was works manager he used the ground floor room next to the kitchen as his office.

These offices became a student hostel for a brief period after Acrow built a new office block in 1974 on the Bentall Sports Club Playing Field. The temporary partitions of the student hostel were removed in 1977 when the building was converted into a hotel, opened in 1979 by Malcolm Babbage and Peter Mann. Malcolm Babbage sold his interest and moved on to other ventures in the 1980s. The hotel was expensively refurbished in 2001, again in 2003 and yet again in 2005 when another new tenant moved in who has endeavoured to create a lively pub to attract youngsters. The hotel kept open until 2am on Thursdays, Fridays and Saturdays - perhaps it was too successful since youngsters disturbed neighbours when they left.

Under the new licensing laws of 2005, the administration of licences to sell intoxicating drinks was passed to local councils; Maldon District Council for Heybridge. Formerly, comments were sought from parish councils. In this case it would have been Heybridge Parish Council but now they have no opportunity to comment. It seems that applicants ask for the hours they would like and these are granted in the main; it is only when trouble occurs that a committee of the District Council can decide whether to impose restrictions. After a three month closure following trouble, Osman Rasih re-opened the club with three hundred and fifty members in January 2008. Although the club opened every night, other than Sundays, only members aged 25 and over were admitted on Friday and Saturday nights. This licensee filed for bankruptcy in the spring of 2009. The premises were empty until 2011 when extensive redecoration was carried out and iron railings erected to keep pedestrians on the footpath away from the hotel. Will the new owners make a success of it?

11.1c The Half Moon

This public house opened in 1769; during its time it has been the headquarters of Heybridge Cricket Club, Heybridge Football Club and the United Patriots Benefit Society had a skittle alley. Robert Sadler was the licensee in 1842 when his rent was £20 per annum. He moved across the road to run the Anchor. He was a shipping agent in 1851. Older people will remember Reginald Frank Cronk licensee after 1926.

It sold Shrimp beer, brewed in Kent and shipped to the cool warehouse on the quay at Fullbridge. The shrimp sign is carved in brick in two places on the front of the warehouse. Truman's used this facility as a distribution centre in the 1930s and 1940s until they moved to Daniels' brewery at West Bergholt.

The Half Moon was a working men's public house. Tom Chaney was a character who said his bike always wobbled when he reached the pub and would not let him go home to Goldhanger until he had a drink. Actually he had two pints; he drank the first one straight down and lingered over the second. This is understandable because he worked in the foundry where it is very hot and thirst making.

James Mann greatly altered the Half Moon in 2004 and ran it as a restaurant when tenants tried to make it profitable. It became one of three restaurants that Mason's ran but when it failed it became an Indian restaurant. Refurbished yet again, a second Indian restaurant acquired it.

Numbers 1, 3, and 5 The Square on the north side form a block of listed buildings; number 1 was begun c.1500 as a two storey structure. It is a complex building that was a house and shop. Number 2 is a late 16th century rebuilding of a former open hall in early nineteenth century. Number 1 was originally linked to number 2. In this block, at various times, there have been Luckin Smith, the grocers, part of a small chain of family owned high class grocery shops in Chelmsford, Danbury, Maldon and Heybridge, Charlie Belsher's cycle shop, Arthur Harris, a hay and straw dealer who operated from the present Hill's shop around 1900. He sold the premises to Percy Woodcraft, a corn chandler, who later moved to Going's Wharf and sold the shop in the Square to William (Bill) Woodcraft, the tailor, who later moved to Maldon High Street near Ansells, the butchers, and Mrs. Davies, tobacconist in the early 1930s. In the 1920s, J. W. Collear supplied valves and batteries for wireless sets and charged accumulators that powered wireless sets. Luckin Smith's shops were sold to Budgens who closed the Heybridge shop. It was briefly an independent grocer and then became a motor cycle accessories shop that closed in the spring of 2009. The other shops are now part of Hill's.

Cyril Hill began his tally business from one front room in the Square that he rented from Smith who also owned Woodcraft the tailor's shop. Mr. Hill sold clothes and footwear that he carried on the front of his bicycle. He cycled to Southminster and the Dengie Hundred, to Tollesbury and Tiptree. He often left home at 9am and did not return until 10pm. Usually customers paid 1s.0d. a week over several weeks for the goods; he was very pleased when a customer bought goods that produced 2s.6d. At a time when farm workers often lived in, no cottage doors were locked, customers left the money on the kitchen table and he left the goods. At Christmas time, he took out socks, handkerchiefs and stockings; it was good business when he sold two pairs of socks or stockings. Later, Mr. Hill had a van that often broke down. His father and wife carried on the business while he was in the services during W.W.2. The business expanded into the adjoining shops. His son, John, went into the business in 1955 and now John and his daughter sell furniture displayed in room settings, carpets and electrical white goods. Customers appreciate the friendly reliable service and prompt deliveries. Unfortunately, Cyril Hill decided not to buy Luckin Smith's grocery shop about thirty years ago because he thought £6,750 was too much.

Opposite, in the Square, Mr. Arthur Nelson Alexander had a high-class butcher's shop. The shop had a traditional butcher's lay-out with a small cubicle with a glazed opening half open to the shop in which sat the lady cashier who received money from customers, prepared price tickets to be pinned to meat cut up for the rounds, and did the books. Animals for slaughter were 'finished off' in a field adjacent to Crescent Road. Behind the shop was an abattoir from which blood ran into the creek and yard behind. Two very smart shiny green horse drawn butcher's carts delivered meat to big houses in surrounding villages. Meat was carried in a box with two doors at the back and vents at the side. Mr. Carter drove one of them and took his horse to the canal to paddle in the water, and Porky Green drove the other. Mrs. Alexander was a very public spirited person and a JP. During the war, the Government issued sugar to groups with which to make jam from local fruit. Suzanne Benbow remembers helping to make jam in Mrs. Alexander's kitchen. Harry Pipe, a Maldon butcher, bought the business in 1958; he sold the Heybridge shop in 1975; it was a pet food shop briefly and then a developer converted the property into flats with an extension on the rear.

At one time, behind the Square and Alexander's butcher's shop, there was an inn called the King's Arms.

Heybridge people went over the Hey Bridge onto the Causeway in Maldon to patronise Cooper's, the blacksmith, Ernest Walter Springett's, the wheelwright who was married to Elsie Lappage and Miss Frost's haberdashery shop - no doubt she followed the pre W.W.2 practice of giving change for one farthing with a sheet of pins and charged 2d. for a reel of Sylko. (In 2011 a small box of pins cost £2.61 (25g) and a reel of cotton £1.45).

11.2 Last's Yard, formerly Crane Wharf and now Benbridge Court

The Belsham family owned land c.1753 to 1827 on north and south of Black Bridge. Tenants held the land from the Belshams south of Black Bridge; they had cottages, a coal yard, a wharf and a malting on the site. It was known as Crane Wharf by 1897 and was a coal yard until about 1922. Last's transferred their business there on the sale of their Hall Road site to Crittalls in 1928. In 1940, Last's asserted that since they had occupied Crane Court in 1927 and had used the site for twelve years without challenge and the land supposedly had no known owners, they were entitled to legal ownership by the process of adverse possession. The process takes ten years now.

At right angles to the road, adjacent to the former Last's Yard and facing the canal is Bridge Terrace - a line of five houses occupied by William Dedman, James Arundell, John Glover, John Sibley and William Bentall in 1799, craftsmen connected with the wheelwright's trade. Near the cottages was a wheelwright's smithy.

Five cottages in Bridge Terrace were sold by Samuel Bignold in 1872 and were bought jointly by Robert Worracker, a butcher, and Frederick Worracker, a grocer, and occupied by Henry Stacy, Morecroft, Bevis Ashley, Buckler and William Bentall.

1 Bridge Terrace faces Crane Court and is built at right angles to 13 The Square, the old breakfast room. The brickwork of number 1 Bridge Terrace has been painted cream. In the 1940s sweets were displayed in large jars in the window of number 1 Bridge Terrace and sold there.

11.3 Anchor Lane

This lane was formerly known as Mill Lane until Heybridge was incorporated into the Borough of Maldon in 1937 when it took its name from the Anchor public house on the corner of the Square and Mill Lane. On 3rd August 1799, it was recorded that the land from the River Blackwater where the coke oven and Counting House stood, and all the ground where terraced cottages stood, belonged to Richard Dixon of Wickham Bishops, barge owner and miller.

Brightwen and Swinbourne, brewers from Coggeshall, had been founded in 1803. At one time they acquired all the land between Fullbridge and the Anchor in Heybridge Square. The Anchor was built on the site of the Feathers Inn in 1760. Jeremiah Holloway, 1782 - 1827, a maltster, was the licensee of the Anchor at one time. From 1773 - 1802 Robert Barnard owned all the land as far south as Mill Lane. This land was sold to Isaac Brightwen in 1804. He owned the nearby Hoy Inn, the Chelmer Brig in Heybridge Basin and other public houses in Heybridge and Maldon. Brightwen's widow was declared bankrupt in 1828 when the Hoy and Anchor public houses were bought by Wells, the brewers of Chelmsford. June Holland has the indenture and deeds of the bankruptcy sale of the Hoy Inn in 1829 when it was sold for £1,030.

In 2007, the Anchor was closed by magistrates for two months after seven customers were found guilty of selling hard drugs including cocaine. Ownership and the name were changed in 2009 to Patrick's Bar and Restaurant when the premises were painted a pleasing shade of light green but it closed soon afterwards. Then, a short lived pizzeria was attempted and after that yet another Indian restaurant opposite the former Half Moon.

Harold Freeman bought a piece of land on the east side of Anchor Lane in June 1959 from Mr. Arthur Nelson Alexander and built a bungalow for himself that he finished in 1966. There was a two storey brick building on the site that had been built in 1819; it fronted Anchor Lane and was on the tidal River Blackwater. There were iron rings on the wall where horses had been secured while loading and unloading barges and it had a hay loft on the first floor. Mr. Freeman's son-in-law, Bruce, had been apprenticed at Sadd's as a mechanic and later worked at Doe's before starting his own business in this building in 1981, repairing and maintaining grass cutting machinery. In 2009, after Bruce's reitrement in 2005 and the death of the widowed Mrs. Freeman, the bungalow and workshop were sold and demolished and a terrace of three substantial houses has been built on the site.

On the opposite bank of the River Blackwater in Maldon, there were wharfs used by barges for bringing grain into the mill and for flour leaving it.

11.4 Heybridge Mill

The mill was at the head of tidal River Blackwater; it is now called Heybridge Creek after Sadd's Dam cut the waterway off from the river; sometimes it is even referred to as Heybridge Ditch. The three storey mill was driven by water from the River Blackwater. The Dean and Chapter of St Paul's Cathedral owned the mill for centuries. In 1792 it was operated by Robert

Barnard, in the 1820s by T. R. Webb, by the 1830s, George Gepp Ward who ran it until c.1885. The miller was Frederick Cock until 1908; c.1900 he supplemented the traditional water power with steam power. In 1911, the tenant Mr. B. Frost was able to buy the mill and Mill House for £1,000 at the 1911 Milbanke sale at which time the mill "had a water-wheel and four pairs of stones and gear". The mill was last worked in 1942. Unfortunately, the attractive white weather-boarded Dutch style mill was pulled down in 1955. The listed Mill House is a small Georgian house built in the late eighteenth century or early nineteenth century. It is timber-framed and rendered with a plain tiled roof in the front-range and slate roof at the rear with five bedrooms. It is situated on a 2 acre island. It was the home of the miller and the Foster family lived there until 2009.

11.5 Hunter's Garage

The garage replaced a little wooden cycle repair shop that had been built on the site of the Hoy Inn known to have existed in 1815 and owned by Mr. Brightwen of the Coggeshall Brewery.

A two storey building of brick and timber became part of the garage that was reached by a tall pair of wooden steps where Mr. Hunter stored oil and tyres. In 1910, the top floor was used for government sponsored woodwork evening classes. The teacher was Mr. Sidney King of Hall Road who was a Bentall's wheelwright. Six woodwork benches were installed that accommodated eighteen to twenty men and the room was lit by six paraffin lamps maintained by Mr. Springett. They had to work on small pieces of wood and learn basic joints before they could choose what they wanted to make. The government provided the wood for exercises free but students had to supply all the other materials. The building was demolished in the mid 1990s. Evening classes were held at St Andrew's School, Heybridge for pupils who needed extra tuition.

In 1929, Jack Hunter built his garage on the site and employed a qualified mechanic, Mr. Frederick Came, Peter Came's father, for motor repair work. Mr. Came had six sons and lived in Danbury. Mr. Hunter sold petrol and oils.

11.6 The Street

Heybridge Creek (formerly the River Blackwater) flowed immediately behind The Street. Raw sewage was deposited from the premises backing onto it as well as blood from Alexander's abattoir. The Square and Hall Road housed most Heybridge people until the 1930s. The Street was known as Church Street until Heybridge was incorporated into the Borough of Maldon in 1934 when it was named The Street. There were no houses on the Maldon side of the Street before 1830. The tidal River Blackwater (Heybridge Creek) used to flow almost parallel to the Street behind the buildings, under the Hey Bridge and up to Heybridge Mill. Hall Road and the Street suffered severe flooding until Sadd's Dam was built across the Creek near the end of Hall Road in 1954. The Creek is no longer tidal and the 2.3 hectares of river bed is bordered by the sea wall and the Creek. This former waterway supports a large bed of common reed sea club with rush and reed mace, sweet violet, primroses and morchatel.

The strip of land between Heybridge Creek and The Street was common land. As Heybridge developed, these narrow strips of land were built on. In 1894, on the south side of the road from the bridge, George Fuller agent for Daniel and Sons (ale, stout, porter and spirit) operated from the first cottage in a terrace of cottages. Further along was the post office for a time and a general shop run by Frank Mulley (opposite the vicarage). This was at a time when Bentall's workers were paid in vouchers and the vouchers were redeemed at some of the shops in The Street. This was extraordinary since the Truck Act of 1831 had decreed that wages were to be paid in the current coin of the realm. Eileen Cannom remembers her grandfather in the 1930s when he would go to Mulleys to cash his vouchers ready for his evening's beer and buy a pie for the family's tea. These cottages have been demolished.

In the 1930s, the south side of The Street starting at the Square was Essex County Council Highways yard until it was transferred to Hall Road. Previously, it had been a wharf; there are iron rings in the wall that had been used for tying up vessels. Next to this was Mr. Cockell's café - later owned by Mr. Barnard - then Miss Rosie Cutts' general shop that sold bread made at the family bakery in Holloway Road. Mr. Everitt repaired shoes; Peter Newton recalls that football players visited the shop on Friday evenings to buy twelve studs for their football boots, six in each of the stout, stiff leather boots. Mr. Everitt's garden was in the gap between his shop and the Waring Room that had been built onto the Memorial School. Between Miss Freeman's general shop and the Queen's Head, Mr. Smith began by selling eggs through his front room window; later, he sold sweets and general goods.

Around 2000, Heybridge Parish Council placed a seat in the memory of Olive and Jo Heathfield in the grassed area that was formerly the Essex County Council's Highways yard. Olive and Jo had started their business in a shop next to Mitchells' Post Office. Later, they had new premises built nearer to the Square. Their shop was packed with a huge range of goods; china, picture frames, haberdashery, tools, stationery, Christmas tree decorations, fishing tackle and bait and much more. They were always friendly and helpful; some nicknamed the shop Harrods of Heybridge! Earlier, when the river was tidal up to Heybridge Mill, coal was unloaded on the River Blackwater wharf (now Heybridge Creek). The second half of the row belonged to Walter Waring in 1847 and was part used by Stephen Bickmore, a carpenter. St Andrew's Memorial School was next, to which the Waring Room was attached in 1888. The entrance to the Waring Room used to be from The Street through a half door.

St Andrew's church on the north side of The Street was surrounded by Bentall's works. Abutting the churchyard was a two-storey building; on its second floor were the blue-collar workers' breakfast rooms. One of Bentall's workshops ran along the edge of the pavement to a row of buildings; the first was Mr. Bert Minter's sweet and paper shop, where Peter Newton and friends dilly-dallied about spending their Saturday pocket money of a penny. After much thought, and to Mr. Minter's annoyance, they spent a halfpenny. In the 1940s, Mr Minter met a train that arrived in Maldon at 10am and collected his newspapers. Chris, aged 10, collected newspapers for Barnfield Cottages, Stock Terrace and Boulton Cottages. Customers paid her 1d. or 2d. a week, one lady gave her 3d. She carried the newspapers over her forearm that became black from the printers' ink. Mr. Minter's three daughters taught at the Sunday school in the Waring Room and in St Andrew's Church. Next to Minters was 'Oily' Guymer's fish and chip shop. Tony Newton remembers that they had no money to buy chips but Oily used to give them a bag of crackling. Then came the cottage where Mrs. Clark and her daughter lived (they owned the little sweet shop at the top of Hall Road - that was another meeting place for the lads). There were two entrances: one for inwards and one for outward goods. All these buildings have been demolished and a blank 2 metre high brick wall built between the church and Going's Wharf. Behind the wall is a car park for the workers and customers of the buildings that have been built at the back of the site. Tenants have included Sarac Engineering, Bekers Motor Cycle Division,

Mars Manufacturing Company selling work clothing and safety wear, Blackman and White and Mr. Plastic: these firms are housed in new buildings or former Bentall's factory premises.

11.7 St Andrew's Church and the Churchyard

The history and description of the church have been covered in "History of St Andrew's Church" by Mr. Shortland and C. M. and J. D. Griffiths and L. and P. Wood and others. This brief entry seeks to give a glimpse of the place the church has had in the history of Heybridge.

The first parish church of Tidwaldington was built by the Saxons c.950. According to the Domesday Survey, Tidwolditune, and Tidweald's settlement had belonged to Brihtnoth's widow, Aetheflaed, and her sister who had inherited the manor of Heybridge, the gift of the living and great tithes under their father's will. They had willed the manor to the Dean and Chapter of St Paul's in 1002. In 1067, the Domesday entry of St Paul's records "the agricultural community of Tidwalditune as 8 hides of land housing 24 population (including 2 serfs at the Manor), 150 sheep, woodland enough for 50 swine, 8 beasts (horses), 1 mill and 1 salt-pan and 3 hives of bees". A survey of 1222 records Tidwalditune as a marsh of 60 acres; Edward II's survey of the Causeway records Highbridge as a swamp. From 1243, Heybridge had its own vicar who collected tithes from farms, Grapnells (1255), Canterbury (1381), Heybridge (1323) and Boucherne (1285).

The Saxon church has been greatly altered in succeeding centuries: Roman tiles, Norman walls and windows, Early English lancets and some attractive modern additions. The church was re-built during the reign of Henry II (1160-1181).

Around 1450, the tidal waters flooded the estuary for several miles; the receding water caused the river bed to be partially silted and diverted the stream of the Blackwater to join the Chelmer at Beeleigh. The vast volume of water undermined the foundations of the tower that collapsed onto the nave leaving only the chancel. The obvious reminder of this catastrophe is the reduced height of the rebuilt tower and nave and internal re-arrangements in the chancel with remnants of a Norman doorway and a Norman window. Electric light was installed in the church in September 1928. Memorials to Mrs. E. H. Bentall are to be found at the church and a new lych-gate was installed in 1959.

St Andrew's was a Peculiar of the Dean and Chapter of St Paul's Cathedral London until 1845. They are still the patrons of the church because they owned most of the land in Heybridge until the nineteenth century. They have a duty to find and present someone to be the Incumbent of the Parish when a vicar leaves. Heybridge is united with St Giles, Langford whose patron is a member of the Byron family with whom they share this duty.

The St Andrew's church yard was closed for burials on 11th November 1887. The burial records state that the last person to be buried was Mary Coe, aged 90. She was described as a cow keeper in the 1881 census. However, burials took place in the churchyard of people who had reserved grave spaces:

> 1891 Reginella Fairhead (Rev. Waring's daughter)
>
> 1895 the Rev. Thomas Wren
>
> 1905 Abra Maria Waring (daughter of the Rev. Waring)
>
> 1913 Emily Harriet Wren (widow of the Rev. Wren)

There is reference that Samuel Bates too was buried in churchyard after 1887.

Before 1954, a clock was dedicated to the memory of Mrs. Bentall. June Holland was given a photograph of the occasion. The photograph shows the tidal River Blackwater passing under the bridge which, for centuries, has been the boundary between Heybridge and Maldon and the entrance to the Waring Room on The Street frontage.

The Very Rev. Oswald Trellis invited Roman Catholics to celebrate Mass in the church at mid-day every Sunday in the 1980s.

Extensions to Heybridge Ironworks (Bentall's) stretched along the north side of The Street as far as Going's Wharf in the 1860s and surrounded the church. The factory buildings were demolished in 1975.

11.8 The Vicarage

The seventeenth century picturesque vicarage was demolished c.1906 because the vicar needed larger accommodation for servants which Rev. Sandra Manley found amusing at the beginning of the twenty first century. A red brick structure of three-storeys in 1908; the top floor used for staff accommodation. Telegraph poles were put in the vicarage garden in 1906 and 1920.

The Diocese sold the building and it is now Firstlings Residential Care Home which was greatly extended in 2004. The third vicarage was number 61 Crescent Road but the bishop thought it was not big enough for a vicarage so 1A Crescent Road was bought and extended and is the present vicarage for the united benefice of St Andrew's Heybridge, St Giles Langford and St George's Heybridge Basin.

11.9 Memorial School and Waring Room

The Memorial School was built in 1869 in remembrance of a former vicar, the Rev. Francis J. Waring who died in 1833 aged 62, by his son, Walter Waring JP. The Rev. Waring left a widow and nine children. He was an eccentric, responsible for services in Heybridge, Mundon and St Mary's, Maldon. He tended to rush through each service and conducted the prayers so quickly that the congregation seldom had time to make the responses and his sermons got shorter and shorter. It is said that eventually he put a travelling clock on the pulpit before starting his sermon. He was vicar for thirty-six years and a master of Maldon Grammar School from 1810 to 1832.

"His domestic arrangements were peculiar. The vicarage was furnished with rough hewn logs instead of chairs. His children ate their meals from a trough next to the split-log dining table. He and his wife slept in an enormous wicker cradle suspended from the ceiling" according to Wikipedia.

At the Memorial School, parents paid one penny a week for tuition (Mr. Ted Wire) during the 1880s and June Carpenter's father paid a half penny a week around 1884. Education did not become free for children up to the age of 13 until 1891. One account says the school closed in 1900 but Eva Mott, born 1906, told the author she attended the Memorial School. The new Heybridge School was not built until 1913.

The Waring Room was added to the Memorial School building in 1888. June Carpenter's mother helped in the W.V.S. canteen in the Waring Room during W.W.2 for soldiers billeted in The Towers.

The Conservative Women's organisation held a meeting in the Waring Room in the mid-1980s that was addressed by Howard Flight, the former MP for Arundel and South Downs who spoke out of turn and was not allowed to stand for the 2005 election. Mrs. Grant, the constituency chairman, was appalled that the hall only had a chemical toilet and no mains drainage. The hall was connected to the sewer soon after.

In the 1950s, popular regular rummage sales took place in the Waring Room on Saturdays. The author donated a suit; on the next Monday; one pupil came to Maldon Secondary Girls' School in the jacket and another in the skirt. There came the time when it was decided to introduce school uniform at Maldon Secondary Girls' School. After consultations, a grey pinafore dress available from Wenlocks was chosen. Hill's had tally rounds in the villages from which pupils came and Eunice Hill pointed out to the author that a basic colour and design should have been chosen that could be bought at shops of parents' choice. It was a lesson the author remembered at the next two schools where she taught.

11.10 Horse trough outside St Andrew's Church

The granite horse trough was erected in 1909 with the inscription 'Miss Leo Thomas 1900'. It is one of many connected with 'METROPOLITAN DRINKING FOUNTAIN and CATTLE TROUGH ASSOCIATION' as stated on the side facing the road. Eileen Cannom who has lived in Heybridge all her life, has found out that Miss Lucy Eleanor Constance Thomas died in 1907 and left £350 to the Metropolitan Drinking Trough Association (£350 in 1907 was the price of two houses). Miss Thomas lived in London and had no known connections with Heybridge; her name is on another trough in Bayswater Road, London.

11.11 Heybridge Inn, formerly The Queen's Head public house

This public house was opened about 1845 and named after Queen Victoria; it is a listed building. The landlord in 1882 was James Witney who was also a lime burner. A branch of the Foresters Court 'Pride of Essex' met there once a month in the 1870s. A large room upstairs has often been used as a meeting place for various clubs and, at one time, was the rehearsal room for a dance band. Sue Baker, a Maldon resident, recalls her great, great, grandfather Rudlin kept the Queen's Head Heybridge and had daughters who all married and ran public houses:

Nellie Eliza married Jim Rivers and kept the Rose and Crown, the Red Lion and the Dolphin,

Annie married Mr. Sewell and ran the White Hart at Fullbridge,

Rose married Basil King and ran the Swan and had a son Baden Savill who became successful selling and repairing wirelesses in Maldon High Street,

Another daughter married and ran The Hope in Tottenham Court Road in London.

The Ancient Order of Buffaloes branch met in the small hall upstairs in The Queen's Head.

Frank Frost left Sissons, the bakers, to become the licensee of The Queen's Head just after W.W.2. The public house then was very damp and frequently flooded; water came in from the creek (River Blackwater) at the back and from The Street at the front. When the cellars flooded, beer casks bobbed about and even hit the ceiling. The Fire Brigade used to pump the cellars out. Mr. and Mrs. Frost's second son, Robin, was born in hospital in 1950 but Mrs. Frost was not allowed home with the baby because of the damp. The family had to split up for several months. Mrs. Frost pestered Mr. Robinson, Maldon Town Clerk, and was allocated a new council house on Glebe Road. The builder went bankrupt when the house was only half finished and the Frosts had to wait for it to be finished. They moved in and lived there for over fifty years.

The Royal Antediluvian Order of the Buffaloes met in the Queen's Head; to outsiders the organisation seems to be a combination of a Masonic Lodge and a Friendly Society. It is not a description the Buffs like because it is not a secret society; their rituals, ceremonies and regalia are not secret and their philanthropic and charitable works are noteworthy. The Buffaloes now meet in the Ship and Anchor in Maldon High Street, the large stuffed buffalo's head which used to be in The Queen's Head is on display there. The Buffaloes used to give the children a party at Christmas in the Headquarters which was a great event for many children. The tea was followed by an entertainment, usually a ventriloquist, and the parting gift included an orange. Children sang a "thank you song" before leaving.

There have been shops on either side of the Heybridge Inn: east of the inn the shops have been converted into dwelling houses, on the other side are small shops, a take away food shop, a butcher and a hairdresser's salon. There are many food outlets in Heybridge to cater for the workers from the many large and small businesses and workshops on the former Bentall's factory site.

Brian and Chris Stubbings retired and closed the butcher's shop in 2010 after trading in the Street for twenty-six years. Their son, Liam, used to deliver orders to the author on a trade bicycle until a van had to be used for health safety reasons. Brian believed "if you sell the right product at the right price, people will support you" and he could have added that real butchers can advise customers on the cuts to buy and how to cook them.

A survey of parking carried out during the week beginning 30th June 2003 recorded that residents of Hall Road and The Street leave their vehicles on the road day and night. Traders lose business because there is nowhere for customers to park; they have difficulties loading deliveries to customers; delivery vehicles cannot stop near their destinations and drivers have to carry heavy, bulky goods too far or double park causing traffic hold-ups; and buses cannot draw into the bus stop because of parked vehicles thus causing hold ups when they stay out in the road while they collect fares. Busy routes into Maldon and out to Colchester, to Witham, to Tollesbury and surrounding villages converge in Heybridge Street. The Parish Council suggested various measures to tackle this problem but the police claimed the restrictions could not be enforced.

11.12 Sign post and fried fish and chip shop

The fingerpost at the junction of Hall Road and The Street was manufactured at Maldon Ironworks. The S shape at the top originally supported a gas lamp. 90% of all cast iron direction posts in Essex were the work of Maldon Ironworks; they received the largest contract ever awarded to a local foundry in the 1920s and were one of the few manufacturers of them. John V. Nicholls of the Milestone Society believes "In May 1940 the arms would have been removed as part of the measures in case of invasion. Due to the way that the arms are fitted this would have involved the removal also of the gas lamp. It is not known if the lamp was refitted after the war".

The late Ron Wells was asked to remove this finger post when redesigned fingerposts were being installed in Essex in the 1960s and 70s. He refused because of its historical interest and location. It is one of one hundred and forty-one surviving by the roadside in Essex. John Prime, who has been assembling photographs of Maldon and District on the Maldon Society computer, has seen many of these sign posts in Ron Wells' Maldon and District Agricultural and Domestic Museum in Goldhanger.

Mr. and Mrs. Copsey moved from the fish and chip shop at the junction of North Street and Maldon High Street to take over a small fish and chip shop in wooden premises next to Bullock's coal yard in The Street. The business prospered; they built a most successful restaurant and car park on the former coal yard but the business has changed hands several times since their son retired and the restaurant closed. These premises were next used as a Turkish barber's shop.

11.13 Heybridge Post Office

Heybridge Post Office has moved around The Street many times. In the twentieth century, the three storey building with a black weather boarded top storey has had many occupants. In 1906, John Payne ran a shop there; later Mrs. Wood ran a general shop there selling a range of goods, including ice cream in the summer. Mr. and Mrs. South, an elderly couple, ran it for a short time followed by their two sons-in-law who ran it until Nell Ripingale bought it in 1928 when she gave up the licence of the Queen's Head. Her nephew, John Mitchell, lost his job at Marconi's and came to live above the shop and run it. John had been born in Scotland in 1890 but came south to London before he moved to Chelmsford on his marriage in Silvertown to Emily in 1915; they lived in Writtle Road, Chelmsford. Soon after arriving in Heybridge, he applied successfully to become sub-postmaster in Heybridge. Mr. Mitchell retired in 1962 and went to live temporarily in Wayside, a former W.W.1 naval hut in Goldhanger Road, before moving to a modern bungalow in Crescent Road. His son, Norman, and his daughter, Kathleen, became school teachers.

When Maldon Co-operative Society got into financial difficulties their many stores in Maldon High Street and on the outskirts of the town including Hall Road, Heybridge were taken over by the Colchester Co-operative Society who closed them all except for the undertakers in Maldon town. New premises built on the site of the Co-op grocery and the butcher's shop in Heybridge became a Barclay's bank. Mr. and Mrs. Farrance ran the shop and Post Office until Graham Mott bought it. He had been a chartered quantity surveyor who changed careers. When the bank closed in the 1970s, Graham Mott transferred the Post Office and general shop, including the news agency, into the bank premises. Later, he split the business in two and ran the Post Office and stationery business in the shop next door while Mixa and Kishor Patel continued to run the news agency and general shop. Kishor was an electrician who died from a heart attack at the age of 32 and his widow went to live in the USA. Their very intelligent son, Katan, followed a successful career in the city of London. After the death of Graham Mott and the sale of his two shops to James and Nicolas Mann, Mixa Patel departed and the Post Office became a fishing tackle shop while the Post Office moved to Bentall's complex. The fishing tackle shop closed down in 2009. The general shop became Corals' betting shop.

Wood Road Alldays sold newspapers but ceased deliveries. Cluttons, who had a general shop in Wickham Bishops and milk rounds in Heybridge, devised delivery rounds in Heybridge since they understood no one else intended to do so. They had not contacted the Rowan Drive Co-op which began rounds in Heybridge. The competition was too great for Cluttons and their rounds became unviable. Rowan Drive Co-op is now the only Heybridge shop that delivers newspapers; it was part of the Colchester Co-operative Society which became part of the East of England Co-operative Society. Chelmsford Star Co-op is one of the few in the country that stands alone.

The Street today no longer has shops selling groceries and every day home supplies. There are five shops selling take away food, a fish and chip shop and the Queen's Head public house. Their customers are the workers from the various units on the former Bentall's factory site and passing vehicles. John Hill is the only local shop left in the village.

11.14 Bentall's warehouse

A magnificent four storey yellow stock brick warehouse on the Navigation's banks, this building has a slate roof. Inside, there are seventeen nobly proportioned bays in the Classical style. The building is listed Grade II and Ian Nairn described it as one of the finest industrial buildings in England. It is scheduled as an industrial monument. It was built in 1863 as a warehouse especially for the export trade next to a passing place on the Navigation which was later used as a dock by Bentall's. Finished machines numbering 12,000-15,000 were stored there as well as agricultural machinery manufactured in the winter ready for sale in the summer. Bentall was already producing catalogues in German by the mid nineteenth century.

In the 1950s, a contractor was secured to paint the windows, guttering and fascia. The scaffolding had been removed when it was discovered that some guttering and fascia had been missed and a helicopter was hired so that the missed bits could be painted. (After ICS acquired the premises the warehouse's wooden window frames were replaced with powder coated aluminium window frames that do not require painting.) Matt Hill secured the contract to paint the sofitt and gable ends of this four storey building. He obtained the second tallest cherry picker available in England; the hydraulic arm was operated from the cradle but even when the arm was fully extended, he needed a milk crate to reach the top of the gable end. Several times gusts of wind blew the cradle away from the building and he had to wait for the wind to subside and for the cradle to bounce back near enough for him to continue painting. A visiting health and safety inspector told him to wear a hard hat; Matt found he could not keep it on even when he wore it back to front because it blew off. He demanded that Matt strap himself in but Matt refused because, in an emergency, he wanted to try to jump out. He invited the inspector to join him in the cradle so that he could demonstrate the difficulties but the inspector admitted he was too scared.

The warehouse became ICS administrative headquarters around 1990. The building was carefully remodelled. By its acquisition, ICS owned a large continuous site on the north side of Hall Road between the warehouse and the former Crittall's building. ICS constructed car parks in Heybridge House and across the creek and was able to insist their staff used them. When the firm was sold to become part of Alchemy at the end of the 1990s, part of the warehouse continued to be used by the firm but much of the rest of the site is leased to other firms, or empty. See 12.2 for ICS history.

Next to the warehouse, and adjacent to Wave Bridge, was a boathouse of wood and corrugated iron construction that contained a boat meant to be used by the Bentall family but they never went out in it.

11.15 Going's Wharf

This building nestles beside Wave Bridge on the Navigation and opposite the warehouse and had started life as a granary in the 1790s. It is listed in the document 'Award of Rent-charge in lieu of tithes in the Parish of Heybridge 18th of May 1843' when it was rented to 'Richard Going and others by the Chelmer and Blackwater Navigation Company'. Richard Going was a merchant of Springfield; Joseph Going, corn, oilcake, guano, and salt merchant operated from Going's Wharf from 1860-1874. He owned canal barges and ships and lived in Heybridge Basin. Pigot's Directory 1850 entry describes Joseph Going as 'ship owner, sail maker, coal merchant and agent in Heybridge Basin'. He was married to Robert Parke's eldest daughter Ann. They imported 6,000 tons of coal and chalk from Kent in 1863. The 1851 census states that Joseph Going's daughter boarded at Miss Wilmshurst's and Miss Banger's Seminary in Maldon. None of the other pupils came from Maldon.

Percy Woodcraft, known as Ned, a corn chandler, moved from the Square into Going's Wharf where he traded as 'Farming Supplies and Services'. He had rounds delivering things such as chicken feed. His shop on the corner of the wharf, known as The Granary, sold sweets newspapers etc. He owned a parrot that stayed in the shop; the parrot whistled when someone came in and greeted the customers with "hello". He let out rowing boats at 9d. an hour just before W.W.2. Boating must have been popular because John Playle remembers hiring a boat with his wife to be and rowing up to Beeleigh. Dennis Fenn said that if two men rowed furiously they could go to Beeleigh Falls and back in an hour. Mary Bright's mother, Mrs. Alfred Playle, the electrical contractor's wife, came from Salcott where she had learned to row sturdy boats and rowed her young daughters up to Beeleigh. Mary remembers being scared of the swans' noise and wing flapping. Suzanne Benbow enjoyed going to Beeleigh by boat.

Percy Woodcraft and his wife and daughter continued to live upstairs even after the business was sold. The new firm's owners were Green and Silley Weir. Mr. Silley invested in more machinery to manufacture animal feeds. Kitty Roberts worked for Farming Supplies and Services when it was managed by Kenneth Kidd who was followed by Mr. Bee from Epping.

Percy Woodcraft's daughter, Ethel, known as Tup, married Harold Gill, known as Chink (it was a time when nicknames were very commonly used). After his wife died, Mr. Woodcraft went to live with Tup and Chink in Holloway Road. The bungalow was bought by Harold Springett after the death of Tup when Chink went to live in the Little Oaks Care Home in Wickham Bishops.

Going's Wharf was in use until round 1960. It was derelict for ten years but the building could not be demolished because it was listed. The owner, Mr. Donald Surguy, initiated an eighteen month renovation to convert it into small workshop units. It was nearly complete when the building was virtually destroyed by fire on 10th August 1979 in what the police regarded as an arson attack. The replacement building has often been empty. It is scheduled to be used as offices so an application to turn it into apartments was refused.

12.0 Hall Road

12.1 The Co-op and Hall Road Terrace

Hall Road Terrace, (locally known as Jumbo Row), was a terrace of thirteen Bentall's houses fronting Hall Road. George Coates, merchant of Springfield, had owned the land and sold it to Bentall's on which they built the terrace in 1860. Water from the Bentall's well was supplied to outside taps. Only one house had an indoor tap. A path separated Hall Terrace from the blocks of two and four earth closets which had buckets and wooden seats. The toilets were not exactly opposite the house to which they belonged. There was a tall wall behind the toilet blocks. Latterly, the buckets were emptied on Wednesday and Saturday nights by the motorised 'night soil carts'. Bentall's sold Hall Road Terrace in 1930 as well as 2 and 4 Lime Terrace, Myrtle Villa.

The Blackman, Challis and Fell families lived there in the late 1930s. Fred Dalton, a tinker, worked in a corrugated iron lean-to shed adjacent to Hall Road Terrace. He walked everywhere, even to Heybridge Basin, to collect and return the kettles and saucepans he repaired.

At the junction of Hall Road and The Street was a Co-operative Society grocery shop that sold some greengrocery. The shop was built in 1905 and later it was extended on the site of the first Hall Road Terrace cottage where Mr. Hinton had lived. He and his family, including June Carpenter, moved to Springfield Cottages in 1934.

In the 1930s Mr. Asa Joslin managed the grocery shop assisted by Colin Thurston, Jack Bright and a delivery boy. The Co-op delivered milk, bread, coal and paraffin etc. The Co-op butcher's shop was situated beside the back entry to Hall Road Terrace. The first manager was Basil Frost who lived in Boulton Cottages; the last manager was John Cocking who later drove the mobile butcher's shop. The two Heybridge Co-op shops were demolished in 1968.

Maldon Ironwork's employees had founded the Maldon and Heybridge Co-operative Society in 1873 at 19 Market Hill Maldon. In 1923, the Jubilee Hall at the top of Market Hill was built by W. A. Claydon and Son to mark the 50th anniversary of the founding. Maldon District Council bought the Jubilee Hall in 1970; which was closed in 1993 supposedly for safety reasons and Maldon Town Council built the new hall in 1999.

12.2 The Limes, Last's Yard, Crittall's and Myrtle Villas

Robert Parke was born in Norwich in 1781. He is recorded as a fisherman, owner of the Sally in Heybridge Basin in 1801. He married Elizabeth, the daughter of Richard Tovee and they had 12 children. He prospered and bought two plots on the Navigation side of Hall Road in 1811 and built The Limes on one of them. The Limes was an elegant house, in appearance it is one house but it is two. It is listed and of rendered brick with a hipped slate roof. The present owners have painted the two halves in different colours.

Extract from letter from Susan Watkins dated 2007:

"My great great great grandfather, **Robert Parke**, lived and owned land in Hall Road from 1815 until he died there in 1849 at the age of 67. In his will, dated 1848, among other things, he leaves 'my maltings, granaries, wharfs and lime kilns' that I believe were still in use in the 1930s.

His grandson, Edward Parke, lived in The Limes from his birth in 1851 until his death in 1938. My mother, now 86, stayed at The Limes with Ted and his cousin, her great aunt Jemima Jane Parke, who lived in the other half of the house, during the 1920s and 1930s".

Edward Parke 1851-1938, an iron planer and fitter, lived on the left of The Limes, his cousins Jemima Jane 1853-1942 and Horatio 1850-1932 lived next door. Jemima Jane had worked in London and Suffolk and returned to Heybridge to run a sweet shop at the top of Hall Road. Horatio was a mechanic and iron turner. All were born and died in The Limes.

Robert Parke was the great great great grandfather of Joy Joslin, Susan Watkins and Sheila Bremner (nee Playle). He farmed Heybridge Hall from 1843 to 1848. Joseph Going, another successful business man, was the son-in-law of Robert Parke by his marriage to Robert's daughter Anne.

In the grounds of Miss Parke's part of The Limes stood an octagonal building of fairly small proportions which was reputed to have been a school. The building was a well-built wooden structure having a large ball at the centre top. The teacher was Eliza Rudlin who taught the younger children of her sisters and others. She lived with her sister Jane, who had married Thomas David Parke, at The Limes for about forty years. Joy Joslin has an arithmetic book, dated 1833, containing worked examples by Eliza who used the 'school' during the 1920s and 1930s for storing her rhubarb wine. The 'school' was demolished around 1970.

Robert Parke purchased land on the opposite side of Hall Road in 1815 through the Commissioners of the Inclosure from the Dean and Chapter of St Paul's. It was on this site that he built his wharfs on the River Blackwater for his ships carrying timber from the Baltic and coal from Newcastle; he owned nine ships and two sea-going barges. He built lime kilns and granaries on his wharfs on the Blackwater. He was a coal merchant and farmer and was farming Heybridge Hall when he died in 1849.

Highfield timbers erected a new factory with a timber yard on this site early in the twenty-first century. Timber products were manufactured: mouldings, picture frames, wooden flooring etc. It is said that foreign competition caused the firm to close.

Lime burning had been introduced by the Romans and was carried out on the riverbank. Lime, calcium oxide, was used for the manufacture of mortar and as a fertiliser. In medieval times, it was discovered that lime improved soil structure and neutralised excessive acidity leading to increased crop yields. Only broken limestone was used for lime burning.

William Jarvis was a farm worker in Kent and a lime burner where he was granted two wage increases; his third request was refused so he applied, and got, the job of managing a lime burning firm in Colchester. For further promotion, he came to **James Last's** in Hall Road as manager of the lime kilns and the builders' merchant. Mr. Last lived in a villa on the Causeway.

The land between Spring Lane and Lime Terrace was owned by Last's; approximately half was marsh and on the rest were the lime kiln and builders' merchants. Last's had a steam wagon that Mr. Bright and his son drove as well as a number of horse drawn carts. At least one sailing barge, the Mermaid, used to bring lime from Kent for burning. William Jarvis married Emma Lee and their daughter, Ada, married William Wiseman who worked for Last's; he ran the yard and looked after the horses. Ada and William Jarvis had two sons, Walter William and George. William

Jarvis lived in a bungalow adjacent to The Limes but when he wanted to buy that site there was some delay until the deeds could be traced. It was as manager of Last's that William Jarvis negotiated the sale of part of Last's site in Hall Road to **Crittall's** together with the meadow on the opposite side of Hall Road in 1927.

Last's continued to operate from Hall Road but in 1940 they had acquired Crane Wharf adjacent to Black Bridge on the south side of the Navigation by adverse possession since they had occupied the site since 1928 - twelve years - without challenge. Tim Hawkins remembers playing there around Air Power's dumper trucks and ground works machinery in the 1940s. Later, Last's established their builders' merchants business on the site but houses have now been built there named Benbridge Close.

Crittall's built a modern factory for the manufacture of metal windows on the former Last's site in Hall Road; the main factory was on the north side of the road. Later, windows were galvanised in another factory on the south side. Crittall had begun making metal windows in 1893 in Braintree. Some products were transported by tractor from Heybridge to the Silver End Works to be finished. Crittall built Silver End as a model village in the 1930s in the German Bauhaus style of Dessau.

John Crittall, grandson of the founder of the Crittall window manufacturing firm, worked in the Heybridge factory at the beginning of his long and successful career with the firm. His wife, Ariel, writes that the experience was not a happy one since he was daily stricken with frustration because he was not getting on at all well with his immediate boss and came home dejected. Ultimately, he became managing director of Crittall's.

Harry Wareham grew up in Mundon Road and served an apprenticeship as a welder in Crittall's; he was promoted to the setting out bench and finally worked in the drawing office in Braintree. His career at Crittall's tracks the history of the firm: he began as an apprentice in Hall Road, went to work at Silver End, then Witham and finished up at the Braintree factory.

When Crittall's transferred the manufacture of window frames to Braintree, the factory was sold to **Ever Ready**, the battery manufacturers, who employed many unskilled female labourers. Apparently, making batteries was a dirty job involving soot. Ever Ready employed six hundred workers at one time. The same batteries were packed in different cartons bearing such names as Ever Ready and Exide.

Mrs. Nicholls remembers them as good employers; they paid fair wages, provided facilities such as showers (that few workers used), a marvellous canteen and lawn with an arbour where workers could sit during breaks. Mrs. Nicholls worked the evening shift from 6pm to 10pm as she was bringing up her three sons and a daughter. Bernard Hall completed machinist's training at Sadd's before securing a job at Ever Ready who sent him on various courses, some in the training school attached to the factory. He ended up as departmental manager. Ever Ready left Heybridge to go into a new purpose built factory in Tanfield Lee built by the government to create jobs in the north east of England after the coalfields had been shut down, the firm also received employees' wages at the start.

ICS Industrial Control Services - Peter Hall and Jim Wilkinson established the private company, Industrial Control Services to manufacture alarm annuciators used in the petro-chemical industry in 1966. They had met at Crompton Parkinson's factory in Chelmsford and worked in Jim Wilkinson's home in Maldon to devise shut down equipment that gave early warning of malfunction of oil rig equipment.

ICS moved to the site of the present Eltime opposite the former Ever Ready factory by 1977 when there were around forty employees. The business expanded quickly; the company designed all the electronic products, manufactured the steel cabinets that housed the systems and installed the equipment and provided support services in Heybridge. It was the time of the boom years of the UK offshore petro-chemical industry and the global expansion of the industry.

In the late 1970s and the early 1980s the company bought the old Ever Ready factory together with three other firms in Colchester.

Frederick Jarvis, son of William, started a haulage business with a Model T Ford next to his bungalow. His father joined him and the firm traded as W. Jarvis and Sons. The firm delivered coal and carried on general haulage work. Frederick died at 41 of lung cancer when his daughter Linda was six weeks old. Walter William and George Wiseman, grandsons of William Jarvis, bought the haulage firm around 1944 after his death and carried on the business until 1968 when it was sold to Harry Frostick. A car parts firm now occupies the site that sells from their shop and delivers to garages by van.

Walter William Wiseman worked part-time for Sissons the bakers when he was a schoolboy. He went to Heybridge School where he was taught by Winifred Keeble. Mrs. Keeble taught Walter's son, Alan, at Maldon Secondary Boys' School where she was a respected teacher and specialised in English. She was a Maldon Borough Councillor and Mayor of Maldon twice from 1961-2 and from 1963-4.

Myrtle Villas, opposite Spring Lane

The villas had been built in 1885. Mr. Adlard bought Myrtle Villas in 1930; he was a baker from the North. Mrs. Sissons Senior rented number 2 and her son, Herbert, and his wife Vera, went to live with her in 1931. Mr. Adlard gave Mrs. Sissons one week's notice to quit the house so that a friend could have it. This was not as catastrophic as it would be today because houses were available at reasonable rents and she moved to Spring Cottage in Hall Road while Herbert Sissons and his wife moved to a cottage in Spring Lane that belonged to May and Butcher. They moved to a council house in Fitches Crescent in March 1936 at a time when many council houses were built in the Borough of Maldon. Fitches Crescent had been built in 1934 and had won an architectural award for the design. Mr. and Mrs. King rented number 1 Myrtle Villas. When Mrs. King developed breast cancer, her daughter, Mrs. Jack Playle, came home to nurse her and stayed on with her father after Mrs. King's death. Jack Playle was the brother of Alfred Playle, the electrical contractor, and John Playle.

Mrs. Vera Sissons was 92 years old in August 2005 when she told the author the history of their baker's business in Hall Road. Her husband, Herbert, was a Co-op bread roundsman when he bought the bakery opposite Myrtle Villas from Mr. Adlard in 1936 and they moved into number 2 Myrtle Villas. Herbert Sissons had helped in bakeries when he was a boy as he was a friend of Basil Frost. Basil was a butcher who had come from Earls Colne to manage the Co-op butchers in Hall Road. Frank Frost, his brother, was a very good baker and this is how he came to work for Sissons until he left to become landlord of the Queen's Head Inn in The Street (Frank died at the age of 99 in October 2008). Mr. Pearson had owned the bakery before Mr. Adlard acquired it. Rumour said Mr. Pearson used to put a sack over the dough and trod it like grapes. Mr. Adlard had installed a new baker's oven in the late 1920s and Mr. Sissons used the old bakehouse as a garage. He bought three Ford vans for £100 each and they were painted green and cream but during W.W.2 they used a horse and cart to deliver bread. They had no shop but sold bread from the bakery. Customers had a book in which bread supplied was entered and Sissons gave a discount of 1s.0d. in the £ from this record keeping. When Cutts' bakery closed down in the 1930s, Mr. Sissons bought their rounds. Doug Whybrow and Gerald Swann, Cutt's roundsmen, did their rounds on tricycles. In the 1930s, bread rolls cost ½d. and a 2lb loaf 4½d. (2½d. = one present day penny). Bread rolls were shaped by hand until Sissons bought a machine, which shaped thirty-six at time. They also made doughnuts. In the 1930s, the bakers cooked customers' cakes on Friday afternoons - Mr. Sissons did it free, the charge in Maldon was 2d! Sometimes, Mrs. Sissons worked with Frank Frost in the night to let Mr. Sissons have more sleep. Older Heybridge residents remember the calendar which had a pocket below for letters that Mr. Sissons gave his customers at Christmas time. A basket maker rented a room next to the bakehouse.

Bread rationing was introduced into Britain in July 1946 and lasted until July 1948. Many believed the measure was a political ploy to bring pressure on the USA at the time of negotiations about ending of wartime Lend Lease and negotiation of the Marshall Plan. Britain was dependent on North America for essential supplies of grain and did not have the means to pay for them. Although there was a world wide wheat shortage, the level set for the British rations did not reduce the quantity of wheat Great Britain imported. The measure was very unpopular. The author remembers attending the heated debate in the House of Commons on this controversial issue. The coupons were tiny; Mrs. Sissons disliked the job of counting them. She and her daughter used a needle and cotton to thread them on string and they had to be sent to the Food Office.

Sissons delivered bread with a horse and cart. A woman told me that when she was a child she and a friend called out "Gee up" to the horse and it did. They were very frightened as it went towards a wall and only just stopped in time. Mr. Cutts cooked his Christmas turkey in the Sissons' oven after he closed his business. Mr. Sissons gave him the key to let himself in so he did not have to get up too early.

In 1953, the bakery site was sold to Crittall's who made it into a car park. Mr. Sissons went to work as a clerk at Doe's, the agricultural implement suppliers, and when he developed cancer in 1971 Doe's allowed him to work part-time until he died in 1974. Mrs. Sissons lived in Myrtle Villas for forty nine years before she moved to a sheltered flat in Maldon.

Mr. and Mrs. Chapman lived next to a meadow owned by Mr. Harrington who owned the grocer's shop that was later bought by Luckin Smiths. They paid Mr. Harrington 1s.0d. a year to use the field as a short cut to their earth closet and for their linen line. Essex County Council acquired this meadow to use as a Highways Depot; the Council stored a tractor there at first then they built offices and a garage in 1934. The manager was Mr. Manaton and the clerks were Mr. Hammond from Holloway Road who died young, leaving a widow and a young son, Michael, who became a primary school headmaster, and Mr. Beech. Mr. Chilvers and Mr. Matthams worked from the yard. Later, when contractors tendered for highway maintenance contracts, the work was organised from these offices and the yard was used as a base for heavy machinery, supplies and equipment. The site has been derelict since 2010.

12.3 Maltsters' Arms

This beer house was built for Heybridge Brewery in 1839 and it is now a public house. In the 1930s when Mr. and Mrs. Perkins were the landlords they used to allow Peter Newton and his friends into the jug and bottle (the off licence) for a 1d. glass of Tizer and an Arrowroot biscuit. If they made a noise, they were told to leave quickly. Mr. Bevers, a relation of Mrs. Feeney, was the landlord at one time.

12.4 Spring Lane

Spring Lane stretched from Hall Road to the River Blackwater before the 1953 flood. There were nine tenanted cottages along the lane. Two cottages in Spring Lane were sold by Mr. Adlard with the bakery to Mr. Sissons; Linda Hawkins's grandmother lived in one of them. Mr. Sissons bought two more cottages with the intention of expanding the bakery premises. When this did not happen the cottages were leased to Mr. Holliday and Mr. Hill who was a violin teacher. Ray Burns remembers seeing Peter Jarvis going to the house with his violin on Fridays after school in Heybridge.

Early in the 1950s, Olive Blyton took Dennis Fenn, a Maldon Borough Councillor, into her Spring Lane Cottage to show him the raw sewage under the ground floor. A series of tenants had rented these sub-standard houses as a means of securing council houses as their families grew. The rent was 6s.0d. a week. Tenants of cottages in Spring Lane were re-housed by Maldon Borough Council after the 1953 floods. The Cannoms were not re-housed because they owned their house.

Mr. and Mrs. Cannom's house was behind the sea wall. Mr. Cannom patrolled the sea wall during W.W.2 when it was feared spies would enter the country via the coastline of the River Blackwater. His orders were to shoot on sight anyone he met on the sea wall. His other duty was to enter Bentall's factory if the invasion by the Germans was signalled and open the valves on the oil storage tanks. The Cannom family went to their Anderson air raid shelter in the garden during air raids and the children were told not to talk so that enemy spies walking on the creek shore would not hear them.

Worshippers from outside Heybridge spent the whole day at Bethel (Baptist) Chapel in Spring Lane. Mr. and Mrs. Osborne, who lived in a villa on the Causeway, seemed to be the organisers and lay preachers conducted the services. In summer the congregation brought picnics which they ate in the grounds of the chapel where there was an iron seat. Mrs. Chapman was the caretaker and made them tea. When the congregation dwindled, Mr. May and Mr. George took over the chapel and converted the front into a workshop. Later, it was locked up and left derelict but children played in and around it and felt it was eerie. The lane can be seen now; it is a narrow grass and dirt track between Eltime and the former Bridge Communications.

The frontage on either side of the lane is now the site of industrial premises. Police raided the premises of Bridge Communications in November 2010 on the east of the lane, believed to be empty, and found 6,000 cannabis plants with an estimated street value of £2 million. The plants were growing in ten individual rooms; 1,000 lights had been installed using £10,000 of electricity a month and must have involved an investment of about £250,000. Four Vietnamese illegal immigrants were found guilty of growing the plants and sent to prison for a total of 16 years 4 months and then to be deported.

On the opposite side of Spring Lane ICS built a modern factory and offices. Eltime Controls, founded in 1979, moved into these premises in 1987. The managing director, Donald Hurst, explained that around twenty people manufactured and assembled specialist measurement, protection control equipment for global industry. Meters, transformers, timers and time switches etc are exported to forty-five countries worldwide; the firm has become a leading global manufacturer in this field. Foremost Financial Services rents offices above Eltime's offices at the front of the building.

12.5 Lime Terrace including Heybridge Creek, Sadd's Dam, Bath Wall and Maldon Marine Lake

Two pairs of semi-detached houses are named Lime Terrace. Originally owned by Bentall's, deeds tell the story of their sales:

Mrs. Clapham bought a property for £240 in January 1929 after Bentall's had gained the written approval of three quarters of the debenture holders who had invested £80,000 on condition no freehold property could be sold without their permission. By then, Bentall's were part of Agricultural and General Engineers Ltd. In October 1959, Mrs. De'ath inherited from Mrs. Clapham, her grandmother, who had died twelve months previously. The property was sold to J. K. Nicholls and Stella M. Cardwell from Springfield Cottages in July 1978 for £7,950 and bought in November 1981 by S. C. Bland and Carol A. Clark for £16,750, sold again in June 1984 to I. Morris and Tracey A. Turnell for £21,500 while K. D. Page and Miss C. A. Charwin bought it in December 1986 for £32,950 and Ms. L. Davies purchased it in July 1991 for £48,000. This is an example of the history of house price inflation.

Frederick Jarvis acquired his house in August 1930. On his death, it passed to his widow, later Mrs. Skerrett.

Number 4 was acquired from Bentall's in June 1959 by Miss Lydia Bacon, daughter of Alf Bacon.

Four members of the Eve family acquired neighbouring industrial premises as an investment in April 1930. Marks and Spencer were leasing the sheds that had been maltings for fruit packing and grading in January 1940. Judy Betteridge remembers earning pocket money by hulling strawberries to fill a tall can of wide diameter, about 10ins. high and 7ins. in diameter, for 2s.0d. in the early 1950s. The hulls were quite rough, difficult to remove and the fruit was acidic which made the tips of the fingers very sore. No processing took place in Heybridge and Judy thinks the cans may have been used to calculate earnings. In those days, the fruit varied in size before new varieties were bred to be disease resistant; looks and flavour do not always go together. Eileen Cannom remembers hulling strawberries onto a conveyer belt after school while others picked strawberries off the belt into punnets or cans. The premises were sold to L. A. Packers in December 1946 but acquired by LAC (Fruits) in November 1958 when L. A. Packers went into voluntary liquidation. Ever Ready Battery Company bought the premises in 1991. The premises deteriorated making them unfit to be used as offices. There have been unsuccessful planning applications for houses to be built on the site.

Heybridge Creek, the River Blackwater, was still used after the building of the Chelmer and Blackwater Navigation. It is recorded in the 1930s that the Mermaid, owned by Last's and May and Butcher, brought chalk from Kent up the River Blackwater to the limekilns in Hall Road during spring tides when there were northerly winds. The mate went ashore on the saltings with a line to tow the barge up while the skipper steered.

Heybridge was supplied with electricity from a substation on the Maldon side of Heybridge Creek on Potman Marsh. Mr. Wisbey was a member of the Home Guard in W.W.2 and his duties included guarding this substation. When an escaped barrage balloon became caught in electric wires, the military came and tried to shoot it down but the balloon broke free and cut the wires that carried the supply of electricity to Heybridge.

Before 1954, June Holland was given a copy of a photograph recording the dedication of the clock on St Andrew's Church to the memory of Mrs. Bentall. The photograph (below) shows the River Blackwater flowing beneath the bridge which forms the boundary between Heybridge and Maldon on its way to Heybridge Mill. The entrance door to the Waring Room has since been re-located at the west end of the hall into the car park and not directly on to The Street.

The dedication of church bell in memory of Mrs. Bentall. SOURCE June Holland

A June Holland; B The Rev. Whitford; C Church Warden Fred Minter; D Church Warden George Free; E Graham Mott; F Wallace Binder; G Eric Major

The River Blackwater was tidal up to Heybridge Mill until 1954 when a dam was constructed to stop flooding in Hall Road. The course of the river is now known as Heybridge Creek and is shallow; this has led to the formation of a significant reed bed and is the home of many breeding warblers in spring.

On the Saltings outside the Sadd's Dam, are two barge hulks; the remains of the Scotia of London left there in 1899 and the Oxygen of Rochester discarded in 1895.

Vic Springett's barge Emma was damaged by enemy aircraft action in the River Thames in W.W.2, the wreck was brought round to Heybridge Creek where she lay until she rotted since it was too expensive to repair her. After W.W.2, Sadd's stored pitch pine logs, 14 to 18 inches square and anything up to 60ft. long afloat in rafts on Heybridge Creek.

Trees were cut into planks, chained to form a raft and left to season near the present Sadd's Dam. Cyril Wisbey remembers swimming from the floating rafts of wood.

12.6 The Manor of Heybridge

St Paul's Cathedral and the Milbanke Estate

Archbishop Augustine of Britain sent Mellitus in 601AD to the province of the East Saxons, north of the River Thames. He appointed him the first Bishop of London, the capital of the East Saxons in 604. Following Mellitus' success in securing converts, King Ethelbert built the cathedral church of St Paul's in London. From this time on, the acquisition of land was the only means of providing an income to fund clergy's work both centrally and throughout the diocese. By 1850, Tillingham, a foundation estate of St Paul's, became their most valuable country estate with an estimated rental value of over £2,000.

Brihtnoth's widow, Aethelflaed, and her sister inherited the Heybridge Manor from their father and they willed it and its land holdings in Heybridge to the Dean and Chapter of St Paul's Cathedral London. At the time the manor of Heybridge was given to the Dean and Chapter of St Paul's Cathedral, a manor meant the manor house and the land over which they had authority through a court. Heybridge Hall was the only manor in Heybridge. This will is the only genuine known will in existence from before 1000 since the original rolls listing grants had been quietly lost and later forgeries were not regarded as accurate. It was not until 1000 that the first genuine list of the St Paul's estates was made. As a foundation estate, the Cathedral was administered by a College of Secular Clerks since the city of London did not allow monasteries within the city walls.

By the seventeenth century, rents levied by the cathedral were traditionally below market rates. Most tenants renewed their leases before they expired; usually for seven years. A premium or entry fine had to be paid reflecting market improvements during the lease or when a new lease was granted. This was calculated by multiplying the improvement by the number of years of the lease. This system produced an unbroken series of tenancies as is demonstrated by the Freshwater family's stay in Heybridge; they came originally from Tollesbury. Parish registers record that the family lived in Heybridge Hall from the early seventeenth century to mid-eighteenth century. Interesting memorials to the Freshwater family can be seen in St Andrew's Church. They were classed as yeoman farmers at the beginning of their tenancy but had been elevated to the rank of esquire by the time the family died out.

The Rev. Julius (Julines) Herring (1694 to 1775) lived in Heybridge Hall. Herring Point at the end of the Reach, where a small piece of land has been lost to the sea, is named after him. At low tides, the original sea wall is still visible with a row of wooden posts sticking vertically out of the mud. Recently, a seat has been placed here as a resting place for walkers from Heybridge Basin to Hall Road where they can enjoy a view of a wide sweep of the river. Heybridge Hall had its own wharf on the river. Half a mile further along the sea wall, a much larger piece of land has been abandoned where it is possible to spot the remains of an old embankment out on the far edges of the saltings.

The Rev. Julius (Julines) Herring bequeathed the lease of Heybridge Hall to his nephew, Captain Juline Herring, a wealthy Jamaican plantation owner, in 1775. He also owned land in Westmorland. Captain Herring married Mary McCall in Philadelphia in 1761, and their youngest surviving son, Oliver, born in 1768, inherited Heybridge Hall and the Jamaican plantations in

1797. This was at a time when tenants were responsible for maintaining the property and the arrangement encouraged them to improve their holdings. Tenants of large holdings were able to sub-let sections. The tenant's right to renew a lease was a valuable privilege and could be assigned for a price.

During the 1830s, reform was sought which resulted in the Ecclesiastical Duties and Revenues Act 1840. This Act confiscated land donated to cathedrals such as St Paul's and placed it under the control of the Ecclesiastical Commissioners. This central body would manage the estates more efficiently for the spiritual benefit of distant parishes including the new industrial parishes in the north of England. The wishes of the donors were ignored. Cathedral deans were relieved of managerial duties of the cathedral property and the income from them; the deans were given a salary of £2,000 per year and the canons £1,000 in lieu. St Paul's suffered badly from the confiscation of their separate estates and the reduction of their corporate income.

The tenants of Heybridge Manor were liable to fines on entry to copyhold; copyholders were slowly buying the freehold interest in their land in the nineteenth century. Heybridge tenants were copyholders in 1850. Their leases were granted for twenty-one years and were renewable after seven years on payment of a fine. Although this resulted in a steady income, it did not reflect the market potential and the management of the estates was a distraction from the business of running the cathedral as a place of worship.

A further Act of Parliament, allowed St Paul's tenants to buy the freehold of their leased land by paying the difference between the value of the lease and the value of the land. The profits went to the Ecclesiastical Commissioners for redistribution to the wider church. By this time, 'manor' applied to a large country house and its lands. It would seem that the owners of Heybridge Manor were able to buy this freehold.

Sir John Ralph Milbanke, the 9th Baronet, inherited Heybridge Manor, the farm and a lot of land in Heybridge and Maldon. He was able to arrange for the estate to be entailed as part of his marriage settlement with Elizabeth Margaret Denman in October 1859 by which the trustees were to pay the widows of baronets £100 annually for life. Sir Ralph died in January 1870.

The original owner of an entailed estate would specify in his will who would inherit the property in the future; for example, the eldest son of the eldest son; a procedure known as primogeniture. The possessor might not dispose of any part of the estate. This has meant that for centuries the great estates of England remained intact while the main residences of the property on the various estates were rented out. The Milbanke estate owned a lot of land in Heybridge and Maldon, as a map of 1887 shows, when land was acquired from the estate for the Witham/Maldon East railway line's connection with the Maldon West station. To avoid cattle crossing the railway line, a cattle grid 19ft. wide and 8ft. in height underground had to be provided at a cost of £60 making the total cost of the necessary land from the Milbanke estate £1,360.

Heybridge Hall was a Grade II* listed building. The timber framed, plastered house dated back to the fourteenth century with additions at later dates. The principal range was a long, rectangular block, but additions made the plan extremely complex including a tall, gabled staircase tower. Derek Maldon Fitch remembers the lovely entrance hall with its staircase that was panelled like the dining room. The landing had corridors off it and seven bedrooms, one was huge, and there were attic bedrooms for the servants. The back stairs led to a huge kitchen. Within the house, there was a self contained flat with kitchen, bathroom, one bedroom and a separate entrance.

Christopher Oxley Parker (1774-1843) acted for the Milbanke estate in the management of Heybridge Hall. He had taken the lease of Woodham Mortimer Place in 1796, aged 22, which became his family home. The last member of the family to live there was Miss Maria Parker who died at the age of 90 in 1939. He built up a good reputation as a land agent throughout Essex and beyond and travelled on horseback between the farms he managed. All his correspondence was handwritten and handwritten copies were retained. His son, John Oxley Parker (1812-1887), inherited 2,500 acres from him in 1843. Charles, his younger son, accepted Edward Strutt's invitation to become his partner in a land agency named Strutt and Parker, founded in 1885.

Sir John Ralph Milbanke's grandson, Lieutenant Sir John Peniston Charles Milbanke, born in 1872, won the VC at Colesburg South Africa in 1900. The citation says that "On 5th January, 1900 during reconnaissance near Colsburg when returning under fire with a small patrol of the 10th Hussars, notwithstanding the fact that he had been seriously wounded in the thigh, rode back to the assistance of one of the men whose pony was exhausted, and who was under fire from the Boers, who had dismounted, Sir John Milbanke took the man up on his own horse under the most galling fire and brought him safely back to camp."

Major Sir John Milbanke Bart VC instructed Alfred Savill and Sons, in conjunction with Strutt and Parker to sell the Heybridge estate, Heybridge Hall Farm, Heybridge Mill and valuable freehold land on Monday, 12th June 1911 at 2pm in eleven lots. (The ancient measurement of land was acre, rood and perch until metrification. One acre was 4 roods or 160 perches. An acre was the amount of land tillable by a man in one day):

Heybridge Hall Farm 210a 3r 10p 3 cottages, and extensive farm buildings between Sadd's wharf and the River Blackwater let to Mr. Frank Stebbing.

Part of Canterbury Farms and Daisy Meadow larger than the present car park of that name.

46a 3r 39p north of the Navigation, around Hall Bridge and fronting Goldhanger Road.

Heybridge Mill let to Benjamin Frost with "a nice old fashioned residence". The mill of brick and timber is tiled with an office and ample store rooms, a water wheel, four pairs of stones and gears, useful out-buildings. Included in this lot was rich meadow land with a railway siding close to Maldon Railway station and frontages on the Navigation since the parish boundary then was a ditch west of the Causeway. Benjamin Frost, the tenant, was able to purchase Heybridge Mill and the Mill House for £1,000.

Paddock Field 1a 2r 8p a small field opposite the mill across the Navigation ready for building.

12a 1r 4p Land abutting the railway at Langford Junction and the Navigation, pasture land, on either side of the railways Maldon East to Witham and Maldon West to Woodham Ferrers.

27a 2r 10p including Stoney Meadow west of the railway and the present Elms Farm.

31a 2r 38p pasture land and valuable willow plantation which abuts Langford Railway Station and is a long distance along the railway and the Navigation.

17a 2r 18p between Maldon East Railway and the Navigation including Maldon Ironworks site and access to the River Chelmer; all then in the parish of Heybridge.

39a 2r 28p between the River Chelmer and the Navigation let to Maldon Golf Club on a seven year lease from Michaelmas 1910 for £40 per annum. It was sold to Maldon Golf Club for £800. Heybridge Parish boundary was then River Chelmer; this land is now in Langford since the boundary is now the Navigation, it represented more than half of Maldon Golf course. The rest of the course was then owned by Lord Byron.

Various plots of land suitable for building houses and factories were withdrawn from the sale.

Sir John, a friend of Sir Winston Churchill, was killed in action on Scimitar Hill at Gallipoli in August 1915 at the age of 42. There is a memorial to him in St Margaret's Church, Eartham, in Sussex. His infant child inherited the Heybridge Hall and the remaining estate, which the trustees, Lord Lambourne and Mark Richard Milbanke, sold in 1919 when the widow agreed to forgo the £100 annual income arranged in the marriage settlement of 1859 and the entail was broken. The widowed Lady Milbanke married Sir Bryan Mahon in 1920. He was from an ancient Irish family and had held high military office in Ireland.

Tenants of Heybridge Hall have been Robert Parke, William Clift who was married to Robert Parke's youngest daughter, Mrs. Simpson (who left in 1872), Edward Faux and Frank Stebbing. The Stebbing family lived at Heybridge Hall during W.W.1. Their eldest daughter, Ethel, married Thomas Maldon Fitch who became the parents of Derek Maldon Fitch who lived in Baker Mews, Maldon around 2000. Soldiers were billeted in Heybridge Hall during W.W.1 and lived there at the time of Ethel's wedding and during the Zeppelin raid when bombs were dropped on both sides of the Hall and all the windows were blown out. More incendiary bombs fell on Heybridge Basin. When Heybridge Hall, farmland and three cottages etc. were sold on 30th May 1919, the lease of the Hall was in the name of Mrs. Stebbing and the lessee of the extensive farmland was Mr. Frank Stebbing. The leases were due to expire at Michaelmas 1919.

In 1935, Mr. Brown, the then owner of Heybridge Hall and farm, died. He had lived in the flat in Heybridge Hall while the Williams' family and their children; Dilys, Haydn, John and Cecil lived in the rest of the house. Mrs. Williams had nursed Mr. Brown and he bequeathed Heybridge Hall and farm to her. Mr. Williams had previously been the tenant of Elm Farm, Hazeleigh. Later, Mrs. Williams returned to live in Dolgellau in Wales.

The Chelmer and Blackwater Navigation cut Heybridge Hall Farm in two and this is the reason for building Heybridge Hall Bridge. It is around here that the canal is higher than the fields on either side. Part of the farm's good grazing land was only suitable for dairy farming and the Williams' family became noted for their fine herd of cattle. The farm was flooded in 1953 which left a residue of salt on the arable land that is very stony. It became uncultivatable for six years.

12.7 Alan Brush, sand and gravel extraction

Alan Brush negotiated an arrangement in the 1960s under which he installed heavy equipment to extract sand and gravel, processed it and paid the Williams for it by the yard. Alan Brush's lorries were painted green with his name on them. One customer was the contractor who was making the underground car park in Hyde Park.

John and Cecil Williams purchased sand and gravel from Mr. Brush and had two red lorries to deliver it to their customers; they employed a driver who worked usual hours but Cecil started deliveries at 4am and worked until late at night, he was assisted by his brother John. Later, Cecil had his own pit in Southminster.

Alan Brush installed a £10,000 crane on concrete blocks near Herring Point but the scheme failed when loaded barges would not float at high tide. After that, Brush's lorries went to Fullbridge to load barges and he installed his main office in 1963 in the nearby former public house. The premises have become a public house again and are now called the Welcome.

Alan Brush had secured planning permission to extract gravel before the days of 106 agreements which stipulate how pits are to be reinstated after the gravel has been extracted. Much of the heavy equipment used is drowned at the bottom of the 48.5 hectares of the worked out pits. In preparation for building houses, an outfall was constructed to lower the level of the water in the lake, this exposed straggling wires and projections from the equipment caused the drowning of two dogs that became entangled in the machinery. The water level has since been restored but cormorants perch on bits of the machinery above the water line.

"Heybridge Hall Lake is situated south of the Chelmer and Blackwater Navigation, it is partly enclosed by the Blackwater estuary and its open water habitat is of particular value to nesting coastal birds being a quiet water haven. There are patches of common reed and reedmace". Maldon District Council's Replacement Local Plan, 2005.

Cecil Williams used a field on Heybridge Hall Farm to school show jumping horses and he became famous as a shrewd judge of young horses and well known on the international show circuit in the 1970s and 1980s. His most famous find was Beau Supreme whose career came to a tragic end when a leg was broken in a jumping accident at the Courvoisier International Championships at Wembley Arena. His stable jockey was Peter Charles who beat famous contestants at the Royal International Horse Show in 1985 on April Sun and followed this up with other equally prestigious international wins. Cecil Williams moved to Tiptree to create Tiptree Equestrian Centre in 1984.

12.8 The chalet site

The selling name for the new development at the end of Hall Road is The Lakes.

When the Brush's gravel pits were worked out, one hundred and twenty attractive Norwegian style chalets were erected in 1969-1970. They had small gardens and were situated next to the lakes formed in the former gravel pits. Buyers had a thirty-five year lease on their chalets which were bought by people from all walks of life: East Enders from tower blocks enjoyed the peace and quiet, a Norwegian doctor bought two and let out one and used the other himself, a local doctor had three for letting out, two local school teachers used theirs themselves, a Billingsgate wholesaler and a Ford Trade Union official stayed there between 1977 and 1982. The site was administered from a site office located in one of the chalets. Users were only allowed to sleep on Friday, Saturday and Sunday nights from 1st November to the end of February because of the greater flood risks in the winter time. The site manager told the author that she had to turn off water and electricity supply to the chalets during the rest of the week which made her office rather uncomfortable to work in.

Miss Moody and Miss Jenkins bought their chalet in 1985. Rabbits chewed through the electric supply cables causing the chalet to burn down in 1998; they did not rebuild the chalet.

Heybridge Hall development was meant to become a members' club with a restaurant and hotel with a swimming pool but that venture did not materialise. The site was sold to a developer who applied for planning permission to build one hundred and twenty-four houses. Heybridge Parish

Council objected on the grounds of the danger of flooding; at certain times of the year, the wind and tide have been known to cause the river to reach within an inch or two of the top of the sea wall and the Navigation is higher than the fields on either side as it passes through Heybridge Hall Farm and Heybridge Marsh where the grass is greener near the banks of the canal suggesting leakage in summer.

A traffic survey was undertaken through the Parish Council on 1st November 2001, at the junction of Hall Road with The Street to highlight the traffic problem that the houses would create:

Between 8am and 9am
  The Street - toward Maldon 1,145 vehicles, toward Great Totham 730.

Between 4pm and 5pm
  The Street - toward Maldon 863 vehicles, toward Great Totham 972

Between 8am and 9am
  Leaving Hall Road - toward Maldon 43 vehicles, toward Great Totham 13

Between 4pm and 5pm
  Leaving Hall Road - toward Maldon 95 vehicles, toward Great Totham 28

The traffic survey was carried out by volunteer enumerators on clip boards sought to highlight the problems of traffic entering and leaving Hall Road. It quite often took fifteen, even twenty, minutes get out of Hall Road and that was before the houses were built on the chalet site. During the time of the survey, drivers travelling from the Colchester direction saw the enumerators and unfortunately stopped to let vehicles out of Hall Road. An alert local councillor noticed that the developers submitted a survey carried out during a school holiday which gave a false result. The volume of traffic has increased since that time and continues to do so.

The first planning application was refused and the developer appealed. Heybridge Parish Council spent £21,243 on experts' fees at the various days of the Government Inquiries, eleven in all. The developers challenged the Inspector's ruling against the application for two days in the High Court and they eventually succeeded in gaining planning permission in January 2004. Heybridge Parish Council expressed grave concerns to the Quality Assurance Unit of the Planning Inspectorate about the handling of this case and the time and money spent by the Parish Council. Their representations resulted in an ex-gratia payment of £7,067.28 attributable to the professional fees of two of the Parish Council's consultants in connection with the second and third inquiries. Redrow secured planning permission for one hundred and twenty-four houses. Two and three storey houses which are very obvious from Maldon Hythe are being built behind the sea wall, in a variety of styles and finishes but progress has been hindered by economic conditions.

Heybridge Hall, an important historical Grade II* listed building, burned down in the 1997. The Maldon and Burnham Standard reported that "A criminal investigation concluded that it was very likely that the fire had been started deliberately but nobody was ever charged". This left the owners under an obligation to rebuild the house. In 2007 Essex County Council delisted the site and building and developers have applied for planning permission to build houses with garages. Objections were submitted reiterating the fears of flooding and pointing out again that the only access to the site is along Hall Road with factories, office buildings and old established houses on either side. More traffic would be generated from one hundred and twenty four houses for which planning permission has been granted.

The Inspector at the first appeal rejected the application to build. At the second appeal, the Maldon District Council's calculations for sites which could be developed were not accepted by the Inspector who believed they were inadequate and permission to build was granted.

12.9 Hall Cottage

Department of National Heritage lists Hall Cottage number 3 Hall Road, south side. The house part was formerly a barn, built between mid to late fourteenth century to eighteenth century. It has an interesting interior plan. Gill Tully, who lives in number 1 Hall Cottages, has seen deeds referring to Heybridge Hall Farmhouse Cottage; it is likely that this goes back to the time when a farmer farmed the land while the owners lived in the manor house. At some time, this black weather boarded cottage has been a groom's cottage. Later, the attached building became the Hall House garage and the lodge to Heybridge Hall. There used to be a gate between number 3 Hall Cottage on the south side and numbers 1 and 2 Hall Cottages on the north side of Hall Road guarding the entrance to Heybridge Hall. Numbers 1 and 2 Hall Cottages were originally the homes of the butler and cook at Heybridge Hall.

The Williams family developed a caravan park opposite Hall Cottage in the 1970s. The caravans were destroyed in the 1987 gale and a small housing estate has since been built on the caravan park. The houses have car ports; planning applications to make these into garages have been refused because of the likelihood that they would be used as stores and cars would be parked in the roads

12.10 Hall Road today

Since ICS was taken over by ICS Triplex, some manufacturing has been transferred and various Heybridge buildings have been let out to other firms. The former factory building originally built by Crittall, the window manufacturers, and later used to manufacture Ever Ready batteries, remains vacant apart from short lets of some parts of the property and a timber firm using the large car park to store timber. A successful firm, Highfield Timber that manufactured timber products and mouldings in a new factory building was put out of business by foreign competition and closed in 2004. Bridge Communications was thought to be empty but found to be growing cannabis and the Highway depot is deserted and their office buildings boarded up.

The Co-op, Hall Road Terrace
known locally as 'Jumbo Row.
SOURCE Ellen Hedley collection

Tenants at The Limes -
the Parkes:
Edward, 1851 - 1938
Jemima Jane, 1853 - 1942
Horatio, 1850 - 1932.

Jemima had been a servant in
London and returned to live
with her brother Horatio in The
Limes and ran a sweet shop in
Hall Road.

SOURCE Susan Watkins

13.0 Colchester Road

Until quite recently, Broad Street Green Road used to extend to Wave Bridge. It was even used, erroneously, in the address of The Towers Lodge by English Heritage when it listed the building in 1990. Today Colchester Road stretches from the junction of Scraley Road with Colchester Road to Wave Bridge.

13.1 Wave Bridge, Navigation Cottages and Navigation Place

13.1a Wave Bridge

Wave Bridge was originally named Goldhanger Bridge. The 108 ton schooner, the Wave, had been built on the quay wall at Sadd's Maldon Warehouse and launched in 1848. The Wave is pictured with a powerful rig that seems to suggest that she was designed to carry perishable cargoes. She was owned by Smiths of Kings Lynn and skippered by Joseph Isaac Paul from 1856. She was engaged in the Baltic timber trade and, occasionally, carried coal into Maldon Harbour as a winter stop-gap cargo. J. I. Paul was still in charge in 1863 but soon retired. He bought the brick-built cottage next to the Wave Bridge and turned it into a beer house that he called the Wave. He kept it until 1888 when his wife Emily took over. Ted Wire's parents kept the Wave around 1900 and Ted was born there. Captain Paul's nephew, Mr. H. Whybrow, a shipwright, kept the Wave in the 1940s. He had two tables in his taproom from the old schooner's mess. It became a private house in the 1960s. Older Heybridge residents called the area Wave.

13.1b Navigation Cottage

On the west side of Wave Bridge and north of it, there are two weather-boarded cottages, Navigation Cottages, formerly known as Riverside Cottages. They were built around 1797, owned by John Russell in 1815 and William Russell in 1847 but occupied by Charles Rayland and James Frost. This pair of cottages has been knocked into one house now. The listed timber framed, black weather-boarded house has a pan tiled, gabled roof. The stack pierces the front roof slope on the former party wall. One of the original cottages was occupied by Mr. Easter in the 1940s; he let out rowing boats at 9d. per hour. Peter Newton said this was popular, especially with a girl friend. In the 1930s, a 6d. fee gave enough time for June Carpenter and her cousins, the Wagers, who lived in the former adjoining Navigation Cottages, to row to the Basin. In winter, they went to the Basin on the ice when the canal froze over. A Wager family photograph shows blackcurrants spread on a cloth to dry in the sun. Lighter men used to stop at Mrs. Wager's for a free glass of dandelion wine and a piece of cake on their journeys from Browns at Chelmsford to Heybridge Basin.

13.1c Navigation Place

On the south side of Wave Bridge and east of it is Navigation Place. Earlier this group of cottages had been known as The Rookery. The cottages were built about 1800 and had once formed Heybridge Brewery. There was a terrace of four pairs of back-to-back cottages with another pair at right angles to this block; a house has been converted from the first two pairs of back-to-back cottages, two pairs are now two cottages and the pair at right angles is now one house. Earlier, the Clark family, who lived in the part of the house adjacent to the canal used to let out boats for 9d. per hour.

As the canal passes the Bentall's famous warehouse, the Navigation widens out on the south side to provide a passing place for lighters and a place for Bentall's to load machinery into lighters. There used to be more wharfs on the bank opposite the warehouse. This stretch of the canal is known as the Long Pond. Later, Mr. Chaney ran separate ladies' and gentlemen's hairdressing shops in a wooden one storey building there. Residents of Navigation Cottages had to walk along the tow path and up steps to fetch their water from an outside tap near the hairdressers' shop. This shop was demolished and ten two storey flats, Wave Bridge Court, have been erected on the site.

13.2 Bentall's Complex - former Acrow offices, Tesco convenience store, ASDA (formerly Netto), chemist offices and surgeries

Acrow, the firm that took over Bentall's, built a modern office block on Bentall's Sports Ground in 1974. Padge Wakelin had kept cows and sheep in the field adjoining the sports field and behind Boulton Cottages. This field was criss-crossed by streams.

This modern office block was converted into a shopping centre in 1986 by Nick Mann. Originally, the office block was extended in a partial U shape to create a small courtyard with children's play equipment in the centre with shops and kiosks around it which created a friendly feeling. The kiosks were demolished and a large two storey pavilion type of building was erected at the entrance to the courtyard that seems to be out of scale and hides shops and businesses around the courtyard. Various tenants have tried to create retail businesses in this large building as well as in the smaller shops in the vicinity but some units always seem to be unlet. Shops come and go but usually there seem to be four or five on the ground floor selling take-away food, a veterinary practice, estate agency plus a chemist's shop (the result of local campaigning), and a dentist's practice; on the first floor a podiatrist and other offices. Originally, the biggest ground floor premises were Pembertons; a privately owned supermarket that was one of a chain of three; the other two were in Maldon High Street and in Tiptree. They were rather idiosyncratic and probably failed because they were confusing; shelves had cheap goods mixed up with luxury items. Dillons replaced Pembertons in 1995 with a convenience store; one of 1,400 they owned in England. The owner of the complex, Nicholas Mann, bought the Post Office premises in The Street when Graham Mott died and moved the post office into Dillons.

Tesco bought the Dillon chain in 2003 and runs the Heybridge shop as a convenience store. Unusually for Tesco at the time, they retained the Post Office which is a busy one serving the many large and small firms in Heybridge and a population of nearly ten thousand.

Initially, the two Maldon doctors' practices had planned to share specially designed premises in the complex with shared administrative staff. The arrangement did not come to fruition and other uses were found for the premises. A small, separate, single storey building houses one of the practices - when there are staff shortages in Maldon surgeries are cancelled at short notice. The other practice built a surgery off the centre of the village between Goldhanger Road and Scraley Road. It is odd that some Maldon and outlying residents prefer to come to surgeries in Heybridge when Heybridge people find it difficult to get appointments in the village. Heybridge is badly served for medical facilities; for routine matters such as injections, patients often have to go to the Maldon surgeries. One practice does not even do flu jabs in Heybridge. The bus fare from Maldon High Street in front of W. H. Smith's newsagents to Bentall's Complex in Heybridge, one mile exactly, is rather expensive - £2.80 and the return is £4.20 (2011), mothers with children and the elderly have to struggle on and off buses and walk some distance from Maldon High Street to the surgeries. The Primary Care Trust recognises the problems and made the provision of improved services and facilities a top priority in 2008. One must wonder when this will happen.

Netto is a Danish firm and part of an international conglomerate that owns Maersk, the Sally Line and widespread transport interests. Netto brought their discount grocery shops to England in 1990 and established stores in large industrial cities of north and central England. One of their first stores in the south came to Heybridge in January 1995; it attracts customers from far afield. Netto stores had no storage facilities. Goods were brought in by lorry as needed and boxes are torn open immediately to reveal goods and placed on the sales floor, often on pallets. The number of lines stocked was smaller than the big name supermarkets and is one of the reasons why their goods were cheaper. The firm asserted that it was very selective about suppliers, was careful to avoid trading with international hot spots, that they followed good environmental practices and aimed to sell locally sourced greengrocery on the same day. Netto charged for carrier bags long before their rivals to encourage customers to limit their use. In 2007, Heybridge and Witham were their only stores in Essex. Very few staff are employed and one had to be patient at the check out when only one or two check outs were open. Only cash or debit cards were accepted. It is said that the firm followed European employment practices that were more generous than those of Britain. Shoppers travelled from far afield to stock up in Heybridge.

In May 2010, ASDA, the second largest food UK supermarket chain owned by American Wal-Mart, bought Netto's 193 UK discount shops to add to their 374 ASDA shops. They seek to challenge Tesco for the first place in food retailing. They have changed the shops into small supermarkets to satisfy the public liking for smaller stores. Their shops offer 10,000 products while Netto stocked 1,800 and there are more staff. Shop fitters have transformed the store with smart shelving and clear signage. This set up differs from the next door Tesco convenience store, where many goods are more expensive than in their supermarket stores.

13.3 Wyndeham Heron Print Works

W. T. Heron and Company was founded in 1885 by Edward Thomas Heron who had been apprenticed to printing at the age of 14. He started his own letterpress printing business in Tottenham Street, London. With a staff of six and working 70 to 80 hours a week, the firm flourished. In 1900, he brought out 'The Optical Lantern Journal' to cater for the increasing popularity of the magic lantern. In 1903, he started 'The Talking Machine News'. He founded 'The Kinematrograph Weekly' following the invention of the cine film and the newspaper grew to 300 pages in ten years. There were difficulties during W.W.1 and afterwards; skilled staff were difficult to find. Although work was hard to come by, the contract from the publishers of the 'Nursing Times' journal was a landmark; this contract lasted for forty years.

Mr F. H. Crittall purchased jointly with E. T. Heron the old established printing business of A. Page and Company of London in 1928. The entire plant was moved to Western Road, Silver End. Printing production continued in London until 1965 when some of their work transferred to Silver End. Various extensions were made to the Silver End premises to accommodate senior staff and the accounts staff where quality catalogues, booklets, house journals, sales promotion material and general printing was being produced. Mr E. R. Heron became managing director in 1966 and, in the next few years, the firm introduced machinery to keep up with technical changes in the industry.

The firm bought Tindal Press of Chelmsford and a letterpress and lithographic printing house. The introduction of photo-typesetting and litho plate processing at Silver End meant the end of letterpress printing in 1976.

E. T. Heron was sold to a property company called RKF in 1988 which invested heavily and moved the firm to Heybridge. Three years later, the parent company went into receivership and a management buy-out by Prudential Venture took place in 1991. In 1996, the company was bought by Wyndeham Press Group. The investment in new machinery and the expansion of the firm on the Heybridge site meant that "E. T. Heron is ... acknowledged as being one of the United Kingdom's best equipped and well respected web offset printers" according to Mr. Rob Austin, the systems manager.

Many of the factory buildings on the former Acrow site were demolished after the closure of the Acrow business in Heybridge but the large, modern factory building, behind the Bentall Complex became an intervention store for the European Common Market 'grain mountain' after the 1984 harvest. Heron was part of the RKS Group when they bought this building and their activities spread on the north side of the Chelmer and Blackwater Navigation.

Dick Heron bought the firm back in the early 1990s, it became part of the Wyndeham Press group in 1993, Dagsbrun Baugur bought it in 2006 and sold it to Icelandic investors and Landsbanki in 2007. Landsbanki went bankrupt and was nationalised. Walstead investments bought Wyndeham Heron to become part of their group of printing companies in 2008. Sixty-three Heybridge workers were made redundant due to restructuring in 2008.

Wyndeham Heron is now one of the United Kingdom's premier web offset plants. They are in operation 24 hours a day, six days a week, producing hundreds of medium and long runs of prestigious weekly and monthly magazines, travel brochures, mail order catalogues, as well as one off publications. Among the titles they print are Marie Claire, Reveal, Marketing, Your Horse, Autosport and 'How It Works'.

The press hall has five high speed web presses printing up to 40,000 copies per hour, four high speed binder lines dealing with up to 10,000 copies per hour, and five stitching lines dealing with up to 12,000 copies per hour. The biggest lorries bring in paper supplies and take out the printed material. The smallest print run is 10,000 copies per hour, the largest print run is 750,000 copies and the average run is circa 50,000 copies.

13.4 Alan Collins, restorer of Jaguar E Type cars

There used to be various other firms on the print works site but Wyndeham Heron acquired their premises, erected new buildings and demolished others to create storage and car parking but Alan Collins has carried on his business of Jaguar E type restoration in the premises where the Bentall car was manufactured for over thirty years.

Alan was apprenticed at Jaguar. He became part of the Marlboro McLaren race team when James Hunt won the Formula 1 World Championship in 1976 and was involved in building their car. Subsequently, he led the race team of Noel Edmunds, the Radio One DJ and Mike Smith for two years. He worked with Phil Dowsett who competed regularly in the British Touring Car Championships during the 1980s and won the up to 1600cc title in 1988 and 1989, he came second in the championships overall in 1988. He was a successful saloon car driver and single seat driver. Alan prepared and looked after the cars. Alan won third prize at Pebble Beach with the Ford Mercury special racing car in 2003. He is now well known for his superb restoration of, in his words, the timeless E Type Jaguars. The cars can be seen in his garage in Heybridge at various stages of refurbishment. His son, Oliver, trained at McLarens and has two British Touring Car titles with Honda. Oliver now manages Airwaves Racing Team for Motobase preparing two Ford Focus cars challenging in the 2011 British Touring Car Championships (BTCC). At other times, he works with Alan, his father.

13.5 St Clare's Hospice

Farleigh Hospice opened in New London Road, Chelmsford in August 1988. A survey in 1989 showed the need for a Hospice Day Centre in Maldon District. After years of fund raising, St Clare's Day Hospice opened July 1995 in Heybridge, local trustees had negotiated a 99-year lease on the former Bentall Sports Club pavilion. It was named after a nun at St Francis Convent who had suffered from cancer. While it was effectively part of Farleigh Hospice services, it had a separate Board of Governors and did its own fund raising until it merged with Farleigh in 2001. The name was changed to Farleigh Day Hospice in 2006. Since that time, Farleigh has built purpose built extensive premises on a site adjacent to Broomfield Hospital.

13.6 The Triangle

The junction of Colchester Road and Goldhanger Road was known as the Triangle because there was a triangle of grass at the junction on which there were three chestnut trees and a seat surrounded by slender iron railings. It was the young people's meeting place in the 1930s and where they went to throw bits of wood up to bring down the conkers. Old men gathered there to smoke their pipes and put the world to rights. The present mini roundabout was installed in the late 1980s but this junction should not lose its historical name, 'The Triangle'

13.7 Edward Lee Baker and the Wakelins

Edward Lee Baker and his wife, Susanna Harvey Smith, came to Langford from Sudbury to the re-built mill at Langford in 1879. The original flour mill was built in 1776. 8,318 sacks of flour were sent to London annually via the Langford Cut and the Navigation by mid nineteenth century. The original mill was destroyed by a disastrous fire on a bitterly cold, clear March night in 1879 when the flames could be seen as far way as Chelmsford. The Chancellor practice of architects in Chelmsford designed the new mill which was completed in November of that year. The building had four storeys; the lower two storeys are in red brick and the others in stock brick with red dressings in Victorian style and was owned by Lady Byron.

Edward Lee Baker's eldest son, **Edward Thomas Baker, 1869-1948**, was born at Liston when his father was connected with the Sudbury mill. After his father's death in 1889 at the age of 42, Edward Thomas Baker was running Fullbridge Mill as a corn rolling mill as well as Langford Mill. Edward Thomas Baker married in 1893. He built New Trees in Wellington Road as the family home and had seven children and was Mayor of Maldon six times when prominent business men became borough councillors to serve their communities.

Fullbridge Mill had been built by E. H. Bentall's sons, Frederick and Edmund, to manufacture nuts and bolts c.1879. They traded as "Bentall Bros, Drill Makers, Fullbridge". Oliver and

Lewis Belsham converted the building into a roller flour mill in 1891.

The Fullbridge roller mills were described as absolutely modern in design and equipment in 1900; they were a complete plant for cleaning wheat and of rolling machinery, including separators, trunks, dust collectors, aspirators, rolls, flour and offal worms, purifiers etc. of the most modern type. The machinery produced four to five sacks of flour of the finest grades an hour. Roller mills could produce sixteen times more per day than traditional grinding methods; they increased productivity, cut costs at a stroke and were the death knell of traditional wind and water mills. The buildings are now offices with a conspicuously large metal fire escape on the Maldon side of the building that was prefabricated for installation.

Three flour mills in the Maldon locality were owned by the Baker family: Langford, Fullbridge and Green's.

Green's Mill, Rayleigh Flour Mill, was erected by Samuel Garrett in 1896. He had previously owned Hoe Mill in Woodham Walter, one of the thirteen mills on the Navigation, but inland water mills were no longer profitable since foreign wheat could be imported into steam mills on the river frontage at Maldon. Garrett's Mill went bankrupt in July 1914 and the mill was empty for two years. In 1916, William Green bought Garrett's Mill for £2,000 after his Rayleigh Mill was burned down. Two of his five sons, Walter and Leno, ran the mill successfully after William Green died in 1921. Walter died in 1943 and the business was sold to Robert Baker, Edward Thomas Baker's cousin for £36,000. Mr. Leno Green worked for the firm until 1960; he attended the Corn Exchange in Chelmsford dressed in striped trousers, a black jacket and a bowler hat. Bernard Lewis became manager on 15th January 1947 when he was demobilised. Manitoba wheat came to Green's Mill in two barges: the Ethel Maud and the Mayflower before W.W.2. One skipper was only 18 when he came to Green's Mill.

Since that time, Green Brothers (Maldon) has been a successful business that expanded with the acquisition of Franklin's Mill at Biggleswade; subsequently their operations were closed down and their modern machinery was brought to Maldon. The Maldon premises have been modernised with new machinery and storage facilities, it is the only flour mill left in Maldon.

When Edward Lee Baker died in 1889 at the age of 42, his family continued to live in the Mill House until 1905. His eldest son, Edward Thomas Baker, operated the Langford Mill until 1918. James Bettley believes the Mill House was probably built at the same time as the original mill in 1776 but the front is nineteenth century. The building has been used by asylum seekers, as a care home and is now a comfortable hotel run by a good friend of Langford Church.

Edward Lee Baker and Susannah Harvey Smith's daughter, Natalie, married William Frederick (Padge) Wakelin in February 1904; the ceremony was conducted by the rector of St Giles, Langford the Rev. Hon. Byron. Suzanne Benbow, Padge Wakelin's granddaughter, does not know how he got this nickname but he was known by it for the greater part of his life. Padge grew up in Langford Hall behind Langford Church in Witham Road Langford. The house is mostly late seventeenth century brick that has a delightful front dated 1748 with a fine central Roman Doric doorcase. Padge was a farmer who rented Draper's Farm, then Lofts Farm and finally bought Home Farm (also known as The Farm) from E. H. Bentall. It is named Hobbs and Steele's Farm in documents. This was the farm that Edward Bentall had bought in 1805 for the site of his new works; he retained the meadows adjacent to the Chelmer and Blackwater

Navigation, the present site of the Bentall Complex and the Wyndeham Heron Print Works. The rest of the arable land connected with the farm, the farm house and farm building was let. The farm house and land were never part of the Bentall Company assets; a map of 1874 confirms that E. H. Bentall owned it personally. Padge was granted a thirteen year lease on Home Farm, the farm buildings and the farm house in 1920. He was able to buy the farm house, farm buildings in one lot and more land in a second lot when they were auctioned in 1930. The farm house is of typical Bentall concrete construction and the extensive outbuildings, cart sheds and barns in the farm yard were surrounded by Bentall type concrete walls. Home Farm was the centre of Padge Wakelin's farming activities; some knew it as Wakelin's Depot. The photograph below shows ranges of farm buildings, cart lodges and animal stalls in the farm yard.

The Triangle

Home Farm was bought by Houldings after Padge Wakelin's death.

PHOTO supplied by Ron Houlding

Padge Wakelin was contracted to provide a horse and tumbrel and to repair roads for Essex County Council. Mr. Gooch used to arrive at 5.30am to feed and groom the black horse; he left at 6.30am in the green two-wheeled tumbrel to repair roads. Padge always wore breeches and highly polished, laced up brown buskins, these leggings were cleaned by his boot boy. Such gaiters were worn by A. N. Alexander and George Free. Padge made nightly visits to the Crown on Broad Street Green Road in a pony and trap. The pony knew the way home, dropped Padge and settled in his stable to await the horseman next morning who removed the harness. Padge rented other arable land in Heybridge including Draper's Farm. It is said he sowed the fields, shut the gate and left it for a year when he harvested the crop. He found it necessary to sell pieces of land during his later life to maintain his standard of living. King George V Memorial Playing Field was created on land he sold. Padge was an early motoring enthusiast who bought a car from Sir Claude de Crespigny. Suzanne remembers that the interior was luxurious with leather upholstery, deep pile carpets and enormous headlights and there was a dicky seat at the back.

Padge was very fond of his grand daughter, Suzanne. He was pleased when she stayed at Home Farm where she had her own bedroom. She remembers spending about half her time there.

Suzanne attended Mrs. Knowles' preparatory school in the Knowles' home on Cromwell Hill. Mrs. Knowles shut her school at the outbreak of W.W.2 and she taught at Maldon Girls' Secondary School in the late 1940s. When Suzanne left Maldon Grammar School where Mr. Knowles was senior master, she went to work at Green's Mill and set up a laboratory to test flour. Old hands were amused at the need for testing but became interested when she posted the extraction rates daily. Later, Suzanne qualified as a children's special needs social worker for Essex County Council. She married Richard Benbow. Retirement at the compulsory retirement age did not mean an end to her concern for the children with special needs; she was persuaded to do the work voluntarily part-time, but part-time spread over very long hours until she finally ceased work.

Family life in those days involved the extended family and people who needed care were helped within the family. It would seem Natalie Wakelin did her share of caring. Olive Berridge had been adopted by Natalie's sister, Ethel Rawlinson, and lived with her at Langford Lee but they went to live at Home Farm after Ethel was widowed and became ill. Later, Daisie, another of Susanna's daughters who suffered from Alzheimer's disease went to live at Home Farm.

The Civil Defence Headquarters moved from The Towers early in the war to Home Farm outbuildings. Ambulances and other vehicles were housed in the main barn; the two other big buildings were used as stores while men on duty slept in one and women in the other. However, since Olive Berridge lived in Home Farm, it was decided she could sleep at home. Attached to her bed was a rope that was pulled when she was needed on duty.

Home Farm was sold on the death of Padge in 1953 and his widow, Natalie, went to live with Miss Wyatt in Moat Lodge until she died in 1963, aged 67.

The Sabbath

Natalie Baker, Mrs. Susannah Baker's daughter, played the organ in Langford Church nearly all her life. Suzanne remembers sitting on a rush seated chair next to the organ with Mrs. S. Baker, her grandmother, during the services. Petrol was rationed in W.W.2 and Suzanne cycled from Heybridge to Langford Church for the services since she regarded Langford Church as her parish church. William Claydon travelled by bus to the Sunday morning service from Doe's Corner; the bus was scheduled to arrive at Langford a few minutes after 11 o'clock - the service was delayed for his arrival. He walked home. Sometimes his granddaughter, Beryl, accompanied him. William Claydon was a bricklayer who became a foreman. He cycled to jobs wherever they were, often quite a long way. His grandson told the author he cycled from Ulting to evening classes at Chelmsford Technical College after work. He started a building and contracting business from an office in Hill Crest at the top of market Hill, Maldon. W. A. Claydon bought Moor Gardens which stretched from Witham to Little Baddow when the Butler Estate was split up. He acquired 140 acres of ancient woodland, a plantation and two fields and he transferred his building and contracting business to Ulting from Hill Crest, Market Hill in Maldon.

William Claydon allowed no card games, Sunday newspapers or sewing or knitting in his house on the Sabbath and he read the Sunday Companion. Friends tell me these beliefs were sincerely held by their relatives right into the 1960s: no washing could be put on a line outdoors on Sunday; Marilyn Green was forbidden to use her roller skates and had to wear her best clothes although they did not go to church and she was stopped from going to a dance; Sheila Rosewarne's grandmother did no housework, listened only to Songs of Praise on the radio, allowed no card games, sewing or knitting, insisted best clothes were worn and the children attended Sunday school; Kathy Lang's parents sent all children living at home to Sunday School, she had six brothers and five sisters. Many girls were not allowed to wear trousers on Sundays. Two people said they were not allowed to cut their nails on the Sabbath.

No shops were open on Sundays with the exception of newsagents. Sunday newspapers were distributed through different traders from weekday papers. Mr. Hardy King had taken over the shop on the corner of Chequers Lane in 1912 which had been a draper's shop since 1691. It is now the site of Iceland. In Maldon, Mr. Hardy King 1 and 2 received papers for the area from a wholesaler. Mrs. Tony Newton, a week day newsagent, remembers her father, Mr. Wadley, collected his Sunday newspapers from the Hardy King's draper's shop, 62 High Street, run by Mr. Hardy King (2)'s two sister where they sold London Evening Standards on weekdays in the early afternoon. Mr. Bittern of Goldhanger collected Sunday newspapers from Mr. Hardy King and organised rounds. Len Wakelin's round included the council houses in Goldhanger Road and Mill Beach; he was fined 7s. 6d. pence for selling newspapers on the street without a licence.

In Heybridge, money for Sunday newspapers was collected from doorsteps. There used to be restrictions on the location and number of newsagents' shops that sold newspapers: they had to be more than 100 yards apart, unlike today when all kinds of shops sell them.

13.8 The Triangle: Houlding's Garage

Dick Houlding, (Dick was his baptismal name) worked in Bentall's foundry. He drove Bentall's lorry which had a windscreen but no sides and went to various markets. Bentall's other lorry was driven by Alf Bacon around 4pm daily to Maldon Railway Goods' Station with manufactured goods for delivery. When Dick left Bentall's in February 1930, he and his wife, Minnie, bought a small piece of ground that was formerly part of The Towers vegetable garden; two high gates pierced the typical Bentall walls on the south of Goldhanger Road. The Houldings started their business in a small way; Dick repaired bicycles and expanded by buying and selling them. His wife, Min or Minnie Florence, was the driving force, her name was on the site deeds, she kept the books and organised the business. Dick had lived in The Street but he erected a bungalow incorporating a Bentall boundary wall at the back of the site which was in existence until 2008. Dick started out with just one petrol pump, later he installed more petrol pumps and a workshop in the garden and called the firm the Triangle Garage. The petrol pumps were right on the footpath. In those days, petrol pumps had a handle that was moved from side to side pumping petrol into a glass dome at the top, a lever released it from the dome into the petrol tank of a motorcar. Sid Linnet, Min's brother, was a carpenter who had helped in the building of the Bentall car and later worked on the restoration of one of the cars. He had installed beautifully made shelving in the garage premises.

Dick and Min's first employee was Joff (Walter) Newton whose father was a carpenter and joiner. Joff, the eldest son, served an apprenticeship at Bates Garage in Spital Road, Maldon. After W.W.2, following service in the army, he moved to his wife's home town in Yorkshire where his father-in-law had a garage business. Joff had five brothers; four won scholarships to Maldon Grammar School but Tony chose to go to Chelmsford Technical School.

Dick Houlding bought a Model T Ford motorcar which he returned when it did not sell. Then Min and Dick Houlding went to Cowley and in 1930 secured the main dealership of Morris motor cars. Min and Dick made plans to build workshops behind the original garage on a piece of land they bought from Mr. Crouch, sometime Mr. E. H. Bentall's head gardener, who owned the Colchester end house in Well Terrace. They gained access to it by demolishing the end of their bungalow.

In the 1930s, few people owned a motor car. Dennis Fenn's listed car owners in the 1930s: Mr. Woodhead of Lofts Farm, Padge Wakelin (a big Hillman), George Free (a Morris), Jack Mitchell (a Morris 12), later Reg Cronk from the Half Moon, Stanley Frost from Heybridge Mill and Miss Packe JP.

Houldings shelved plans to expand the existing facilities when the opportunity to buy Home Farm on the opposite side of Colchester Road arose after the death of Padge Wakelin in 1953. The farm buildings adjoining Stock Chase fronted an unmade road. This road was due to be adopted by Maldon Borough Council and the owners of the farm were liable for the charges of making it up. This was unfortunate for Mrs. Wakelin since the farm and farm buildings were sold for less money. The barn was demolished and tiles from the barn were used to re-roof the Anchor public house. Dick and Min Houlding moved into Home Farm House and the bungalow was let to Len Nardy. He lived there for some years until his son died in the bathroom when fumes from a paraffin heater killed him.

Dick and Minnie's son, Ron Houlding, expanded the business and became a Rover main agent. He was joined by his three sons; finally his twin sons, Richard and Charles ran the business. A showroom was built on the Home Farm site; cars were serviced behind the showroom and office administration carried out on the first floor. Petrol was sold on the original site on the Goldhanger Road side where there was a second car showroom.

By 2000, Charles and Richard Houlding, Dick and Min's grandsons, were running the business. They decided to stop selling and repairing Rover cars. Richard said "So many independent garages are closing … because of the massive investment needed to run them" and "It's now very difficult for independent retailers to trade profitably in the fuel business". However, Charles and Richard sold petrol on the forecourt of the original garage premises and created a general shop behind the pumps selling newspapers, confectionery, soft drinks, tinned food and much more. Such general shops on garage forecourts fulfil a need as village shops disappear and make the business viable. The car showroom on the original site was rented to a firm selling mobility aids which moved to the Causeway when the site was cleared.

Twins, Richard and Charles, continued to run the Shell petrol filling station and convenience shop until March 2008. The first planning application on that site was refused because the Environment Agency objected on the grounds of the high flood risk. The second application for eight 3 bedroom houses, four 2 bedroom apartments and two 1 bedroom apartments with twenty-four parking spaces was granted and site preparation began in 2010.

The various buildings on the Home Farm site have been split up into small workshops where small firms operate but the main building, that housed the offices and a showroom, has been occupied by a tyre and exhaust centre.

Houldings owned a tract of land, adjoining the original garage premises that included the orchard, to the Navigation, that was compulsorily purchased by Essex County Council for a playing field for Heybridge Primary School. A County Councillor and two other Heybridge residents told the author that the land had to revert to Houldings if the school was not used for educational purposes. Richard Houlding had never heard of this but two other Heybridge residents confirmed it. When this covenant surfaced, the sale of the school and the playing field had to be abandoned. Initially, people starting new businesses were able to rent small units in the school buildings but leases were not renewed. The Heybridge Children's Support Centre is now housed in the building and has catered for pupils with special educational needs since 2008.

13.9 King George V Memorial Playing Field

E. H. Bentall had owned the plantation privately in 1874. The 1874 OS map shows the tree planting. Fred Mott records that fifteen poplars and fifty-three sycamore, maple, ash and firs were felled in November 1925. E. E. Bentall sold the plantation to Padge Wakelin who sold it to the King George V Trust in 1937 to create a playing field to commemorate the King's Silver Jubilee. The great uncle of Janet Smith, a Heybridge resident, was a blacksmith in South Woodham Ferrers who made the attractive main ornamental gates to the field. The brick pillars on either side of the gates are embellished with plaques showing a lion shield on the right and the King's name with the date of his reign 1910-1936 and a unicorn shield on the left naming King George's Field.

John Playle sketched a scene which showed that a Bentall wall of medium height formally protected the boundary on two sides and came up to the edge of the road. Tony Newton says that the wall was demolished and the footpath was set back from the road adjacent to the iron railings because there was a plan to widen the road there which never happened. The playing field is higher than footpath and road. Trees were planted on the greenswards that are now mature and most attractive.

In the spring of 1992, Heybridge Parish Council created the popular children's play area. The seats in the field are used for picnics and as a resting place by shoppers on their way home to the big estates beyond the field. Teams hire the football pitch and use the changing room facilities in Plantation Hall.

13.10 Plantation Hall

Maldon Borough Council had erected a prefabricated building, called the Community Centre, on King George V Playing Field in the 1960s. The building could hardly be called luxurious; the author knew a similar building that was used as a tractor shed at the Warren Golf Club. The District Council was anxious to be rid of the building because of the financial burden and the problems of managing it so the new Heybridge Parish Council was able to acquire the building on advantageous terms. Heybridge Parish Council made an early decision to replace this spartan building as soon as possible. The money to pay for the new hall came from: Bovis £145,000 planning gain from the Elms Farm Development, grants from Maldon District Council and money Heybridge Parish Council set aside over the years. The new hall was opened in 1999 by John Whittingdale MP, was designed by the architect, Ben Downie from the Inkpen Downie practice, and built by the Maldon builders, Capon, at a cost of £312,000. The main hall has a wooden floor, underfloor heating, a loop amplifying system, a kitchen that is fully equipped with a catering cooker, refrigerator, double sinks and hand wash basin with ample storage for china, cutlery and cooking utensils, two committee rooms and an office. Cupboards are available for storage of equipment to regular hirers. Plantation Hall has changing rooms for football teams and referees who use the King George V Playing Field, and a spacious, floodlit car park. The hall had been fully paid for by 2004.

Community Centre is a much disliked name; it does not look good on invitations to wedding receptions or golden wedding anniversary parties. Heybridge Parish Council sought naming suggestions and a local resident suggested that the hall be named Plantation Hall since it was built on the former plantation, now King George V Memorial Playing Field. This name linked generations of children who had nicknamed the field the Planny and still invite their friends to play with them on the 'Planny'.

In 2007, the Parish Council added a larger committee room named 'The Claydon Room' to mark Beryl Claydon's and her parents' contributions to the village.

The Plantation Hall is owned and managed by Heybridge Parish Council which makes it possible for the council to subsidise the running costs of the hall, purchase equipment for it and deal with maintenance. The council sets the hire fees and aims to be very competitive. The building is well used throughout the day and evening - the council's staff prepare and clear up the premises to hirers' wishes; the premises are centrally located in the village; there is easy access to various bus routes and the car parking is free.

13.11 A wartime incident - Heinkel Crash

On Saturday 24th August 1940, 15 year old Harry Yuill stood in the back garden of his home number 11 Oak Road watching German bombers coming over in formation. Suddenly, a Hurricane came from nowhere, went right up underneath a Heinkel and fired three bursts; this caused smoke to come from underneath the plane that wavered from left to right. The plane dropped down but was unable to climb. The youngest crew member baled out and floated to the ground. During the descent his boot came off that landed in the Yuill's garden and frightened Mrs. Yuill who feared it was a bomb. Then the plane pulled out of its dive, went over Heybridge Woods struck a large tree near Howell's Farm, pulled down telephone cables on its way and exploded igniting an adjacent corn field and a pile of rubbish in the back garden of Ravens on the west side of Maypole Road. (Ravens, the two old L shaped cottages, were owned by Lord Byron and have been refurbished and incorporated into one house with ornate entrance gates and tidy garden which some people think has destroyed the historical character). The other four crew members perished. The explosion was caused by the bomb load the plane was carrying, wreckage was scattered all over adjacent fields. Harry reckoned there were fifty or sixty souvenir hunters on site within a short time.

This plane was part of a huge Armada; thirty-six Heinkels and fifty Dornier bombers escorted by seventeen Messerschmitts sent to strafe and cause as much damage as possible to twenty-eight airfields in Essex north of the Thames estuary especially Hornchurch and North Weald. Six Hawker Hurricanes were launched from North Weald followed by nine from RAF Kenley, they shot down German planes at Bulphan, Layer de la Haye, 13 miles off Brightlingsea and at Great Wakering. After hospital treatment, the German survivor was sent to a POW camp in Canada.

13.12 Social housing; council houses, Colne Housing Association, Plume/Moat Housing Association, outer London boroughs

John Playle's family moved into the first pair of council houses built on the west side of Colchester Road in 1924. Building started in the middle of the row and worked outwards towards Maldon and Colchester. Council houses at that time were pebble dashed because there was a shortage of bricklayers after W.W.1. Some victims of the floods from Hall Road were rehoused in these houses in 1928.

Glebe Road and Towers Road council houses were built on Glebe Farm east of Colchester Road soon after the end of W.W.2. This land had been farmed by George Free and then Padge Wakelin and was also the site of allotments. Larger families from all parts of Essex came to live in Heybridge, many from the sixty-five chalet bungalows along Mundon Road.

Maldon Borough Council built council houses in Oak Road and Wood Road in 1957. The local nickname for Wood Road was First Avenue and Oak Road was Second Avenue. Diane Marsh moved into 38 Wood Road when it was new and has lived there ever since. She was able to buy the house in 1985.

The houses in Colchester Road had kitchens added onto the rear of their houses in the 1970s and later pebble dash removed and the walls plastered. In 1993, Maldon District Council voted to transfer their stock of council houses to a housing association so that the Council would be relieved of the debt burden and maintenance and would no longer be responsible for setting rents (always a policital hot potato).

The Council interviewed various housing associations and chose Moat, who set up Plume Association, to run the Maldon housing stock. In 1993, the 2,000 houses formed one of the largest transfers at the time. Early on, the Association was fortunate to recruit David Robinson as chairman and John Wheeldon as chief executive - they created a most effective team. The set up they negotiated included a board with three tenant representatives; (this was an innovation at the time but their contribution was to prove invaluable), two Maldon District Councillors (including John Cocking) as well as independent members. One tenant, who gained experience by participating in management, was led to study further and gained qualifications leading to an important career move in this sphere. The team had much to learn in these early days of housing associations. They arranged many consultation meetings with the tenants during which Plume undertook to spend £1 million installing central heating, £1 million replacing windows, £290,000 on refurbishing kitchens and bathrooms and to peg rents for five years subject to inflationary rises plus 1%.

A total of £42 million was raised by Plume to finance the cost of buying the council houses and the planned improvements. The actual transfer took place in 1995. One hundred and sixty-two houses in Heybridge were taken over. There had been years of neglected maintenance of the council housing stock and tenants soon began to appreciate the changed set up since Plume had but one task: to manage and maintain the housing stock. Decisions were not subject to committee and council consideration and local government cash restraints. Plume was very proud of the fact that it met every one of the promises it made to tenants for its first five years. Tenants were involved in deciding priorities for the spending of available monies.

Development plans allow few houses to be built in Maldon District due to inadequate road links with the A12 and the high cost of building land. Moat Homes maintains the register of housing applicants for the whole district. Homeless people were given priority and after that a system allocated points according to such criteria as over crowding, family difficulties, place of work etc. There is a shortage of houses for key workers and the needy. The earnings of Moat tenants are low and something like 70% receive housing benefit. There have been changes.

Today, there are wardened bungalows for older people in the vicinity of Sycamore Road and residents appreciate the help the wardens give them. Tenants can seek information and advice and gain access to computers from the resource centre in the King's Head Yard in Maldon that has been managed voluntarily by Pam Crewes and paid for by Moat Homes. Their help with computers is not restricted to Moat tenants.

The Colchester Co-operative Society returned to Heybridge when they bought the Alldays convenience store in Wood Road. It is first in the row of three shops; the Co-op convenience store, a fried fish and chip shop and a laundrette.

Heywood Way, which is half a mile long, was built behind Wood Road in the 1950s. The houses were mainly privately built but there is social housing leading off it including flats built by Colne Housing Association, a charitable housing association that was established in 1973 to own and manage homes in North Essex for those in social need. They built houses behind King George V's Memorial Playing Field for people from places outside Heybridge including Colchester, Tiptree, the Dengie Hundred and Maldon. The present chief executive, Mark Powell Davies, reported that, in Heybridge, Colne Housing has over seventy-seven properties made up of two bedroom houses and flats and a few three bedroom houses. Colne Housing is involved with sheltered housing schemes where people over 55 have the benefit of a local manager to support independent living. Tenants have emergency careline connections.

Colne House was built in 1967. Each of the twenty-four flats has a bedroom, bathroom, a lounge diner and kitchen. Flats on the first floor can be reached by lift and there are laundry and drying facilities. There is a resident manager.

In 2009, Colne Housing Association owned or managed 2,100 affordable homes throughout Essex. Colne Housing Association built Tensing House and Edmund House to cater for people with special needs. Heybridge families and families in north Essex are helped by Home-Start, a charity that works with volunteers through a donation received from a Colchester Housing Society. Colne Housing Society passes this money on to the local branches of this national organisation which helps families with young children. The volunteers receive 40 hours' preparatory training, continuous up-dating and their work is confidential.

Some outer London boroughs have bought housing in Heybridge which is managed by London Quadrant to provide housing for those who wish to leave London. Gateway Housing Association aims to meet this need and private landlords work through London Quadrant to provide rented accommodation.

13.13 Sheltered housing

There are two privately run care homes in Heybridge: Boucherne which has accommodation for twenty-four residents and Firstlings with thirty residents.

Runwood Homes PLC took over Brewster House from Essex County Council and has over one hundred single rooms.

13.14 Black Cottages

These were also known as the Black Huts and stood on a lane known as Black Huts Lane. This lane has become the entrance to Wood Road. It used to go from the Broad Street Green Road/Wood Road entrance to Heybridge Wood which was private, past Grapnell's Farm, along Wood Lane and into Holloway Road. The Enclosure map of the mid nineteenth century shows the lane turning left along former Langford Road for a short distance and then left into the present Crescent Road, into what is now known as Green Lane and it has become a pedestrian entrance to Elms Farm development. Since Green Lane is a generic name for such a lane, Heybridge Parish Council decided to adopt this name for the short path between Crescent Road and Elms Farm. Historically, this route was designated as a bridleway and Wendy Titheridge, the veterinary surgeon, remembers riding a horse along part of it.

Black Cottages consisted of two 2 storey semi-detached cottages for two families, followed by few metres gap, then a single storey building for four families. The next gap contained a hand pump to draw water up from the well. A further single storey building accommodated four families. At the end of the plot, approximately in line with the Isolation Hospital (see section 13.15), was a further small building that served as the washhouse for the community. These cottages were of tarred Essex weatherboard. The single units had cast iron-wheels put on them and Harold Lewis said teams of horses towed them from what became Bentall's Sports ground while Evelyn Wood Last in his account of Broad Street Green from 1879 said they came from The Towers site close to the triangle to Wood Lane.

Ev wrote that farm workers starting at Bentall's and newly married couples lived in the Black Cottages for 1s.6d. a week rent. They would be moved into other Bentall houses, Barnfield Cottages or Woodfield Cottages (the flat tops), as their families became larger. The next step up was a five roomed house, or even a villa, where the rent required a wage of 30s.0d. a week. Since most worked for Bentall's in the factory, few got further than the flat tops.

Ev recalls that the best known resident of the Black Cottages was the preacher, Mr. Hart, a heavily built man whose watchword was kindness. He was noted for his generosity and often discreetly gave the 5s.0d. burial fee to the bereaved when he really needed the money. Mr. A. Gooch and his new wife moved into Black Cottages and, after a lifetime's service to Bentall's, spent their final years in Springfield Cottages.

Black Cottages were condemned just before W.W.2. Local families put up their bombed out relatives from London and then put pressure on Maldon Borough Council to house them. The council refurbished some of the Black Cottages into which the evacuees moved. The Baker family arrived in 1942 after their London home was bombed; they lived with their relatives in Woodfield Cottages until they were allocated housing in Black Cottages. They remained in Heybridge after the war. Local people were housed there temporarily during the housing shortage after the war as well as illegal squatters. The cottages were demolished around 1949 when plans for Heywood Way were made. Henry Lewis bought the site for £15,000 and sold a plot for a bungalow to his nephew, Stanley Twinn. OS map 1824 shows the location of the Black Cottages.

Heybridge Wood close to the Black Cottages is largely planted with conifers interspersed with birch. Maldon District Council's Local Replacement Plan 2005 says that ground flora and wildlife in general would benefit by replacing the conifers with native broad leaf species.

Ev Last recalls that Mr. Dickerson, the farmer, Bill Rowlands and Bill Baker were out shooting on farm lands near Heybridge Wood when one of them shot a pheasant. They were seen by David Gibson, the old gamekeeper, and his son, Bert, and the case came before Witham Bench. Each man had a different version of the events and the case went to Chelmsford Assizes; all three were found guilty of perjury and sent to prison for three months.

13.15 Isolation Hospital

In 1900/01, with thirty-five cases of typhoid in the Heybridge area, a tented isolation hospital was set up along Broad Street Green Road. In 1903, the brick isolation hospital was built on the site with ten beds, a substantial house for the matron, a caretaker's house and a laundry. The site was surrounded by a close boarded green painted oak fence 8ft. high with two sets of double gates.

During an epidemic of scarlet fever in 1911, tents were erected in the grounds because the hospital was full and the tents became full. There was no electricity so gas and oil lamps were used. One night, an overturned lamp set fire to a tent necessitating the evacuation of all patients but no tragedy occurred. The medical superintendent was Dr. Henry Reynolds Brown who was the Borough Medical Officer of Health and a general practitioner in the town up to the 1930s. At the time of the outbreak, he was in a London Hospital suffering from scarlet fever.

Mrs. Watling, nee Nurse Cobb, served there from 1943 to 1946 when the elderly matron was assisted by a Sister Davies and ten nurses. Dr. Phillips was the medical officer. There were two main wards; north and south, each main ward had a smaller room attached that was necessary since patients with different infectious diseases had to be nursed separately. For example, scarlet fever patients were nursed apart from diphtheria patients. Similarly, there were two separate kitchens for their food preparation and washing up. There were two ward maids, two laundry maids and the cook, Mrs. Barrett, came in the morning. Mr. Hume was important; he was caretaker, carried out maintenance work, created gardens, drove the ambulance, mowed the lawns and managed the on site sewage works.

A 2½ year old boy was treated for typhoid in 1928. Scarlet fever was the scourge of the time. Eric Willsher remembers he was sent to the Isolation Hospital in 1933, aged 3½, when he contracted scarlet fever; his clothes and all his soft toys were burnt to stop the spread of the disease. As late as 1945, Shirley Burns suffered from scarlet fever and was nursed by Mrs. Watling. Mrs. Kemp, the ward maid, consoled her mother when she left, after seeing Shirley through the window. Subsequently, all Shirley's clothes were ruined by compulsory fumigation. Mrs. Watling remembers when seven airmen from Bradwell on Sea aerodrome were nursed at the Isolation Hospital during the war.

When patients were out of quarantine, they were taken back home in horse drawn ambulances, later the hospital owned a Model T Ford ambulance. Ordinarily, if only one patient was due to go home, the Matron, Nurse Miles, drove them home in a dog cart. Nurses did not accompany returning home patients in ambulances and no companions were allowed in the ambulance. Nurses attended incoming patients. Later, the navy blue ambulance with opaque windows was driven by Mr. Hume, the caretaker, in a navy blue uniform with a peaked cap. Ambulances rang a bell on their journeys.

A fine TB hospital was built at Broomfield in 1937 to which the Isolation Hospital became an annexe where about twenty-five TB patients were treated. By 1946, TB was a leading cause of death among adults in Europe and North America; the disease thrived in the close quarters of military barracks and refugee shelters. Before the discovery of streptomycin, tuberculosis was treated by years of bed rest and unpleasant surgery which saved barely half of those infected. Streptomycin was the first antibiotic that cured the disease; it was isolated in October 1943 and mass produced around 1950. The author remembers visiting Black Notley when streptomycin was first being administered and patients found it very unpleasant to take. Sir John Crofton led a team at the Brompton Hospital to investigate the effectiveness of this new antibiotic streptomycin against tuberculosis; it was found to curb the number of deaths but soon the disease became resistant to the drug. Sir John discovered that by combining with a newer medicine, para-aminosalicylic acid and, later, isoniazid, TB rates were halved by 1957. Since Sir John became chairman of Respiratory Disease and Tuberculosis Department in Edinburgh University, this treatment became known as the Edinburgh Method and the standard method of treating TB. Sufferers were able to continue work during treatment and they felt better after three or four weeks of treatment but had to take the full course of the drugs. Nowadays, the drugs cost only £10 but even that is a lot in the Third World where the disease is prevalent.

John Playle entered a TB hospital in September 1951. He was transferred to Heybridge Isolation Hospital in 1952 because he was a Heybridge man and was kept in bed for twenty-one months. He was then allowed up for short periods and stayed in the hospital for three years. Patients were smoking; John asked if it was alright to smoke and the doctor said "Yes provided you don't cough" so he began to smoke with the other patients.

Black Notley Hospital opened as a small pox isolation hospital; it became a TB sanatorium in 1912 and was enlarged from 1939 to 1946. It became an emergency hospital and temporary buildings were erected in the grounds where soldiers were treated. The author's mother was a member of VAD (Voluntary Aid Detachment) working voluntarily in these wards. It was often a very harrowing experience. Wounded soldiers from the Dunkirk evacuation were nursed there. Soldiers who had been badly burned recovered more quickly if they had waited in the sea; the author was told this was one of the reasons for changing the treatment of burns victims. In the 1950s, some wards were opened for TB patients and orthopaedic operations were carried out there. Heybridge people tell of their hip replacements. In 1957, plastic surgery operations were carried out but the hospital was obsolete, the temporary buildings were dilapidated, food was distributed to wards in containers and staff recruitment difficult in this location. The hospital closed down in 1998 and three hundred new homes have been built on the site.

Heybridge Isolation Hospital was being painted when news came that it was to be demolished. Mr. Hume's house stands at right angles to Broad Street Road while opposite and parallel to the road, is the larger matron's house and nurses' home that still exist. The rest of the site was sold for £15,000 and twenty-one bungalows have been built, even one on the site of the morgue. The development is named Scylla Close after Scylla House that used to be on the opposite side of the road next to the Congregational Chapel. Latterly, this detached very square sizeable house with bay windows on the road side is remembered as grey looking with the main entrance facing the chapel. The house was owned by three ladies; Jimmy and Mollie ran a cafe, a shop selling sweets and cultivated a market garden behind the house which Nic Hughes from Lofts Farm says was $5^1/_2$ acres (large when one remembers that an acre is the size of a football pitch), Eileen worked in London. They kept chickens, ducks, and pigs, grew vegetables and flowers for sale. They made Chris Wareham's wedding bouquet in 1957. When Julian Lewis helped, one of his rewards was a duck egg. Rows of fruit trees grew along the Chase for the length of the holding which was their boundary with Lofts Farm where, in 2011, hay was the sole crop. On one of the lakes on the other side of the Chase, there were many cygnets and ducklings. Scylla House was demolished when sand and gravel had been exhausted from Lofts Farm and the three ladies went to Cornwall to run a guest house. Jimmy died there from a fall over the cliffs.

Colchester Road c.1932 showing Plantation wall left and The Towers' wall to the right.

A Bentall wall enclosed the Plantation which became King George V Memorial Playing Field in 1937 commemorating the Silver Jubilee. Note gas street lights

The original Going's Warehouse at Wave Bridge, Heybridge. The Going family were substantial ship-owners in the port of Maldon and their warehouse was situated on the banks of the canal enabling goods to be moved to and from ships moored in Heybridge Basin.
By kind permission of the Maldon Society

14.0 Broad Street Green

14.1 Heybridge Enclosure Act 1811 - Jeffrey Grimwood's entail

This hamlet lies between Great Totham and Heybridge and is partly in both parishes. The 1777 Chapman and Andre map showed it consisted of five small homesteads in a corridor: rough, common land with vegetation which stretched from Captain's Wood to Scraley Road and along Scraley Road; this is the green in the hamlet name. A dotted lane through the middle of the green is a track or footpath. Another lane north of Captain's Wood links up with Maypole Road. Broad Street Green became a hamlet when it was laid out after the award of 7th December 1815 under the Heybridge Enclosure Act of 1811. It would seem that some of this land belonged to Jeffrey Grimwood of Cressing Temple. The common land was marked off; spacious plots were bought cheaply and cottages were built close to the new highway with long gardens. Families arrived steadily and a community was created. The deeds of Pleasant Cottage on Broad Street Green Road show that the land on which the cottage was built formed part of the Grimwood estate. Jeffrey Grimwood died in November 1842; in his will he appointed his son-in-law, James Brewster Cozens of Woodham Mortimer Lodge and others to be trustees for the management of his estate that covered extensive holdings in the County of Essex. He bequeathed £600 a year and Woodham Mortimer Lodge rent free for life to his daughter, Elizabeth Richardson Cozens, and the remainder of his property was invested in a trust for his grandson, Jeffrey Grimwood Cozens, and, thereafter, to the eldest son of the eldest son. His grandson had to adopt the surname of Grimwood. Land might be sold but the proceeds were to be invested or used to purchase land of the same value.

14.2 Grimwood entail broken legally 1938

This arrangement concerns Heybridge because the entail was legally broken in 1938 after Jeffrey Grimwood of Annini Tal in the Empire of India, a colonel on the retired list of His Majesty's Army and a late colonel of His Majesty's Regiment of the King's Royal Corps, died in 1938. His son, who lived in Hove and was born on 4th January 1911, inherited the estate. He sold a large number of properties including fifty-six cottages; William Ager Springett bought Pleasant Cottage, George Free was able to buy Canterbury Farm and the market garden and house rented by Mr. H Miller.

Harold Lewis grew up next door to Pleasant Cottage in Wood View Cottage. The outhouse at the end of the garden served the two houses with a copper for each house. Harold's father, Albert, collected two buckets of water from the well for their daily needs and an extra on wash days. There was a faggot oven at the rear of the wash house where bread was baked for the hamlet. Faggots were thrown into the oven, set alight and after the ashes were cleaned out the bread went in. Every Whit Monday, a gooseberry pie, 2ft. across, was cooked in the oven. Later, Albert Lewis and William Springett demolished this oven.

Harold bought Pleasant Cottage from William Springett where his son, Herbert, the Maldon photographer, and his daughter, Dorothy, were born.

14.3 Life in the hamlet largely based on Ev Last's memoir 'Broad Street Green from 1879' written in 1948

Ev Last wrote that "although consisting of less than 50 homes, this little hamlet . . . could fill many pages with history".

One account says that the Green Man was built round 1833 and became known as the Crown in 1839 to mark Queen Victoria's Coronation, celebrated two years earlier. The first proprietor was Henry Whitmore who ran the Crown for sixteen years. Men cycled past on boneshakers and penny farthing bicycles - they had to avoid deep ruts in the unmade road.

The Green Fair was held on Whit Monday at the Crown; it was a time of great fun. Old Mrs. Wardley sold rock, toffee apples, ginger bread and other things from her wicker pram. Ginger beer was one penny, a brown stone bottle with a marble in the top. The greasy pole with a leg of mutton at the top of the pole was a great attraction. Men used to get Bill Jarvis drunk, urge him to climb the pole but when he was a few yards up others tried to pull him down because they thought he was going too fast; they only succeeded in pulling his trousers off! Wise guys waited until many had attempted to reach the mutton and had wiped off all the grease, then one of them was able to climb up to get the leg of mutton. Cigarettes were known as 'willies', no doubt after Wills Woodbines that were sold in the 1930s in green paper packets for 2d. in machines.

Ev Last ran a complicated 100 yard potato race against Billy Pratt. A potato was laid at each yard, competitors picked up the first spud and returned it to the start, ran back to the second yard, and returned it to the start and so on until one hundred spuds were in the bucket. This was only 160 yards short of 3 miles and there was only one prize, 3s.0d. which Ev did not get.

Wilky and Nanty Playle once ran the four miles round Maypole Road and then finished the last 100 yards at sprint speed. An eye witness said they rode in the cart that accompanied them.

At the back of the Crown, in a large cart shed, there was a skittle alley lit by a hurricane lamp. At the further end, there was a 5ft.sq. board on which nine skittles stood. The thrower stood 20ft. away and threw the 'chess', a wooden disc, if he knocked down all the skittles, his opponent had to buy a gallon of beer. Usually there were many spectators so a gallon did not go far. The Crown was demolished in the 1990s and large houses have been built along the road on the site.

William Baker, assisted by an old man called Peeler, made fine hurdles that were stacked near the road ready for transport to farms. Many said that this very thirsty work prompted Peeler to drink a pint of beer for every nail he put in a hurdle.

Tom Springett was a moulder at Bentall's whose wife was busy at all hours of the day and night. She would be called on to help someone taken ill or to assist with a new baby. They had two girls and two boys. On Saturday afternoons, the family walked to Maldon to shop and returned loaded.

Charlie Last was born in and lived at number 2 and worked at Bentall's for fifty-six years. He was a keen gardener, a parish councillor, a prize winner at Maldon Flower Shows, a member of the Ancient Order of Foresters and the chief ranger of the Colchester District and President of the Maldon Co-op Society. He was a great believer of self help and thrift. He grew fine flowers and introduced a new plant, tomatoes; they were red and bright yellow, the size of pigeons' eggs and the same shape. At first, no one liked them and they were dispatched to the 'Bumby Hole' a square hole 6ft.sq. and 4ft. deep where they rotted down and were, probably, the reason for many of Charlie's successes.

William Charlie Last was the fifth child of Charles Last, a turner at Bentall's. He was born 23rd June 1873 and attended the Headquarters School until he was 13. He became odd job boy with Mr. Ward, the Totham builder, then under Fred Cox, a prominent sportsman. He worked in a flour mill using water driven grinding machinery but the dust caused him to become a farm worker in Salcott before working in Dagenham for three years. He returned to Heybridge at the age of 24 to work at the Co-op for forty-one years as horseman, roundsman, baker, and warehouseman in the grocery stores before retiring in 1941. The list of his public service is lengthy; inaugural president of the Old Age Pensioners' Association, keen trade unionist through his membership of the National Union of Distributive and Allied Workers Union and active member of the Maldon Trades Union Council, staunch Congregationalist, member of the Band of Hope as a life-long teetotaller, member of the Board of Guardians for Heybridge, parish councillor, School Board member and office holder of the Independent order of Foresters for sixty years.

Ev Last, another of Charlie's sons and a staunch member of the Labour Party, grew up in Broad Street Green Road and wrote an unpublished memoir 'Broad Street Green from 1879' in 1948. He lived in Springfield Cottages because he was a tool maker at Bentall's. Ev Last describes taking a basket of linen to old lady Pratt who had a mangle and mangled it for one penny.

In another cottage, Phoebe, the daughter of Charlie Wood, kept a private school where the children peeled potatoes, dusted the furniture, polished the knobs, lit the fire and so on. When a little boy was asked to spell cat he couldn't but offered to spell kitten! Phoebe sold pins, buttons, cotton thread, sweets and many other things including tape which has today been replaced with elastic. She 'played' the organ at the chapel - not always pleasant listening.

Fred, a school friend of Ev's, played buttons, a game which must have entailed forfeiting buttons since Fred in his desire to win ripped all the buttons off his clothes rather than give in. Unfortunately he often lost at many things but always tried hard. Fred had extra large feet, needing size 14, but when the shop keeper had none that size, Fred said, "I'll take two pairs of sevens". All the boys mentioned in Ev's memoir were called by their nicknames.

William Barbrook was born 1854, he married Catherine Lewis from Broad Street Green; they lived in the Flat Tops, (Woodfield Cottages) and had thirteen children. Their son, Leonard Barbrook, worked in the foundry at Bentall's and married Margaret Eavery whose family came from Fingringhoe. Their only child, Colin, married Barbara Tilbury in 1955. Colin and Margaret came back to live in Heybridge when they retired. Margaret Eavery's brother, Jack, worked in Maldon Iron Works and married Polly; one of Arthur Butcher's five daughters. Jack Eavery managed May and Butcher's after Arthur Butcher (1) died. He was secretary of Maldon Golf Club for many years. Of the other daughters, Lucy married Thomas McPherson who was created a Labour life peer, Joan who married Roy Lappage of Woodlands Farm, Norah and Doris the eldest. The son of Arthur Butcher (1), Arthur (2), was a director of May and Butcher's and drove a lorry. There was a small holding past Pleasant Cottage which used to be cultivated by Harry and Charlie Barbrook who concentrated on strawberries. Charlie would not frighten the birds away for fear that the poor things might be hungry. John and Jack Handley who lived on Broad Street Green were Crimean veterans.

William Springett lived in Pleasant Cottage in the 1930s. When his wife was ill, straw was put on the road to lessen traffic noise. All was well the first time this was necessary but on the second time, a lorry skidded into a ditch opposite the house and shed its load of fruit. Harold Lewis remembers eating some of the fruit: "There was a large crab apple tree near and, although we grew a dozen of the best apples in our own garden, such as Cox's Orange, Lord Derby, Blenheim Orange, Lanes Prince Albert, Lord Suffield, Dr. Harvey etc., to us (Ev and his brother, Frank) a pocket full of pinched crab apples was more fun that all the fancy named ones". Billy Pratt lived in a cottage with his wife and three daughters and five sons; there must have been a crush around the table. They sold sweets and ginger pop.

Ev Last described the games they played: Hot pies, Leap frog, Buck Buck, tying two door handles together, setting fire to someone's coat tails, tying a parcel on a long string for somebody to pick up and then snatch it out of his hand. Cricket and football were played. Ev Last skated along the Navigation when it froze.

Ev tells the story of a widow and her daughter. Two brothers; Jim and Charlie were both in love with the daughter. Jim won her. To recover from the shock, Charlie married the widow and, subsequently, both had daughters. Try to work out those relationships. The younger brother had a nut tree and sold the nuts twenty for 1d.

Ev Last describes a black barn which used to be a blacksmith's shop where Maldon Iron Works started; ploughs and harnesses were made there. Afterwards, in Victorian times, it became a chapel where old Joseph Sadler regularly preached. He would walk from Maldon every Sunday dressed in a tail coat and silk high hat with his white beard flowing. He was accompanied by Parson Hart who had a deep commanding voice, and James Bevern about whom many stories are told. He once walked three miles because someone told him they had dropped a penny. He led the chapel singing many times, once singing Abide With Me while the rest of the congregation sang The Old Hundred.

Poplar Hall used to be called Butterfly Hall; it had an ornamental pond surrounded by attractive planting.

Broad Street Green had two communal wells for fresh water. The hamlet children attended the Iron Works School.

Mr. Fred Willey would be seen in his general shop, on the corner of Scraley Road and Colchester Road, wearing a long white apron buttoned to his waistcoat; the traditional clothes of grocers in those days. His son, Norman Willey, who was succeeded by Mr. Nicholls, used to open on a Sunday. Opposite the shop fronting Scraley Road there was a small playing field provided by Mr. Free. The shop ceased trading in the 1960s. At this junction, there used to be two tiny white cottages.

Each summer, Dr. Barnardo's boys spent a two week holiday as guests in Broad Street Green. The local boys played tricks on them, fought them and, in one case, pretended a house was 'aunted to keep them off their patch.

14.4 Broad Street Green Church

North of the present Outreach Church across the chase there used to be a pair of cottages lived in by a farmer, Haywood Henry Rush, and his son who had the same name. In 1870, Mr. Rush

Senior erected a window-less building as a place of worship on May's Farm. He said "If religion does not catch on, I will use it as a barn".

Sir Claude de Crespigny and two others names appear on the indenture (deeds) as the buyers in 1885. This was the time when Sir Claude left Great Totham Church; John Playle told Pastor Sylvia Tappin that his mother had told him this was after Sir Claude had had a disagreement with the vicar of Great Totham, the Rev. Eyre. Windows were installed by Mr. Stratford, a Maldon builder. Harry William Sadd bought the church in 1898 and sold it for £125 to twenty-three trustees of the great and good of Maldon Congregational Church including three members of the Sadd family in 1899. The church still belongs to trustees from the Congregational Church. Fitch records it as Heybridge Mission (Congregational) Chapel in 1898. Leonard Bentall, the draper, one of the original trustees, became the first superintendent of the chapel.

Mr. Spikel was a mystery man and an eccentric. Cups and saucers were purchased from funds that had been collected but they disappeared as well as the church funds when Mr. Spikel did a moonlight flit. He was a great favourite of Lady de Crespigny who supposedly paid for the chapel in 1900 but Sir Claude became bankrupt at that time.

Mr. Springett was superintendent from 1927-30 when there were two services every Sunday, morning and evening, 11am and at 6.30pm, attended by forty adults. Sixty to seventy children attended the Sunday school. Occasionally when the lay preacher was not available, Mr. W. Springett presided over the services. Harold's mother, Mary Lewis, attended the services regularly and played the organ in the absence of the organist. The author has spoken to people in their 70s who fondly remember attending the Sunday school. Harold Lewis attended the Sunday school and belonged to the Band of Hope in the 1930s. Ivy Woodcraft and her sister, Phyllis, helped with the young children at the Sunday school. Ray Burns remembers attending Sunday school before the morning service and his parents lighting oil lamps for the services. Many families worshipped in this chapel; the Burns family, Mr. and Mrs. Barbrook, Mrs. Evans and Mrs. Laura Woodcraft. Every summer, Sunday school children had a treat; they went to Mersea several times on a Green's lorry and sat on forms placed across the width of the back of the lorry. They played games on the beach and had a picnic. Pastor Glen Tappin was told that a Sadd's lorry also took the children on this annual excursion.

Mr. and Mrs. Chilvers became superintendents in 1935, they had originally come from Heybridge Basin to help out with the Sunday school but they continued to help with the Sunday school at the Basin Chapel and attended their evening service. Their son, Dereck, told Pastor Sylvia Tappin he had to attend all these services whether he liked it or not. Mr. Chilvers died in 1966. By this time, the Sunday school children were treated to several day trips by coach; they went to Whipsnade Zoo, Oxford, Box Hill Surrey, High Beech Epping Forest, Windsor, Dovercourt and Walton on the Naze in as many as three coaches for a family day out. Mrs. Chilvers (1901-1993) fulfilled many roles in the church: secretary, treasurer, organist, communion steward and she booked speakers.

Mrs. Chilvers in her later years

In 1971, Maldon Congregational Church voted to join the United Reformed Church but Broad Street Green congregation voted to stay as they were. By 1987, there were only four to five elderly in the congregation including Mr. and Mrs. Horace Weaver, Mrs. Eavery and Kitty Roberts. The Rushes' cottages and Scylla House were demolished but the continued worship of this small group ensured this church was not pulled down.

Glen and Sylvia Tappin came to Heybridge in 1987. The married couple had trained to be pastors at the Christian Life Bible College in London and came to be ministers in Broad Street Green Church, taking over from Mrs. Chilvers. The church was in a dilapidated state. However, Glen had been a bricklayer and refurbished the building and built the kitchen at the front of the building to match the original brickwork and laid a new concrete floor. The inside of the church has been completely renovated, wooden pews removed, the floor recarpeted, new chairs and the paintwork tastefully renewed.

The church is next to the site of Scylla House. Access to the site across the fast moving traffic was hazardous. The new owner of the land was hoping to build houses on the site after sand and gravel had been extracted. When Glen Tappin skidded on diesel as had the car in front, the owner of the first car turned out to be the manager of the new land owners. By the end of the week, the church had permission to use the site of Scylla House as a car park; subsequently it was gifted to the church.

In 2009, after a successful ministry, the Tappins moved on and their help in compiling this account is appreciated. The church joined the worldwide Christian Outreach Centre in 1997.

14.5 Sir Claude Champion de Crespigny (1846-1935)

Sir Claude was a descendant from one of the many Huguenots who settled in Essex in the sixteenth and seventeenth centuries. His family was an aristocratic Huguenot family that had to leave France after Louis X1V revoked the Edict of Nante in 1685 - withdrawing religious toleration from Protestants in France. Sir Claude inherited the 4th Baronetcy at the age of 21. His great grandfather had been awarded the title in 1805 by the Prince Regent who had spent a pleasant weekend at Champion Lodge. Sir Claude was one of five sons who were all named Claude, they were known by their second Christian names.

Sir Claude is remembered as a daring all round sportsman whose childhood was spent in Wivenhoe. He was a naval cadet on the training ship Brittania in 1860 and, when he was 15, he was posted to the Warrior, the first iron clad ship to go to sea in 1860. He went to Ireland in 1867 and became an officer in the 60th Regiment; for four years, he helped to suppress the Fenian uprising. He followed this by walking through the French army lines to join a Prussian Regiment of cuirassiers in the 1870 Franco-Prussian War. All this time, he accepted any ride he was offered on the flat and steeple chases; he often won his races and was called 'a mad rider'. He saw service in India where he could only afford snipe and pigeon shooting.

He complains in his memoirs that his father's will had infamous terms causing him to be hard up and he had to spend much time sorting out the legal complexities. Sir Claude brought an unsuccessful action against his father's estate in an effort to get the money to buy a commission in the army. The first of his two bankruptcies happened in 1871 but it would seem that by 1883 he was able to pay his creditors in full. His financial difficulties are confirmed on a legal document Mrs. Nicholls received when she and her husband bought number 11 Springfield Cottages. The document traces the ownership of land acquired by E. H. Bentall north of Hobbs and Steele's farm, the original site where William Bentall built his works in Heybridge. One parcel of land was part of Grapnells Farm, 13 acres 3 rods and 13 poles on which Springfield Cottages were built, the second parcel, 13 acres 3 rods and 13 poles, formed part of Hobbs and Steele's Farm. The owner, Sir Claude de Crespigny, had mortgaged the land and the names of the lenders had to appear on the lengthy document. The second bankruptcy was due to his extravagant lifestyle and impulsive gambling on horse racing which forced him to flee to France to avoid his creditors.

Sir Claude married Georgina in 1872 and went to live in County Clare in West Ireland where he joined the Limerick Artillery Militia. In 1876 during their annual training he was awarded the Bronze Medal for Bravery from the Royal Humane Society for saving the life of a drowning man. He lived in Wiltshire near Pewsey from 1876 to 1879 and hunted with various hunts on four, five and sometimes six days a week. As a member of the National Sporting Club, he trained as a pugilist and boxed in their ring. In 1880, he made Champion Lodge in Broad Street Green Road, Heybridge his main residence. The house had been built by E. H. Bentall for his son. Sir Claude filled it with many trophies of his sporting life - hundreds of stuffed animals he had shot. In the census of 1881, three sons, three daughters and nine servants are listed as living there. He was a member of the East Essex Hunt for years. He created a cricket ground in the grounds, walked many miles and exercised daily. Mrs. Jean Wright hilariously recalls that Lady de Crespigny dressed in her swimming costume was driven by her butler to Blackwater Sailing Club daily to swim in the River Blackwater and returned to Champion Lodge wrapped in a towel. Sir Claude used the diving board in Maldon. There was a ladies' splash pond at Champion Lodge that is now a pond, the gentlemen had a larger one in the woods.

Tony Mandara's researches show that Sir Claude's three sons served in the Boer War; Lieutenant Claude de Crespigny of the 2nd Life Guards, who was severely wounded at Kleinfontein, Paul de Crespigny with Third Battalion of the 2nd Grenadier Guards, and Vierville with the Imperial Yeomanry. In his autobiography, Sir Claude recalls his visits to the battlefields with his wife. Nineteen men from Maldon, Heybridge, Witham and Hatfield Peverel enlisted and served in South Africa where 24,000 died.

Sir Claude created a one mile steeple chase course at Champion Lodge and the first meeting of the Champion Hunt and Military Steeple Chases took place on 30th May 1881. He participated on that occasion and for many years afterwards. The last meeting was in 1903. Sir Claude wrote that "some thousands of spectators favoured us with their presence and the vehicles were most remarkable for their variety". Ev Last records that all roads led to the Champion Lodge estate on race days. Trains, stage coaches, cabs and carts of all sorts brought people to the races. Brewers' vans loaded as never before with barrels, vans with tents, tables and eatables, bookmakers with their goods and chattels, the old man with his tin of pies calling out "Meat or fruit all hot". Twenty barrow loads of horse manure were collected from the road after the meetings. The atmosphere was lively with a bookmaker trying to steal away, the three card tricksters, the Crown full with 'racking' men enjoying beer and skittles while parties at the Lodge imbibed champagne and wine.

At this time, Sir Claude was competing in steeple chases regularly further afield and had a good share of wins. He was a regular competitor at Galleywood near Chelmsford. Racing took place in Galleywood from 1759 until 1935. The original course was constructed on the 175 acre common. A new ovate two mile steeple chasing course was built in 1880 with nine hurdles and a water jump and the prize or plate was £50. It was the only course in England that crossed a main road. Steeple chasing had become the sport of gentlemen while professional jockeys engaged in flat racing. The Galleywood hilly, narrow track wound through woods and across the common and had a challenging hill near the finish that was the downfall of many riders. A second grandstand was built in 1922 when the course was widened. Galleywood is the only race course to encircle the village church which had been erected in 1873.

The two three day meetings took place annually on Tuesdays, Wednesdays and Thursdays. Later, the number of meetings varied. They were a great social occasion in Chelmsford where there were balls, concerts and other entertainments. Sir Claude competed in boxing bouts. The village school closed on race days. Racing ceased in the 1930s. The 1923 grandstand was converted into a Heritage Centre in 2009.

Unbelievably, in 1886 Sir Claude became assistant to the public hangman under a false name and was present at a triple hanging at Carlisle Prison which caused an outcry.

Sir Claude became interested in ballooning and made the first ascent from Maldon. He had planned to accompany Simmons, an aeronaut and civil engineer, on the first ever flight to France in June 1882 but his assistants held onto one side of the basket too long and it was flung against a wall crushing a spectator who sustained broken ribs. Sir Claude was thrown from the basket and suffered a broken leg, cracked ribs and concussion as he tried to fend the balloon car off a wall. Simmons managed to stay in the basket and decided to continue the flight. The 170 mile flight to Arras took one and a half hours which was the second fastest time at that date. The next year Sir Claude and Simmons took off from Maldon, crossed the North Sea and landed on Walcheren Island near Flushing in Holland without incident. Simmons continued his hair raising exploits and was killed in Ulting when his balloon crashed into trees in 1888. Sir Claude was the last man in England to fight a duel.

He did have a serious side shown by his service as a magistrate and appointment as a Deputy Lieutenant of Essex and he was a friend of royalty.

Sir Claude died in 1935 at the age of 88 and he was buried in the grounds of Champion Lodge. Champion Lodge was sold and became Totham Lodge, a residential home for the elderly licensed for twenty-eight residents and registered for dementia patients. The family coffins were transferred to Hatfield Peverel churchyard where a modern monument records the burial. One older Heybridge resident told the author that it was an impressive sight to see the hearses drawn by black plumed horses on their way to Hatfield Peverel. There have been three owners of the home, the first stayed there for ten years, the second for fourteen years and the present owner, Mrs. Page, has been running the home for eight years.

Sir Claude had five sons and four daughters. One of the daughters; Crystal, Mrs. Matthew Ffinch, lived at Langford Meads on Langford Road Heybridge.

In November 2010, Captain Richard Champion de Crespigny, aged 53, saved a Quantas Boeing 747 when a Rolls Royce engine disintegrated in mid air. He calmly dealt with the situation, gave the four hundred and twelve passengers regular updates and landed the plane safely. Surely with that name he must be related to Sir Claude Champion de Crespigny! Qantas did not reply to a letter of enquiry.

14.6 The Huguenots in Essex

Elinor Roper, writing about the history of Essex seed growing, records that Flemish, Walloon and French Protestants started to seek refuge in England from 1540s; some came to Harwich and families bearing their names are spread over Essex: the Marriages, Pertwees in Colchester, the Birkins in Tiptree and Coggeshall (the author's sister-in-law which was news to the family) and Ralph Gould, the world-renown Essex flower seed breeder. These people are descended from Huguenots, Protestants, in France. In addition, acquaintances have told the author of their Huguenot ancestors: an Irish woman had discovered recently that her ancestors were Huguenot who had married into an Irish Roman Catholic family, a member of NADFAS on a visit to Windsor said her French sounding surname was Huguenot, a Heybridge friend said she was descended from Huguenots, another Heybridge friend, who grew up in Manchester has Huguenot ancestors. It is amazing how often it happens.

On a visit to Woodham Mortimer Church, Sholto Morton, a local historian, told the author that he had discovered his family was of Huguenot descent. His cousin had found the house in Montauban France in 1914 where his ancestor had lived in the sixteenth century and viewed his Huguenot Palairet's family marriage register. By the 1720s, the family had moved to Holland from where a member of the family came to London as the agent of the Dutch States General and became tutor to the children of George II and founded the English family.

Two local famous families of Huguenot descent are noteworthy:

14.7 The Du Cane family

The Du Cane family left Flanders in the reign of Queen Elizabeth I because of the cruel persecution of Protestants by the Duke of Alva. The family settled first in Canterbury and later in London. They were wealthy merchants and fostered wool manufacturing by their countrymen in this part of England.

Peter Du Cane of Coggeshall was Sheriff of Essex and Member of Parliament for Colchester in 1745. He purchased Braxted Lodge in 1751. On his death in 1803, his son, Peter Du Cane 2, lived there for twenty years. Pete 2's son, Peter 3, extended the estate and had the $4^1/_2$ mile brick wall with six lodges guarding entries erected by Braddy, the Kelvedon builder. Then the estate became known as Braxted Park. White's Gazetteer and Directory 1848 records that "Braxted Park now comprises about 500 acres, richly clothed with wood, and having a fine lake of 20 acres, and 10 acres of ornamental gardens and pleasure grounds, in which are seen a great variety of rare and valuable trees, shrubs, flowers".

At that time, park meant a large house and the surrounding park. Locally, White Notley Hall was rented by Mrs. Jean Wright's family, the Du Canes rented out Braxted Park, and both Felix Hall, Kelvedon and Woodham Mortimer Place were leased at various times. Langford Grove had a series of tenants. Younger sons of land owning families went into the Army or Navy, the Church or emigrated.

A cousin, Sir Charles Du Cane, 1825-1889, inherited the estate and became Lord of the Manor of Braxted. He was a Colonial Administrator and Governor of Tasmania from 1868-1874. He was elected Member of Parliament for Maldon in 1852 but the election was declared void when it was discovered his agent had been involved in bribery of which Sir Charles had been unaware. He held various public offices and died in Braxted Park.

Captain Charles Du Cane RN was Lord of the Admiralty. Sir Edmund Du Cane was Surveyor General, Director of Convict Prisoners and a prison reformer. The Du Cane family were important landowners in Witham; they owned the Manor of Newlands and Great Witham. The Rev. H. Du Cane lived in the Grove and Captain Du Cane was a principal landowner.

The fortunes of the Du Cane family declined and the Braxted estate was sold to Sir William Boulton MP in 1919. During his ownership, the author remembers going to skate on the lake in the 1930s.

The Plessey Company had been acquired by Byron George Clark after the end of W.W.1. He was joined by his son Allen who turned the company into a manufacturer of radio sets under contract to Marconi. His son Michael was put in charge of the electronics division which he built into a dynamic international company in the field of military electronics. He placed great emphasis on research and development and used Braxted Park during W.W.2 for scientific research when entrance to the park was denied to the general public. Plessey Company bought Braxted Park, the Queen Anne house and park, in 1947 as a home for Sir Alan Clark. On his father's death in 1963, Michael Clark lived there. Braxted Park is now owned by a Clark family trust. When Michael retired, he directed the investment of over £2 million to diversify the facilities for weddings and events, cookery demonstrations and cookery school with noted chefs, a pheasant and partridge shoot, the management of the properties, a nine hole golf course and arable farming. These enterprises are managed by Michael's son, Duncan Clark.

14.8 Chamberlen - inventors of obstetrical forceps

Dr. William Chamberlen was Huguenot surgeon who left Paris in 1569 to come to London. His first and fourth son were called Peter; hence Peter (1) and Peter (2). He taught his first son, Peter (1), (1560-1631) medicine and he qualified as a barber surgeon at 18. Barber surgeons were not allowed to prescribe; only men with doctorates from Oxford and Cambridge Universities were allowed to be physicians and to do so. Peter (1) was arrested in 1612 for prescribing and imprisoned in Newgate from where he was rescued by Queen Anne of Denmark, wife of King James I, who paid the fines. Peter Chamberlen (1) treated a number of rich and powerful people; he attended the wives of Kings James I and Charles I and assisted at the birth of King Charles II. He invented the obstetrical forceps which doctors in the family used secretly and lucratively in difficult midwifery cases for over a century when labour was complicated. There was a ritual when they were summoned to a patient. Two men carried the wooden box containing the forceps into the patient's room. The patient was blindfolded and all others left the room while a Dr. Chamberlen went to work. Peter (1)'s brother, Peter (2) (1572-1626) used them when he worked as a surgeon and obstetrician.

Peter (2)'s son Peter (3) (1601-1683) was the first in the family to qualify as a physician. He studied at the universities of Cambridge, Heidelberg and Padua and gained doctorates at each to become a member of the Royal College of Physicians. He carried on the secret use of the forceps and tried to start a scheme for training midwives that put him at odds with the Royal College Physicians. This caused him to move to Woodham Mortimer Hall but he visited London frequently.

Dr. Peter Chamberlen, the son of the inventor of the obstetric forceps, maintained the family secret since all the other people in the delivery room were made to leave when he used the forceps. The story of his life is told in his own words on his tomb-chest in Woodham Mortimer churchyard but since the inscription is difficult to read, Sholto Morton typed them using modern lettering. A copy can be seen overleaf.

In 1688, Dr. Hugh Chamberlen, Peter (2)'s son (1630-1720) arrived an hour late for the birth of 'The Old Pretender' to Mary of Modena, Charles II's second wife, and had to refute claims that an unknown baby had been smuggled in a warming pan to replace a dead child. His attempts to sell the forceps to Francis Moriceau in Paris were unsuccessful but he came back to England with a copy of Moriceau's book "Diseases of Women with Child" which he translated into English; it made him a profit of thousands of pounds. Later, he sold the secret of the obstetric forceps to doctors in the Netherlands; their design and use entered the public domain in the 1720s. Pairs of the forceps were found hidden in a little tin box in the floor of the attic of Woodham Mortimer Hall in 1813 with books, old letters, pieces of jewellery and some coins.

A blue plaque on Woodham Mortimer Hall records the fact that "Dr. Peter Chamberlen 1601-1683 and Dr. Hugh Chamberlen 1638-1720 Pioneers of obstetrics lived (t)here".

14.9 Museum of London 400th Huguenot exhibition

The author visited the fascinating 400th Huguenot anniversary exhibition in the Museum of London in 1985 where the curator said that information about Hugeuenot history in England was difficult to acquire because the refugees had assimilated so well. The exhibition showed how thousands of skilled artisans, wealthy merchants experienced soldiers as well as gardeners who brought new and improved seeds fled to Protestant England in the sixteenth and seventeenth centuries bringing with them their skills and loyalty to this Protestant country.

Du Cane family servants

Sir Claude de Crespigny

Dr Peter Chamberlen (1601 - 1683)
of Woodham Mortimer Hall, near Maldon, Essex

Inscriptions on the tomb in the graveyard of the adjacent St. Margaret's Church.

NOTES: (1) The spellings are as they appear in the Inscriptions except that the old forms of s, I and U have been, for clarity, replaced by the modern versions. (2) The means of O and h in the first and second lines of Panel are not known.

North face - panel 1

Here lies ye body of Doter Peter Chamberlen, who was borne on O ye 8th of may 1601, & dyed on h ye 22th of December 1683: being aged 82 years 7 months, & 14 dayes. He had 2 wives, & by ye first Jane Middleton had 11 sons, & 2 daughters & amongst them 45 grand Children, & 8 great grant Children: whereof were living at his death three sons: Hugh, Paul & John, & his two daughters, and 20 grand Children and 6 great grant Children.

By ye second Anne Harrison had 2 sones & 2 daughters; whereof onely Hope was living at his Death who hath Erected this Monument in Memory of his Father

North face - panel 2

The said Peter Chamberlen toock ye Degree of Docter in Physick in fever att Universities both at home & abroad and lived such above three score years being Physician in Ordinary to three Kings & Queens of England.viz King James & Queen Anne; King Charles ye first & Queen Mary; King Charles ye second and Queen Katherine; & also to some for = raine Princes; having travelled most partes of Europe, & speaking most of the Languages.
As for his Religion was a Christian kee = ping ye 7th day for ye saboth 32 years

To tell his learning and Life to Men Enough is said by here lyes Chamberlen

South face - panels 1 and 2

The inscriptions on these are in poor condition and appear to contain a long poem about the life of a Christian person. Along the bottom of the panels these lines are clear:

These verses were found made written and ordered by Docter Peter Chamberlen here interred for his Epitaph

SOURCE Sholto Morton, assisted by his brother, deciphered the inscription on the tomb-chest in Woodham Mortimer church yard telling the life story of Dr. Peter Chamberlen

15.0 Goldhanger Road

It is surprising to learn how recently roads have been tarmacadamed; David Clements, who lived in a council house in Goldhanger Road, remembers Goldhanger Road being metalled in the early 1930s. No path was made but pedestrians walked on the greensward and flattened the earth to create a footpath.

15.1 The Towers' Vegetable Garden

In the 1930s, at the start of Goldhanger Road, next to Houlding's Garage, George Whittaker bought part of The Towers' vegetable garden. This 1.506 acre section was surrounded by an amazing 8ft. high cavity wall made of yellow gault bricks.

He sold the plot, number 21, next to the cemetery gates which later became the site of Mr. and Mrs. Doves' house. The sidewall to their garden runs parallel to the cemetery entrance road; it is 16½ in. wide. They have put 17½in. square paving stone on the top of the brick wall to prevent water entering the cavity. Mr. Whittaker lowered the wall in front of his house (number 9) and re-used the bricks to build the house. Number 17, was sold to Mr. Pedley and the present owner is Mr Philip Gill.

Jubilee Cottages, numbers 13 and 15, are a pair of semi-detached houses built by Mr. Sullivan, an Irish Roman Catholic policeman who lived at number 15, with his two daughters Betty and Kathleen. George and Queenie Borrett lived in number 13; Mr. Borrett carried out maintenance in Bentall's factory. Mrs. Borrett, nee Wells, came from Woodham Mortimer where her parents lived in the Lodge of Woodham Mortimer Place. Betty Chittenden remembers being taken into Woodham Mortimer Hall gardens to see figs growing when she accompanied her mother for Sunday afternoon tea. Mr. and Mrs. Borrett looked after Betty Chittenden on the day her father had all his teeth extracted at home just before W.W.2. The Borretts had two evacuees, one of whom was named Columbine, billeted on them at the beginning of the war; the Borretts' daughter was born later. Jack Gill's parents built the last house, number 11, in 1936. Jack Gill had been educated at Maldon Grammar School, trained at Crompton Parkinsons, served in the RAF as a Spitfire pilot in the Far East and returned to Cromptons. He made number 11 his home when he married and became an insurance agent.

15.2 Heybridge Cemetery and the Fitch family

In 1848, E. H. Bentall had bought The Well House with yards, gardens and appurtenances and one little meadow and one croft lying near the highway leading to Goldhanger containing about 4 acres from the Dean and Chapter of St Paul's. It was from 2½ acres of this land that Heybridge cemetery was formed at a cost of £1,300 in 1887. In January 1888, a 50ft. strip outside The Towers vegetable garden, by that time allotments, was purchased for £50 by the Heybridge Burial Board to provide an entry road to the cemetery. The eastern boundary was to be properly fenced, no trees or shrubs were to grow more than 10ft. high, and the western boundary was part of the 8ft. high cavity brick wall that surrounded the Towers' vegetable garden. Heybridge cemetery was opened on 1st November 1887.

In the 1930s, pupils at Heybridge School were disgruntled because they were not allowed on the playing field adjacent to the cemetery at playtime during a funeral in case the noise disturbed the mourners.

The Rev. John Wade, URC minister in Burnham on Crouch, states that the iron grave markers manufactured by E. H. Bentall in his Heybridge Works are to be found in Heybridge Cemetery and other local cemeteries. They show the name of the deceased and date of death.

The parish records state that Richard Norton, aged 17, was killed when he fell off the mast of the ship Leander in 1856. In 1812, a photograph shows a coffin and male mourners in a barge that journeyed from Heybridge Basin to the cemetery. Thomas Fletcher, a young seaman from the Hartlepool ship 'The Standard' drowned in the sea lock when he fell from his vessel in Heybridge Basin. Ned Woodcraft, Andrew Woodcraft's great grandfather, is at the helm with top hatted undertaker. His father is in the bows before the coffin and relatives and residents of the Basin, including the six men permanently available as pall bearers surround the coffin. Ned Woodcraft's coffin was one of the last Basiners to be carried by boat from the Basin to the cemetery. Later, John Kemp, who grew up in Heybridge Basin but lived in the former Wave Bridge public house after his marriage, had his wish when his coffin was carried by boat from the Basin to the cemetery.

The Company of Proprietors of the Chelmer and Blackwater Navigation sold 2½ acres of land north of the canal to the Heybridge Burial Board in 1887 for £1,300 to form the main part of the cemetery. They imposed the following conditions: the gate entrances to open inwards during such hours of each day to the public and persons authorised by the Navigation Company, the company to have a private waterside gate, the Navigation Company not liable to repair or maintain this section of the towpath and the Heybridge Burial Board to pay an annual rent of 10s.0d. from 29th September 1888.

George Free bought 46 acres, 3 roods, 39 perches of Milbanke land between the canal towpath and Goldhanger Road opposite Jacobs Farm, in October 1919, for £1,800. It would seem that Mr. Free created allotments on part of the frontage and then sold 8 acres, 3 roods, 28 perches that were adjacent to the entry road into the cemetery including the allotments to E. H. Bentall and Co Ltd in April 1920 for £383.11s.0d. After W.W.1, there was a shortage of houses and the Housing Act of 1919 made it the duty of local authorities to build houses; a state subsidy was granted for the purpose. Maldon Rural District Council bought the frontage of this land in June 1921 on which to build council houses. There was no sewer system in Heybridge then. Money to purchase the land acquired by E. H. Bentall and Co Ltd from the Milbanke Estate had been borrowed by them in the form of £80,000 debentures at an interest rate of 8%. Agricultural and General Engineers, the conglomerate of which Bentall's had become part, had taken over this liability in July 1921. When the Bentall company decided to sell the remainder of the land that had not been used for council houses, they had to secure the written permission of three quarters of the debenture holders first and Mr. Free bought back the remainder of this land for £275.

Mr. Free sold a further side strip of land, 1.58 acres, in August 1955 to the Joint Burial Board (Maldon and Heybridge) to extend the main cemetery. The Board borrowed £1,250 from the Public Works Loan Commission for the transaction. A small chapel, with a vestry that has an oriel window and wooden seats for thirty-five people, was built at the same time. The windows are leaded and delicately coloured; the one above the door is circular. The yellow-bricked chapel has a timbered, vaulted ceiling. It is non-denominational and it is not consecrated. There are no religious symbols so that memorial events for those of various religions, or none, can be commemorated there. The author was told that not long ago, and to avoid publicity, a funeral service was held in the chapel for a person who was notorious.

The building was restored in 1996 when the wooden panelling and floor were renewed and electricity installed. There is no charge for using this chapel. By the entrance from the canal towpath there is a memorial garden for cremation burials and next to this an area reserved for woodland burials.

The records of burials in Heybridge cemetery and the Maldon cemetery were combined. The task of separating them was deemed to be so complicated that Heybridge Parish Council did not take back the ownership of the Heybridge cemetery in 1987 when the Council was revived.

Heybridge Parish Council refurbished the entry gates to the cemetery from the canal towpath to mark the Queen's Golden Jubilee. Two of the famous Maldon Fitch family graves are located beside the main path opposite the chapel. Major Fitch, the son of the man who gave land to create the Promenade Park in Maldon and who wrote the important history of Maldon, married Julia Stebbings. They started their married life in the home of his wife's parents, Heybridge Hall. Their first son died on 2nd June 1917, of meningitis. The family moved around the district to Limbourne Farm, Hazeleigh Grange, Maldon Hall and Brickhouse Farm. Major Fitch died on 29th April 1931 aged 42; he chose to be buried in the same grave as his infant son. Major Fitch had been gassed in W.W.1 and had suffered greatly although he carried on the family tradition of service to Essex local government. His son, Derek Fitch, lives in Baker Mews and remembers a zeppelin raid in W.W.1. when bombs were dropped either side of Heybridge Hall blowing out all the windows. Derek's mother, the widow of Major Fitch, died on 29th October 1978 and is buried in a grave next to her husband and son. Derek has no descendants, he has chosen to be buried in the same grave as his mother hence the inscription "Derek Maldon Fitch" with no dates!

Heybridge Parish Council met in the Cemetery Chapel in 1898 according to "Maldon and the River Blackwater" by E. A. Fitch, published in 1898. This publication is still referred to as the definitive history of the district.

15.3 Council houses

Along the frontage of Goldhanger Road four pairs of council houses were built and, after a gap, twelve more pairs in 1921. Today, the first eight houses have various external finishes. Some have the original stone dashing; the stone dashing of some has been renewed, while others have been rendered in various colours. The next twelve have all been rendered in various colours; in some cases two adjoining pairs have stressed their individuality by choosing different colours and shows they have bought their council house. Rendering not only smartens the appearance but covers any cracks.

15.4 Jacobs' Farm, George Free and others

Frank May, who lived at Saltcote Hall, advertised for a farm manager in 1910 and George Free, aged 28, from Thaxted was appointed. Saltcote Hall Farm had poor soil underlaid with gravel and was the reason why Frank May rented Jacobs' Farm with its good land from the executors of J. R. Grimwood. George Free worked enthusiastically and was determined to have his own farm. Frank May influenced the executors of J. R. Grimwood in 1914 and they sold Jacobs' Farm to George Free. Previously, a Mr. Jacobs had owned it at some point, hence the name. George Free married in Thaxted Church on 28th March 1910 after cycling from Heybridge to court Ethel on Sundays and they lived in a bungalow near the sea wall at Mill Beach until Jacobs' Farmhouse could be renovated because it was in poor condition. William Collier, a former horseman for

Frank May, had lived on the ground floor while the first floor had been the home of chickens, cats and dogs. William Collier moved to Middle Farm. George Free moved into Jacobs' Farm in 1914. Jacobs' Farmhouse is a listed building erected in the fifteenth and early sixteenth century; it is a substantially complete small in-line hall house of late fifteenth century. There is a late nineteenth century pump in the front wall of the cross wall of the cross wing.

Ethel and George Free had three daughters; Laura (Peggy) who married Francis John Macmorland, Madge, and Joan who married Norman McCready, a local bank manager. Joan McCready inherited Jacobs' Farm.

Mr. Free rented Canterbury Farm from the Grimwood Estate and farmed there traditionally for over fifty years. He was able to buy Canterbury Farm in 1938.

David Macmorland writes that during W.W.2, the meadow between the farm shop and the houses in Cedar Chase was requisitioned by the War Office. Six large billets were erected backing onto The Towers' wall separated by flagstone paths. Hard standing was laid for lorries serving the site, a machine gun emplacement was established next to the pond, an anti-aircraft gun was placed at the north end of the paddock and a large searchlight was operated in the centre of the field. Many soldiers were stationed there who willingly helped on the farm during their time off. It was during harvest in 1943 that a Spitfire crashed where the cows had been put temporarily while the meadow was being used by soldiers, narrowly missing Jacobs' Farm House. The pilot baled out but was killed. Afterwards live ammunition, jettisoned on impact, was collected all over the yard and surroundings.

George Free was a public spirited man and much respected in Heybridge. He was a JP, Parish Council chairman, regular worshipper and churchwarden at St Andrew's Church, benefactor to Heybridge School and the Swifts Football Club. He died in 1968.

The McCready family, George Free's grandson and great granddaughter, now run a successful friendly farm shop in the cow shed of Jacobs' Farm. Shopping at Jacobs' Farm shop is a joy for young children who love to see the chickens, Muscovy ducks, geese, billy goat and two nannies wandering around the farmyard.

Milk used to be cooled in the adjoining room by water running over the milk in pipes and customers came to fetch milk in jugs that was served from the churns with long handled metal ladles. After the advent of the Milk Marketing Board, milk could not be sold in this way and milk was collected daily in ten gallon galvanised iron churns from farms. Because the churns were so heavy, they were tilted on one side and rolled about, the churns had a brass plate near the top to identify the owner and a white paper label was attached to record the producer. Latterly, with refrigeration, tankers collected the milk every other day.

Ted Wire was born in the Wave public house when his father was the landlord. He had a sister, Gladys (who was a cook at Maldon Grammar School) and two brothers, Cyril and Thomas (who was killed in W.W.1). Ted enlisted in the Royal Norfolk Regiment at 17, he returned to work as an electrician at Bentall's. He moved from Barnfield Cottages to Beechway, which he rented from George Free, in Goldhanger Road. Later, he regretted not buying the Barnfield Cottage but, at the time, did not like the idea of borrowing money to buy a house.

Joe Brown remembers working with horses for eighteen years on a farm in Heybridge, drilling, ploughing, rolling, stacking corn and threshing. His hardest job was sugar beet lifting that needed three horses. His typical day began at 6am when he prepared the horses, braided their tails and gave them breakfast. He harnessed them at 7am, left the stables at 7.20am for the day's work in the fields. He breakfasted at 10.10am and had his dinner between 12.30 and 1pm. He returned to the stables, cleaned, fed and bedded down the horses at 4pm. This was a time when a horseman was expected to harrow 10 acres a day walking ten miles and plough an acre a day.

Since October 1979, Wimpeys estate built on agricultural land off Goldhanger Road has matured - the pleasant estate has an attractive layout with trees and shrubs. Originally, a new four bedroom detached house sold for £33,650 and a two bedroom semi-detached house cost £19,395.

15.5 Nursery Cottage

Nursery Cottage in Goldhanger Road is a seventeeenth century listed building. It is a timber framed, white weather boarded cottage, with a tall off-centre chimney stack on the ridge, which used to be known as Gooseberry Hall and by the family as GH. Harry Miller grew vegetables behind the cottage during and after W.W.2 and had several greenhouses where he grew delicious white grapes. It was part of the Grimwood Estate that was put up for sale in 1938. Norman McCready, son-in-law of George Free, bought it and his family now let it out.

15.6 Draper's Farm House

This is a listed building; the eastern end was built in 1450 as an in-line hall house, the roof supported by a queen post. The original wattle and daub is visible. In 1550, a second storey was added. The floor has a central truss with heavy oak bracing. A two storey extension was added in 1780 as a two bay hall. This extension was lived in while the original structure became a store or a dairy. The farm was called Pratt's Farm before 1800. Then William Draper, a watch and clock maker, whose workshop was in Butt Lane Maldon, bought it and it became known as Draper's Farm. On the wall of the two-storey extension a piece of paper was found with the following:

> "5th day of March 1883
> Bill Gymer mixes the mortar
> W Holt drinks the porter
> T Cudmore chops the sticks
> C Baxter lays the bricks
> O Sardeant tickles the gals
> These are the best of pals
> Signed O J C
> and the builders above"

Electricity was laid on in 1931 and mains water was put into the dairy in the 1940s but farming priorities meant the farm house did not get mains water until later. The pump in the kitchen continued to be used for cooking and making tea!

Edward Wakelin, his wife, and daughter, Suzanne, lived at Draper's farm house which was owned by his father Padge. He oversaw Draper's Farm while running a haulage business. His lorries carted bricks from Maldon East Railway Station to Langford Waterworks for the building of the tall chimney that was demolished in 1965. Edward Wakelin bought the farm in the 1940s.

The farm house was bombed on 27th July 1944: the bomb destroyed the front of the house exposing the rooms and caused the house to tip forward. Edward Wakelin cut down two large trees and used them as props. The damage was repaired after the war but, before the days of listed buildings regulations, concrete was used not timber, lathe and plaster.

Padge gave lambs that needed hand rearing to his grand daughter Suzanne who could be seen walking them on a lead around Heybridge when she was a child. These lambs were taken to join the flock when they were grown. Betty Chittendon remembers David Wakelin, Edward's son by his first wife, in her class at Heybridge Primary School. The first Mrs. Edward Wakelin left in 1947 and Edward married Sheila Doig in 1952. She had worked for the BBC in London and visited her parents locally at weekends. Edward and Sheila had a son, Mark, now Harbour Master at Burnham on Crouch. Edward died three years after his marriage. Sheila had tests to see whether there was sand and gravel on Draper's farm land; the results were negative. Sheila sold the farm, farm buildings and farm house in 1955 to Derek Birkumshaw for £3,500. He was not a very capable farmer and sold up after three years for a far greater sum when it was discovered that the land was indeed gravel bearing. Baker Bros. and then Essex Aggregates extracted sand and gravel.

Houses were built on another part of Draper's Farm and Maldon District Council acquired the farm house, barn and 17 acres of land in front of the barn as planning gain for sport and recreation acres in the 1980s. Maldon Rugby Club and Maldon Cricket Club developed facilities for their sports on the land and the big barn was converted into a club house for Draper's Farm Sports Club.

Ralph Gill and Laurence Cunningham rented a small piece of land behind council houses in Goldhanger Road where they kept a few pigs while continuing with their daytime local jobs. They bought fields that were part of Draper's Farm opposite when they came up for sale. Laurence built a bungalow in Draper's Chase and Ralph rented Draper's Farm House, which he later bought. Helped by their wives, they grew lettuce under glass on one field, grew strawberries and kept pigs. Abbey Homesteads bought these fields in the mid 1970s and built houses on Draper's Farm in the early 1980s.

Many houses were built in the developments off Goldhanger Road by Wimpeys and Abbey Homesteads. They include Lawling Avenue and Coopers Avenue and the roads that branch off them including Maple Avenue. Lawling Avenue and Rowan Drive were separated by the Co-operative car park and shop in the mistaken belief that this would stop vehicles using it as a short cut to Goldhanger Road and Scraley Road. Along the south side of Scraley Road are twenty-six larger detached houses backing onto the Bovis estate built by Claydons.

15.7 Middle Farm House

This is a listed building. The house was built circa seventeenth century or earlier. Bernard Shortland's mother knew this as Frogs' Hall.

15.8 Basin Road and illegal tolls

There was no road access to Heybridge Basin until 1811 when the Heybridge Enclosure Act made a road link to Goldhanger Road possible. However, in 1823 a gate was erected at the junction of Goldhanger Road with Basin Road beside Tollgate Cottage. Illegal tolls were payable until 1836 for access to the Basin by Borough Marsh Road (now Basin Road). We know this from a sketch map of 1847 that calls this road Borough Marsh Road. It is not known who kept the tolls. Two Justices of the Peace supervised the crowd taking down the toll gate in 1836 and drove a cart down to the Basin and back to emphasise the right to do so at all times. E. H. Bentall bought adjacent land and Tollgate Cottage and allowed free access to Heybridge Basin. More houses were built behind the Basin in the second half of the nineteenth century. There is an Essex County Council boundary post on Goldhanger Road east side that was erected in the late nineteenth century which has a cast tubular shaft and knob-like finial.

15.9 Naval huts Osea Island in Goldhanger Road and Basin Road

There were five barrack huts along Basin Road from Tollgate Cottage toward Heybridge Basin and five more single storey barrack huts from the junction of Basin Road along Goldhanger Road towards Heybridge. These huts had housed sailors during W.W.1. Jack Chaney and Tom Cottis, with a gang of sixteen men, dismantled them on Osea Island and re-erected them here where they were converted into homes:

In Goldhanger Road

Mr. and Mrs. Mitchell lived temporarily in a hut, Wayside, on the Heybridge side of Spickets Brook after they retired from the Post Office in 1962. This hut was demolished and a brick bungalow has been built on the site.

Oakdene has the original red corrugated iron roof and outer walls but replacement windows have been inserted.

Mrs. O. J. Clark converted Brook Lodge into a general stores and tea room licensed to sell tobacco, postage stamps and Mill Beach rock in 1918. She opened her shop around 6.30 in the morning to catch the valuable trade from workmen cycling to work at May and Butcher's and Blackwater Timber who had to report at 7am. Later, she sold Walls' ice cream which was a great luxury then. The next owner used the large commercial oven for his outside catering business. The hut was demolished and has been replaced with a modern brick built bungalow.

Mr. Little told the author he had lived in Oaklea for thirty years. In that time he has rebuilt around the original hut so that only the chimney is original.

Devonia has the original roof and Briar Bank is largely unaltered other than by the addition of a glazed veranda.

In Basin Road

Number 2 of the first pair of semi-detached bungalows has a slate roof with green plastered outer walls and new wooden windows and porch. Number 4 has been much altered with a slate roof, plastered outer walls, new wooden windows and porch.

Number 6 of the next pair has a slate roof, pale green plastered outer walls and UPVC windows while number 8 has replacement windows and front door with leaded lights.

Mr. and Mrs. Jack Eavery lived in number 10. The author used to visit the property which had retained much of the original structure. It had been well maintained and rooms went up to the sloping roof with no ceilings until it was demolished and replaced by a smart, modern, large bungalow with red tiled roof and white weather boarded outer walls.

15.10 Colliers' Reach and Ballast Hole

Colliers Reach is that part of the River Blackwater between Hilly Pool Point on the northwest corner of Northey Island and Herring Point on the Basin side of the river as it turns toward the port of Maldon. From about 1847, sailing ships made a habit of lying against the sea wall so they could dig clay from the meadows as ballast for the return journey. Later, deeper draught brigs and barquentines unloaded their cargoes of coal in Heybridge Basin and Maldon and returned to Colliers Reach. Here, they moored while lighters filled their hulls with large quantities of soil and stone dug from the river bank to use as ballast needed to maintain the ship's stability on the long voyage back to north eastern coal fields. These efforts weakened the sea wall so much that it collapsed during one of the great tides, probably in 1856. This abandoned area is now known as Ballast Hole. It is covered by water at high tide. As areas were abandoned to the sea, the sea defences had to be built further inland to protect the fields. The present sea wall has a series of sharp bends but the original coastline is visible at low tide from Saltcote Mill and Blackwater Sailing Club.

Two hulks lying in the mud are the 1882 former gunpowder barge, Betsy, that was part burned in 1864 and the last remaining frame of Rawreth from 1866.

15.11 Saltcote Mill

The Blackwater estuary is saltier than the sea itself because the saltings and mud flats are covered by sea water for a short time at high water when salt is deposited on them by evaporation, and this is again taken up in solution twice in 24 hours causing the River Blackwater to be the saltiest water in the kingdom. Salt production pre-dates the Roman conquest of Britain. The Domesday Book of 1086 records forty-five salt pans in the Maldon area and one in Heybridge. Basically, pure salt is manufactured by heating the water to evaporate off the water causing pure white crystals to form on the surface. The reddened earth that forms the Red Hills of Essex is evidence of early salt production identified along the Rivers Blackwater and Crouch where forty two salt pans have been located. Red Hills can be up to 4ft. high and 40ft. in diameter or much smaller. Red Hills have been identified where clay that lined the fire and the broken earthenware pots holding the salt water came into contact with the fire.

The large Heybridge Salt Works was set up in 1810 by Messrs. Bridges, Johnson and Company at the farm known as Saltcote Farm. Coal was delivered direct from Newcastle and salt water flowed along a channel to the works. Salt was extracted by boiling seawater over coal fires. In the early nineteenth century, salt was heavily taxed and the tax had risen to £30 a ton by 1805. There was no chance of avoiding payment because there was an excise man based in the Salt Office in Heybridge Basin. Salt was essential for food preservation before the days of refrigeration and freezing. The company went out of business after the repeal of the salt tax in 1825 when cheaper rock salt from Cheshire flooded the market.

The Maldon Crystal Salt Company is the only company left carrying on this age old tradition which it has been doing for over two hundred years. Today, it is said that the Maldon Salt Works use siphoned off water from the middle of the River Blackwater where the concentration of salt is highest.

Messrs. Bridges, Johnson and Company's warehouse was converted into a maltings by Hayward Rush. Since there was no kiln at this time, it is likely that he took the grain to the germination stage. The germinated barley was then taken along the Navigation to the nearest kilns in Chelmsford where there was a brewery. A strong floor is needed during the germination stage because the soaked barley is heavy. It was spread about 1ft. deep across a well-scrubbed floor with broad malting shovels to keep the temperature even. The strong floor of the salt warehouse was ideal for malting. Later, George and Frederick May built the large stock brick maltings with two kilns alongside since the coastal site was convenient for the import of barley and the export of malt. R. Boley of Bury St Edmunds supplied separating plant to the new maltings at Saltcote in 1903 and 1913. Ernie Vince, who worked at Little Totham Hall, remembers that their barley went to the Maltings at Heybridge from where the malted barley was sent by barge to London for beer making. George and Frederick May, maltsters, acted as agents for Watney, Combe Reid and Company's cask and bottled ales. Frank May was a flourishing farmer with a large successful dairy herd and the manufacturer of lemonade. He lived in Saltcote Hall. Barges made their way from Saltcote with hay to feed the thousands of London horses. John Howard, the Maldon ship builder, built the barge, Saltcote Belle, for Frank May who lived at Stisted in 1895. A painted white hoist housing on the front of Saltcote Mill was used to transfer coal, grain and malt to and from the boats and barges. Corn was sucked up in wide tubes that swung out and transferred it into the Ethel Maud and the Mayflower barges. Later, Newman and Clarke used the mill premises to receive and store corn from farmers; huge shovels were used to spread the load. Jack Rayner used to collect the wheat that fell through gaps in the suction tubes for the family's chickens. A big barge got wedged in the creek beside the mill and had to be broken, much wheat was lost before the rest could be shovelled into smaller barges.

The maltings were served by sailing barges until the 1940s. The premises were then split into industrial units housing, at various times until the 1990s, car repair workshops, offices, Den Phillips' photographic studio, and for the promotion of boxing matches.

Since then the red brick salt store has been converted into a six house terrace behind the sea wall and the maltings and salt works have been converted into apartments. The two and three storey dwellings must be difficult for families with young children and not very convenient for older people. New houses have been built on the site while the timber framed, weather boarded malt workers' cottages have been refurbished. One cottage, dating from the seventeenth century, is thought to have been the salt master's home and is a listed building.

15.12 Mill Beach Hotel

Mill Beach Hotel was built in 1894 on the site of the miller's cottage and it was in the parish of Heybridge. The public house has held a licence since that time. The licence was bought from the Chelmer Brig in Heybridge Basin for £200 when that public house was losing business. The first landlord was William Chambers who ran the hotel from 1904 until the 1920s.

Mill Beach became a favourite watering place; by c.1900 James Loveday was advertising the Mill Beach Hotel and Major Charles Williams of Heybridge was operating conveyances from Maldon East Station to Mill Beach that met guests by appointment. Later, every train was met.

The 'Ideal Riverside Resort' boasted good fishing. A boating lake was created in the third pound of Barrow Tide Mill next to the Mill Beach Hotel car park. The Mill Beach bathing machines for ladies were sold to Benjamin Turnage Handley who moved them to the Bath Wall in Maldon. There were paddle boats and rowing boats on the lake and Pat Yates recalled that children from the camp sites learned to row there. The boating lake was filled in the 1990s and the site was grassed over, family cricket was being played there on a sunny summer afternoon when the author visited. The third pound was connected to the other two by a ditch.

Arthur Butcher (1) owned the hotel by 1951 when his grandson Ivan and his wife ran it for six years. Arthur's wife, Hilda, opened a café in 1951 selling teas and coffee while her father managed boats used by children. There were paddle boats in which handles were rotated to make the paddle wheels go round and propel the boats and rowing boats on the lake. The son and daughter of Mr. Clark from Benfleet sold shell fish from a stall where shrimps, prawns, cockles, winkles and jellied eels were displayed on glass trays. Holiday makers from the camps used to walk to the hotel along the sea wall or on the road and Pat Yates remember being dive bombed by bats.

Ivan and Maisie Butcher left the hotel in 1957 and Arthur (1) and Hilda Butcher took it over leaving the management to Mr. Courtney. The hotel was sold in 1958 and a series of people have run it since with varying degrees of success. Perhaps it would be an outstanding location for a fine restaurant with views of the river in each direction?

15.13 Barrow Marsh Tide Mill and Wharf Road

The tide mill located in the section of the river known as Mill Reach is recorded in documents as far back as 1819. As the tide rose, water was allowed to flow into three enclosed pounds. (Pond comes from the Old English word pound meaning a small area of still water). When the tide began to drop, sluices would divert the flow past the mill building and drive a large water wheel. Two pounds are visible today and can be accessed from Wharf Road. Saltcote Sailing Club is based in front of one of the pounds and the site was owned by May and Butcher. This is where Arthur Butcher erected seven pairs of army huts from Osea Island; four pairs are on the bank of the largest pound and three pairs front Wharf Road. They were let as permanent residences. In 1938, they were described as comfortable, well equipped with gas lighting and gas cookers. The bungalows are in various states of repair; some brick faced, others lath and plaster, and some have the original wood while some are modernised and in need of attention. One un-modernised chalet was advertised for sale at £200,000 in 2007.

Jack Rayner grew up in an Osea naval hut after his father, Arthur Rayner, a carpenter, returned from working at Rippers in Sible Hedingham in 1934 to work at Sadd's. Arthur Butcher erected seven detached 'houses' on the sea wall that were supported by stilts over the river. Two were ships' cabins from ships that May and Butcher's had broken up. Families used to live in these houses but only two remain. The site used to have some allotments.

The remains of the tidal corn mill and its wharf can be seen at low tide sticking out of the mud at the river end of Wharf Road from the opposite side of the inlet. The mill was converted to steam but demolished in 1892.

Sluice gates were wound up and down by turning a handle; as the gates were slowly raised, a frame of enclosed mesh that captured eels and flounders was placed in front of the sluice gate. The eels were placed in a bucket with eel shears and covered with sacking to prevent their escape. The eel traps were stored in Wharf Road. A stubby little paddle steamer tug lay up off Wharf Road for many years until it was cut up with acetylene cutters. Saltcote Sailing Club is now based on the site of the wharf.

15.14 Barrow Marsh Farm

Douglas Wakelin, Padge Wakelin's younger brother, rented the farm in 1915 and managed to buy it in 1918. Later, brother Richard, and his brother-in-law George Bunting, took over the mortgage. Richard was in business in London. Douglas had to give up farming during the 1929-31 agricultural depression when Buntings took over the cultivation of the farm which they still do today. Douglas lived in the farm house with his mother and sister and when he married Ivy Speakman in 1926, she moved in. They had two sons, John and Peter, who run the caravan park today on three of the farm fields near the road. The farm house was destroyed by bombs in W.W.2. It was not rebuilt and Mrs. Douglas Wakelin moved into Barrow Marsh bungalow.

15.15 Mill Beach

Mill Beach is the area that, since the Middle Ages, was known as Barrow Marsh. It is known that Barrow Hills Mill, a windmill built there in 1703, was destroyed in a hurricane. Another mill built on the site was destroyed by gale force winds on 30th June 1831. The replacement was a two-sail tower windmill built in the same year. John Leather records that the miller was required, early in the nineteenth century, to provide his landlord with a turkey at Christmas and to keep a dog. The miller had to be paid a toll when sailing barges discharged and loaded grain, and often hay or straw, on the quay.

Fitch records in 1898 that "F. and G. May were responsible for the commodious Mill Beach Restaurant, a convenient rendezvous for the picnicker and sea bather in summer, along the delightful beach stretching away on the shores of the Blackwater ... and for the sportsman or naturalist in winter".

C. R. B. Barrett sketched Barrow Hills Mill in 1891 when the mill was in the Parish of Little Totham. Then access to the River Blackwater allowed goods to be taken in and out of Little Totham by sea. Parish boundaries have changed at various times and now this land is in Heybridge Parish.

The smock mill was owned by local farmers while the miller was self employed. The last miller was Abraham Springett, who was Harold Springett's grandfather. Major Williams suggested to Springett's wife, Emma that she provide refreshments for the day visitors he brought from Maldon East station. Mrs. Springett bought bottles of lemonade from Markhams in Maldon for 8d. a dozen (3p) and sold them for 6d. each. The mill was pulled down in 1892.

A sketch in 'Maldon and the River Blackwater by E. A. Fitch 1898 shows Mill House and Mill Beach Restaurant.

15.16 Mill House

This listed building has a seventeenth century rear range and around 1830 there were alterations and additions. There is a nineteenth century timber framed pump in the rear garden with a columnar pump of cast iron; the pump is approximately 1.2 metres high and has a spout and handle with acorn finial. The upper part of the shaft is fluted with fluted cap. The house had two pounds of Barrow Tide Mill on the west and a ditch that connected to the third and largest large pound beyond Mill Beach Hotel that became the boating lake on the east.

15.17 Chigborough Lakes

The lakes came about after the extraction of gravel in the 1960s, first by Baker Bros. from Great Totham who later sold out to Essex Aggregates. When the site was abandoned, Essex Wildlife Trust and their warden, Phil Luke, with dedicated conservationists, cleared ponds, cut scrub, pollarded trees, mowed grass, and provided nesting sites and reptile refuges to attract wildlife on the 23 acre site. Now, there is great diversity of wildlife: including two hundred and thirty species of plants, including the common spotted orchid, the southern marsh orchid, grass vetchling, blue fleebane and sneezewort. Fine aquatic flora is developing including greater pond sedge and marsh horsetail that covers large areas. Breeding birds include the great crested grebe, dab chick, tufted duck, coot, sedge and reed warblers. In winter, the lakes attract a large number of other duck species; the gadwell and pochard being the most numerous, as well as water-tail snipe, hen harriers and long eared owls. There are one hundred and twenty types of birds, many amphibians, reptiles, butterflies, dragon flies and damsel flies, some deer, fox and badgers. This nature reserve welcomes visitors who may wander through the paths.

Mill Beach Windmill
SOURCE Lloyd Blackburn

Lock Hill, Heybridge Basin. The spoil dug out of the locks raised the bank on either side of the lock.
PHOTO by kind permission of Mersea Museum

WILLIAM BRIGHT & SONS LI
THE OLD SHIP
FINE AND
ALES STOUT

William Bright, the Coggeshall brewer, leased the public house after 1906

16.0 Heybridge Basin and the inland port of Heybridge

16.1 Three families

The original Chelmer and Blackwater Navigation was built by three families: the **Clarks** from Suffolk, seamen, the **Chaneys** from Newcastle and the **Woodcrafts** from Hull. They stayed in the Basin and their descendants form a family network today. Mrs. Twinn (nee Chaney) believes the Willis family were early Basin residents. In the 1960s, Ben Willis worked at May and Butcher's as did his sister, Babe; she was a machinist in the wood mill but there are no Willis's in the Basin today. 'The Story of a Waterside Community' by Denys Harrison is an account of the growth of Heybridge Basin on land owned by the Dean and Chapter of St Paul's Cathedral and of people who lived there.

16.2 The eel trade

Businesses of note that operated in the Basin were May and Butcher (see below) and the Dutch eel firm started in 1926 by Dutchmen, Johan and later, Hans Kuijten. It became the biggest eel business in Europe before it closed in 1968. May and Butcher built the eel ships which had porous hulls that kept the eels in salt water during their voyages from Friesland in Holland. Typical boats carried 30 tons of slippery eels in the well. Eels came from the Baltic in Danish owned small wooden motor ketches. The water in Heybridge Basin is brackish so that eels could be stored in the cages until they could be sorted. Each eel had to be weighed and measured! Darby Stebbens earned £12 a week sorting eels which was pretty cold on the hands in winter. George Clark worked for the eel company until it closed, at which time he became lock keeper.

16.3 Blackwater Timber

Walter Burr left English Timbers to found Blackwater Timbers which traded in the Basin from 1946/7 until 1986. Walter was joined by his brother, Thomas. Initially, the firm ran from a site in May and Butcher's yard. Afterwards they bought a chicken farm opposite as their base where they built workshops. The firm dealt in English timber; they felled oak, ash, poplar, and elm. The timber was brought to Heybridge on the firm's two big timber whims that were serviced and maintained by the firm's mechanics in their workshops.

The trees were felled by sub-contractors, brought to Heybridge Basin in the round and cut as required for specific purposes: for barn repairs, coffin boards, to form the structure of boats, for fencing, gate posts, and pallets and for roofing props for the National Coal Board. The timber was not planed but rough cut.

From the age of 17, Carol Whitworth worked as a tree feller in a team dealing with dangerous trees. He remembers when the firm felled the line of elm trees in front of the Lodge of Langleys at Great Waltham due to Dutch elm disease. After five years, he was made redundant and worked as a builder's labourer but left the job when building work fell off due to a hard winter and he returned to the mill. He operated a band saw until he was made redundant after twenty-two years. The firm is now run by Walter Burr's son Gordon but the firm has left Heybridge Basin.

Blackwater Close and Burswood Close have been built on part of the timber firm's site while the remainder of the site is zoned for industrial use. Planning applications for houses have been refused.

16.4 Samuel Purkiss

Samuel Purkiss set up business in Heybridge Basin in c.1900 as a shopkeeper; by 1912 he was a grocer and postmaster. His son, Jim, worked in the shop while his other son, Clifford, was probably the first tallyman in the area; that is, he allowed people goods on credit and collected weekly payments from them. Later, his horse wagon was advertising Purkiss and Sons, Drapers, Boot Factors and Hosiery. He had extensive rounds north of Heybridge and worked in the shop when he was not on the rounds.

16.5 Wakelin and Leonard, butchers

Robert Leonard was a slaughter man and butcher living in Kent when, in September 1939, he heard of the death of his brother-in-law, Mr. Wakelin, who had recently opened a butcher's shop in Heybridge Basin. He told his wife that they must move to Heybridge to run the butcher's shop to help his sister who had five sons. The Leonard family, including Joyce, were able to live above the butcher's shop since Robert's sister stayed in her home in Goldhanger. Robert Leonard was medically unfit for the services in W.W.2 and carried on the butchers for thirty-two years. Petrol was rationed during the war so deliveries by van were limited. Three of Robert's nephews, in turn, delivered meat on a trade bicycle and have made great success of their lives. Robert Leonard's daughter, Joyce Allum (nee Leonard), helped on the van after W.W.2 and remembers Mr. Blott, who later became chairman of May and Butcher's, a lovely old man, coming in to buy sausages. It is sad that Robert Leonard was unable to sell the business on his retirement. The shop premises have been converted into a house named 'The Old Butcher's Shop'. Now that Mr. Stubbings has retired we no longer have a butcher's shop in Heybridge Street. (There are no butchers in the centre of Chelmsford today). Young people do not appreciate that local butchers know the source of their meat, can cut it to their requirements, advise them how to cook it and are often cheaper than supermarkets. There are no shops in Heybridge Basin today.

16.6 Thomas Richard Polden

Mr. Polden came from Kent and had joined the Royal Navy at the age of 15. He trained on the Trincomalee which had been built in Bombay in 1817 and was the last wooden ship in the Royal Navy. The Trincomalee served as a training ship until 1966; it is the oldest ship afloat in the UK and is now in Hartlepool Maritime Museum. Tom Polden met and married Ivy May Stebbens when he was stationed on Osea Island. He served through W.W.1, and left the navy in the early 1930s when he drove a lorry for Newman and Clarke. He re-joined the navy in July 1939 since he was on the Royal Navy Reserve, and served for the duration of W.W.2; a total of thirty-one years.

Around 1936, Heybridge Basin residents were still carrying their water either in buckets hanging from a yoke or in a bath with a wooden lid carried between two men. When Mr. and Mrs. Polden had their bungalow built in 1937 on Basin Road, it was connected to mains water.

Tom's son Tom describes himself as a modern blacksmith. His business is based in Sheepcotes Lane, Great Totham where he carries out a wide variety of work in metal. He created the Basin's new village sign, a seat in memory of George Clarke and used to repair the railings around King George V playing field when he noticed that they were broken. Tom is the youngest of the family, he has sisters; Mollie, who worked at Maldon East Railway Station and Betty, the eldest, trained as a nurse and went to New Zealand where she married Norman McDonald and returned to live in Maldon and work at St Peter's Hospital.

16.7 Frederick Austin

This family's history has strong links with Heybridge Basin. John Austin, barge master, was running a fortnightly sailing service to London around 1800. Norah Austin's grandfather, Frederick Austin, had nine children, he had three homes in the Basin; the first next to the Ship on Lock Hill, then a cottage opposite, and last, he had a bungalow built further up the road. He bought Saltcote Cottages for two of his sons, one was Norah's father. Frederick Austin piloted ships and barges to London Docks where he met his wife, Tilly, from Poplar. He worked at Blackwater Sailing Club when he retired from the sea.

16.8 David Clements

As lock keeper at Heybridge Basin from 1881 to 1914, David Clements lived in Lock House. He lost his first wife when he was 19, later his second wife died and he married Emily his third wife. Grace, Norah Austin's mother, was among the five children of this third marriage. Grace married Charles Austin and had two daughters: Norah and Barbara. The third Mrs. Clements, Emily, was sad when she had to leave Lock House on the appointment of Mr. Ellis as lock keeper because she had understood she would be allowed to continue to live there.

16.9 The bombing of the Basin, 11th January 1943

Norah Austin was educated at Heybridge Primary School and then went to Maldon Girls' Senior School. To fill in the gap before she could enter nursing training at 17 (the lowered age of entry during the war) she worked at May and Butcher. She thinks they had around fifty employees then. Norah Austin completed her training as a State Registered Nurse at the Royal Waterloo Hospital in London. Later she trained as a mid-wife at St John's Hospital in Chelmsford and in Ipswich; she did a post-graduate course in 1952 in Manhattan, New York. During her thirty-five year nursing career, she rose to be in charge of district mid-wives in the Dengie Hundred, Maldon and Burnham on Crouch and maternity wards of St Peter's Hospital Maldon, the William Julian Courtauld Hospital, Braintree and the Maternity Home in Burnham on Crouch.

Norah saw the bombing of Heybridge Basin: A German bomber airplane flew over Maldon Boys' Council School in Wantz Road and fired bullets; the holes on the building were visible for several years. Fortunately it was in the school holidays. The plane then came in low over Heybridge Basin and dropped four bombs at 9.35am on 11th January 1943. The first destroyed Arthur Butcher (1)'s car and garage, the next one struck the cottages opposite Mr. Purkiss's shop killing Mr. and Mrs. Wisbey, Mr. and Mrs. Everitt, Miss Jones and Ida Bailey (Jim and Cliff Purkiss's sister), as she crossed the road. Norah says that she and John Staines from May and Butcher were the first on the scene. Bernie, the postman, was having his usual cup of tea in the post office when an explosion caused the lids to be blown off the tins of cocoa covering him from head to foot in cocoa. The cottage opposite the car park entrance is an odd shape today because it was part of a row that had a direct hit. This cottage escaped; internally, extra brick work strengthened the structure and externally the walls were permanently propped up. There used to be a small area of garden created as a remembrance of those who were killed.

The third bomb passed through the chapel and exploded further up the lane while the fourth bomb landed harmlessly in the Navigation. Lord Haw Haw reported the raid on a broadcast to England saying that "the submarine pens at Heybridge Basin had been attacked". There have never been submarine pens in Heybridge Basin. Was he trying to promote his worth to the Nazis by seeming to have local knowledge and seeking to confuse the Germans with the submarine activity on Osea Island in W.W.1? Denys Harrison said "He should have known better as, between the wars, he kept a boat in the canal". The house opposite to the entrance to the car park, then owned by Mr. Handley the taxi man, looks more modern because it replaced a cottage destroyed by a bomb. Reg Mansfield was brought up in The Gables, a children's home in Maldon High Street. When he left school in 1942 he was apprenticed to Mr. Reeve, the Maldon plumber; he remembers accompanying Mr. Reeve to the Basin to repair the bomb damage.

Mollie Polden was at Maldon Girls' Senior School. Girls who went home for dinner returned to tell stories of how everyone in the Basin had been killed so the headmistress, Miss Samuel, sent Isa Chaney and Mollie home in a taxi.

16.10 Stebbens' Boat Yard

Cecil Stebbens, the son of Charles Mott Stebbens, started the boatyard in the 1960s. He had married Jill Butcher and based the business on part of May and Butcher's yard. Their daughter, Judy, and son-in-law, Adrian Robinson, have taken over the business. They crane boats up to about three tons over the sea wall for storage and engine repairs, fitting out, can accommodate about forty-five boats and have moorings, mud berths as well as the chandlery.

16.11 May and Butcher

This firm was the major employer in Heybridge Basin in the first half of the twentieth century. Arthur Butcher (1), 1872-1934 was a shipwright at Howard's boatyard in Maldon. He left Howard's in 1898 to be a boat builder and chandler at the Lock House. He was married to Annie Eliza Chaney. Before W.W.1 Jack Chaney, aged 12, joined the firm when much of the work was connected with agriculture and the workforce numbered about twenty, including apprentices, who made field gates and a variety of wooden buildings. The firm expanded into sheds in fields behind the sea wall.

In 1911, Arthur Edward May from Langford Cross, a timber merchant, farmer and businessman, bought half the shares in the business and became a partner to form May and Butcher Ltd.

Two steam-powered engines supplied the firm with electricity in 1914. Later, this unusual 80 volts DC electricity enabled many Basin cottages to have one bulb in the parlour and there was a lamp at the lock side. Commercial electricity came to the Basin in 1933.

When war broke out, Mr. Butcher was commissioned to build net submarine defences. Later, he went to Felixstowe Docks, erecting boom defences and he continued this until the end of the war.

Arthur Butcher (1) was a dealer. The Government's Disposals and Liquidation Board attempt to sell more W.W.1 tentage by tender had failed. The Board realised that auctions would be a slow process so Arthur Butcher had become involved. As tentage was declared surplus, he was given a detailed schedule of what was to be disposed; he inspected the goods at the various depots and paid £77,000 in 1920. Large marquees were erected and every available building in the Basin was rented to store the tentage that was sorted by twenty women.

Again in 1920, Arthur Butcher purchased a large quantity of surplus tentage but things went wrong in 1923. The money Mr. Butcher offered for the available tentage was deemed to be too little by the Commission. Mr. Butcher claimed he was not given a detailed schedule of the tentage on offer which prevented him from ascertaining the condition of the goods because of the way they were stored. As a large scale buyer, he should pay less than small retailers because of the risks he was taking on the state of this huge amount of tentage. When his offer was not increased, the goods were sold elsewhere. Mr. Butcher mounted a case in the High Court claiming the Commission had broken the contract with May and Butcher to purchase all surplus tentage. It is extremely rare for a private individual to obtain permission to mount an appeal in the House of Lords Court of Appeal. The Board contended that the price was to be settled by agreement as each lot became available; no agreement - no sale, which meant there was no contract. One of the three Appeal Judges would have allowed the appeal but the other two Appeal Court Judges threw out May and Butcher's case. It was an expensive affair because May and Butcher had to pay the respondent's costs. This did not put him off dealing and he subsequently bought a million toothbrushes and sold each one for a profit of a farthing, around £250,000.

When the tentage transactions ended, May and Butcher bought old battleships for breaking up as well as the entire plant on Osea Island. The huts used by the navy on Osea Island were taken to Wharf Road, Mill Beach and along Goldhanger Road and Basin Road. The large corrugated iron sheds were floated down the river from Osea to May and Butcher's yard in one piece; lifted over the sea wall by crane and used as offices by the company.

John Blott, a colourful character who had made his fortune manufacturing leather goods for the army in W.W1, joined May and Butcher in 1920 when the firm undertook ship breaking. He later became company chairman. His wide business connections were valuable to the firm. Mr. Blott bought Howbridge Hall in Witham around 1924 and created a beautiful garden where he employed four gardeners. He was married three times having been widowed twice. Older Basin residents remember him with affection. His first yacht was the Alpha and just before W.W.2 he had a luxury fishing trawler type of vessel built that was requisitioned during the war. His skipper was George Brand from Tollesbury. Maisie Butcher remembers visiting his yacht at Mersea. Mr. Blott spent three months of every year in South Africa.

Ships were brought to a wharf along the sea wall for breaking. It was no easy task and the seamen bringing them were in danger from bad weather and the dilapidated state of the old ships. For example, the Saltcote Belle was towing a ship from Harwich when a gale blew up and the tow rope gave way; the wind took the ship to the French coast with Jack Chaney aboard. Another ship sailing from the Humber ran into bad weather and two crew men were drowned. Among the ships broken up were the yacht St George, one of the finest and largest of the Royal Yacht squadron, a man-of-war from Dover, while the largest was HMS Dido, a cruiser built in 1896 that lay along the sea wall for many years. Valuable material was removed and then the hulls were broken up. HMS Marlborough was a 63,000 ton sailing three decker carrying one hundred and thirty-one guns and had been built in 1855. One of the largest wooden ships of war ever built, she had been converted to steam. The hulk of the Marlborough had been acquired by May and Butcher in November 1924. The ship was to be towed from Portsmouth to May and Butcher's yard at Heybridge Basin for breaking up. In a violent gale, the vessel became flooded, broke in two, and sank near the Owers lightship. The captain of the tug, Vanquisher, Captain H. Pascoe, immediately let go of the hawser; the engineer, Harry Wilkinson who was an engineer on a yacht berthed at the Basin, described how "the water came in quickly and flooded the three decks. The water burst in forward and put out the dynamo lights. We had to rush about with candles. After a time, the boat gave a list to starboard and finally toppled right over. She seemed to break clean in two. When the water rushed in forward, we all went aft and scrambled through the aft window. I was floating about in the sea clinging to pieces of wreckage for about three quarters of an hour. I saw most of the crew swimming about in the sea. I think the skipper must have been lost with the ship, being unable to get out of her". Captain Pascoe heard a voice shouting "Save us" in the darkness and headed that way where he found two men, James Stubbings and Harry Wilkinson, clinging to a large piece of wreckage. The rope Captain Pascoe threw fell short; Cecil Stubbings, aged 22, who was some distance away, sprang for it from another piece of wreckage and risked his own life to stay and put the line around his uncle, Harry Stubbings, aged 56, from Lock Hill, Heybridge Basin. Both men were hauled aboard the tug that rescued Harry Wilkinson. The other four crew were drowned including Arthur Dowsett from Heybridge Basin and George Johnson from Goldhanger.

There were several unemployed men in the Basin in 1924; thirty had already been signed to break up the ship during the winter and several more would have been needed. Denys Harrison on page 29 writes that the Astrid Gloriana, known locally as Gloria, was built in Canada in W.W.1 to replace shipping losses. After the war, she was used as a fish processing plant in Brightlingsea until she was brought to Heybridge Basin where May and Butcher stored scrap metal in her alongside the sea wall. Two cranes in the stern and prow loaded the scrap. The Gloria was deliberately set on fire on Guy Fawkes Night when Ivan Butcher (1) lost a finger through a firework. The ship burned for two weeks causing anxiety when the wind changed direction.

Local people were able to buy things from these ships. Items such as cutlery and china and small souvenirs may be seen in Basin homes today. Daphne Shortland remembers cutlery from the ship named the George in her mother's home. Salvaged timber was made into park seats for London County Council, each seat bore a plaque naming the ship from which it was made.

Arthur May published May and Butcher's Mail on 7th February 1922 to celebrate the ten years' trading of the company. In this edition, John B. Gill, the secretary of The National Farmers' Union, Essex County Branch, reported that a journal would be published monthly in future giving news of the NFU County Executive, the Local Branch and the National Farmers' Union Council in London and any matters of interest to farmers. The NFU membership subscription was 2d. an acre minimum, £8 maximum and 5s.0d. each for farmers' sons at that time. May and Butcher's Mail advertised oak field gates for 26s.6d. The firm is described as Timber Merchants, Manufacturers of Fencing, Gates and Farm Appliances and traders in Government Stores in the May edition and announced they would be in attendance at the Suffolk, Essex and Royal Agricultural Shows.

During W.W.2 May and Butcher manufactured parts for the Mosquito fighters and Handley Page aircraft, manufactured MTB (motor torpedo boats) that were repaired and tested at HMS Osea, repaired minesweepers, made moulds for prefabricated houses, oilrigs, bridges and Twickenham grandstand.

Jack Rayner and John Price, who have become successful builders, served five year apprenticeships as carpenters and joiners at May and Butcher. John Price started his apprenticeship on 17th September 1945 at the age of 14. He worked a 52 hour week, including Saturday mornings, for 5d. (2 pence) an hour. A skilled carpenter earned £4.10s.0d. (£4.50 pence) at that time. John left May and Butcher to do his National Service in 1950.

Men worked a five day week in the 1950s starting at 7.30am and finishing at 5.30pm with an hour off for lunch. The wage for a skilled carpenter was £11 a week in the 1960s. Many of the employees spent the whole of their working life at May and Butcher. Jack Eavery, the husband of Arthur Butcher's daughter, Polly, managed the firm with Roy Gurton after Arthur Butcher (1)'s death. Jack Eavery lived in an Osea hut in Basin Road and Roy Gurton lived in one in Wharf Road. Later, Roy Gurton worked at Mr. Kuijten's eel business at the Basin. Tony Pitt followed Jack Eavery. He was the husband of Arthur Butcher's granddaughter, Lyndal (Joan Lappage's daughter) and Evan (Hefin) Roberts was the last manager. Mrs. Stella Wisbey, the company secretary, backed up these managers and her knowledge and expertise was an invaluable asset to the firm. Arthur Butcher's son, Arthur (2) was a director and drove a lorry.

Ship breaking had finished by the 1960s but the firm continued to grow. As a result of advertising in the Construction Gazette, goods were produced for the Far and Middle East, for example Kuwait. The firm began to diversify by making wooden moulds and shuttering for Anglian Building Products which supplied pre-cast concrete beams and bridges for Essex roads. Skilled carpenters created accurate wooded templates for bridges that were waxed to protect the wood when concrete was poured into them and then assembled. In the unlikely event of a bridge of the same design being ordered, the moulds could be used again, otherwise they were smashed up. Seed trays and wheelbarrows were made for Carters of Surrey during Jack Eavery's time.

The voluntary liquidation of the firm took place in 1984 by which time no family members were taking an active part in the firm. The contents of the Timber Yard were sold at an auction sale on 28th March 1984. The works' site was sold by auction on 28th July 1986 after residential outline planning permission had been granted for the 4½ acre site; houses in Maritime Avenue and Spinnaker Drive have been built on the site. The Colliers was built on former allotments that used to be a shortcut to the river by St George's Church in Basin Road.

16.12 Public houses in the Basin

There were at least six public houses or beer houses in the Basin at various times in the nineteenth and twentieth centuries, now only two remain.

The **Jolly Sailor** was built in 1788 by Woodcock and Hedges Writtle Brewery (later Wells and Perry of Chelmsford) before the hamlet or Basin existed, to cater for sailors on ships moored in Colliers Reach, workers from the nearby saltern and nearby farmers. Later, it was used by men digging out the Basin from Heybridge Marsh.

In April 1839, Dengie magistrates heard a complaint that Edward Tovee, licensee of the Jolly Sailor, kept his house open during the hours of Divine Service and sold spirits and porter on 31st March. They convicted him and imposed a fine of 6s.6d. and costs of 13s.6d.

On 24th June 1893, John Thomas Wilding, the licensee of the Jolly Sailor, was convicted of selling the Police Superintendent, Thomas Gillis, a pint of gin below proper strength, because he had watered it down, He was fined 2s.6d. and 8s.0d. costs.

Among the notable landlords was 'Tishy' Clark who came ashore in 1886, took over the pub and married Jane Woodcraft, they had ten children. When he died in 1927, his widow took over the licence and retained it until her death in 1952 at the age of 92. Then their daughter, Mona, ran this popular pub successfully with quiet dignity and a good sense of humour until 1962 when she retired. She was assisted by Rena Burrell who had stayed on after the war, coming originally from Cumberland to join the Land Army in W.W.2 when she had been assigned to allocate prisoners of war to farms in the locality.

Later, beer was shipped down the Navigation from the Chelmsford breweries and the Jolly Sailor remains in use; it is an important meeting place for locals and visitors including members of the Blackwater Sailing Club which, even today, has no everyday bar.

The **Old Ship** started life on the canal towpath. The present Myrtle Cottage was part of the original Old Ship public house built in the 1790s, the large ground floor room was the taproom. The upstairs room was used by Chelmsford lightermen to 'doss' down between trips. Stables were alongside the Navigation. Mollie Graham (nee Clarke) was born on 11th November 1946 in the private house, Myrtle Cottage. Men filling in a small pond on the canal bank that had been used by horses to ease their feet after dragging lighters from Chelmsford ceased work when they heard Mrs. Clarke was in labour. Sheila Wakelin lived in this cottage in the 1960s.

The **Chelmer Brig** was built on the site of the present Old Ship in 1799 by the Chelmer and Blackwater Navigation Company. At one time, Mr. Brightwen owned The Chelmer Brig. Joseph Going was the landlord of The Chelmer Brig in 1845 when he combined the roles of landlord with the duties of shipping agent and sail maker with selling Best Sunderland and Seaham coals from the Springfield Wharf. Other public house landlords were similarly shrewd business men.

The Chelmer Brig was partially demolished in 1858 and rebuilt for £552.10s.4d. to give a larger front over looking the river. The older part was converted into a separate cottage for £20.6s.4d. and sold to Robert Thomas Smith on 30th July 1898 as a Home for Motherless Children. He was the founder of that organisation and ran an orphanage there for twenty-four children with a matron. Later, it was called Lock House by David Clements who rented the house when he was lock keeper until he moved across the canal to the house built for lock keepers. The original part of the Chelmer Brig is now Miranda Cottage. Lock Hill cottages next to Miranda Cottage are listed and were the offices of the Chelmer and Blackwater Company at one time. William Filby, the landlord of the Chelmer Brig, was fined for 'selling gin not composed of ingredients in accordance with the demands of the customer' in March 1883.

The Chelmer Brig ceased to trade when the 1880s' depression failed to provide a living. The original Old Ship licence was sold for £200 in 1894 to the Mill Beach restaurant which henceforth traded as the Mill Beach Hotel. William Bright of the Coggeshall Brewery took a ninety-nine year lease on the Chelmer Brig and reopened it as the Old Ship in 1906 when tourism was becoming popular. He sold out to the New London Brewery in 1921. Charles and Alice Stebbens were landlords of the Old Ship in the 1930s when stabling was provided for horses that plodded along the tow path and pulled the flat bottomed barges along the Navigation to and from Chelmsford. The public house remained in possession of the Chelmer and Blackwater Navigation Company until the administrators sold it in 2005.

Basiners value their separateness from Heybridge. There is a flourishing Conservation Association which keeps a watchful eye on development in the village.

17.0 Mains Water, Sewerage and Gas Lighting, come to Heybridge

Many people will be surprised to learn that sewerage did not come to Heybridge until the 1950s and that mains water was not available until that time.

17.1 Water

Heybridge is located above a layer of London clay below which is chalk. London clay forms a crust that slows water percolating through and above this is a layer of gravel of varying thickness into which shallow wells can be dug.

Bentall had a deep well to supply the Towers and the estate where cucumbers, melons and vines were grown with this water. The company had two deep wells that supplied the factory and their workers' houses; the one near the church was probably sunk by E. Bentall in 1859. This well was in the yard below the blue collar workers' breakfast room. It was 18ft. in diameter with a steel reinforced wooden cover. Water was pumped to provide water for the works and Bentall's houses. This well was replaced in 1872 and was said to be capable of supplying sixty houses with water of excellent quality. E. H. Bentall refused permission for the Maldon Rural Sanitary Authority to tap into Bentall's water supply in 1876 for non-Bentall houses in Hall Road and the residents drank Navigation water.

The second well was behind Stock Terrace. It seems likely that this well supplied the nut and bolt factory. Christine Wareham (nee Marshall) lived in Boulton Cottages and remembers a ground floor wooden building with a corrugated iron roof which housed an engine that pumped water into a tank resting on girders above. There were 3in. round holes 3 - 4 ft. from the ground with a spout that spurted water now and again. The pump was operated and maintained by Mr. Chapman who walked from the Causeway morning and evening to switch the electric pump on and off; the pump was driven by wide leather belts. Mr. Chapman cleaned and polished the engine until it gleamed. Children raced to the building when they saw him arrive and they were able to peep inside the building; he gave the children very strong small peppermints from a tobacco tin.

There was a low iron pump between numbers 134 and 135 Woodfield Cottages which is now listed. The pump in Well Yard was turned on daily to provide water for Stock Terrace, Boulton Cottges and Barnfield Cottages. There are four pairs of cottages named Boulton Cottages; between each pair there was a tap, four in all. There are twelve houses in Stock Terrace; six shared one tap and the other six houses another tap. Maggie Lloyd's family kept a china jug in the kitchen for drinking water, her father collected water in a pail for the other needs. Understandably, clothes were washed much less often than today and more than one person used the water in the tin bath on Friday nights. All Bentall workers' houses enjoyed water from a nearby tap and the firm employed their own plumbers.

Typical of a family collecting water 1920s

SOURCE David Williams

The rest of Heybridge depended on many bore holes and shallow wells that were often polluted. Drinking water had to be boiled.

The 1916 report stated that there was a well 100 yards from the Navigation near Heybridge Hall which could supply 600 gallons per hour but it had been abandoned in 1908 because of the infiltration of tidal (salt) water. A new well had been sunk but suffered from the same problem.

The first houses on the Causeway to have piped water had to have an outside tank which stored 30 - 40 gallons of water from which supplies were collected, there were no taps indoors. Next, water was pumped from Southend Waterworks to Southend and then pumped back to Maldon. In Heybridge, the Essex and Suffolk Water Company took over supplying more houses and those houses had to have a tap indoors. Reg Mansfield joined Reeves, the Maldon plumbing firm, in 1942 and worked for them for fifty-two years. He remembers connecting the houses to the mains in the late 1940s and early 1950s. Houses were without water when the pipes and taps froze in winter.

Heybridge Basin had a public well 100 yards from the lock gates. A new bore hole was sunk in August 1908 and the 1916 report stated it could supply fifty to sixty houses.

Around 1900, six villas were built from Crescent Road along Holloway Road towards Langford Cross. Water was laid on to these houses and also to the villas being built along Crescent Road by Southend Waterworks after 1927. Bentall's signed a thirty year agreement to supply houses in Heybridge in 1942.

David Williams sums up the situation between 1860 and 1970. Before 1860 supplies were from rainfall, springs and ponds, afterwards the supply of water to Heybridge was predominately from chalk. The Southend and South Essex Water companies combined to become the Essex Water Company in 1970. Maldon Borough and Maldon District Councils were incorporated to form Maldon District Council in 1974 and Southend and South Essex Water Company became responsible for the district including Heybridge.

17.2 Sewerage

Main drainage came late to this locality. Houses built along the Causeway in Maldon around 1912 were not connected to the sewer until 1956; even then not all houses were connected. Night soil was collected in Heybridge in the 1950s; the author remembers hastily winding up her car windows when she saw the night soil cart along Holloway Road. The vehicle was known, colloquially, as 'the last bus', others knew it as the 'Lavender Wagon' or 'the night soilers'. The story goes that Mr. Ruggles and Mr. Pennick were collecting in their handcart when one of them put his arms into the tank. His colleague asked, "What are you doing?" The reply was that his coat had fallen in the tank. "You will not be able to wear it". He responded: "No, but my sandwiches are in the pocket". They used to put their jackets over the back of the tank to sit on when eating their sandwiches in the lay-by in Goldhanger Lane. Later, a motor tanker did the collections. Mr. Houlding got a surprise one night when his vehicle ran into the back of the tanker and the contents spilled out. Users of earth closets had to be wary because the small door at the back of the shed could be opened and the bucket whipped away regardless of whether someone was sitting on the facility. It was common until way into the 1960s for older houses to have privies in a small shed outside the house where, inside, would be squares of newspaper hanging from a string on a nail.

The big pipe crossing the Navigation on the north side of Wave Bridge is the Heybridge main sewer, constructed in the late 1950s. Permission for the sewerage scheme had been obtained after a delegation from the Borough of Maldon: Mr. Blow, the Borough Engineer, The Mayor, Cllr. Tonkin, Alderman D. Fenn, Alderman Mrs. Brewster, Alderman Dines and the Town Clerk, Mr. Robinson, met with representatives of the Ministry of Housing and Local Government in London. Reg Mansfield spent the late 1950s converting earth closets into water closets in brick buildings.

17.3 Gas Lighting

In 1965, electric street lighting was installed in Holloway Road, Crescent Road (the final part of Crescent Road was not made up until the 1960s), Oak Road and Wood Road. Maldon Gas Light Company was established in Maldon High Street in 1839. The times of lighting up and going off had to be changed throughout the year. They were controlled by wind-up clocks and there were two hundred and fifty lights in Maldon and Heybridge including Heybridge Basin. Maldon and Heybridge were the last places in England to be lit by gas. The last gas lamps were not replaced by electricity in Heybridge until 1972. Each street gas lamp had to be lit and William Alford was employed as a lamp lighter in Maldon and Heybridge until 1976.

Houses and the school were lit by gas until the 1930s.

17.4 Housing yesterday and today

Before W.W.1, Heybridge clustered around what is now Holloway Road near Black Bridge along The Street and in Hall Road. Bentall's had built nine groups of houses for their workers outside this centre.

Maldon Rural District Council bought land in Goldhanger Road for council houses in 1921. John Playle moved into the first pair of council houses to be built in Colchester Road in 1928. In 1957 council houses were built in Oak Road and Wood Road. In the 1960s, Heywood Way stretched for half a mile behind Wood Road with side roads, houses, flats and special needs accommodation. They were built by Colne and Moat Housing Association and private developers.

In the early 1960s, Crescent Road was extended to reach Langford Road. Houses were built on the frontage, on A. N. Alexander's field, on Langford Cross land, allotments and Mr. Moore's grazing meadow.

Detached houses were built along Scraley Road followed by a through route along Rowan Drive and Lawling Avenue to Goldhanger Road over half a mile in length, eastward to Drapers Chase and westward to Colchester Road.

Hazelwood Court, between Oak Road and Wood Road, is an attractive development of nineteen flats and bungalows for residents over 55 built by the Salvation Army in 1986.

In Heybridge Basin, the yards of May and Butcher, and Blackwater Timber were built over.

Around 600 houses have been built on Elms Farm.

Building has begun on the one hundred and twenty-four houses on the chalet site on Heybridge Hall farm land. Some of the residents of these houses may be employed in the small and medium sized businesses on the Bentall factory site and in Maldon but many commute to the surrounding towns and further afield.

Railway carriage being transported along the 1½ mile causeway between the mainland and Osea Island.
SOURCE Lloyd Blackburn Maldon Society

Rivermere 'Ideal home for inebriates' 3 guineas a week. SOURCE Ellen Hedley collection

18.0 Osea Island in the Parish of Heybridge

18.1 The island

In 2009, Osea is in the parish of Heybridge. A record shows that in 1873, it was in the parish of Great Totham. It is 330 acres in size with stony, gravelly, light soil that is farmed. Osea Island is over a mile in length and is never more than a few hundred yards across. It is about five miles from Bradwell on Sea at the entrance of the River Blackwater (where the Romans built a huge fort, Othona, to guard the approaches to the River Blackwater between 40 and 400AD), and four miles from Maldon Harbour, the river's navigable head. The Romans had salt works and a pottery on the island. There was a wharf on the north side of the island from which barges traded agricultural cargoes.

It has been a strategically fortified encampment throughout the centuries, guarding the upper reaches of the river and the settlement and port of Maldon from Saxon pirates to attacks by the Germans in W.W.1 and W.W.2.

Osea is linked to the mainland by a 1½ mile causeway built by the Romans. It is usable for only four hours during every low tide. The causeway begins at Fauley Point which became known as Decoy Point when there was a large decoy pond on the headland. Decoy ponds were located away from villages and ploughed fields so the birds would not be disturbed. The central pond had offshoots leading away in different directions like spokes from a wheel. These offshoots, or 'pipes', were around 70 yards in length and 8 yards across where they leave the central pond but they gradually narrowed to a channel a few feet wide. The whole pond was surrounded by tall reeds or rushes to shelter the birds. The Decoy Point headland attracted passing birds that fed on the pond, especially at dawn and dusk. A fence or hedge screen was built around the pond to hide the decoyman who approached down wind and unseen while 'tame' ducks or wooden decoy ducks lured the birds into the 'pipes'. The twisty 'pipes' were covered with nets supported by large semicircular hoops. The decoy man's dog would come out and dance about luring the ducks into the pipe or scaring the birds into flying up the narrowing pipe where they were caught in the nets and the decoy man wrung their necks.

In the nineteenth century, marshes were regarded as a rich source of food; the size of the bag in the nets varied enormously from two hundred to up to one thousand in the 1890s. Wildfowlers caught wild geese, duck teal and widgeon and some plover, curlew and dunlin. The birds were taken to Leadenhall Market where the prices varied widely, depending on the season. The numbers of professional wildfowlers dwindled. Walter Linnett of Bradwell on Sea was another sort of wild fowler who made his entire living with his punt and gun, often working at dawn on the salt marshes, until he died in 1958. Sportsmen still go duck shooting along the Blackwater Estuary at dusk. There is evidence of one decoy pond on Osea and possibly two. Numerous brent geese feed on grass in the fields and there are gulls, pheasants, wading birds and rabbits.

Visitors to the island need to know the tide times since the incoming tide covers the road at a very fast rate. At low tide, the River Blackwater dries out almost completely between the shoreline and Osea Island, leaving just the tiny channel of Goldhanger Creek snaking its way across the wide plains of mud. When the tide is in, the causeway is covered by water up to a depth of about 14ft. The time taken for this varies with the tide and the direction of the wind.

Osea is privately owned and there is no right of way onto the island. The causeway is not straight; there are bends as the 'road' wends its way across the treacherous mudflats and is almost level with them. The bends are there to break the fast running currents. The track is maintained in remarkably good condition with a firm surface up to 8ft. wide. Small boulders define the route but they are covered with sea weed and the mud on each side is dangerously soft.

As sub-postmaster at Heybridge Post Office, Jack Mitchell was responsible for delivering and collecting mail from Osea Island. The author has seen a picture of a photograph of the post box in 1948 which says collections "According to Tide". From 1928, Jack cycled from Heybridge Post Office, across the Causeway and back - a total of eight miles daily in all weathers. He retired in 1962 but, when the ride was too much for the man who took over, Jack resumed the task for a further three years until he was 80 years old. Peter Roope, a Royal Mail Inspector, remembers accompanying Jack Mitchell to Osea Island and cycling across the one and a half mile causeway. Jack told Mr. Roope that he greased the wheels of his bicycle to stop salt damage.

Jack Mitchell had to go to Osea Island even if there was no post to be delivered in case there was mail to be collected from the pillar box. He varied the rest of his 'walk' around the tide. The author remembers that her mail deliveries in Crescent Road were unpredictable for this reason. Jack's daughter, Kathleen, told me she carried out this round about half a dozen times with great trepidation when her father was unwell but was reassured because she realised her father knew the times of the tides to the minute.

The very fast, incoming tides trap the unwary: many stories are told of victims. A postman named Ruddick almost drowned when the ice on which he was crossing the Stumble gave way in the great frost of 1888. Recently, a taxi driver had to get on the top of his car and use his mobile phone to be rescued. Woodley's acquired a new van and the next day the driver delivered goods to Osea, he misjudged the tide on his way back and the van was a write off. The author recalls seeing a man rolling up his trousers midway across and later removing them and holding his clothes in a bundle above his head.

The island has mains electricity via underground cable from the mainland and drinking water.

18.2 Frederick Nicholas Charrington

The director in the Charrington's family brewing firm in Mile End saw a drunken man repel his wife's appeal to come home to the family one Saturday night. Her husband struck her across the face, lurched into the bar and slammed the door. Charrington saw his name on the inn sign, he was conscience stricken and resigned from the firm. He wrote "it knocked her into the gutter and me out of the brewery". He decided to use his wealth, £1 million from the sale of his brewery shares, to tackle the problems of alcohol abuse and poverty in the East End. He used the Maldon estate agents, Spurgeon, to buy Osea Island in 1903 with the intention of developing it as a seaside and health resort for middle class alcoholics, mainly from London. The population on the island numbered seven when he bought it. The charge for a week's stay was £7.10s.0d. and the large staff was recruited mainly from Dr. Barnardo's Homes.

Londoners who had lived in the East End for twelve months who could not find employment elsewhere and whose families were in immediate need of relief applied to the Mansion House Relief Works. Those whose application was successful were sent to Osea for a month. They lived in wooden huts with free board and lodging while they worked at road-making, ditching and other tasks for 6d. a week, while their wives received 10s.6d. and 2s.0d. for each child a week. Some could not face the rural life, disliked the work or were lazy but others stayed the month and good workers were allowed home for a few days and could then return.

Mr. Ocoomore was the foreman, superintendent, and dispenser of castor oil to the relief works colony. He conducted Daily Graphic reporters on a tour; they saw the roomy huts where the men lodged with bunks one above the other with good bedding, and a stove in the centre. There was a dining tent where the men were having a good substantial meal and a new hut was being prepared to accommodate one hundred and twenty men.

'Osea Island' an illustrated guide, price 6d., advertised to "inebriate cases for 3 guineas a week and visitors from 8s.0d. per day. Rivermere has been recently erected as an ideal home for ladies and gentlemen suffering from the insidious and baneful effects of alcohol and narcotics".

Avenues of trees, palms and fuchsias were planted, houses and bungalows were built and a pier erected opposite the doctors. A large ornamental lily pond was constructed in front of the doctor's house. In the 1930s, Miss Stone ran the village shop that Mr. Charrington had opened and stocked. It did not sell alcohol; the manufacture, sale and consumption of alcohol were forbidden. However, it is rumoured that local boat-owners earned a lot of money rowing out with booze that they hid in bushes under the cover of darkness, friends of the inebriates hauled up boxes of booze tied to the doctor buoy by rope, and fishermen ferried patients to the Mill Beach Hotel and Maldon public houses. Even today hidden bottles are discovered by Osea residents. Mr. Charrington hoped to divert the alcoholics by setting up a zoo with cockatoos, emus, three kangaroos, wallabies and seals which he hoped to acclimatise to English conditions. His plans for a convalescent home for children were only half completed when W.W.1 broke out and he had to close down the project.

Before W.W.1, Charrington bought the little steamboat Annie that had been used on the River Orwell. Cook's boatyard adapted her to carry one hundred and fifty-one passengers on the Blackwater estuary. There was a little steam engine with boiler and coal bunker amidships, fore and aft saloons and an awning over the after deck. There was a crew of three. Passengers boarded the boat from a floating landing stage on Maldon Promenade and they disembarked on the Osea pier. Timetables show various itineraries as well as two voyages an hour to Osea and back, voyages allowing two hours on the island and a trip around the island, all subject to tides. These trips were popular. Occasionally, when there was a full moon, moonlight trips with the boat lit by lanterns in the aft awning attracted romantic young couples. The Annie was laid up on the north shore of Osea Island during W.W.1. After the war, Mr. H. C. Lamont bought her, refurbished the stripped out boat, installed a petrol paraffin engine to replace those which had disappeared, and renamed her Maldon Annie. He ran trips from Maldon Promenade luring customers with a sign saying "Bar open all day" until 1925 when she went to London and took passengers from Westminster to Greenwich. She was lost at Dunkirk. In the 1930s, Conqueror and Britannia, 40ft. open motor launches, took passengers on trips down the river. These boats were commandeered in the war and never heard of again.

18.3 Sea plane trials, 1913

Aviation history was made when Lt. Porte RN, managing director of British Deperdussin Aeroplane Company, tested their newly developed seaplane; a single-engine monoplane fitted with two large floats, which took off from the deep water channel south of the island, and made a successful ten minute flight.

18.4 W.W.1 secret sea plane base

In W.W.1 Osea Island became an important naval base known as HMS Osea where up to 1,000 self-supporting naval personnel were crammed in temporary huts and barrack blocks. Engineering and carpentry workshops, stores and boat sheds and a mechanically controlled slipway for launching boats, living accommodation for sailors and WRNS, and a chapel, were built on this substantial naval base for motor torpedo boats. Pure water was obtained from underground supplies and stored in two water towers. The number of passenger trains from Maldon to Witham was reduced from seven to five from 1914 to cope with the supplies needed on Osea and for military establishments in the neighbourhood.

In 1914, three officers suggested that small motor boats carrying a torpedo might be capable of travelling rapidly over protective minefields and attacking ships of the German Navy at anchor in their bases and retire before being detected. The Admiralty gave tentative approval and produced a specification for a boat which, complete with its torpedo, should not exceed the weight of the 30ft. motor boat, 4.5 tons, then carried in the davits of a light cruiser. The speed of the boat when fully loaded was to be at least 30 knots and able to carry enough fuel to give a considerable radius of action. John I. Thornycroft considered it would be possible to meet these requirements and, in co-operation with the Admiralty, produced a suitable design in January 1916. The firm received an order for twelve boats and completed it in August 1916. Weight restrictions meant the one torpedo was carried in a trough built into the after part of the boat's hull and was fired backwards by means of a long steel ram operated by a cordite cartridge. The torpedo's propeller entered the water first and, as its engine warmed up, the torpedo built up a great speed going in the same direction as the boat so that the boat had to be steered away very smartly to avoid being hit. These boats operated from Osea Island where a railway and long jetty were built to receive large vessels in connection with the venture. Approximately 1,000 naval personnel were living on Osea while the boats were being constructed, with several large workshops, factory buildings and accommodation blocks. The grey painted, wooden boats with their oak frame, African mahogany planking and copper fittings were known as CMBs - coastal motor boats - or skimmers; they had a crew of two or three and could skim over booms and shallow cables because they lifted high out of the water at full speed and needed less than 3ft. of water. CMBs were stored on dry land until needed since the wood would have soaked up water that would have increased the weight. Between 1914 and 1918, CMBs attacked German naval bases in the North Sea.

After W.W.1, this base was retained. Lieutenant Agar of the Royal Navy volunteered to go to Finland with two CMBs and their crews to contact Paul Dukes, a British spy working in Russia during the civil war that followed the Bolshevik Revolution. Counter espionage had captured British agents and the job of the volunteers was to land and pick up British agents. The sailors dressed in civilian clothes and knew that the British Government would give them no help if they were caught. The CMBs had been towed from Osea to the West India Docks in London and then towed by the cruiser HMS Voyager to the secret British base at Terrioki, three miles from the Russian border in Finland.

The Bolsheviks controlled the former Czarist fleet that was moored in Kronstadt Harbour situated on an island in the Gulf of Finland near Petrograd. Lieutenant Agar (1890-1968) launched the attack on the Russian Fleet from Terrioki with CMB4 that was 40ft. long with the torpedo 18ft. long on 17th June 1919; he was accompanied by Sub Lieut. J. W. Harshire, second in command, and Chief Motor Mechanic, M. Beeley. Captain Agar got through the screen of six destroyers without being seen and discovered that there was only one large warship - the Oleg - in harbour since the other eight warships had been withdrawn. CMB4 was manoeuvred over the chain guarding the harbour with only an inch or two to spare, crept past forts with the engine noise muted and Lieutenant Agar ordered the firing of the torpedo when some one hundred yards away. Something went wrong; the cordite charge fired early without propelling the torpedo and a new cartridge had to be put in, which took twenty minutes in close vicinity of the enemy. Lieutenant Agar got the Oleg in his sights and fired the torpedo at half a mile range. As they escaped, ships in the harbour fired at the CMB on all sides and a huge column of water rose from the sea as the Oleg turned over and sank in the shallow water. It took twelve minutes for the cruiser to sink; five of the warship's crew were lost. Lieutenant Agar received the Victoria Cross for sinking the Oleg and the DSO for his second raid and Sub Lieut. Harshire and Chief Mechanic Beeley were awarded the DSC. During his career Lieutenant Agar moved up the ranks to Captain, and then to Commander. From June to August 1919 Captain Agar made six hazardous trips to Soviet Russia to land and pick up agents, CMBs made a total of nine.

Seven more CMBs from Osea joined Lieutenant Agar to attack the Russian Fleet in Krondstadt Harbour on the night of 18th August 1919. They sank two battleships and a supply vessel but eight officers and men were lost and nine taken prisoner. The voyage from Terrioki to Petrograd entailed a voyage of thirty five miles through minefields, past searchlights and the guns on forts. The forays were carried out because many British ships were being sunk by ships from the naval base at Petrograd. A CMB is displayed at the Imperial War Museum Duxford where Captain Agar gives a recorded account of the voyage.

The Imperial War Museum produced a film of service life on Osea during 1920 and 1921. They show sailors and WRNS at work and play dressed somewhat informally. The base was retained until 1926. In the 1930s the author's family visited Heybridge Basin on summer Sundays; her parents would chuckle when passing a certain house in Heybridge because it was a maternity hospital to cater for the WRNS from Osea. Which house? Nothing about this has been found but Hillside on Market Hill, Maldon was a maternity hospital from 1909 to 1927.

18.5 Between W.W.1 and W.W.2

Large corrugated iron sheds were floated from Osea Island Naval Base to Heybridge, lifted over the sea wall by crane and used as offices by May and Butcher's who were engaged in ship breaking.

Between the wars, motor launches plied from Maldon Promenade; Tom and Bill Handley's Britannia carried sixty-eight passengers, and Dick and Fudge Phillips' boat carried twelve. Hedgecock Bros.' 1923 boat drew up on the sea wall on the Promenade with wheeled contraptions to help the passengers board the boats. The pleasure boats did not return after W.W.2. The island was sold to Major Alnatt, who farmed the land after Frederick Charrington's death in 1936.

The author remembers her family holidayed at Bradwell on Sea in the 1930s and visited Osea Island in Daniel Burch's motor launch for the day. On one occasion, she saw a large Baltic timber boat anchored in Stansgate Hole off Osea Island. While they picnicked near the pier, they watched timber being unloaded. Sets were made up manually for discharge into lighters by ships' derricks; there was no "packaging". Lighters had no power and had to be towed by tugs to Heybridge Basin. Unloading was piece by piece ashore into black tarred storage sheds (before the days of cranes) or loaded into lighters that were pulled by horses along the Navigation to Browns at Springfield. Lighters with timber for Sadd's were towed by tugs to their wharf in Maldon Harbour.

Stuart Joslin told the author that Sadd's converted the lighter Alice (known as Black Alice because she was tarred all over) to accommodate men unloading the ships and was moored near Stansgate Hole. Alice was fitted out with bunks, had a shed on the deck and basic cooking facilities for men who stayed on her for up to a week.

During W.W.2, Italian prisoners of war were brought in from Colchester by lorry; the lighter was moored in Heybridge Creek and used as a mess. The man designated as cook was not allowed to do any other task, as Harold Springett, Sadd's manager in charge of the unloading, found out when he offered the cook other work for extra money. The Geneva Convention does not allow this.

During W.W.2, soldiers were based on the Osea Island; a pill box is still visible at East Point to watch out for enemy intruders up the River Blackwater. Flt/Lt. P. S. Weaver was killed on 31st August 1940, when his Hawker Hurricane crashed in the mud at West Point. The pier was demolished during W.W.2.

The 28th Company of the Royal Army Service Corps was stationed in Heybridge Basin during W.W.2. They had three or four motorised wooden barges to carry their machinery and a 'Tid' tug. In preparation for D Day, a dozen or more Thames lighters were tied up along the sea wall between the Basin and Mill Beach. Soldiers were billeted in The Towers and Manor House on Osea Island. The yacht Francis II was commandeered, moored off Osea Island, and turned into a river patrol boat.

There are many tall tales about Osea. Rodney Hill from Mersea recounts that early in W.W.2 a group of Mersea fishermen acquired sacks of raisins and rowed ashore on Osea. They laid a trail of raisins to the shore where the sea dipped before a spit of land; turkeys crowded onto the spit of land where they eventually drowned. The fishermen collected the carcasses, rowed back to Mersea Island and sold the turkeys in local public houses at a cheap price which made the fishermen popular. They were arrested but the police could not produce sufficient evidence to charge them.

18.6 Later history

A newspaper reported that David Shayler, the journalist and former M15 officer, retreated to Osea Island while waiting for his trial after being charged on 21st September 2002 with passing secret documents to the Mail on Sunday in September 1977. He was found guilty and sentenced to three months in prison in November 2006. He appeared in the news again in 2009 when he was dressed as a transvestite calling himself Dolores and living in a squat. He proclaimed himself a Messiah and declared the world will end in 2012.

There was a time when Wembley Stadium greyhounds were kept on Osea Island.

Osea Island was sold to brothers David and Michael Cole for £70,000 in 1960 who used to reach the island in their private plane. They sold Osea to Cambridge University in 1968 for study purposes, experimental farming and the breeding of rare sheep and as an investment. The contract stipulated that the Coles were to be given first option to buy it back if the university decided to sell.

David Cole and his wife Hilary bought it back in 1986. They planted 3,000 new trees and began to renovate the buildings clustered around the high ground in the centre of the island along a short stretch of road known as The Chase. The first building is the Manor House and nearby is the estate office with black weatherboarded Pine Cottage just beyond. A couple of small buildings stand on either side of East Street.

The Maldon builder, Arthur Baxter, erected Rivermere, the convalescent home, an imposing Edwardian building on high ground. It was converted into ten luxury apartments in 1989 overlooking the old naval chapel, now two flats. There were twenty residents in 2005. Mr. and Mrs. Cole lived on the island in the Captain's House.

Brendan Quin, a psychiatric nurse, opened Causeway Retreat, part of the Priory Hospital Group, as a rehabilitation centre on Osea Island in 2004. The medical director was Dr. Mike Phillips. Patients were treated for drug and alcohol addiction as well as for general psychiatric conditions including depression, bi-polar disorder and stress related illnesses. Treatment cost £5,000 to £10,000 a week. The internet reported that among the famous people who have been treated there are Nicholas Knatchbull, Earl Mountbatten's great grandson, Count Gottfried von Bismarck, grandson of the Iron Chancellor and Amy Winehouse who alludes to this in a song. Staff travelled to Osea by boat when the causeway was covered with water but times varied according to tides. Sometimes, staff stayed overnight when shift hours did not coincide with tides. New staff were required to sign a confidential clause in contracts forbidding them to divulge the names of patients, and visitors could not go to the island since it was privately owned.

At the end of 2009, the Care Quality Commission investigated the Causeway Retreat for eight months to ascertain whether services were being provided as an independent hospital without the necessary registration. Since May 2010, only patients requiring non registered treatment were admitted while the Causeway application for registration is being considered. The Causeway Retreat was closed and fined in the autumn of 2010 because it did not hold the necessary licences to give these treatments. This was during the ownership of Nigel Frieda a music producer.

In 2011, the island is being advertised as "an exclusive private island enclosed by 4 miles of beaches and coastline ... abundance of wildlife and rare birds ... unspoilt and tranquil with a wide choice of accommodation; from the ten bedroom manor house, the small hamlet of fourteen beautifully appointed cottages in the village around seventeenth century farm buildings to seven courtyard apartments and the Old Chapel which are let weekly and for short breaks. Just relax or choose from a range of free sporting or outdoor activities; the gym, heated outdoor pool, tennis, art studio and many more activities. For a fee, a fishing boat can be hired; an instructor will guide bird watching, etc. Catering can be organised in the chapel for large parties, otherwise it is self catering".

19.0 Langford, our near neighbour

19.1 St Giles Church and the Byron Family

St Giles in Langford is part of the united benefice of Heybridge with St Andrew's Heybridge and St Giles, Heybridge Basin. The link with the Byron family goes back to the Westcombe family. They were lords of the manor of Langford and owned most of the land in the parish from 1680 when Nicholas Westcombe bought it. J. E. Westcombe died intestate and his property descended to his nieces; the three Misses Westcombe, daughters of Langford's rector, the Rev. W. Westcombe. One of them, Mary Jane Westcombe, married the Hon. Frederick Charles Byron MA who was the second son of Lord Byron in 1851. Her son, the Hon. Rev. Frederick Ernest Charles Byron, born 1861, became rector of St Giles Church, Langford in 1890. She was the patron of the living. Frederick moved to the family seat Thrumpton Hall in Nottinghamshire in 1914 and was the vicar of Thrumpton until 1941. He became the tenth Lord Byron on the death of his brother in 1917. (The British Romantic poet, the sixth Lord Byron, lived from 1788-1824.)

The restoration and extensive rebuilding of the Norman church between 1880 and 1882 by Edward Browning was paid for by the Hon. Mrs. Mary Jane Byron. Since apses are usually at the eastern end, the church is unique in England and rare in Europe because it has a semi-circular western apse. The bell tower was added on the chancel's north side. The reredos by Gerald Cogswell is elaborately carved with two angels in low relief, brightly painted in silver, red and blue. There is a stained glass window to the memory of Mary Jane Byron who died in 1909. The window has a small but detailed picture of the restored church in the uppermost portion.

19.2 Langford Grove

John Johnson built Langford Grove for Nicholas Westcombe in 1782. "The fine house had five bays of two and a half storeys with single storey connecting passages and then three bay pedimented outer pavillions." Buildings of Essex, Pevsner and Bettley. This elegant house and its surrounding ancillary premises were set in a finely wooded park.

John James Strutt was born in Langford Grove in November 1842 when his parents were tenants. He inherited 7,000 acres in Essex when his father died in 1873 and became the third Baron Rayleigh.

Langford Grove had various tenants; in 1923 Mrs. Curtis opened it as a high class girls' school attended by girls from the Continent, especially France. The school existed until 1939 when buildings were requisitioned by the army who caused damage so bad that the main building was demolished in 1953. Then Colonel Claude Granville Lancaster, Member of Parliament for the Fylde from 1938 to1970 used one of the outer pavillions as shooting lodge. His mother was a member of the de Crespigny family.

19.3 Langford and Ulting Village Hall

Langford and Ulting Parish Council's plans for creating a village hall in the old Victorian cow shed were well ahead when they received a devastating blow. The rating system that replaced the poll tax resulted in only domestic premises rates going to Maldon District Council while business rates went to central government. Central government redistributed this money to parts of the country according to their judgement of need. Wealthy Essex lost some of this money to other parts of the country, for example the poorer former industrial regions in the North. Langford lost the rates from Southend Waterworks and Doe's agricultural business. The plans to transform the cattle shed next to Langford Mill into a village hall had to be postponed until alternative sources of funds were found. The conversion was planned by the architects, Plater Claiborne, and won a conservation award in 1984. The attractive new hall opened on 5th November 1993.

The hall is used as a nursery school during term time and is heavily booked by various organisations at other times. It is away from houses and suitable for small private parties. The author was puzzled to see cars in the car park one Christmas day and learned, much later, that a family had used it for the day. They had cooked Christmas lunch in the kitchen and their young children had been able to play in the hall with more freedom than in their small homes.

19.4 Lady Byron and The White Hart, Langford and council houses

Edward Eavery ran the White Hart public house in Langford from 1832 to the early 1840s when he went to the Flying Tinker, a beer house, situated on a narrow site along the roadside on what is now the car park for Doe's shop; it closed down in 1950.

Langford village was part of the Lord Byron estate and Lady Byron, a strict Methodist, refused to allow a public house to continue in the village. She closed it and provided a cottage, Turners, for the Goodey family who had run the public house from 1845 to 1867.

What is left of the White Hart is now called Mill Cottage; it is opposite the main entrance to the Waterworks Pumping Station on the corner of the road leading to Maldon Golf Club. The cottage is all that remains; the stables, chaise-house, coal house and brew house have disappeared.

Lady Byron would also not allow council houses to be built in Langford. Ken Russell, verger at All Saints' Church, Maldon, grew up in a council house just over Langford Parish boundary.

Langford Mill. SOURCE Ellen Hedley collection

20.0 Business in and around Heybridge yesterday and today

We learn of the major industries in parts of Great Britain that have disappeared but little publicity is given to places like Heybridge and Maldon which have lost their major employers since the mid twentieth century.

20.1 Bentall's

Their story is told in Section 4.0

20.2 John Sadd and Sons

Little remains of the timber yards, wharfs, sawmills and joinery works and builders' merchants of Maldon's biggest employers from 1729 which can be glimpsed from Fullbridge and behind the Causeway. Sadd's became the largest employer in Maldon following two and a half centuries of growth after John Sadd, a carpenter, moved from Chelmsford to Maldon in 1729.

Confusingly, the eldest son of each John Sadd was called John. John Sadd broadened the firm's activities between 1780 and 1820 when he purchased a number of Thames barges and hoys to transport imports of building materials by sea. He bought a considerable land holding in Maldon including a part share in a wharf.

From 1823, a large variety of goods were carried to and from Harrison's wharf in London every week. This continued through the nineteenth century but gradually decreased with competition from the railway. By 1831, Sadd's had acquired considerable wharfage from Colonel J. H. Strutt. John Granger Sadd guided the firm for forty years; a time of phenomenal growth. He brought the firm to the forefront of the country's timber trade. Soft woods sawn into planks were imported from Norway, Finland and Quebec while British hard woods were traded and had to be sawn up in Maldon. Large quantities of Welsh roofing slates and other building materials were brought by sea to Maldon Port as the firm became the largest builders' merchants in East Anglia. Steam powered machinery for woodworking was introduced in the works and included replacing the old saw pits. Sawn and planed timber was sold to the building trade. Gradually, joinery was discontinued.

In 1871 Sadd's bought their first steam traction engine for hauling great baulks of timber to their saw mills. This monster engine weighed about 12 tons and was a novelty. There were many complaints about the amount of noise it made: the smell and glaring fire, the black smoke that belched from its tall chimney, that it frightened cattle and terrified horses, it damaged the roads and bridges. Indeed, it destroyed Battles Bridge at Rawreth in June of that year. In several cases, the firm was fined by the Courts for the damage done by the machine.

Sadd's acquired a fleet of barges to bring timber from large ships off Osea Island to the Fullbridge wharfs. The expansion in scale and size of this family firm by 1889 made it advisable to seek the legal protection of incorporation as a private limited company. John Sadd and Sons Ltd. was created with capital of £38,000 divided into 7,600 £5 shares held by the Sadd family. Alfred Thorn was appointed company secretary at a salary of £20 per month. John Granger Sadd was chairman until his death in 1900. John Price Sadd, his eldest son, became responsible for the importation and processing of soft wood, Harry William Sadd, the next son, looked after the buying, carting and sawing of home-grown hard woods. Herbert Eustace, the third son, had a varied career abroad before he became the company's chief engineer.

In 1873, the new saw mill was destroyed by fire, the replacement cost £1,797.6s.8d. This mill was extended many times over the next ten years. The works were reconstructed following a disastrous fire in 1909. The lay-out was redesigned with two mills; a resawing and planing mill on the same site and a log mill at the opposite end of the yard. New machinery was installed, powered by electricity instead of steam. There was electric lighting throughout the works; the electricity was generated using wood refuse from the saw mills as fuel. The plant and three directors' homes were lit by electricity. By 1912, all Maldon and Heybridge could receive electricity for lighting, cooking and heating from the Sadd's generators and the first water heater was installed in the town. John Sadd and Sons were the sole suppliers of electricity to Maldon and Heybridge between 1912 and 1931. Customers had to pay 2d. a unit for heating and 3d. a unit for lighting. In 1931, Sadd's sold the supply rights to the County of London Electric Supply Co. Ltd.

During W.W.1 joinery was resumed and women were employed for the first time to produce War Office hutments, doors, sashes and frames. After the war, the firm expanded rapidly establishing branches in Southend, Clacton, Wickford, Hornchurch, Chelmsford and a London office off Park Lane to which the manager commuted daily from Maldon. They owned and used several Ford trucks and articulated lorries, next they acquired their first Foden lorries with diesel engines and later, articulated Bedford lorries with petrol engines.

An account of 1937 described how gangs carried lengths of timber on leather shoulder pads from the holds of barges and coasters up the angled gang planks to the timber stacks. There is a permanent display of scale models in Maldon Museum in the Park. Brenda Wombwell lived in Wantz Road and remembers hearing Sadd's hooter going off at 7.40 in the morning and her mother prompting her to hurry since the final hooter sounded at 8am and workers arriving after that were penalised.

During W.W.2 Sadd's fulfilled a large contract for army huts; they manufactured motor launches of the Fairmile type, motor torpedo boats, air sea rescue craft, pontoons, small assault craft, and motor fishing vessels as well as aircraft parts. Their barges went to Dunkirk to assist in the rescue. Harold Springett spent his whole working life at Sadd's; he started as office boy at 14 and eventually became foreman of the Sadd's Southend on Sea works timber yard and later went to Clacton on Sea to do the same job. He was called back to Maldon to manage the yard and transport in Maldon at the outbreak of W.W.2. Women worked on the saw benches for the first time as men were called up and he found them very good workers.

When Sadd's acquired Maldon Ironworks and converted it for the manufacture of radio and television sets, Mr. Springett became manager there. During the 1960s Causeway Meadows were developed; storage sheds were erected, a new soft wood mill was created and production flow lines were installed to make standard windows, kitchen cabinets and door frames. The wharf was re-aligned allowing three ships to discharge at a time.

Boulton and Paul originated in Norwich in 1797 from an ironmonger's shop. They grew to undertake large building contracts and were a general manufacturing firm. From 1915, they developed into an important aircraft manufacturer until 1934 when this side of the firm was sold and transferred to Wolverhampton. In 1956, they decided to concentrate on standard joinery. Boulton and Paul were acquired by the Dowty Group in 1961. In the late 1960s Boulton and Paul acquired John Sadd's and were able to add flush doors to their range. Robert Shanks, a Boulton and Paul main board director was drafted to Maldon to be managing director of the Maldon business. Boulton and Paul acquired Stephens and Carter, a ladder manufacturer, from High Wycombe in 1974 their whole operation was installed in new factory premises in Causeway Meadow. In 1980, it was decided that the Maldon operation should be administered from Norwich and Mr. Shanks was made redundant.

John Sadd's Merchanting Division was sold to Jewson and Sons, a Norwich based timber and builders' merchants, a subsidiary of the International Timber Corporation in 1978. After big losses in 1996, the Rugby Group took over Boulton and Paul who sold it to Jeld Wen Inc., a privately owned worldwide joinery manufacturer. During these times, Sadd's works were closed down and the site became derelict as did Boulton and Paul's Norwich works. The closure meant that skilled workers and training opportunities were lost from the biggest employer in the district. A Heybridge hairdresser told the author that two members of two generations of her family were thrown out of work by the closure. The port of Maldon declined.

20.3 Maldon Iron Works

A letter heading: Maldon Iron Works Company Ltd

                                        Iron Founders and Manufacturers
                                        Carts Vans and Wagon Builders
                                        Maldon Essex

Joseph Warren had a foundry on Broad Street Green in 1833 although the whereabouts of the site is not known. Warren manufactured the Goldhanger plough which William Bentall had not patented; it sold for £2.7s.6d.

In 1853, Joseph Warren re-located his foundry to Fullbridge, Maldon adjacent to the railway line and opposite Station Road and the business prospered. He built Foundry House in 1863 for himself on the Maldon side of the works. It was double fronted and 'Georgian' in style. The house was occupied by John Charles Float, the manager, in 1891.

Foundry Terrace, a terrace of twelve houses was built at right angles to Fullbridge behind Foundry House for the workers in 1865. This is where the entrance to Tesco is today. Four of the cottages had six rooms and eight had four rooms. A photograph of the work force in the late nineteenth century shows that the cottages housed only a few of the workers. The cottages were used as temporary housing before their demolition in the 1960s at the same time as Foundry House. James Bettley describes the later factory building as "Two three storey yellow brick ranges of 1875 in parallel with gabled ends to the street, with oculi and windows set in round arches. Inside, cast iron columns support deep transverse beams".

Warren invented a plough that was a commercial success which was re-designed by Baker of Writtle, estate agent, surveyor and auctioneer.

Maldon and Heybridge Co-operative Society had its origins among the labour force of Maldon Iron Works in 1873.

New works premises were erected in 1875; offices, warehouse and finishing shop behind which there was a turnery with lathes and a Ransome circular saw. There was a foundry with three furnaces and a small scrap furnace, a steam engine and boiler house and a nut and bolt shop and various milling shops. There were stables, a cart shed and blacksmiths' and wheelwrights' shops beside warehouses for iron and plough shares on the site. The exhibition Maldon Museum mounted in 2010 about Maldon Iron Works displayed advertisements for:

Stacking elevators, Water carts
80 gallon £7.15s.0d., 100 gallon £8.10s.0d., 120 gallon £9.5s.0d., 150 gallon £10.0s.0d.,
Handsome wooden cart for two horses and one horse

Essex County Council placed an order for cast iron direction posts in 1920. It was the largest contract ever received by the foundry and led to 90% of all cast iron direction posts in Essex being made in Maldon. A rare example is to be seen at the junction of The Street with Hall Road. The author raised the question of listing this example of Maldon Iron Works direction posts in a Heybridge Parish Council meeting around 2000 and believed this had been achieved until she sought the wording of the listing. The Heybridge Parish Council considered the issue again in 2010 and decided to seek listing from Maldon District Council and to approach Essex Heritage Trust with a view to applying for a grant from them towards restoring the sign with its gas lamp. The application was turned down.

Root shredders or graters were being produced in 1885. Smaller products displayed included grave markers, a shoe repairer's snob iron kept in most homes for repairing shoes, padlocks large and small, and a tool resembling a small lawn rake that was pushed into the mud and, with luck, lifted an eel when it was withdrawn.

Maldon Iron Works manufactured farm implements and machinery until early 1955. Sadd's, substantial shareholders since 1947, bought out other shareholders in 1954 when they adapted part of the building to produce veneered radio and television cabinets. Later, more of the building was used to manufacture flush doors including doors for the Queen Elizabeth II liner.

Boulton and Paul took over Sadd's and continued to use the building for the manufacture of TV and radio cabinets until 1981 when it was closed and sold. Foundry Terrace was demolished while the main building has seen various adaptations; the first floor became a snooker club, part of the ground floor a restaurant for a short time and later Cash Converters and Wickham Flooring moved into the ground floor. In 2010, Domino Pizzas opened to sell take away pizzas.

A plaque outside Maldon Ironworks commemorates Stephen Knight, a Protestant, who was burned at the stake there on 28th March 1555. Researchers now believe he was not a Maldon man but was executed there to frighten heretics.

20.4 The loss of employment in and around Heybridge in the last quarter of the twentieth century

Bentall's made Heybridge a 'factory' town where agricultural products were manufactured from 1805 until the site was finally closed down in 1985 by the parent company, Acrow. Six to seven hundred people had been employed there at one time; now the site has been taken over by many small firms.

Sadd's was taken over by Boulton and Paul in 1969 who transferred much production to their other branches. When the Rugby Group acquired Boulton and Paul, they ceased the majority of the old Sadd activities. The site and the wharfs became derelict. Sadd's had employed twelve hundred workers at their peak.

Maldon Ironworks was part of Boulton and Paul when it closed in 1981. The main factory building has been retained; the ground floor has retail outlets and the first floor leisure businesses.

The former Crittall's and Ever Ready factory buildings, were used by ICS to manufacture oil rig equipment. When the firm became part of ICS Triplex, most of the manufacturing went to their other factories and little remained in Heybridge. ICS Triplex continues to use part of the site including the warehouse but various units have been let to small firms and the original Crittall building remains empty other than for short lets as storage. In July 2011, the assembling of equipment ceased to be carried out in Heybridge, it was carried out on site. This means more empty premises in Hall Road and the loss of skilled workers.

Houlding's Triangle garage closed in 2000. They had employed around forty people. See Section 13.7

Doe Bros: Ernest, Hugh and Hubert Doe bought the garage on the corner of Spital Road in Maldon in 1937 and became Ford main agents. They traded as Doe Motors from 1962. A fine showroom with workshops adjoining operated on the east side of the Spital Road. Later, a big showroom was built on the opposite side of the road with extensive car parking space behind it. A Chelmsford firm, Underwood's, bought the business but they sold it to Lookers who closed the Maldon business and sold the sites to developers who have built houses on both sides of the road.

Heybridge Shops

In various places in this account, shops have been mentioned, often only in the front room of homes. All, except Hill's, have disappeared by the first decade of the twenty-first century and even Hill's now sell only furniture, carpets and electrical goods. The Street now has a fish and chip shop, the Queen's head public house where food is sold, two Turkish barber's shops, a hairdresser, a pet shop and five or six shops that sell food to be taken away to be eaten. There used to be a variety of shops on both sides of The Street; now on the north side there is a long blank 2 metre high brick wall behind which are various workshops and their sales outlets. There are no shops in Heybridge Basin today: gone are the little shops in the front rooms of houses or

Brian and Chris Stubbings started their butcher's shop in 1984 and retired in 2010

PHOTO by kind permission of Brian and Chris Stubbings

in huts in garden. The four caravan parks have closed their shops.

Thousands of skilled jobs were lost in Heybridge and Heybridge Basin in the last quarter of the twentieth century resulting in men and women having to travel afar for work. Valuable opportunities for training with skilled, experienced workers have disappeared locally. Money, wages, investment and trade have left the neighbourhood. It is fortunate that there are many small firms based in units on the Bentall's factory site. Only Hill's furniture, carpets and electrical shop is locally owned and run now.

21.0 Education provision

21.1 Schools in the first half of the nineteenth century

Schools were generally sponsored by a benefactor or affiliated to a church in the first half of the nineteenth century. In 1839 Rev. Crane reported to the London Diocesan Board of Education that no schools existed in the parish (of Heybridge) but considerable numbers attended an inter denomination school for dissenters in Maldon and some at a Meeting House in Heybridge Basin. After 1870, the newly established enlarged inter denominational school boards could make school attendance compulsory for 5 to 13 year olds (with some exceptions).

21.2 Chapel Reading Room

The Heybridge Basin census of 1841 records Mary Huring, as a school teacher. No further details are known.

21.3 Reading Rooms and the Heybridge Ironworks School for Boys and Girls

This school was opened by E. H. Bentall in August 1864 in the Drill Hall at the end of the large building known as the Headquarters. The school log book records that on the first day, 29th August 1864, fifty-three scholars were formed into four classes. By October of that year, there were one hundred and two on the roll.

The school had the distinction of being inspected by Matthew Arnold HMI (Her Majesty's Inspector of Schools) in July, 1867. He found "the standard below the usual average in British schools, but there is much demand for the children's labour and it is difficult to keep the pupils in school". Matthew Arnold was an eminent poet and critic who became an HMI from 1822 to 1888 because he needed the income. He travelled constantly on tours of inspection across England and studied education on the Continent. His reports as a school inspector and his observations on education in France and Germany had an important influence on English education.

Mr. Joad, a certified teacher, became headmaster with his wife as infant mistress in June 1893. In 1894, there were two hundred and forty pupils and the headmaster was Mr. W. T. Holmes.

Basin children attended the (Bentall's) Iron Works School. Many walked along the Navigation path four times a day as there was no school for children under 9 in the Basin. Basin children could go to The Towers for coffee or chocolate at lunchtime. Jill Babbage's mother attended this school.

Special twenty-five day holidays were granted by the school so that mothers could take their children fruit and pea picking and a further ten days to help with the harvest.

21.4 Rev. Walter Waring's School Room

The 1870 Education Act decreed that children should attend school between the ages of 5 and 10 but it was not free. St Andrew's Church School was a small, red bricked Victorian school built in 1869 by the Rev. Walter Waring at his own expense. The school stood on waste land adjoining the River Blackwater in Church Street (the present Street) and pupils were either the children of Bentall's employees or of local farmers. The Act of 1880 made school attendance compulsory for 5 to 10 year olds but children under 13 could be employed if a certificate from the headmaster was obtained saying that the child had achieved the standard decreed by the local school board. One pupil who left before his appointed time to work at Bentall's was ordered to return to school by a factory inspector. The school opened on two Saturday mornings in May so that Frederick Austin could attain the necessary 250 half-day's attendance in five years to qualify for leaving school. His granddaughter, Norah Austin, remembers him as a very strict parent of his nine children. He became the Heybridge Basin River Pilot; the only one listed in the censuses from 1841 to 1901.

The Rev. Waring's School grant was reduced by one tenth in 1880 when the teaching of arithmetic fell below standard. The school was enlarged in 1888 when the average attendance was seventy-nine children and Mr. Hoskins was the headmaster.

The Rev. John Wade, the United Reformed minister in Burnham on Crouch, who grew up in Heybridge, reminds us of the harsh conditions of life in Victorian times; The Street and Hall Road were often ankle deep in mud in winter and a dust bowl in summer that would be sprayed daily with water from a horse-drawn water cart. These roads were subject to flooding when high tides forced water up through drains and water swept through the school and houses. Indeed, on Monday, 24th February 1882, water swept through the school leaving a tide mark on the classroom walls and the dampness of the walls necessitated the school closing. The Rev. Wade wrote that dampness and poor living conditions caused ill health on a big scale; Rose Miller was frequently absent because of ill health, Frances James stayed at home to look after her sick mother, Matilda Bignall left school on 10th December 1880 when she was not yet 10 years old. The school was closed from 10th May to 15th June 1883 because of measles. In 1888, Emily Nichols died of typhoid, Frank Mulley, Stanley Buckley and Elizabeth Chaney were removed from the register because of ill health and the Medical Officer of Health visited the school when there was a bad outbreak of croup. Very bad weather affected school attendance in March 1878 and February 1879 and few pupils could reach the school due to flooded roads in the following June and October.

There was a holiday of two weeks at Christmas. Children helped their mothers pea picking for three weeks in June. It is recorded that in June 1892, children sat slumped in their wooden desks on a hot afternoon because they had been awake since 4am picking peas. There were further odd days off for the circuses, fairs and the Maldon Agricultural Show. In August, the Iron Works School joined St Andrew's School for tea and games together. At Christmas 1889, Mr. Harrington, a Heybridge grocer, gave St Andrew's children oranges - a rare treat.

The parish rates paid for education but parents had to contribute a sum called School Pence that Mrs. Wren, the vicar's wife, collected. The poor were excused this. The fee was abolished in 1891 by an Act of Parliament. The school day began at 8.30am but not until 9am in bad weather when the registers were marked. The children were taught history, poetry, knitting, arithmetic, writing, and singing.

In 1893, the Evening Continuation School started when thirteen young men began evening study, followed the next evening by nine young ladies.

Before W.W.1, children were allowed to leave school at 13 if they passed the school leaving examination; otherwise they had to stay on another year. Girls from large families often went into domestic service. Flora Thompson wrote in Lark Rise that this eased the overcrowding in the cottages. The author was told of one large family in the 1950s where six girls slept in one bedroom where the father had welded two double beds one above the other to accommodate five of them sleeping head to tail while the eldest girl had a single bed. The boys slept in another bedroom. Each child had their daily allotted tasks; the eldest girl who was still at school had to get in the coal, peel the vegetables before she could join her friends.

21.5 Schools in the vicinity of Heybridge

At the beginning of the twentieth century, school holidays were geared to seasonal farm work of fruit and pea picking. Twenty-five days were granted for this seasonal work.

21.5a The Old Dame School House Heybridge Basin

The Old Dame School was housed in Basin Road. The teacher known as Aunt Alice charged 1d. a week. A pupil was sent to the pub for three pennyworth of beer on a Monday morning after the fees were collected. One night, the old lady was tarred and feathered.

21.5b Woodham Walter School

William White records in his History, Gazetteer and Directory of the County of Essex of 1848 that the school was built in 1829 and had sixty children in attendance who pay 1d. a week or 2d. a week when only one is sent by a family.

21.5c Great Braxted School

The school was built in Tudor style in 1844 by Captain Du Cane.

21.5d Langford School

The school was designed by Frederick Chancellor in 1874. It was National School for forty boys and girls. The brick building had a bellcote at the west end and the master's house at the other. The school became a public elementary school in 1900. After W.W.1 only a small number of pupils were on the roll and it closed on 29th January 1922. Frederick Chancellor was a renowned Victorian architect, with offices in Chelmsford and London, who designed churches, schools, houses and many public buildings in Essex. He was Mayor of Chelmsford seven times.

21.5e Ulting School

The school was built in 1865 with a capacity for sixty pupils. It closed in 1910, leaving Ernie Doe and Reg Claydon having to walk 2½ miles to Hatfield Peverel School.

21.6 Heybridge School 1913

In 1913, the new all age school designed by Mr. P. M. Beaumont to provide accommodation for four hundred and sixty-eight scholars, opened on Monday, 2nd June 1913. The tender of Messrs. Parren and Sons of Erith for £5,667 had been accepted but was largely exceeded (Maldon Advertiser 30th May 1913). The accommodation consisted of an assembly hall, a drill hall and nine classrooms, a babies' room, masters' and mistresses' rooms, heating chamber, three cloakrooms, ample lavatories, cupboards etc. The average attendance then was three hundred and thirty pupils.

21.7 The pupil teacher system of teacher training

21.7a Beginnings

The pupil teacher training system was established in 1846. Originally, pupil teachers were indentured to the school head for five years. The head was responsible for training them in methods of teaching as well as furthering their academic studies. It was an arduous route into the teaching profession. Centres were established and apprentices attended up to half the week in school time. Wendy Robinson (National Union of Teachers Headquarters' staff) records that the Colchester Centre complained that heads failed to release pupil teachers due to staff shortages.

Teacher training centres had two main tasks; to teach the professional expertise of teaching and to further the pupil teacher's academic studies. The centres were staffed by educated people. The centre curriculum varied but the courses were demanding; as many as thirteen academic subjects were studied and the too frequent examinations were held quarterly as well as annually and finally the Queen's (later King's) Scholarship examination took place. All girls had to be proficient in needlework!

In November 1888, St Andrew's School, Heybridge closed for one week to allow a teacher to sit the Certificate of Education examination. Successful King's Scholarship students had the opportunity to go on to training colleges for two year courses. These colleges were residential and many colleges were supported by the Church of England (C of E) as well as other denominations. Many Essex teachers went to Hockerill College at Bishops Stortford, a C of E college.

It is not known where the Pupil Teacher Centre in Maldon was before 1907 but Rodney Bass records that his grandmother, Elizabeth Jane Fisher, cycled to and from Althorne Hall to this centre. She was born in 1885 and had come south with the family from Goosnargh in Lancashire in 1893. She was educated at Mayland School and then at a private school in Southend. Rodney records that "she inherited the Fisher gift of music and was very good with children and so it was natural she became a teacher". She taught at Burnham on Crouch Infant School where she "so inspired the children that she taught them to sing as a choir while she sang alto and they gave performances" (which was unheard of in those days). Elizabeth Fisher married Henry Lister Bass in 1906.

21.7b Maldon Grammar School

Alderman Ralph Breeder, a successful Maldon business man, bequeathed £300 for the "mayntenance of a schoolmaster to teach a grammar school within the town" in 1608. This money was used to purchase several properties in and around Maldon High Street and the rents were to be used to supplement a schoolmaster's income even until the end of the nineteenth century. The Maldon Grammar School has had a long list of headmasters; it has occupied various properties in the town and the number of boy pupils has fluctuated. There were only five boys on the roll when the Rev. Ryland was appointed head in 1895. His success may be measured by the quick rise to fifty-two boys but the trustees were unable to finance the new buildings needed. A new scheme for the governance of the grammar school with a wider spread of representatives failed to finance new buildings.

It was fortunate that the 1902 Education Act could be used to solve the problem; it aimed to provide more secondary education. The Act abolished school boards and created Local Education Authorities to organise funding, employment of teachers and the allocation of school places, resulting in Essex County Council taking over Maldon Grammar School and merging it with a new boys' County High School and the school became a Pupil Teacher Centre to which girls were admitted. Essex County Council erected new buildings on Fairfield land adjoining Fambridge Road in 1907. Robert P. Mumford MA was headmaster from 1904 to 1912. It would seem that Mr. Mumford ran a boys' preparatory school in 1910 in The Gables in High Street Maldon at the same time.

The 1907 Grammar School buildings can still be seen today amid the many extensions that have been made since the formation of the Plume Comprehensive School in 1970. The school leaving age was raised to 16 in 1972 with one leaving date each year; the last Friday in June.

In 1906, pupil teachers had an extra year at school when the school leaving age was 13 and began their apprenticeship at the age of 14. 60% of teachers in elementary schools were trained following the pupil teacher route. This method of recruitment was a necessary way of solving the acute shortage of teachers especially in rural areas; it was cheap (the clue to many educational "reforms"!) but success depended on the head teacher's calibre and own academic education. He had to teach and carry out the dual task of professional and academic education of the pupil teacher. How to find the time was the problem.

21.7c 1902 Education Act

After the implementation of the 1902 Act, girls (and it was mainly girls) were recruited from secondary schools as pupil teachers at 16 years of age and their apprenticeship lasted two years.

Success depended on close co-operation between centre staff, the pupil and the head. It was not unusual for pupil teachers to take small groups at first before being responsible for whole classes and they taught younger children (the lower standards) and later older children (higher standards) at a time when class sizes were much larger than today.

Pupil teachers came from "independent, respectable, religious, hard-working, upper working class" families. It involved a financial burden on the family; pupil teachers' earnings were low, books were costly and there were the travel costs. The majority of pupils went into schools as uncertificated assistant teachers.

Chelmsford Girls' High School was opened in 1907 and Colchester Girls' High School in 1909 as part of the expansion of secondary education due to the 1902 Act of Parliament. Girls were not admitted to Maldon Grammar School until 1919.

The Board of Education designated the new Heybridge School as a pupil teacher training centre in 1913 because Mr. Benjamin Peacock ACP(Hons) had been successful as head of the Iron Works School in Heybridge for the previous seven years.

It would seem that local teachers who trained through the pupil teacher route included Ethel Whittaker, Mrs. Eva Mott (nee King) who told the author that she cycled from Heybridge to Latchingdon School and later married Mr. Mott the Heybridge builder, Mrs. Duce (nee Withams), Mrs. O'Shaughnessy (nee Collins) who cycled to Great Totham School. Jill Climie's mother told the author about the training days in Maldon when she was teaching at Great Totham School, she had to resign when she married in 1935.

The early twentieth century grammar schools provided education for aspiring teachers and, eventually, led to the closure of pupil teacher centres. In Wendy Robinson's view, "The pupil teacher system did turn out many competent and efficient teachers for elementary schools".

21.8 Reminiscences of Heybridge School

Many Heybridge ex-pupils will remember Mr. Gibbins, headmaster from 1920 until 1945. He wore a navy blue suit and a stiff rounded white collar. Head teachers taught full-time in those days. Mr. Gibbins taught the top class of this all age school. He was proud that all the pupils from Heybridge Basin, between ten and twenty per year, could read and write when they left school. Betty McDonald remembers Mr. Gibbins as a very strict headmaster; boys and girls feared his cane. Harold Lewis regarded him as a very good headmaster. Betty Chittenden recalls that in wartime there were special War Savings Weeks to raise money for ships or planes etc. Mr. Gibbins played a big part in these campaigns and during his frequent absences his class was squeezed in with Miss Fitzgerald's class. Miss Fitzgerald married Mr. Peck, a well known local window cleaner, whom the author remembers seeing cleaning the shop windows in Maldon High Street before 9am.

Miss Grimmer claimed that all the pupils from Heybridge School left being able to read. She used to give pupils scraps of fabric that they frayed; Jill Babbage believed she used the threads to stuff cushions.

The football team of 1924 with Mr. Gibbon on the right side. He was head teacher from 1920 to 1945.
SOURCE Booklet to commemorate the official opening of the new extension and school

The Italian prisoners of war billeted at the Towers seemed to come and go as they pleased. They liked children and played football with them on the Planny. One day, when Jill Babbage misjudged the time and arrived late for afternoon school, she was severely told off by her teacher. Another ex-pupil told me she had a three penny piece decoratively engraved by a prisoner-of-war, one of many they gave to children.

During the W.W.2 school children received one third of a pint of milk at morning break time and Sheila Bremner remembers drinking the milk of children who did not like it. The government provided a teaspoonful of malt extract daily that Miss Wright issued which was disliked by many.

At the age of 11, Sheila Bremner, who was John Playle's grand-daughter, secured a place at Chelmsford Technical School where she specialised in art. There must have been inherited artistic ability in the Playle family because John Playle's son's sketches form a pictorial historical record of Heybridge and his grandson, Andrew Fawcett, is a professional artist.

William Wiseman was taught by Winifred Keeble and Eva Mott. Mrs. Winifred Keeble went on to teach at Maldon Secondary Boys' School where she was very popular and she later became Mayor of Maldon.

The author's great uncle, Dolph Parker, attended the boys' preparatory school run by Robert P. Mumford MA(Oxon) in The Gables, High Street Maldon when the family lived at Bradwell on Sea. In the early 1900s, Dolph boarded in the Gables during the week. His mother brought him to Maldon on Sunday evenings and collected him on Fridays in a pony and trap - she was noted for driving fast! At the same time, Mr. Mumford was headmaster of Maldon Grammar School from 1904 to 1912. Dolph Parker served in the Essex Yeomanry until he transferred to the Royal Flying Corps. He was killed in a flying accident in Norwich in 1918.

In the 1940s, people who wished to be recognised as intending teachers had to do one month's school practice at the age of 15. The author went to Witham Secondary School. When the science master was called up in 1943, she had to take over his classes. Many of the pupils, aged 14, towered above her but the master in the next door laboratory gave her a valuable piece of advice: "quiet teacher, quiet class".

In 1925, the head of Heybridge Junior School was Miss Wright who lived with her brother in Goldhanger Road; other teachers were Mr. Mills, Mrs. Banks, Miss Read, and Miss Whittaker. Miss Whittaker was cousin to Betty Feeney who called her Aunt Ethel. She lived with her parents in Well Terrace, until she joined her W.W.1 widowed sister in Goldhanger Road. The infant teachers were Miss Grimmer, a very popular teacher who lived in Victoria Road, Maldon and Miss Pratt. Later, Mr. Cannel came to teach the older pupils; he was very popular and wore heavy tweed suits with plus fours and lodged with Mrs. Min Houlding.

Betty Feeney started at Mrs. Cloughton's private school next to Ruggles' garage on the Causeway. Pupils at Heybridge School ostracised her at first when she transferred to the council school. In those days, there were a few private schools in the Maldon area including one run by Mrs. Knowles, wife of the deputy head of Maldon Grammar School.

Betty Chittenden entered the infant school in 1938 where she remembers Miss Seager from Great Totham who taught her in the reception class. Miss Grimmer followed, then Miss Wright (who Betty Chittenden found formidable) and in the junior section part of the school, Miss Ethel Whittaker, Miss Read, Mrs. Peck, and finally Mr. Gibbins. Betty was in his class for two years and then went to Maldon Grammar School in 1944.

Mrs. Bentall was a governor and gave every school child a bag containing sweets, oranges etc at Christmas time. Oranges were a luxury few had tasted. John Price, the Tollesbury builder who married Joy Wire, recalls he had a Saturday job, around 1950, at the Co-op greengrocery shop in Maldon High Street when he tasted his first orange and banana.

Mollie Polden recalls coming out of school after the morning sessions and running home along the towpath to Heybridge Basin to eat her dinner and running back afterwards. Her sister, Betty, took sandwiches. Darby Stebbens remembered how he used to walk along the towpath to Heybridge School, and at the end of the day he raced to Wave Bridge to hitch a ride on a canal barge which nearly always arrived around 3.30pm.

Jill Babbage recalls that in 1940 Mrs. Fisher would prepare children's own food, for example boil an egg. School dinners were started in the school in 1943 when one of the infant classrooms was converted into a kitchen and the meals were served in the Assembly Hall. This was the way school children received extra food in wartime while canteens in workplaces supplemented workers' rations and the general public could go to British Restaurants and buy a two course meal for 10d. The Maldon British Restaurant was in the café run by Alice Bees on the Prom.

Ivan McLauchlan used to cycle from Rivals Farm, Tudwick Road, Tolleshunt Major to Heybridge School from the age of 8 to 11 before he went to Maldon Grammar School.

Linda Hawkins remembered, with distaste, the lavatory block outside Heybridge School with bucket toilets that were closely monitored by the teaching staff. The sewer came late to Heybridge.

Past Heybridge pupils from before W.W.2, who had left school at 14, have succeeded in reaching important managerial, technical and professional positions.

Mr. Fenn had been a pupil at Heybridge Primary School, trained to be a teacher before the war and taught there when he left the RAF after W.W.2.

21.9 Changes in 1937

Grammar School admissions

Until 1937 Essex Grammar Schools admitted fee paying pupils and some pupils who took an examination to compete for free scholarship places. After 1937, pupils were only admitted if they passed an entrance examination and fees were paid on a means tested basis until the 1944 Education Act abolished fees.

Heybridge senior pupils went to Maldon Boys' and Girls' secondary schools in 1937. Senior pupils had been attending weekly cookery and woodwork classes in Maldon while Heybridge School was an all age school until 1937. In September of that year, ninety-two senior pupils transferred to Maldon Senior Boys' and Girls' Schools in Wantz Road, Maldon.

Betty McDonald lived in The Basin and had to walk to the Tollgate to board the free school bus. This bus was withdrawn around the end of the war when children had to pay their fare on the service bus at 8.30am from the Basin or cycle. Pupils attending Maldon Grammar School always had to make their own way to the school, many cycled.

Harold Lewis was in the first intake. His form master was the newly qualified teacher, Charles Tait. The senior boys' and girls' schools were in one building but had separate heads and teaching staff. The schools were built in 1911 next door to Maldon Junior and Infants School. They were extensively enlarged in the 1930s into fine premises. The senior schools became Maldon Boys'

Secondary Modern School and Maldon Girls' Secondary Modern School as a result of the 1944 Butler Education Act.

From 1912 to 1963, the boys and girls and the schoolmasters and mistresses never walked through the doors separating the two parts of the building or crossed the imaginary line across the playing field. One 60 year old ex-pupil recalls jokingly that she and her husband did their courting across the line and a young school mistress told the author that she was called into the headmistress' office to be rebuked for talking to a schoolmaster on the field.

The facilities of the building were shared; there were two halls one was an assembly hall with a stage and the other had physical education equipment. Each school had the use of them month and month about. There was an evening badminton club in the PE hall with members from both staffs as well as outsiders. Examples of this plan can be seen in many schools in Essex including Witham, Colchester St Helena's, Moulsham and Rainsford in Chelmsford and Margaret Tabor in Braintree.

In the 1950s there were about three hundred and thirty girls in Maldon Secondary Girls' School. At the end of the Christmas term, the girls' staff entertained the pupils with pantomimes. The scripts contained the usual corny jokes about school life and school dinners, productions were greeted with gales of laughter. Marjorie Curtis, the deputy head, played Prince Charming and the head, Miss Thody, was the Fairy Godmother, the author, whose figure was never sylph like, was in the corps de ballet in a tutu with two other staff who were heavily built. Would this fun be possible today?

School attendance was enforced at various times by the School Board Man, the Educational Welfare Officer or the Attendance Officer. Maldon was served in the 1940s by Sid Harris. He was a real character with a robust sense of humour feared by those playing truant and quite a few of their mothers.

When the school leaving age was raised to 15 in 1947, the author remembers teaching a very reluctant class Religious Education first lesson on Monday mornings. They had not expected to be back at school. She used to draw herself up to her 5ft. 3in. and say to herself "It's them or me, and it's not going to be me".

The boys and girls continued to be educated separately until 1963 when the two schools were combined under one head.

21.10 Heybridge Primary School 1990 to 2010

The all age school built in 1913 served as such until 1937 when boys and girls transferred to Maldon Senior Boys' and Girls' Schools in Maldon. The junior school moved to Rowan Drive new premises in 1971 which had nine classrooms and a hall. In 1986, architect, Bryan Macnamara, was briefed to design nine additional classrooms and an additional hall suitable for community use. This extension was officially opened in 1990.

A group of Heybridge residents produced a report in August 1999 as part of their campaign to secure a second primary school for Heybridge. At that time, vast numbers of houses were being built in Heybridge, especially in the west. Five hundred and eighty-four houses had already been built/approved on Elms Farm, more were expected there and in other parts of the village. 'The Essex School Organisation Plan (ESOP)' stated that they preferred schools with two hundred and ten, and four hundred and twenty pupils. This figure was favoured by primary head teachers known to the author but plans for school provision for Heybridge were based on a primary school of five hundred and eight-six by the then chairman of ECC, or six hundred and nineteen in the ESOP report. Parents contended that the proposed school would be too large and the village needed a second primary school.

There had been plans to build another primary school on Elms Farm when the site was designated as housing land not agricultural land. Some councillors made enquiries to authorities outside Essex and learned that those authorities would have classified it as agricultural land. This may have been the slip up that made it too expensive for Essex County Council to buy the site for a school. Furthermore, it was intended that the school would be built on the proceeds of the sale of The Street School but a covenant surfaced shortly before the proposed sale that said the previous owners, Houldings, must have first option to purchase if the site was not used for educational purposes. These facts were told to the author by a County Councillor and two other Heybridge people. It made it impossible for the sale to proceed.

By 2010, the school has attracted around five hundred pupils because parents send their children to seventeen schools outside Heybridge. Many are easier to access and Heybridge Primary School is too far east from the centre of the village. Children walking to the school from Holloway Road, Crescent Road, Creasen Butt and Elms Farm have to be accompanied, (usually by mothers who walk the route there and back twice a day) on the long, time consuming walk, a total of around eight or nine miles. Today, these parents with their primary aged children and younger children in a buggy have to start as early as 7.45am or the children are taken by car on their parents' way to work. One Crescent Road mother said she had to run a car to take her children to school.

Had the second primary school been built on Elms Farm where the birth rate then was higher than average, children from houses on the Causeway which attract young families and first time buyers would have been able to walk to school and ease the pressure on schools in Maldon.

The old Street School building was split into Enterprise Start up Units for new business but this was discontinued and a Pupil Referral Unit for pupils with special educational needs from Chelmsford, the Dengie Hundred and Thurstable Hundred (that includes Tiptree) is now sited there. It is staffed by two teams of teachers providing education at the centre or in pupils' homes.

21.11 The Plume Comprehensive School

In 1970, Maldon Secondary Modern School, located in Wantz Road, that had been formed in 1963 with the amalgamation of the secondary girls' school and secondary boys' school, became the Lower Plume for Years 7 and 8 and the former grammar school in Fambridge Road now caters for Year 9 and above where there were 1,844 on the roll in 2011. The school has benefited from the successful headship of Miss Sarah Dignasse who was succeeded by Mr. David Stephenson.

The Plume School became a Specialist Performing Art College in 2003. Fiona Hill, a clarinettist and pianist and a highly respected free-lance musician who regularly appears on Classic FM and Radio 3, now leads a team of specialist staff in this college. With her keen leadership, the school is encouraging enthusiastic students in many aspects of appreciating music of all kinds, people of all ages in and around Maldon enjoy music made by students and their membership of local groups will be hoped for when they leave school.   The Plume School's contributions in and around Maldon:

Students learn about music as part of the curriculum.

Individual pupils can receive individual on tuition on various instruments.

The encouraging atmosphere within the school has led to students carrying on their musical studies. The choir has grown from six students in 1995 to sixty members in 2011. They were adjudged in the BBC Radio 3 the Choir of the Year in the regional heat and, as a result, invited to participate in the Llangollen International Eisteddfod for the third time in 2011. The choir has performed with the Maldon Choral Society.

Three former Plume students performed at the Churches Together July Lunchtime Concert in 2011. Kristian Rawlinson played three Gershwin piano pieces which reflected his two interests, that of musical directing and acting. He has acted in a long list of productions and been involved with workshops in musical departments from several West End shows and has received awards for his musical and acting achievements. Paul Johnson played three organ items. He was in his third year of a scholarship studying the organ at Birmingham Conservatoire with Henry Fairs. As a flautist he has played at Cadogan Hall, the Royal Albert Hall, the Brandenburg Dom, Vienna Cathedral and the Dvorak Hall. In 2010, he was appointed assistant conductor to The Amadeus Orchestra working alongside Philip Mackenzie and the Bournemouth Symphony Orchestra Chorus. In 2011 he will hold the Percy Whitlock Organ Scholarship for Town Hall and Symphony. Ben Markham received a BA(Hons) in History from Essex University in 2011 and will follow that to study for a Masters Degree specialising in African History. The audience were enchanted and amazed by his fine performance of the three movements of Beethoven's Pathetique Sonata no.8 in C minor. He achieved a Diploma in Piano Performance at the age of 16 at the Royal College of Music Junior Department and reached the quarter finals in the Young Musician of the Year Competition and actively promotes music and drama in the local community, conducting the Maldon Youth Orchestra and acting in the Maldon Drama Group.

Plume staff work with local primary schools.   The Plume Adult Music Society offers instrumental lessons, a choir, a band, steel pans and ensemble groups. This year, ballroom dancing has been added to their offerings. 'Pluming Babies' starts them young with 45 minutes of singing, action songs, instruments and parachute games for pre-school children on Monday mornings. Plume Dramatic Society for Adults meets on Wednesday evenings.

Five students followed up the link with Essex Jiangsu Shakespeare/Kun Opera cultural partnership on a visit to China.

21.12 Heybridge Pre-school

Heybridge Pre-school was founded in 1979 and operated in the old Community Centre until 1990 when a ten year old demountable classroom was erected in a corner of the playing field of the new Heybridge Primary School in Rowan Drive. The management committee, staff and volunteers had been seeking funds for a new building for ten years. It opened on Monday 5th September 2011. The building is purpose built to accommodate twenty-two to twenty-six children per session and has a meeting room, staff room, small office and disabled facilities.

22.0 Places of worship in 1898 and later

22.1 Places of worship listed by Fitch in 1898

Heybridge St Andrew's

The church accommodated three hundred, all seats free. Sunday school took place at the Vicarage 10am and 2pm and classes for boys and girls on winter evenings at the Vicarage.

Strict Baptist Chapel

This chapel was situated in Hall Road from 1835 with accommodation for one hundred and twenty worshippers. Services were held on Sundays at 10.30am and 2.30pm. Eltime Controls is sited now at the junction of Spring Lane and Hall Road. The bakers, Adlards then Sissons, fronted Hall Road. Three terrace houses fronted the lane with the Baptist Chapel attached to the one nearest the creek. These houses suffered greatly from flooding in 1953 causing the Cannom family, Linda Hawkins' grandmother, and the Blighton family to move to Orchard Road.

Heybridge Mission (Congregational) Chapel Broad Street Green

See Section 14

Headquarters

Fitch recorded that services supplied by the Evangelisation Society were held on Sundays at 6.30pm and there was a Sunday school.

Black Bridge Mission Room

Service Sunday at 3pm supplied by the Evangelisation Society and on Wednesday evenings. This Mission Room, built on stilts up from the canal edge with steps leading up to it, was maintained by Mrs. O. D. Belsham, a Congregationalist.

Bethel Chapel, Heybridge Basin

Fitch records that the chapel could accommodate one hundred and twenty worshippers. The services were held at 10.30am and 6.30pm on Sundays and supplied by Wesleyans and Congregationalists alternately, Thursdays 7.15pm in 1898.

The Bethel Chapel existed in 1820 but its location is not known. On 17th May 1834, John Copeland Jnr. was granted a certificate of registration and on 11th November 1835 a certificate was obtained "under the hand of John Sadd Jnr. that a messuage in the possession of the same John Sadd was forthwith to be used as a place of religious worship, and was registered in the Commissary Court of the Bishop of London". The Sadd family built the Bethel Chapel in 1836. Later, the villagers collected enough money to build a Reading Room with its library next door. Three years later, a school was operating in the 'meeting room'. In 1867 J. C. and A. G. Sadd bought the chapel for £25 and donated it to Maldon Congregational Church for the use of 'Basiners' which became part of the URC (ed Church).

Mr. F. Cocks was the Bethel Chapel secretary and ran the Sunday School Bible Class in the Reading Room and library. He was also the secretary of the Band of Hope Temperance Society in 1876 when there were sixty-eight members. The last active member of the church, its organist and secretary, Mrs. Rene Chilcott, died in 2004. Her funeral was the last service to be held.

Sunday School Association

They met fortnightly at Black Bridge Mission Hall.

22.2 Later places of worship In Heybridge

Primitive Methodist Chapel

There is a reference to Heybridge Workhouse on the site of the present Jehovah's Witnesses' Kingdom Hall in Holloway Road. Parish Poor Rates were becoming so onerous before the 1834 Poor Law Act that far reaching reforms were necessary. The author researched the out relief granted in Tolleshunt D'Arcy before 1834 that showed an ever rising rate when many rate payers were in difficulties. Lengthy lists of grants for out relief were one of the reasons for the 1834 Poor Law Act. The Act transferred the granting of out relief to old people and widows, the poor, the care of orphans and rudimentary health care from local vestries to a district Board of Guardians. Out relief ceased for able bodied men.

The 1834 Act decreed that parish workhouses were to be closed, the Heybridge Parish Workhouse closed in 1836. The poor of Heybridge were sent to the new union workhouse on Market Hill, Maldon which had been built to accommodate the poor of parishes in and around Maldon. This building was vacated in 1873 when an imposing new union workhouse, now St Peter's Hospital, was erected costing £21,500 to plans by Mr. Frederick Peck and built by Mr. Ebenezer Saunders. The premises covered 5 acres and were scheduled to accommodate three hundred and fifty inmates.

Hillside on Market Hill started out as Maldon Workhouse between 1719 and 1835 when it catered for the poor of the three Maldon parishes - All Saints, St Peter's and St Mary's. It was the Maldon Union Workhouse from 1835 to 1873 for the poor from thirty-six parishes on either sides of the Blackwater Estuary including Heybridge, with a capacity of three hundred and fifty people. In 1836 Mr. Baxter, who had built Maldon Railway Station, was involved in the structural work on the extension to Hillside. While other unions in Essex built new workhouses following variations on a standard government design, Maldon deferred building a new one until 1873 when the grand new workhouse was built on a green field site in Spital Road. Hillside was sold and subsequently divided into six apartments; the maternity hospital occupied only part of the building.

We read that John Playle (1865-1945), who had been a Methodist preacher all his adult life, with his wife, sponsored and built a Primitive Methodist Chapel on the site of Heybridge Workhouse when he retired in 1928. He was responsible for holding, and taking, most of the services. His wife, Lotte, became very active in arranging the Sunday school and Ladies' meetings. The chapel was used for worship until the 1950s. In 1956, Browns of Chelmsford sold the property for £400. It was converted into a six-roomed bungalow. A few months later, the Jehovah's Witnesses bought it for £1,200 and they extended the building in 1975. They were able to buy adjoining land in 1995 and the old building was demolished. The present Kingdom Hall was built by volunteer labour over two long, four day, weekends in July 1995. It has become a thriving centre in the district.

St George's Church

The first Church of England services in Heybridge Basin were held in an upper room rented from Mr. Purkiss for £4 on Sunday, 10th August 1916. Mr. Purkiss ran the general stores and post office in the Basin. The collections amounted to between two and three shillings each week. The Jumble Sale in January 1918 made a profit of £4.1s.6d. that went towards the expenses; the rent, to buy service books, coal and a brush for the stove, a lamp and oil to light the room, matting, broom handles and milk. George Willis was paid weekly 6d., later 9d., probably to prepare the room. Church of England members' baptisms, marriages and funerals took place in St Andrew's church in Heybridge since the Basin is in the parish of Heybridge.

Edmund and Maude Alice Bentall purchased the Royal Flying Corps Sergeant's Mess from the aerodrome at Wash Bridge, Goldhanger and converted it into an Anglican Church. The timber hut was covered with plaster outside; a small bell tower was added and inside a small vestry was created at the west end. The seating was on benches made by May and Butcher. St George's Church was dedicated on 4th March 1920.

Second Lieutenant Ernest Hammond Bentall, the 18 year old son of Mr. and Mrs. E. E. Bentall, was killed on 3rd October 1915 in France and he was buried at Vermelles. Older Basiners believe the face of the saintly figure in the stained glass over the altar resembles him. The church has two good stained glass windows by A. A. Orr. Joan McCready died in 2000 and her family have put in a memorial window to this loyal member of the church. It shows her beach hut, scenes around Jacobs' Farm including chickens, and was designed by Andrew Fawcett in 2001.

After the dedication of St George's, Evensong was held at 4pm and there was a service of Holy Communion on the second Sunday of the month with an average of five communicants. The first baptism took place on 11th February 1923.

The first wedding in the church took place by special licence in 2008. It is now licensed for weddings. Bryan Harker and Brenda Keighley, two Maldon District Councillors, were the first to be married in the newly licensed church in December 2010.

The church has been blessed with long serving parishioners; including Miss Willis, organist in the 1920s and 1930s, Mr. Hume was church warden for seven years and the other church warden, Mr. Francis May, served from 1920 until 1942 and was succeeded by his son, Mr. Donald May, until 1985. Miss Judith Manley is carrying on the good work.

Flooding prevented services taking place in January 1953.

The United Benefice of Heybridge, Heybridge Basin and Langford

Three churches serve the united benefice of Heybridge; St Andrew's, Heybridge and St George's, The Basin that are in the gift of the Dean and Chapter of St Paul's Cathedral, and St Giles, Langford which is in the gift of Lord Byron.

23.0 Parliamentary Elections: Heybridge and Maldon

Maldon Borough was famous as the political cockpit of Essex. It had two Members of Parliament out of ten in Essex from 1328 until 1862; it elected one MP from 1868 to 1885, the borough status was abolished in 1885 when Maldon became a county division of Essex until 1983.

Historically, Maldon Borough's low voters' qualifications permitted wide enfranchisement enabling candidates to appeal to electors with lavish expenditure, bribery and entertainment. John Strutt, Tory, who lived in Terling Place and his son, Joseph Holden Strutt, were able to sway elections in the eighteenth century. In 1763, John Strutt's friend, Bamber Gascoyne, needed to be re-elected as MP for Maldon since he had been appointed to the Board of Trade. Maldon Corporation favoured John Huske and secured his election by creating enough freemen to vote for him. Huske accused Gascoyne of threatening freemen who worked in the Custom House with the sack if they did not vote for him at the 1763 election. The Prime Minister backed Gascoyne who secured a writ against the Maldon Corporation and the Corporation was dissolved by judicial order in 1768. John Holden Strutt represented Maldon as MP for forty years.

By 1807 there were only fifty-eight freemen eligible to vote although Maldon Corporation had created eight hundred freemen but there was no one to swear them in. After thirty-eight years, the borough was granted a new charter in time to create new freemen for the 1810 election.

The freemen would arrive by trap or on horseback wearing their scarves and coloured cockades - blue for the Tories and orange for the Whigs. Booths were erected to record votes. Before Gladstone's 1872 Secrecy Ballots Act, voters had to declare their choice. A poll book was printed and published after every election showing how each elector had voted. Trades people who had voted 'the wrong way' lost customers. Voters were able to sell their votes and even advertised them for sale and it was not unknown for voters to be kidnapped until after the voting was over. Candidates hired armed gangs to further their interests and fighting took place between the gangs. Freemen had the right to vote; they inherited, purchased, and received it as a gift or by marrying a freeman's daughter. Men living as far afield as Southend on Sea, Barking, Burnham on Crouch, Brighton, Dunmow and Colchester as well as Heybridge had bought this privilege.

The Corporation created 1,000 freemen in the 1826 election. 2,527 freemen who lived in 'the town and country' and 586 in London voted (A. F. J. Brown). The contest lasted fifteen days and cost £50,000 in bribes and hospitality and 3,113 freemen voted. The candidates were Winn, Lennard and Dick. Quintin Dick fought and won three elections in 1830, 1831 and 1837 after spending £30,000.

The Reform Act of 1832 extended the Maldon Parliamentary boundary to include Heybridge, while freemen living further than seven miles from Maldon were disenfranchised. 876 freemen were eligible to vote; made up of 699 freemen and 177 £10 householders.

Arthur Brown quotes the Suffolk Chronicle saying that "From 1832 to 1847 every election in the town of Maldon has seen a contest. All have been in character; corrupt from first to last. In 1832, the contest was only comparatively pure. In 1835 the cost was much increased. In 1837 the place was quite corrupt … In 1847 nothing could be worse … Supper parties became fashionable …The candidates attended …Wine, punch, brandy, anything you pleased was the order of the day … for three weeks … drunkenness prevailed in Maldon". David Waddington was elected with 461 votes, a majority of thirty-four.

Sir Charles Du Cane was elected Member of Parliament for Maldon in 1852, but the election was declared void when it was discovered his agent had been involved in bribery of which Sir Charles was unaware. A Royal Commission investigated and found no major scandal; it took two years before the second election took place. It was a time when political agents threw bags of sovereigns into public houses through the doors at times of elections. The second Tory polled only six more votes than his Whig opponent and only six votes separated the first elected candidate from the fourth unsuccessful candidate.

Mr. E. H. Bentall was elected Liberal MP for Maldon with a majority of 153 in November 1868. This was still a time of open voting; electors had to announce their choice publicly so just before 4pm he walked into Maldon High Street to the shouts and plaudits of his supporters who knew he was the new MP for Maldon. He took little part in Parliamentary debates and did not stand at the next election in 1874.

We get a glimpse of the shenanigans at Parliamentary elections when in 1880 Dr. Salter of Tolleshunt D'Arcy and Sir Claude de Crespigny worked together to try get Sir William Abdy, Conservative, elected. The opposing Liberal candidate was Mr. George Courtauld. Both were rich men who were prepared to spend any amount of money to get elected. As polling day approached, desperate measures came into play. Six hundred men from Halstead were enlisted by the Courtauld side to prevent the voters from the country getting to the poll; liquor flowed freely and other means were put into play. Sir Claude went to Plaistow, London, to recruit prize fighters and he also found sixty coal miners and Dr. Salter went to Colchester and came back with Tollesbury blue-jackets in wagons. By noon, Maldon High Street was full of agitated men spoiling for a fight. Dr. Salter recorded that "There was a murderous fracas…in the centre of the town and many heads were broken". By mid afternoon, the Conservatives believed they had won but the Heybridge Basin men arrived and they had been bought by the Liberals. "They were originally to have 10 shillings down and a pound more if the election was won". This last minute manoeuvre helped George Courtauld to secure an 18 vote majority; he secured 679 votes to Sir William Abdy's 661.

This was after the passing of Gladstone's Act 1872 securing secret ballots at Parliamentary elections. However, the Tories were perturbed by Sir Claude's actions. The borough had one MP from 1867 to 1884 and then the borough was disenfranchised and became part of a much larger county constituency. Members of Parliament were unpaid until 1911 when they were granted an annual salary of £400.

A General Election was held on 14th December 1918 at which women over 30 voted for the first time and the franchise was extended to all men over 21; this tripled the electorate.

Maldon seat 1918: George Dallas, Labour 6,315; Sir Fortescue Flannery, Coalition 8,138;

E. W. Tanner, Liberal 1,490.

At the 1923 election Valentine Crittall Labour held the seat for one year; he became Lord Braintree in 1947. In the election of 30th May 1929 women over the age of 21 voted for the first time: Maldon seat 1929: Major Evans (Lab) 11,224; H A May (Lib) 6,748; Lt. Col. Ruggles Brice (Con) 14,020.

Tom Driberg contested the seat as an independent in 1942 following the death of Ruggles Brice the Conservative MP. Political parties did not contest elections during the war. Driberg contested the seat as a Labour Party candidate in 1955 and was defeated by Brian Harrison, Conservative, who was followed by John Wakeham, Conservative, until 1992 at which time John Whittingdale was returned as the Conservative candidate.

Many houses have been built in and around Braintree and Witham since W.W.2 necessitating major changes of constituencies. Heybridge and Maldon suffer from poor links with the A12 and relatively fewer houses have been built so that the make up of the Parliamentary constituency has seen many alterations. Boundaries of the Maldon constituency have changed after each election to reflect increases in population in the county of Essex. Heybridge has always remained in the same constituency as Maldon. The Maldon constituency lost Braintree and Witham and it was combined with Rayleigh, next it had parts of Colchester Borough including a segment of the town, then parts of Chelmsford Borough were added to Maldon. It now has South Woodham Ferrers and various parts of Chelmsford Borough and is known as Maldon Constituency. Major changes occurred throughout Essex in 2010, when the new constituency of Witham gave Essex an extra Member of Parliament and Maldon lost villages that had been in the Maldon constituency for a very long time.

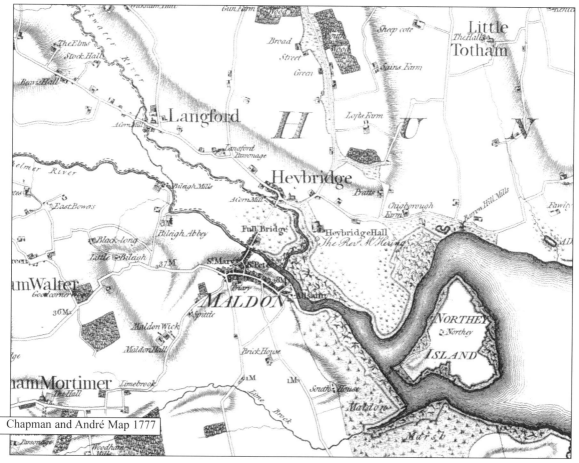

Chapman and André Map 1777

Beeleigh Viaduct
SOURCE Lloyd Blackburn, Maldon Society

A Ford T with a 12 seater horse bus body modified by Maskell of Tollesbury to suit the motor bus chassis.
G. W. Osborne stands on steps. July 1919 PHOTO By kind permission of the Osborne family

24.0 The expansion of travel

24.1 Transport of goods by water

We know that travel on water was easier and quicker than on land in the early nineteenth century. The building of the Chelmer and Blackwater Navigation speeded up the transport of goods and reduced costs to and from land bordering the Rivers Blackwater and Chelmer and Chelmsford. White records that in 1848 vessels left the wharfs (Fullbridge) weekly to voyage to Chelmsford and London etc.

24.2 Walking

At the beginning of the eighteenth century, travel by stage and mail coach was expensive, only the rich could afford it. Journeys had to be pre-booked with fixed stopping points at post houses or inns. Most people walked and many walked great distances. Workers walked a long way to their work; we learn of a Bentall worker who walked from Goldhanger, three and a half miles, to the factory in Heybridge although this was probably thought a short distance then. Other workers came from further afield. Even in the 1960s, only three out of ten households had a car. By 2010 seven out of ten households had a car and fewer people walked or cycled.

24.3 Horse drawn vehicles

Carriers took goods but would pick up and set down passengers en route without pre-booking since they followed a timetable. Edward Moore started his carrier business on 20th February 1815 in Feering. He used a simple, bone shaking springless cart hauled by one horse. The journey to Colchester took three hours since there was a speed limit of 4mph. He served Colchester Market on Wednesdays and Saturdays and Chelmsford Market on Tuesdays and Fridays. Transport magazines credit Moore's with being "the oldest family undertaking in the passenger service industry". The firm moved to Kelvedon in 1844, probably because the Eastern Counties Railways main line reached Colchester in 1843.

John Witterings, a London merchant, established fixed regular posts and Witham became a post town which had its own mail bag in 1635. Maldon was linked to Witham which was on the route from London to Colchester and Harwich. By the eighteenth century the post was delivered by post boys on horseback who rode between postal stages that had been set up along main thoroughfares. John Palmer proposed, in 1782, that the mail be carried along stages in coaches with a guard for protection. Since coach owners would compete for the contracts, he reasoned their charges would result in little extra cost and the journey would be faster, safer, regular and efficient. His plan was adopted.

In 1795, Maldon was made a post town instead of being a sub-post office of Chelmsford and a coach and mail cart went from Maldon to Burnham and Southminster daily.

In 1848, carriers operated from Maldon: J. P. H. Dines' fish wagon from Market Hill travelled to London via Chelmsford carrying fish every Tuesday and Friday, John Lake went from the Swan Inn to Witham daily, W. M. Pond and J. Richardson went to Tillingham and Burnham on Mondays, Thursdays and Saturdays, John Worraker's van went to Southminster and Burnham on Crouch daily, a carrier from the Rose and Crown to Steeple Wednesdays, Ostend Mondays,

Thursdays and Saturdays and Bradwell Tuesdays, while Holmes' van went from the White Horse and Swan to Chelmsford on Fridays and to Colchester on Wednesdays, Fridays and Saturdays. The coach of Mr. Ward of Maldon departed from Maldon at 7am for Whitechapel on Mondays, Wednesdays and Fridays and returned at noon the following days. This is an example of the detail in the timetables and illustrates how the network of routes was developing in the first half of the nineteenth century and demonstrates the growing industrial importance of Heybridge and Maldon.

24.4 Cycling

Stuart Warburton, in a lecture on the history of cycling, described how rich young men rode penny farthings as a leisure activity. They formed clubs and wore clothes reminiscent of army uniforms; knickerbockers and close fitting tunics with military style pill box caps in the club colours. Until the 1870s rich men cycled on penny farthings. Mr. Warburton showed us how to mount and dismount a penny farthing and rode the machine at a surprisingly fast speed. The greatest danger was unexpected hazards hidden at the bottom of hills.

John Kemp Starly invented the first successful 'safety bicycle' in England in 1885. It had a steerable front wheel and two wheels of equal size, the rear wheel that was chain driven and a diamond frame. Dunlop's invention of pneumatic tyres meant that four aspects had been covered steering, safety, comfort and speed.

Cycling was considered unsuitable for ladies and bad for their health until safety bicycles came in. The frames were smaller and the lower seating position made them easier to mount and ride but their voluminous restrictive long dresses were inconvenient. It was unseemly to show legs but later ankles were allowed. Some women joined a movement that campaigned for 'rational' dress to liberate women from corsets and ankle length skirts to the horror of many men.

Cycling gave the working man and woman an affordable form of transport; it widened the range of work opportunities and broadened the scope of leisure activities. Cycling became popular in the 1880s and 90s. Bone shaker was the name given to early bicycles. They were cheap, efficient and quick. Ev Last records that Didles Barbrook who rode a bone shaker from Broad Street Green to Bentall's and back did not mind how many there were in front of him in the morning but coming away he was always first.

When George Free was managing Jacobs' Farm for Frank May in 1910, he cycled to Thaxted to court his future wife on Sundays.

Men from villages around Heybridge cycled to work in Bentall's, to Crittall's factory in Witham, to Sadd's; building workers cycled to jobs around the district. A building contractor at Doe's Corner Ulting employed men from as far afield as Fairsted, Great Totham, Maldon and Goldhanger who cycled to the yard or to jobs in the district for a 7.30am start until the late 1950s. Masses of cyclists crossed the Causeway morning and evening going to Bentall's, Maldon Ironworks and Sadd's; it was like a tidal wave in the 1940s and 50s, and they went home for a hot meal midday. Before bicycles, men working on farms lived in and domestic staff lived in and cycled home on their days off. Bicycles offered women new job opportunities and alternatives to domestic service. They rode machines nicknamed "sit up and beg" on unmade roads. Cycling was hard work because, until recently, few bicycles had gears. Bicycles were the cheapest form of transport.

Before W.W.2, it was not unusual for shop keepers to call at middle class customers' homes for orders that they entered in red leather covered books. Errand boys on special bicycles delivered milk, bread, fruit, vegetables and meat to be followed by monthly accounts. This was changing as war approached and delivery vans replaced errand boys but petrol rationing put this back and it was not until the 1950s and later that errand boys disappeared. We never hear errand boys and newspaper boys whistling today.

Leisure was enriched in the 1890s as cycling opened up the countryside and became an attractive past time for men and women. Groups of men and women cycle club members journeyed to the seaside and other places of interest. This was the first time men and women of various classes mixed; it meant that the gene pool was broadened as men could visit further afield too. En route cafes displayed signs welcoming members of various cycle clubs. Families could visit relatives. More people could enjoy leisure activities, such as cinema going and dances outside their villages.

Local garages began repairing and selling bicycles before opening garages for motor cars; Dick Houlding from the Triangle garage, Heybridge, Mr. T. S. Bates from 1 Market Hill, Maldon before moving to Spital Road and E. G. Claydon from Witham to Hatfield Peverel. Fitch's advertisement boasts of highly skilled mechanics, riding taught free when a 'machine' bought and bicycles 'to let on hire'.

24.5 Maldon to Witham Railway

24.5a Early history

Oliver Herring and E. H. Bentall opposed the building of the railway from Maldon to Witham since Heybridge was served by the Navigation. They believed that the railway would put the canal out of business (they were right). Heybridge tradesmen compiled a petition; E. H. Bentall was one of the first signatories, asking for the railway to go from Maldon directly to Chelmsford, the county town, which the Eastern Counties Railway had reached in 1842. It reached Witham and Colchester on 29th March 1843.

Originally, the railway from Maldon was meant to be a direct link with the market town of Braintree and the quays of the port of Maldon. Braintree was the corn depot for central Essex and the centre of a rich farming area from which hay, flour, corn and malt were exported while timber, lime, slate, oil cake and grain were imported.

A meeting was held in February 1845 at the White Hart, Witham under the chairmanship of the Rector of Cressing, the Rev. Sir John Page Wood. Businessmen from Braintree and Maldon attended. Joseph Locke was appointed engineer; he had worked with Stephenson on the Liverpool and Manchester Railway. James Beadell, a Chelmsford man, was chosen to be the surveyor. In June 1846, Royal Assent gave the company power to run the line from Maldon to Braintree by way of Heybridge, Langford, Wickham Bishops, Witham, Faulkbourne, White Notley and Bulford (later renamed Cressing). Eastern Counties Railway granted running rights to link with their main line from London to Colchester and offered to purchase the company for £6,300 to cover expenses already incurred plus ten shillings per share. This offer was accepted and the purchasers nominated the "Railway King" George Hudson and his deputy David Waddington as new directors, Eastern Counties Railway Company promised to open the line within eighteen months but bad weather delayed the opening until August 1848.

It is not known why Eastern Counties Railway decided to make Witham the junction of the Braintree/Witham and Maldon/Witham branch lines instead of the line being direct from Maldon to Braintree. Thomas Jackson undertook the contract to build the line from Braintree to Maldon. In May 1847, he employed five hundred men for the Witham to White Notley section and one thousand more in July of that year. All hand labour, no machinery then. Good progress was being made when summer rain slowed down the work necessitating great efforts during autumn and winter. Originally, there were six wooden viaducts on this line. In a lecture, Adrian White, the railway historian, said the 1840s were a time when investments in railways were unpopular, the company was impecunious and lines had to be built cheaply. Economies were necessary and wooden viaducts of the simplest construction were one of the economies that were used to carry this railway over rivers and brooks. These viaducts were responsible for the weight restrictions on locomotives on this line. The Wickham Bishops section needed pile driving. The trestle bridge behind Wickham Bishops Mill was restored in 1995 and is the only surviving trestle bridge in England which is scheduled as an Ancient Monument.

Wickham Bishops station served the surrounding small hamlet until the later development of Wickham Bishops took place on higher ground which is the site of the present village.

Cast iron girders were needed on the bridges in Witham and Maldon. Eastern Counties Railway Company had to pay the Chelmer and Blackwater Navigation Company £45.14s.8d. to erect a bridge over the Navigation between the pond and the level crossing and build a wharf on the Navigation adjoining the bridge.

The line opened for freight in August 1848. 300 tons of coal and 350 tons of other freight were carried during one week in September 1848. Captain George Wynne RE inspected the line and passed it for passengers on 30th September 1848. The first passenger train left Maldon at 8am on 2nd October. Five passenger trains a day were timetabled. The journey from Maldon to Witham took 20 minutes, 40 minutes from Maldon to Braintree. The fares from Maldon to Braintree were: 1st class 2s.6d., 2nd class 2s.0d., 3rd class 1s.6d. and Parliamentary 1s.0d. The journey from Maldon to London, 44 miles, took 85 minutes. In 1862, various Eastern Counties connections were incorporated as the Great Eastern Railway. In the 1890s the fares were 11s.0d. first class and 3s.3$\frac{1}{2}$d. third class. There were eight trains on weekdays and three on Sundays.

Originally, Maldon East station was called Maldon East and Heybridge, trains stopped by request at Langford and Ulting Halt. The Halt was renamed Ulting, Heybridge and Langford and Ulting at various times.

Ironically, the Navigation was used to transport building materials for the construction of the railway and this was its busiest time while it contributed to its decline. Coal traffic along the Navigation was subject to delays from floods, frost and mill repairs but in 1863 68% of goods carried on the Navigation was still coal and only 15% agricultural goods. The railway carried passengers, parcels and livestock.

Vehicles entering across the Causeway and leaving Maldon from Market Hill and Station Road had to pass over the level crossing. When a train was due, the signalman left his box high up beyond the underpass, walked along the rails over the underpass and opened the gates on each side of the line, walked back to the signal box and set the signals to allow the train to pass while traffic waited. The procedure was reversed before the gates were opened to allow traffic on their way. In the 1930s, Mr. Bowles, was one of the two signal men; he lived in Station House and had two daughters.

The Causeway from Maldon to Heybridge had rising slopes to a gated level crossing beside which was the 9ft. high underpass originally intended for pedestrians and animals. Before W.W.2, motor cars used this because it avoided the delays of the opening and shutting of the crossing gates. This underpass was the scene of a tragic accident during W.W.2 when soldiers standing in the back of an army lorry were decapitated on the way through the low underpass. After this, it seems more cars used the level crossing.

The underpass at the Causeway
SOURCE Lloyd Blackburn, Maldon Society

Arthur Baxter built Maldon railway station. It was built well above Potman Marsh to avoid the risk of flooding and to give sufficient headroom to the canal, which ran near to the station. The station has been described as a fine Queen Anne style building or, according to Historic Towns of East Anglia, a Jacobean mansion with Flemish gables, ornate chimneys and a nine-arch arcaded loggia. It is now a listed building. The elegance of the building was the result of political expediency.

David Waddington's electioneering included a boast that this fine station building reflected his concern for Maldon. The Parliament elected in 1841 was not dissolved until 1847. The construction of the station was spun out to keep the railway employees resident in Maldon so they would vote for Mr. David Waddington. No secret ballots then! "The building of such a large station kept a large force of Waddington's workers employed and resident in Maldon Borough". Some two or three weeks before the election, Waddington contrived to have a considerable number of persons, chiefly freemen, taken into nominal employment on the railway at a salary of one guinea a week. They were nicknamed 'Waddington's guinea pigs'. This 'workforce' was taken on without regard to age or calling or capacity for work; a man of 70 was engaged, another was a member of the canvassing party and other employees admitted that 'their usual daily vocation was little interfered with by their work on the railway" (Swindale). David Waddington, Liberal, merchant and manufacturer, of Adelaide House, Enfield, Middlesex and Chairman of Directors of Eastern Counties' Railway and T. B. Lennard of 9 Hyde Park Place and son of Sir T. B. Lennard Bart of Belhus were elected.

To celebrate peace at the end of the Crimean War, an excursion train left Maldon for London at 6am. The train was shunted, left on a siding at times and the carriages (cattle trucks with seats) reached Shoreditch about 11am. The return journey was meant to return at midnight but did not leave until 3am and reached Maldon about 7.30am.

There was a serious accident between Wickham Bishops and Langford on Tuesday 15th June 1869 when the fireman was killed, although the fifty passengers and the driver suffered no loss of life or serious injury.

Langford and Ulting Station, actually a halt, had the distinction of having the first station mistress; she sold tickets through a window in the station house, dealt with parcels, attended to passengers, lit signal and station paraffin lamps and dealt with the train. The station house was built around a hundred years before the railway line.

Paddy Lacey states that booking facilities were discontinued at many smaller stations in 1921 including Maldon West. Albert Chapman remembers buying tickets on the train from the guard when he boarded at Langford and Ulting Halt in the 1920s. It is recorded that whole train loads of chaff cutters travelled from Bentall's via Maldon East Station to Warsaw in Poland.

In February 1852, a locomotive, standing at the platform in Maldon East station, burst its boiler. The explosion smashed all the glass in the station canopy which was never replaced.

When the station was enlarged to the east, extensive yards with numerous sidings, a 50ft. turntable and a loco shed capable of accommodating four locomotives was constructed. Close by the level crossing, was the Old Victorian goods shed built of red brick. Mollie Polden worked in the office in the front of the building, described as interesting and attractive with its unique internal ironwork. Rail trucks were shunted into this large building in the 1930s, 1940s and 1950s and unloaded into lorries for delivery. The office had a front door and interesting window. The listing of the goods' shed for its historic and architectural significance was under consideration when it was demolished overnight on Whitsun Bank Holiday 2006. The site owners, Aquila, were fined for this.

24.5b Maldon Dock

In 1848, the original promoters of the Maldon Witham Railway, excavated a large area near the station to compete with the Navigation trade to the Basin. The dock was never completed and Sadd's used the 'lake' for seasoning timber. Later it was filled in and a warehouse erected on the site.

24.5c The Canal Wharf

A 150 yard railway wharf was constructed where the railway crossed the canal on the north side so that goods coming by water for Braintree could be floated up from Heybridge Basin on the Navigation and then transferred to railway wagons at this little quay. Braintree Railway station was little more than a hut then. Later, Bentall's made use of the same wharf when their coal came by rail instead of coasters. There was a turntable so that trucks, once loaded, could be moved along and hitched behind an engine. The last passenger train between Maldon and Witham travelled on 6th September 1964 and the freight service ended two years later.

24.5d The Pond - sometimes referred to as the Ballast Hole

"The long pond was excavated on the south side of the canal with the idea of creating a dock as a direct link between the proposed railway and barges arriving by sea in Maldon Harbour at Fullbridge from which to load and unload freight". This was written in 1845; it was part of plans to redevelop Maldon Harbour after its decline as a port due to the success of the Chelmer and Blackwater Navigation. The idea came to nothing. An alternative version says ballast was taken from here to provide building materials for the triangular junction of the lines from Maldon East and Maldon West. Later, railway engines took on water from this pond, which is now used by fishermen. The marginal vegetation around the pond is sedge and reed dominated but lesser reedmace and greater pond sedge are present. The adjoining section of the railway embankment is bounded by tree and shrub vegetation especially pedunculate oak and hawthorn. The Maldon

District Council's Local replacement Plan 2005 includes lesser catmint, field scabious and lady's bedstraw in the ground flora. The road junction on Heybridge Approach adjacent to the junction is called the Pond Roundabout.

24.5e The Crimean Connection

The British Army in the Crimea in 1854 was badly led, ill clad and equipped and casualty lists were large as men died of wounds, frostbite, cholera and starvation. All supplies for the British Army had to be dragged up over a single-track road, sometimes ankle deep in mud, from Balaclava, the British port, Sevastopol and the fighting zones. On 30th November 1854, Samuel Morton Peto, Whig Member of Parliament from 1847, announced in Parliament that his firm would build a railway from Balaclava to all parts of the front at cost; they would provide men and materials and would run the line when it was finished on a non-profit basis.

Edward Ladd Betts had been Peto's partner since 1842 in the Canada Works Birkenhead and he had married Peto's sister in 1843. This firm had built the Eastern Counties Railway in 1846 to Colchester and Maldon/Witham line that joined this railway at the Witham Junction. It so happened that a double track had been laid between Maldon and Witham but by 1850 the volume of traffic was deemed insufficient for two tracks. Six miles of track were taken up from the Witham/Maldon line, some were used on repairs on the line. Peto and Betts went into partnership with Thomas Bassey, an even bigger railway builder, who was commercially very successful. The firm became famous for their successful railways in Britain and overseas and they were the world's leading railway builders by 1854.

Within three days of the offer to build the Crimean Railway being made, verbal orders were issued to charter twenty-three large steamers to transport the work force and its equipment: five hundred men, fifty horses, rails, sleepers, tools, wagons, medical equipment and even books for the workers. Peto and Betts knew the rails had been lifted off the Maldon/Witham Railway and were ready for immediate dispatch. They were laid on the first miles of the Crimean railway (Swindale). The engineer in charge was instructed by Thomas Brassey to lay the track right to the wharves so that heavy supplies could be directly unloaded. Within a fortnight of landing, Beattie's men had built their base camp and laid seven miles of track. Originally, no locomotives were sent although some went out later; wagons were drawn by horses where the line was level and where steep, by cable powered by a stationary steam engine.

Where there was insufficient time to manufacture items, they were found and purchased. Most suppliers and agents opened their stores to Betts for his unrestricted use at cost price. The scale of the undertaking was accomplished because skilled navvies who had worked for Morton Peto were engaged, transported to the Crimea; their housing and supplies organised, and then several miles of railway were constructed in just over six weeks. The Treasury Bill covered only materials and goods purchased. Originally, it was believed that fifteen miles of railway would be needed. Peto promised that the railway would be operating within three weeks of landing at Balaclava. However, the railway was started on 8th February 1855 and carried stores to the Commissariat Stores in Kalikoi on 23rd February while on 26th March shot and shell were taken to the HQ on the summit $4\frac{1}{2}$ miles away from Balaclava. A total of twenty-nine miles of rail railway track were laid. The railway carried 112 tons of food each day, plus shot and shell, and evacuated casualties in spite of the Army Commissariat allowing the railway to operate only between 8am and 5pm.

"Before the siege (of Sevastopol) ended, the port (of Balaclava) was connected with all parts of the front by railway lines with planks in the 'four foot' and 'six foot'- the spaces between each pair of rails and the two sets of rails - so that horses and men could use the railway like a road" (Jack Gould).

Peto, Brassey and Betts had laid the track at no cost to the government, but after the war, the British government put the whole of the railway up for sale by tender with a the proviso that the minimum tender of £10,000 would include twenty-nine miles of track. The Russians bought the track; they lifted it and sold it to the Turks.

24.5f Maldon West to Woodham Ferrers

The Maldon to Wickford line opened on 30th September 1889. The aim was to provide a passenger link from Southend on Sea to Colchester via Maldon. Maldon East Station was linked with the new Maldon West Station by an extensive cutting that became the line of the Maldon relief road in 1997. A brick bridge was built over the River Chelmer with costly embankments and a string viaduct supported by brick towers carried the railway over the tidal River Chelmer and, with a brick built bridge over the Chelmer and Blackwater Navigation, connected new line from Maldon West with Maldon East Railway Stations. Another short line connected the line from Woodham Ferrers direct to the Witham line forming a triangle of railway lines.

The new line went from Barons Lane Halt, Cold Norton, Stow St Mary Halt (Stow Maries) to Woodham Ferrers where it joined the Southminster branch line. The lines from Maldon, Southminster and Southend met at Wickford and proceeded to Shenfield Junction to join the main line from Colchester and thence to London Liverpool Street Station. This service ran daily from 1890 to 1894 and then on Saturdays only. The through passenger service existed only four years. It was never popular and passenger traffic was light because, although the journey was shorter, the time taken was greater. However, a large amount of freight was carried including market garden produce. It is recorded that 925 tons of green peas were carried in three hundred and thirteen rail trucks to London on 11th July 1891, using both stations. The Woodham Ferrers branch line passenger service ceased on 10th September 1939 never to be resumed but the goods' yards of Maldon East and West were linked until 1959.

Adrian White is of the opinion that Maldon East facilities could not be expanded to cope with the volume of goods from the industries of Maldon hence Maldon West station had four sidings, cattle dock, large goods shed, engine workshops and coal dumps. There were two 30 cwt jib cranes and the station had a goods lift to cope with Maldon's traffic.

The line was closed in 1959 and the tracks were lifted a few years later.

24.5g Later history of the branch lines

The development of the port of Maldon did not take place because the Maldon Harbour Authorities failed to dredge the river. A decline in ships using the port of Maldon caused disappointing freight levels on the trains and Maldon's status as a port was removed in 1880 and the River Chelmer was designated as a creek serving the port of Colchester.

Cheap tickets were available to anglers boarding trains with their fishing rods around 1900. Horse drawn buses met passengers at Maldon East station before 1905. Mrs. Chapman became station mistress of Langford in 1906; said to be the only woman in England to hold the position at that time.

The Maldon/Witham line became part of the London and North Eastern Railway system in 1923. The line made steady progress during the inter-war years; goods traffic, passengers, day-trippers, holidaymakers and amateur sailors used the line. Maldon, Heybridge and Mill Beach were regarded as minor tourist destinations within easy reach of London and the trains were punctual. In the 1930s, Ben Handley met trains at Maldon Railway Station in his blue Humber taxi while Jimmy Patten with his distinctive waxed moustache met trains in his Ford. Many Heybridge passengers and even commuters walked to and from Langford and Ulting Halt across the fields to the trains.

By 1945, the branch line from Witham to Maldon was in a poor state; maintenance and repairs had been neglected during the war. The line was nationalised and became part of the Eastern Region of British Railways. The Maldon West Goods Station link with Maldon East closed on 1st September 1954 and re-opened from 31st January 1957 to 31st January 1959 for freight when the final closure took place. The track was lifted in the mid 1960s. The huge embankments of Maldon's viaduct over the River Chelmer had been constructed with garbage from London brought in by rail. Betty McDonald told the author that as many as fifty people went there on Sundays in the 1960s and found very good specimens of pots.

Two-coach diesel passenger trains replaced steam locomotives after 14th June 1956, and then rail buses carried passengers from 7th July 1958 until the closure of the passenger service on 7th September 1964. It was found troublesome to carry parcels, prams, cycles and other bulky items on the rail buses; this and mechanical problems led to operating losses.

In 1962, the Eastern Region staff magazine reported that the Maldon/Witham Branch line was thriving. Forty wagons a day were leaving Maldon goods yard with merchandise for Woolworths from Goldhanger canning factory, grain for the Continent, oysters, winkles and fertilisers. A year later, the line's closure was announced. Maldon District Trades Council held a public meeting to promote opposition. A campaign committee was formed but Maldon Rural District Council refused to object to the closure while the East Anglian Transport Users' Consultative Committee asserted that the Eastern National bus services would be able to cope except at peak hours.

The Essex Chronicle reported on 11th October 1963, that R. A. Butler and Members of Parliament through whose constituencies the Braintree/Witham/Maldon passed were canvassed by the railway company to oppose the Beeching proposals to close down the line in the Parliamentary debate on the issue. However, the passenger service between Witham and Maldon was withdrawn on 7th September 1964, and the freight service on 15th April 1966. The Braintree/Witham line continued to flourish. A special Eastern National bus service was promised to replace the trains. In the cold, snowy winter of 1963, it was the only way in and out of Maldon for several days. The fare for this rail bus from Maldon to Witham was 2s.6d. The bus could carry ninety-six passengers in 1964 but the service ceased on 2nd January 1970 due, the company said, to poor passenger figures.

After the Maldon West line railway was decommissioned, in May 1965, demolition men placed charges under the massive iron bowstring span of the viaduct. The towering piers remained standing; they were constructed with special industrial blue bricks. The railway track between Maldon West and East stations south of the river was enhanced by the established, wooded railway embankments. The track was removed in 1969 and the rails cut into 2ft. lengths which was a boon to scrap metal thieves.

Torbjorn Hallenstvedt BSc, in a lecture to the Maldon Society, explained that he worked for Essex County Council and was involved in the design of the new bridge that replaced the River Chelmer Viaduct. He became assistant resident engineer during its construction. The railway viaduct had to be demolished. Geological surveys were undertaken and two coffer dams were created in each of which two piers were constructed. Piling was carried out in the coffer dams for the installation of strengthening rods and finally concrete was poured in. Four steel girders were laid across the length of the bridge with K supports resting across the piers on which concrete slab decking was laid. The piers were clad with slim blue bricks resembling the original Staffordshire blue engineering bricks that were used on the original viaduct to preserve some of the character of the original viaduct. Staffordshire blue bricks were salvaged and used for back filling of the new piers. This Chelmer River Bridge was built in 1989 and cost £1½ million.

Two bridges had to be demolished and rebuilt since they were too narrow to carry the by-pass road: (1) The bridge between the Pond roundabout and the roundabout where the level crossing and underpass used to be. It was built in 1989. Volunteers painted murals about the history of Heybridge to discourage graffiti; the objective was not achieved. (2) The bridge between the Pond roundabout and the Chelmer bridge (viaduct) now known as By-pass Gates. Both these bridges cross the Navigation and have parapets of Staffordshire blue engineering bricks.

Eddie Kidd was an English international motor cycle stunt man. He had acted as a stunt performer in many films. On 10th December 1979, at the age of 20, he filmed scenes from 'The Life of a Motorcycle Stunt Man' on the disused viaduct over the River Chelmer that used to link Maldon West to Maldon East stations. He rode a Yamaha 400cc motorcycle in gusty winds and reached the speed of 100 mph on the 400 yard run up to the 80ft. gap, 50ft. above the River Chelmer. He described it as the most terrifying stunt he had ever undertaken. The film crew stayed at the Benbridge Hotel in Heybridge and Eastern Hotel in Station Road. Eddie Kidd's career came to an end when he was seriously injured in August 1996.

The huge embankments of Maldon's viaduct over the River Chelmer had been constructed with garbage from London brought in by rail. Betty McDonald told the author that as many as fifty people went there on Sundays in the 1960s and found very good specimens of pots.

The deserted Maldon East railway station became derelict; it was used for light industrial work for a short time while the yard became weedy and rubbish strewn. Two businessmen restored Maldon East Station building in 1974 and turned it into a public house and restaurant, the Great Eastern. The two bars were known as the 'Main Line Bar' and the 'Junction Bar', whilst upstairs was the 'Oh Mr. Porter' restaurant. There was a beautiful lamp from Wickham Bishops station in one of the bars. The venture did not flourish and was closed in 1976.

Others turned it into a motel and public house that again failed. By the early 1970s, the station had been vandalised; not a window was intact, not a door was on its hinges and there were holes in the roof. Fortunately, another firm came along and converted the buildings into offices that are now used by international shipping forwarding agents who are careful tenants. The nationally important Combined Services Museum has been built adjacent to the station.

Essex County Council bought the remaining 4 miles of the track bed in January 1993 to be a low key multi-purpose linear park; the Blackwater Rail Trail. There are problems to be overcome since parts of the track have been sold off where homes have been built and the Wickham Bishops Bridge has been stopped up with household rubbish. Detours and tunnels are needed to allow walkers easy and safe access to permit an interrupted walk from Witham to Maldon.

Maldon West Station site developed into a light industrial estate during the late 1960s and early 1970s. One large red brick shed remains in the yards amid seemingly successful small units. The underpass between the goods yard and the booking office has been filled in and replaced with a roundabout with three exits; to the A414 part of the Maldon relief road, into Maldon centre and towards the Danbury direction. Remains of the bridge parapet with the characteristic blue industrial bricks have been left on the eastern side of the road. The booking hall was demolished after 1969 following complaints about its dereliction.

24.6 Buses

24.6a George William Osborne

George William Osborne started in business as a carrier transporting fish boxes to Tollesbury from the Great Eastern Railway Station at Kelvedon, initially in a two wheel open cart drawn by a single horse, later with a four wheel cart with two horses. He bought a Model-T Ford in 1919. The body work of this new 'bus' had originally been fitted to a horse drawn van and was adapted by Tollesbury funeral director, Richard Maskell, into a twelve seater bus which had to cope with poor roads, narrow lanes and thick mud in winter.

Osborne's began their first contract bus service to Maldon in 1922 to take pupils to Maldon Grammar School. At first, the bus dropped the pupils at The Ship Public House and they walked up the hill. They had previously gone by train via Kelvedon and Witham to Maldon. This contract led to a service route from Tollesbury to Maldon. The route went from Tollesbury Pier, opened from 15th January 1907 to 1921, to Tollesbury station, Tolleshunt D'Arcy, Tolleshunt Knights, Little Totham, Goldhanger and Heybridge to Maldon.

George and Ellen Osborne had twelve children. Les, the middle son, emigrated to Australia at the age of 14. The rest were involved in the business in some way; Olive, known as Dolly, was the conductress on the Maldon route; her eldest brother, George William, known as Jim, drove the Maldon route; the next daughter, Ivy, took turns with Dolly on the Maldon school bus when they were quite old - a pupil at the time says that the passengers were very cheeky and led them a song and dance. In 1930, the Tollesbury to Witham Railway Station route began, commuters knew that when trains were late the buses would wait for them.

Victor Brown of Tiptree sold Blue Bird coaches to Osbornes in 1932 and they were able to expand their Maldon to Tollesbury route and to operate a daily service. Osbornes acquired two other routes; Tollesbury to Colchester via Birch, Goldhanger to Colchester via Little Totham and Birch.

Pupils from Tollesbury attended Maldon Secondary Boys' and Girls' School after the 1944 Education Act until Thurstable School, Tiptree, opened in 1958. Osbornes had the contract to take children to both schools. One of the entries in 'Tollesbury to the Year 2000' book remembers that Joe, another son, on the Maldon run would stop the bus, get out, and disappear down a cottage path with a parcel. Later, Molly Osborne's husband, Ron Smith, drove the buses.

The Eastern National bus company withdrew their service between Maldon and Goldhanger leaving this road entirely to Osbornes. Previously, Osbornes were not supposed to pick up passengers on this part of the route. The change enabled Osbornes to introduce a diversion to

Heybridge Basin. Heybridge people were able to use Osbornes' buses between 1963 and 1980 to go to Chelmsford Market on Fridays and to Romford Market on Wednesdays. Mary Gregory says that the cinema bus went once a week to the Embassy Cinema in Maldon and the bus driver went to see the film so it didn't matter if the film went over time. Near the cinema, Kathleen's Kitchen used to sell hot pies, a real treat after the performance.

Osbornes ran buses to dances at the Heybridge Headquarters. Many will remember how helpful the Osbornes' drivers were; they waited for regular passengers who were late; did shopping for people who lived on the route and carried messages. Buses were sometimes overloaded at peak times because drivers did not like leaving passengers behind. Breakdowns were not unknown. The author went to Blenheim Palace on an Osbornes' coach that broke down and the passengers had to wait on the other side of London for a relief bus to come from Tollesbury. Bus tickets for future use were collected from passengers as they left the buses.

The company provided the team coach for Colchester United Football Club from 1965. In the 1970s advertisements, Osbornes advertised as private hire specialists for a day's outings, week's tours and continental holidays.

Three grandchildren, Myra (Gilbert's daughter), George and Barry (Joe's sons) carried on the business until 1997 when the firm was sold to the Hedingham Bus Company.

24.6b J. W. Gozzett (Jim) and Quest

After serving an engineering apprenticeship, Jim Gozzett began his bus business at the age of 19 in 1924 with one coach and a loan of £100 from his aunt, Julia Gridley. Quest came from the name of his first coach. The business was first based in Silver Street, Maldon where there were two mechanical pits with a piece of waste land to store the coaches he acquired. These maroon and cream buses were driven by uniformed drivers and had conductors. They provided a passenger service between Maldon and Witham. After two years, the fleet of Quest Coaches was moved to the Causeway and ran a service in and around Maldon from the 1920s until 1935.

Pre W.W.2, Frank Tebbell of Maldon drove a small 20 - 29 seater Gozzett coach from Maldon to King's Cross for 5s.0d. return on Friday evenings. It was he who drove a 36 seater double-decker bus bought from Moore's in 1926 after it was converted into a charabanc with pneumatic tyres and used for private outings. There is a photo of this vehicle pictured outside Heybridge Headquarters with twenty men passengers ready to begin a journey.

Harry Sefton ran a bus service from Maldon Road, Althorne from 1928 daily to Burnham on Crouch and to Maldon, and twice a week to Chelmsford which was taken over by Pride, a company that operated from Mayland. Quest took over these routes by 1933. By this time, Quest operated routes from Maldon to Burnham on Crouch, to Bradwell on Sea and to Wickford as well as providing a half hourly service from Scraley Road, Heybridge to South House Farm on Mundon Road for a fare of one penny.

Jim Gozzett sold out to Eastern National on 1st January 1935 when he owned twenty-six buses. All were sold to Eastern National who wished to expand their services to Maldon and the Dengie Hundred. Jim Gozzett used the proceeds from selling the bus routes to set up a garage in the High Street opposite Wantz Road in Maldon. He was granted the South East Essex dealership for Vauxhall/Bedford vehicles and created a showroom in St George's Place on the corner of Wantz

Road (later Kathleen's Kitchen). On display in the present Quest Maldon showroom is the account of a sale by Quest of a secondhand Vauxhall car in October 1938 to a purchaser for £14.0s.0d. after the purchaser had received £5.0s.0d. allowance for his old Ford car. When Jim Gozzett was able to acquire more land adjacent to the garage, he transferred the showroom to the garage site and all operations, including workshops, were on the enlarged site.

Machine tools and munitions were made in the workshops to great exactitude during W.W.2; the engines of diesel boats from the Maldon Wharf were repaired, and existing privately owned motor vehicles were repaired in the works at a time when there were no new cars. Other garage proprietors, who were skilled engineers, worked full time machining components with great exactitude during W.W.2. in their garages. E. G. Claydon, like Dick Houlding, had started his business in Newland Street, Witham selling and repairing bicycles. In the 1930s, he moved to Hatfield Peverel into new garage premises selling and servicing motor vehicles.

Frank Tebbell was enterprising when he was working full time at Crittall's; he took his fellow workers to Witham in the charabanc for 3s.6d. a week.

After W.W.2 Quest bought a fleet of twelve coaches. Five coaches undertook contracts to take USA servicemen's children from surrounding villages to school on the base at Wethersfield, the other coaches were used for private hire and running private excursions. Frank Tebbell, the foreman coach driver, drove coaches on excursions and tours. A photograph shows two coaches in Goldhanger Road at the start of an excursion. Photographs show charabancs with no roofs.

In the 1950s, Quest undertook a breakdown and recovery service nationally including for Scotland and Wales. Mr. Gozzett developed private car hire and had self drive vehicles as well as a taxi business. The coaches were sold in 1957 in order to finance the purchase of the Rayne Road, Braintree garage site.

At Jim's death in 1969, aged 69, he had three garages; Maldon, Braintree and Halstead and employed nearly one hundred workers. His son, John, took over the running of the whole business which is now managed by Jim's grandsons: Robin who is managing director, and his brother, Martin, the sales director.

Quest Motors acquired the Saab franchise in 2004. The Maldon High Street site became too small and inconvenient and was unable to conform with EU standards. The business transferred to modern premises in Wycke Hill Business Park in 2007 where Quest Saab and Quest Vauxhall cars are sold. On the High Street site fifty-six superior properties have been built on the old Quest garage site; they are traditional in style with modern touches, near the High Street but untroubled by traffic noise. The accommodation varies; there are one, two and three bedroom apartments, two, three and four bedroom homes.

24.6c Moore's Bus Company

Moore's built the Temperance and Commercial Hotel in 1879 in High Street, Kelvedon to accommodate traders doing business in the locality. Moore's provided the traders with carriages. They introduced a horse-drawn omnibus service between Kelvedon and Coggeshall that met trains arriving at Kelvedon Railway Station in 1881 until 1924. This service was the beginning of the network of routes that developed into a bus company early in the twentieth century; the routes radiated from Kelvedon.

Thomas Clarkson had invented a flash boiler that contained a small quantity of water and was able to produce instant steam when needed, using paraffin to heat the boiler. He moved to Chelmsford in 1902. He formed the National Steam Car Company to operate buses in London and later, operated routes to Writtle, Danbury, and Great Waltham from Chelmsford. Moore's order for a double-decker steam bus in April 1914, to operate in North East Essex, was a great advertisement for Clarkson; it was the first such bus in those parts. The arrival in Colchester caused great excitement but the ride was bumpy and rather uncomfortable because of the rough roads, solid tyres and the maximum speed of 12 mph. This steam bus travelled from Kelvedon to Colchester via Tiptree on Tuesdays and Fridays, and to Colchester via Coggeshall on Wednesdays and Saturdays, as well as private hire. It was withdrawn from service in 1919.

Moore's bought their first petrol bus secondhand from the father of Bertram Mills in 1912. It was used for private hire work. Many people were unwilling to travel in the new petrol buses. Reluctance to travel in motor buses meant that horse drawn omnibuses were in use as well as motor buses for a long time.

Private hire charabancs were an important feature of local bus travel in the 1920s. The local bus companies travelled further afield to Clacton on Sea, Southend on Sea, Bury St Edmunds, and a local Mothers' Union branch visited Windsor in 1929. Petrol buses operated daily from 1930 on the main routes Moore's had inaugurated.

The Road Traffic Act of 1930 led to Moore's connection with Heybridge. This Act tightly controlled licences for buses, routes, manning; drivers (over 21), conductors (over 18), testing, timing, fare stages, stops and much else. Evidence for and against licences for routes had to be submitted to Traffic Commissioners at Traffic Courts; their decisions were strictly enforced. One way of securing new routes was by transferring an existing licence but existing bus operators did not want newcomers. Moore's acquired the licence to the bus service from Chelmsford to Maldon via Hatfield Peverel and Heybridge from Vic Brown, proprietor of the Blue Bird Coaches in Tiptree when he decided to cease trading. Bryan Everitt in his book "Moore's, the story of Moore Bros" has a picture of a conductor's ticket rack with printed tickets of various denominations. Bell punch and the shoulder slung leather money bag were inaugurated in 1928.

In W.W.2, because of petrol rationing, all strata of people travelled on buses; young and old, school children, bank clerks as well as bank managers, school teachers, headmasters and shop assistants, friendships developed and ownership of certain seats was respected; buses became rather like a club. Wider car ownership did not come until the 1950s.

Moore's ran a service from Maldon via Heybridge to Chelmsford. The author began teaching at Maldon Girls' Secondary School in 1947 while living in Kelvedon. The first bus travelled from the bus depot in Kelvedon via Hatfield Peverel to Maldon direct. The journey could be delayed by Lappages' cows crossing from Stoney Fields to the dairy at Woodlands Farm in Holloway Road and by the closure of the railway crossing gates.

The Eastern National buses ran an hourly service from Chelmsford to Colchester leaving Chelmsford on the hour while Moores' buses left on the half hour. Return, weekly and season tickets were only valid on one company's buses so a missed connection at Hatfield Peverel was a nuisance.

Many bus routes proceeded along Chelmsford High Street; Eastern National came from their red brick bus station built in the 1930s while Moore's buses stood in Coval Lane before travelling past the Railway Station, down Market Road (Victoria Road South) along King Edward Avenue into Market Road again where there was bus stop outside the Golden Lion public house at the junction of Duke Street, Tindal Square and Market Road. The Golden Lion abutted all three with its curiously rounded elevation and was opposite the Corn Exchange; those two buildings have now been demolished. Buses continued through Tindal Square past John Johnson's beautiful Shire Hall (1789-91) and down the High Street. There was a busy bus stop outside MacFisheries where wet fish was displayed on the counters open to the pavement. Opposite was Luckin Smith (the present Marks and Spencer) open plan homeware shop where the money was put in metal containers and whizzed along wires to the central cashier (as Luckin Smith's grocery shop in Maldon High Street). Moore's buses to Heybridge went up Springfield Road, along the former A12 to Hatfield Peverel, around Nounsley, through Langford, to Heybridge and then to Maldon.

King Edward Avenue, Chelmsford was an important bus route that linked two ends of Market Road avoiding that part fronted by the cattle market. The houses along King Edward Avenue were demolished to provide the site for extensions to County Hall, a public library and the Registry Office for Births, Deaths and Marriages, various other offices and number 9, the house Gordon Digby lived in as part of his job at Brittain Pash's. New bus routes had to be created.

Bentall's clerical staff had to be in at 8.40am so an army of walkers and cyclists passed along the Causeway to work. Later, the author lived near Doe's Corner. She used the bus in winter and in summer pushed the bicycle across the Downs which was less steep than Market Hill.

24.6d Eastern National

In 1902, Clarkson and Capel Steam bus syndicate started in Chelmsford and in 1902 moved into the Arc Works, formerly occupied by Cromptons, where they built steam driven buses. Thomas Clarkson had invented a flash boiler. The first buses carried eight passengers who sat along the sides of the bus. They were sold to established bus companies throughout the country. In 1905 open topped double deckers were introduced. Munnion and Son went from building horse drawn carriages to bodywork for Clarkson's steam buses and the bodywork for Bentall's cars. Charabancs developed at this time, they were open topped and were specially designed for holiday excursions. The author's parents went to the Isle of Wight by charabanc in 1925.

Clarkson and Capel later became Clarkson Ltd and were taken over by the National Steam Car Company which became a bus operator. The company sent buses to London and later operated routes to Writtle, Danbury and Great Waltham from Chelmsford. Internal combustion engines had improved so much by 1919 that steam buses were no longer made.

A successor company became Eastern National Omnibus Company which took over Moore's Bus Company in 1962.

We get some idea of bus fares from ticket prices: Kelvedon to Chelmsford return 2s.0d, Colchester to Kelvedon return 1s.6d., pupil's season ticket from Kelvedon to Chelmsford £1.15s.0d. per term.

24.6e Hall's Coaches

Hall's blue buses were based off Queen Street. They had school bus contracts, one contract brought primary school pupils from Heybridge Basin to Heybridge Primary School where they collected boys and girls attending the Maldon secondary schools in Wantz Road Maldon. In the 1940s and 1950s when few people had cars, privately hired buses ran groups to London theatres and other social functions. Hall's were a popular choice.

24.7 Motorcycles and sidecars

By 1924 over 500,000 motorcycles appeared on the roads of Great Britain brought about by returning service men who had become accustomed to mechanised transport. This affordable method of transport offered employment opportunities, especially in the country, and widened leisure activities.

In the 1930s, families squashed into motorcycles and sidecars; father driving, an older child on the pillion and mother with one or two children in the sidecar and went camping. The author remembers a family whose motor bike and sidecar broke down on their way to Clacton on Sea put up their tent in a field in Kelvedon and camped overnight. The author's next door neighbour, a motor mechanic, used his combination for work and pleasure, while Pat Yates' parents travelled from Chadwell Heath to camp in Osea Road Leisure Park in the summer on a motorbike and sidecar.

Sixteen year olds can obtain a licence to ride a 125cc motor cycle. This has become is a milestone for teenagers who proudly enter school carrying their skid lid (safety helmet). As fares continue to rise and traffic into towns and cities become heavier, people are using motor bikes to commute to work. Motor bikes can weave in and out of traffic, they do not have to pay the congestion charge to enter central London and they are not as thirsty as a car. The AA had 1,500 motor bikes and sidecars on patrol in 1938; they began to use Land Rovers in 1949.

24.8 Motor cars

In 1900, there were 8,000 cars in the whole of Great Britain; in 2000 there were 21 million. The Office of National Statistics said that, in 2007, 75% of households had access to a car or light van, 51% had access to two or more cars. In Heybridge and the villages around, the ownership or access to a car or light van is an expensive necessity for work; Heybridge residents commute all over Essex and to London.

Young drivers who live in and around Heybridge face a dilemma; insurance premiums for secondhand cars are greater than the cost of the car. This leads to too many uninsured drivers since the fines for driving uninsured are relatively low. Others are put on their parents' insurance which is illegal and can invalidate the cover. Nationally, additions are added to other insured drivers' premiums to create a pool from which victims of uninsured drivers can be compensated.

Although quite widespread, the opportunities for car sharing are limited in the countryside. In Heybridge, some houses have two, three or more cars and vans to take people to work, some travel far afield.

One woman told the author that her family of six boys and six girls went on family outings in a van fitted with forms for seating in the 1960s. They were not alone.

In rural areas, buses are infrequent, expensive and circuitous routes are time consuming and can never cover isolated homes; a point London based politicians seem to be unaware as they tax the motorist more and more heavily.

25.0 Leisure Pursuits and Sports

Heybridge members and committee officers play an active part in the large number of leisure and sports clubs in Heybridge and Maldon. Many incomers are attracted to Heybridge because of the wide choice. The following list is not comprehensive, but will give a taste of what is available - time precluded further research.

25.1 Bentall's Sports Club

Bentall's provided the ground that pre-1914 was used for football and cricket as well as cycle racing, quoits, athletics, dancing, fishing in the moat or pond, and tennis. Mrs. Proctor said cycling was taken very seriously; professionals came from London and laps were ridden round the field. Teams from Bentall's sports clubs used to travel to other clubs in the inter-war years in 'Argonaut', an open top bus, run by Crows from the bottom of Maldon Hill. Clubs were always near a public house!

The first changing room was built backing the wall behind the Wave public house alongside Colchester Road near where Mr. Gooch, a Bentall's employee, lived. This hut was burned down on the night Jack Newton and volunteers finished refurbishing it.

Tom Jarvis and Jack Hales put in tremendous efforts to plan and organise the new club premises in the late 1940s and 1950s with the help of club members. Tom Jarvis, representing the football and cricket clubs, went to see David Ransome, the managing director of Bentall's, to ask if the club could build a pre-fabricated building as a pavilion. Mr. Ransome said he would prefer a proper building and offered the two clubs £750 if they could match the figure. Tom Jarvis recommended the clubs to build the pavilion opposite the centre of the football pitch and arranged for the ditches that crossed the ground to be piped. Harold Freeman did the site work and laid the lower brickwork. May and Butcher erected the structure and voluntary workers fitted it out. It had a concrete bath for teams after matches. The Swifts and Bentall's Cricket Clubs formed The Heybridge Fete committee to raise the money. Spectacular fetes were held on Bentall's Sports Club ground. Some were organised by Norman Mitchell, a teacher at Maldon Secondary Boys' School and Heybridge resident. Profits from these fetes went towards providing the money for the sports club pavilion and social club premises. Ted Wire and Wal Gooch used to remove fluorescent tubes from the workshops and put them up in the marquee for the fetes. Maypole Marathons were held on Friday evenings to help with the cost of hiring the marquees, facilities and performers. Competitors left the sports ground and went along Holloway Road, Maypole Road, Captain's Wood Road, Broad Street Green Road and back to the sports ground where they ran a lap. Runners of national standing competed. The fetes were opened by famous footballers including Tommy Laughton, Jimmy Hill, Sam Bartrum, Eddie Firman and the one armed referee Alf Bond. Attractions included an open air display by a high wire act from France 'Les Diables Blancs', a wrestling ring with bouts between well-known wrestlers, contests against the famous Barber Brothers' Tug of War team from Great Totham, a ring for dancing, a demonstration of motor cycle dirt track riding (although on grass) by Rayleigh Rockets team and the Territorial Army with Bofors guns. Many were organised very successfully by Tom Jarvis. Coaches and special trains took spectators home after the fireworks display on the Saturday evening. Each fete in the 1950s made a handsome profit of around £200.

The pavilion became the cricket pavilion for the Cricket Club, changing rooms for the Swifts Football Club and a social club in the evenings with bar billiards. Ted Wire was the part-time steward for fifty years although he was a teetotaller. He received a certificate when he retired in June 1964. His day job was as an electrician in Bentall's Works. The building is now Farleigh Day Centre.

25.2 Football in Heybridge

Heybridge Football Club was formed in 1880 and recognised by the Football Association when it played on a field east of Heybridge Hall which was known as The Plains. The club used the Half Moon as their club house. Ev Last in his booklet "Football and other Sports in Heybridge" price 6d. written in 1948, records that the original team colours were blue and white hoops with

Heybridge football team in 1890: left to right, F. Perry, G. Bacon, G. Flack, C. Hicks, J. Gower, I. Jackson, F. Pollard, H. Maynard; sitting, A. Simkins, F. James, I. Wright, I. Clarke.

stockings and hats of the same colours. Not all players could afford the kit, one player in the first team played in his mother's elastic spring-side boots but he was reputed to be the fastest player on the side. The club moved to a meadow near Bentall's factory where a footpath crossed the pitch. They shared the ground with Heybridge Cricket Club. It was here that the club lost their first cup match against Harwich and Parkeston in 1890. The OS maps 1874 and 1922 show these two fields and the hedges and ditches. F. C. Perry was the honorary secretary of the football and cricket clubs from 1893 and actively supported both clubs for over fifty years. He lived in a house adjacent to the field next to the Wave public house.

In the 1893 season, the football club annual subscription was 2s.0d. (which could be paid in four instalments). The club colours then were black and white 2 inch. vertical stripe, the first of many changes. Friendly games were played then against teams from Witham, Chelmsford, Chelmsford Excelsiors, Brushes (Braintree) and Coggeshall. On 9th December 1893, Heybridge played Colchester Town Essex Senior Cup Tie at 2pm before 2,000 spectators. The referee Mr. W. Cook and friends met in the Anchor before the game. All went well during the first half but some strange refereeing decisions made in the second half favouring Colchester incensed the crowd. After the final whistle, the two captains and the teams strove to protect the referee from a ducking in the pond, from the mud by the gateway, from the Navigation, and from turnips from a farmer's cart before they dragged him into the Half Moon. Mr. Cook escaped through the back door of the Half Moon into a bus escorted by the police that took him to Maldon Station. Heybridge Football Club was suspended for six weeks and fined £2. It was a black day for Heybridge for which they were branded for many years.

A new ball cost 7s.6d. plus and a spare bladder 1s.6d. and a collection on the field during a cup tie raised 4s.10d. The club played thirty matches, winning sixteen. In 1898, the team reached the semi-finals of the Essex Senior Cup and lost 2-0 at the time when O. D. Belsham was the president who kept the club afloat and the captain was J. Woodcraft. On 29th November 1902, Ev Last was knocked out after 15 minutes play and carted off with a broken leg. The team travelled to away matches in a horse brake and had many adventures on the way home in the early hours of Sunday morning.

A second Heybridge club called The Swifts played between 1902 and 1910. The pitch they used was further in the meadow beside the Heybridge pitch. It had a path running across it and a ditch across one corner. When a corner had to taken, the player crossed the ditch and kicked the ball over the ditch onto the pitch. The Swifts club folded when many of their players joined the Heybridge Club.

Heybridge players changed at home and cycled to the ground while the away team changed at the Half Moon public house and ran along the canal path to the ground. On one occasion, in an away match at Tolleshunt D'Arcy, the Swifts' players dashed to the Red Lion while a burst ball was mended. Heybridge Football Club merged with Maldon Town Football Club in the 1930s but the merger was not a success.

It is recorded that two hundred and seventy-six men from Heybridge served in the forces during W.W.2. when Heybridge Football Cub virtually ceased and Mr. Wakelin's sheep grazed on the sports field. Jack Newton left Maldon Grammar School on Friday, 26th July 1941 and began work in Bentall's accounts office on the following Monday. He raised a football team in 1941 just before he went into the RAF and called it the Swifts Athletic Club. Teams changed in the school, crossed the road and climbed over the Bentall concrete wall and played the first half, players went back to the school at halftime and returned to the pitch for the second half. Wyn Wright, a nurse at the Isolation Hospital, remembers lime trees inside the wall, they had a delightful smell as one walked along the pavement. Jack Newton served the team as secretary and treasurer and cycled to Chelmsford to obtain affiliation to the Essex County Football Association. He was demobilised at the end of 1946 and went back to Bentall's in January 1947 where he worked until 1984 when Acrow went bankrupt.

There were seven Gills who have taken part in Heybridge football and cricket teams. Between 1920 and 1923 William Gill, Cliff Gill and Harold Gill each served as captain for a year. Clifford Gill (1895-1987) first played football for Heybridge Swifts in 1912, he received his County Cap when he was chosen to play for Essex in 1922-3 and his proud granddaughter still owns it. He served the Swifts in many capacities and received The Award of Merit from Essex Football Association in 1973, his nickname was Quaff after William Quafe, the batsman for Warwickshire and England early in the twentieth century, whom he resembled in height and build, and who was the quoits champion of England. Harry scored 22 goals for Heybridge in 1907-8, Fred scored 27 in the 1908-9 season and Arthur 17 in 1910-11.

The Swifts Football Club was revived in 1945 with Charles Bentall as president. They had great success and even had a supporters club with a membership of five hundred with the Rev. Whitford as president.

Philip Gill started to play football with the boys' team in about 1954. He progressed into the reserve side and finally into the first team. He was an apprentice instrument maker at Marconi's for five years and did his National Service at the age of 21. Afterwards he returned to Marconi's but retired from playing football aged 25. He has served the Swifts on the committee and in various capacities ever since. He worked at Marconi's for 46 years. When he retired, he and three other men prepared the pitch for matches on a voluntary basis. Even in 2009, the club did not employ paid groundsmen. Philip Gill continued to watch most matches.

Jack Newton told the author that it cost 6d. or 3d. to get into the ground on the Swifts' match days. Mr. Taylor and Mr. Woodcraft hung up canvas strips at mid-day on their way home from work between the wall opposite the school and in the lime trees to stop spectators viewing the matches without paying. Ev Last printed a 'programme' on a double sheet of paper listing team members, something about the opposing team and news and stories about the club. He went around the ground selling them at one penny.

Malcolm Willis joined the Swifts in 1946 from Heybridge Youth side. It seems unbelievable today that when Heybridge and Maldon played each other on Boxing Day and Easter Monday, crowds of 2,000 to 3,000 attended and as much as £80 was taken on the gate when admission was 6d. each. The four Moss brothers played in the Swifts team.

The club paid no rent and had a free hand in the use of the ground because virtually all the members were Bentall's employees. Acrow gave Bentall's Sports Club a subsidy in 1961 but later they gave the club only 15 days' notice to quit the sports club premises and the ground so that the site could be cleared for vast new factory buildings. Len Miller saw Mr. Grimaldy, company secretary of E. H. Bentall's, to negotiate the removal of the Swifts' Football Club and the Bentall's Cricket Club equipment. The cricket club ceased to exist. The Swifts played on King George V Playing Field and then Sadd's ground until Mr. Free sold the Swifts Football Club 7$\frac{1}{2}$ acres of land for £100 per acre in Scraley Road. He made a proviso that the McCready family, his daughter Joan's family, should approve the sale of any of that land for a certain number of years after the death of his three daughters. Donald May, the club's president, officially opened the Swifts' new club house at the beginning of the season in August 1965.

The Swifts are famous in the South of England since they play in the Ryman Premier League (Isthmian), which includes clubs from much bigger places than Heybridge, in and around London and further afield in places such as Basingstoke. Today, the players are professionals or semi-professionals.

25.3 Cricket

In the early years of the eighteenth century cricket had become a craze of the aristocracy. There is evidence that cricket was being played in Maldon in 1755. It began as a gambling game and the members combed the Dengie Hundred for the best players to win the game and the bets. Maldon Cricket Club was financed by a long list of prominent citizens who did not necessarily play the game but who chose those who did. Few matches were played against other clubs but pick-up matches took place regularly. The Maldon Club played on Potman Marsh, southeast of the Causeway that was protected by low sea walls for centuries because of its military value. Potman Marsh had been the venue for the Annual Horse Race in September, and fairs and celebrations for Heybridge and Maldon people before the railway was built in 1847. Sheep grazed on the ground and no special wickets were prepared. Between 1780 and 1800, cricket was played in every school and on every village green. The MCC was not started until 1787, thirty-two years later than cricket in Maldon.

This was a time of country house cricket. In this district, Sir Claude Champion de Crespigny hosted cricket matches at Champion Lodge while other wealthy families at Woodham Mortimer Place (the Oxley Parkers), Downhall, Bradwell on Sea, Baddow Hall, Great Baddow, Felix Hall, Kelvedon and Braxted Park entertained teams raised by the county's gentry as well as some club teams such as Maldon. Public school educated sons and university students plus professionals meant a high standard of cricket. The house parties were fashionable, social occasions and lasted into the twentieth century.

When round arm bowling came in, the game became more dangerous and fashionable clubs, such as Colchester, Chelmsford and Witham, had better wickets prepared by the newly invented cylinder mowers from Ransomes of Ipswich and heavy rollers. The Maldon Club moved to Fairfield, the site of the present Upper Plume School, and made better pitches in 1848 when the railway crossed Potman Marsh.

Facilities were provided by E. H. Bentall; in the early days, the pitch was so rough that mats were laid on the bowling and batting area. The various departments within the factory challenged each other, a match was played between 'Capital versus Labour' in 1848 at the time Karl Marx published the Communist Manifesto. However, later, the significance of the naming caused future games to be between 'Offices versus Work'. There was a departmental programme with teams representing the fitters, the blacksmiths, the foundry men and the turners who played against each other.

The 1874 plan defining E. H. Bentall's personal land holdings separately from the firm of Bentall's shows a cricket field as belonging to the firm on Hobbs and Steele's Farm. The club flourished and played Saturday matches against most local clubs. Maldon Amateurs played Heybridge in 1870 as well as Langford. Fitch records that in 1898; "Heybridge Cricket Club (40th year): Club House, Half Moon Inn. Sub., 2s.6d. and upwards. Pres., E. H. Bentall. Capt. C. Perry. Hon. Sec. and Treas., F. Mott, Heybridge)".

Maldon Club was in decline around the 1900s while Heybridge gained the reputation of a go ahead club of some ability. In 1902, Maldon played Heybridge over three matches, won one and the other two were drawn but Maldon beat Heybridge in 1903. E. V. Last reports that Heybridge played ninety-five games and scored 16,581 runs in 1921. Mrs. Proctor remembers making sandwiches for cricket club teas and Betty Chittenden was the scorer for a short time. The Maldon Cricket Club had bought and played in a field next to the Maldon Town Social and Athletic Club in Fambridge Road in the 1950s. The club wound up in 1958.

Decline of Maldon Cricket Club

The club comprised local traders who played mid-week debarring large numbers of employed men who were working. The subscription of 10 shillings per year excluded many too. Maldon Cricket Club, the descendant of the original town club, was revived in 1923 and played on the Prom until the building of the Bowling Green and tennis courts displaced them.

In 1932, Maldon Wesleyans formed the Strollers Cricket Club. They played Bentall's in 1950 and beat them. The Old Maldonians Cricket Club was founded in 1951 as a section of the Old Maldonians' Association. They played on the school field but when these facilities were withdrawn, they threw open their membership and were known as the Maldonians and became a wandering club until they shared the pitch on the Prom with the Strollers.

Bentall's Cricket Club lost their ground in 1974 when the new Acrow offices were built on the site of Bentall's Sports Club and the cricket club folded.

Maldon Cricket Club and the move to Drapers Farm, Heybridge

The Strollers and Maldonians combined to become Maldon

1953 Bentall's cricket team and Betty Chittenden (nee Askew) the scorer

PHOTO By kind permission of Betty Chittenden

Cricket Club in 1975 and moved to Draper's Farm in 1980. Maldon District Council had acquired 17 acres of land at Draper's Farm as planning gain for the development of a housing estate in the vicinity. The land was scheduled for sport and recreation. The Council brokered a deal with Maldon Cricket Club and Maldon Rugby Club by which the clubs, jointly, invested £10,000 and then developed and managed the facilities for their members.

Recent Maldon Cricket Club news

After fielding four teams on Saturdays with the first team competing in the East Anglian Premier League against teams from Suffolk, Norfolk, Huntingdonshire and Cambridge, the club withdrew from this league at the end of the 2005 season after 250 years of cricket to enable their younger players to receive more coaching and gain experience which, it was hoped, would prepare them for that level of cricket in the future. Their four Saturday teams competed in the Marshall Hatchick Two Counties Championships, which covers North Essex and Suffolk. On Sundays, the Club played in Division C of the Two Counties Championship and the PDQ Cars North Essex Cricket League. This allowed those unable to play on Saturdays the chance to play in the highest standard available at local level on Sundays.

The club had a ladies' section, who played in the Beaumont Seymour Women's Cricket League on Friday evenings. For younger cricketers, there were Friday evening training sessions, which ran from 6.30pm to 7.45pm and helped to teach the game in a fun and enjoyable way, under the watchful eye of the club's qualified coaches. Promising youngsters attended the Winter School of Excellence organised in association with the Plume School and Maldon District Council, which encouraged new players into the game. There were Colts' teams at every year from under 11 to under 15.

In 2011, the club had three teams in the Two Counties Championship on Saturdays; competing with teams from North Essex and Suffolk. Two teams play on Sundays: one in the Piri Piri League and the other in the Warsop Central Essex League. The ladies team play in the Beaumont Seymour Cricket League.

Gone are the days when schools played one sport in the winter and one in the summer; students have tasters of many sports in limited class time. No real in-depth skills are taught, but Maldon Cricket Club has tackled this situation. Coaches have been trained within the club to coach boys and girls. Over two hundred boys and girls youth members are registered with the club. Coaches understand that sessions must be fun and progressive. Weekly coaching sessions are available for boys as young as 5 and matches begin for those under 9, 11, 13, 14 and 18. Sessions for girls under 11, 13 and 15 are arranged but teams for games are few.

The club is proud to have Alastair Cook of Essex and England as a playing member. He played in their adult team at the age of 11 and achieved seven test centuries before he was 23. Maldon Cricket Club celebrated 250 years of cricket in 2005.

25.4 Rugby

Men who had played rugby in the forces and liked it got together on 28th August 1947 to form a rugby club in Maldon. The president was G. R. Williams, then Tommy Harries, and the secretary was Bill Rollinson. The club played on the Promenade Park, Sains' Farm and Primrose Meadow and met in the Blue Boar, the King's Head, the Ship and the Queen's Head before they moved to Draper's Farm in 1983 with their own rugby pitches and a club house shared with Maldon Cricket Club. The three senior teams play their matches on Saturday afternoons and their training takes place on Tuesday and Thursday evenings. Maldon Rugby Club's First Team was top of Essex League 1 in 2007.

Maldon Rugby Club realises the necessity to attract youngsters to ensure the future of their club. They have recruited over one hundred youngsters from 2 years of age and upwards who receive coaching on Sunday mornings; "Little Scrummers" for 2½ to 5 year olds", Tag Rugby for 5 year olds and upwards. The youngsters gradually move, in stages, into full contact 15-a-side rugby. There are teams for the 7, 8 and 9 year olds, under 13, under 14 and under 17 year olds who play mini, midi and youth rugby then the adult game of rugby. Stages include playing on a smaller pitch with a smaller ball, with nine players in a team and tagging not tackling. Mini, midi and youth matches and training takes place on Sunday morning. The club's youth teams have been champions in Essex for various categories of ages.

25.5 Quoits

This ancient game became popular in the nineteenth century. It was played on Bentall's Sports Club Field behind the wall opposite the school. There were two quoits pitches holding clay that had wooden covers. Quoits were thrown from one end to the pin at the other and then the return was made to the opposite pin. Johnny Moss became quoits champion of England. Mrs. Cissy Proctor (nee Wager) now 90, remembers her father, Toby (Albert) Wager playing quoits. He played for England and his son has his medals.

PHOTO By kind permission of Malcolm Willis

25.6 Sailing

25.6a Blackwater Sailing Club

A meeting was held to form the Blackwater Sailing Club at the beginning of 1899 when Edward Ernest Bentall became the commodore. The vice-commodore was Tom Lawrence Eve, Walter Gray combined the roles of treasurer and secretary, and there was a committee of four. They drew up a schedule of rules and sailing regulations for each member and the first race was held on 29th April. Heybridge is 17 miles from the open sea and the Blackwater is a tricky estuary; currents, tides and mud test the skills of an amateur sailor. Members were drawn from local families with long-standing professional or business associations with Maldon District.

The club has remained essentially a sailing club; many of the members are content to stay in the estuary, sail dinghies or race day boats while members of the cruiser section go much further afield. G. H. P. Muhlhauser circumnavigated the world 1920-1923. The club's first regatta was held on 30th June 1900 when Commodore E. E. Bentall gave a prize for the member with the highest number of points.

Blackwater Sailing Club first met in the granary next to the canal locks. They wrote to the Chelmer and Blackwater Navigation Company asking for the use of that building - and they are still awaiting a reply! Until 1903, the club had been meeting in public houses. Their search for a site for the club house was solved when E. E. Bentall, the commodore, offered a site on his property behind the sea wall which had been used for salt panning by Maldon Salt Company in the middle of the nineteenth century. "The only access to the site was by a rough track leading over the fields to Basin Road or along the sea wall to the Basin. The sea wall had been in existence since 1806 when William Lewis built it in ten weeks running from Heybridge Basin past the Sailing Club House site, northwest to Millbeach across the mouth of what is now known as the Ballast Hole. Mr. Lawrence received a silver medal from the Royal Society of Arts for his work which had cost £307.10s.1½d. The area behind the sea wall was meadowland." (Jan Wise).

Mr. A Ward built the new clubhouse at a cost of £140 and there was a grand opening on 4th January 1904. James Woodcraft was appointed steward and caretaker in that year at a wage of 3s.0d. per week and extra for attendance on meals. He did not retire until 1928; he had served the club loyally in various ways. In 1909, he had laid a floor for 6d. an hour, that year he asked for a rise because the increase in the number of members meant that the washing up took longer, he was awarded one shilling extra per week from March to September. Improvements to the clubhouse have been made over the years; in 1906 the balcony was enclosed in glass by May and Butcher for £8.5s.0d. and the dressing room was lined with matchboard for £9.10s.0d.

Mrs. H. R. Brown, wife of a founder member, Dr. Brown, the town's medical officer, was the club's first lady member in 1899. Ladies were involved in the club's affairs right from the beginning but probably with limited rights. Early members included Wedgewood Benn MP, later Lord Stansgate, Sir Norman Angell from Northey Island, winner of the Nobel Peace Prize, Sir Claude de Crespigny who requested a diving board at the end of the club pier since Sir Claude and his wife, Lady Georgina, were keen swimmers. Clem Parker was a member and a regular competitor in barge matches. He had five barges named after his daughters. Barge owners had their own secret formula for dressing the barge sails to preserve and lubricate them; Clem Parker's sails were spread out to dry on the field at the top of the road from the Bradwell Quay after a mixture of linseed oil and red ochre had been brushed over them which took a long time to dry. The workmen's hands and clothes were stained red. After 2000 homes were built on this field.

It was not until 1909 that the club was granted membership of the Yacht Racing Association (now the Royal Yacht Association). The subscription was 2 guineas a year. In 1913 members first attempted to persuade the committee to apply for an alcohol licence; at last a bar was installed in 2005 that opens on special occasions. Before W.W.1, yacht owners were able to buy special rail tickets for travel to their boats, cruise along the East Coast and return to London from the anchorage they had reached.

The sea wall became a popular place for swimming, picnics and parties in the 1930s when the club introduced a bathing category of membership; this is in keeping with the family spirit of the club. Bathing membership was restricted to over 18s at first, then 16 years olds and in 1937 Mrs. Wright, then Jean Reid-Scott, was admitted to bathing membership at 14 years of age.

In 1978, the club managed to purchase 17 acres of land for £28,000, between Basin Road and the club house, from Donald May. The cost of creating a sail training lake on this land and improving the access road came from the sale of gravel. One hundred and seventeen youngsters aged from 10-18 received training there to qualify them to sail on the river in 1986. The lake is used by Newham's Outdoor Centre to train sailors and canoeists and Chelmsford Radio Controlled Yachts race there. In 2007, a pavilion was built overlooking the sail training lake where on shore instruction takes place and safety supervisors, instructors and parents can shelter. The Blackwater Sailing Club had one thousand members of all classes in 2004. It is an RYA training club with an RYA appointed trainer and a cadet section and there is a happy split between cruisers and dinghies. Maldon District Council owns the club's moorings. The club house was sympathetically renovated in 2004 to provide modern day facilities.

25.6b Marconi Sailing Club and Newham Outdoors Activities Centre

The Marconi Sailing Club was formally established in March 1952. The club's first headquarters were based in a boatshed 60ft. x 18ft. on the sea wall at Heybridge Basin in May and Butcher's yard for an annual rent of £50, which included electricity. Denys Harrison says this was the original workshop of Arthur Butcher (1). In 1958, the club acquired the 97ft. barge yacht Mangu. This vessel had been built by Gill and Sons at Rochester for the marine artist W. L. Wyllie in 1904 and used as working barge, then named Cawana, that cruised on the east and south coasts. She was known as the Mangu when R. de B. Crawshay lived on her in Maldon during the 1930s and 1940s. She had been elaborately fitted out below with oak panelling and a brick fireplace. Ron Greygoose remembers that Cecil Stebbens, the water bailiff, towed her round to Heybridge Basin where she was moored bows-on to the sea wall. This boat became the Marconi Sailing Club House instead of the shed. Ground for dinghy storage was rented from local allotment holders.

To ensure the long term future of the club, a three year lease on a small strip of land at Stansgate was obtained in March 1963. It became possible to acquire the present larger site in October 1971 and three years later the temporary wooden club house was replaced by the present day building. After 2003, the club became independent from Marconi Athletic and Social Club when members of the sailing section bought the site and assets.

West Ham Education Committee established a residential centre on the sea wall on premises leased from May and Butcher in 1963 and they acquired the Mangu from the Marconi Sailing Club to use as their Outdoor Activities Centre. Two permanent staff, one of them Dudley Courtman, were appointed and two parties of twenty students pursued week long courses aboard. Cubicles were installed below deck and a store room was inserted. Their activities centred on 13ft. Torch Dinghies and a dozen canoes that had been made in West Ham schools. Later, a toilet block was built ashore with various sheds for boat repairs and storage on land acquired from May and Butcher's trustees.

East Ham had been using Valentine Crittall's (Lord Braintree) home, Crockies, as an Old People's Home since 1952. They had re-named it Fairplay House. Mrs. Wooldridge, who ran the home, said it was a mistake to house older residents in the middle of the countryside as they needed to be able to wander into shops and visit public houses. When West Ham and East Ham were amalgamated to form the London Borough of Newham in 1965, courses in Heybridge Basin became popular and Newham decided to expand the facilities and make the whole of Fairplay House part of its Outdoor Activities Centre. The centre, which is set in 12 acres of grounds, has its own swimming pool and magnificent views from the elevated position. Two groups are based in Fairplay House which has been generously equipped for educational purposes including classroom laboratory facilities and the centre's own minibus while a third group is based on the barge yacht "Mangu" in Heybridge Basin. The centre is supported by the Passmore Edwards Museum Service who stepped in with a grant to rescue the lighter Susan when the Navigation Company wished to dispose of her. She was re-furbished in the Maldon Boat Yard. They restored the barge Dawn which is used for one and two night residential trips by youngsters and is moored on Maldon Hythe. Dudley Courtman, one of the original staff as warden and later principal, ultimately had a staff of twenty-four.

Today, groups canoe on the Chelmer and Blackwater Navigation, sail on the estuary, carry out field studies of the local geography, history and marine biology and visit the Essex Record Office. The art and drama group made a short film about building lock gates and installing them. It was a film making teaching tool but, more importantly, it preserved knowledge about a unique craft.

25.6c Saltcote Sailing Club

This club was founded in 1961 and operates from Wharf Road.

25.6d Mill Beach Marine Club

This was known as Mill Beach Motor Boat Club originally. It is a members' club that was founded in 1967. Their boats were kept in the corner of Mill Beach Hotel car park until they managed to buy a piece of waste land from Mr. Harry Pledger nearby. There are eighty-five members. The club opened a new club house in September 2009; the building work and fitting out were carried out by the members who raised £60,000 in seven months to pay for it.

25.7 Maldon Golf Club

In 1881, Thompson of Felixstowe laid out the course which comprised nine holes and was 2,189 yards long. The club was instituted on 24th November, 1891, the third oldest club in Essex. Originally, forty-two members paid an annual subscription of 10s.6d. Sir Claude de Crespigny was one of the founder members. The club headquarters were at the White Hart Inn at Fullbridge that closed in the 1970s. It was next door to the Welcome Sailor. Shortly after the inaugural meeting, Edmund Ernest Bentall was made captain; he held this office from 1891 to 1895. He became honorary secretary in 1899 in which capacity he served until 1913. Competitions were underway in 1892 when E. E. Bentall had the lowest scratch score in a club competition of 101. In the Monthly Medal, 27th October 1893, he scored 103 less 11, net 92. He participated in matches against Bullwood (Rayleigh) in 1894, Braintree in 1897 and Southend in 1896. By 1900, there was a club house, fifty members and the president of the club was the Rev. E. R. Horwood.

Today, men play for the Bentall Cup presented by E. E. Bentall in 1899 and women play for the Bentall Cup presented by Joan W. Bentall when she was Lady Captain in 1947. Part of the course is leased from Foyle Estate of Beeleigh Abbey. The Chelmer and Blackwater Navigation forms the boundary between Heybridge and Langford but when the River Chelmer was Heybridge parish boundary, part of the golf course was in Heybridge.

25.8 Maldon Bowling Club

The author visited the club and met Jim Thompson, chairman for ten years and Brian Chalk who served as president for eight years. They described the history and running of the club which was founded in 1908 when bowls were played on a green at the back of number 17 London Road, Maldon that was approached by a footpath alongside the house. The pavilion was spartan; trestle tables and forms and no bar. Ladies did not play but did the teas. The club grew steadily, the green was extended and various improvements were made to the club house helped by a fund raising bridge drive in 1932. In that year, ladies were invited to become members of a Ladies' Section paying an annual subscription of 10s.6d. In 1941, the groundsman's wages were fixed at 15s.0d. per week.

In 1942, Major Douglas Brown became the new owner of number 17 and subsequently bought two thirds of the club's land that he leased back to the club. Lengthy negotiation took place culminating in the opening of a new green on the Promenade on Wednesday 30th April 1952 owned and constructed from Cumberland turf by Maldon Borough Council. There were six rinks; the club rented three on certain days of the week and the other three were available to the general public. It was decided that year that players should wear white flannel trousers and shirts. In December 1958, the ladies requested that a ladies section be re-formed so that they could be affiliated to the Essex County Women's Bowling Association. By 1959, the club had a pavilion but it had no lights, no changing rooms, no door or windows. During the next few years, members provided the money and labour to improve the facilities.

Maldon Borough owned the green and the club house. It was discovered that the club paid the council £150, the public had paid £15.18s.0d. while the council's outgoings had been £600 causing club rent to be raised by £25! Later, Maldon District Council granted the club a licence to play on the green, to have the sole use of the facility and be responsible for the maintenance. For around six years, the Maldon District Council team's tender has secured the contract to maintain the green. Entrance is through double iron gates, hedges define the club property, the surrounds of the green are decorated by attractive topiary and wooden seats are available for spectators. Club members care for the club grounds; on the morning of the visit, five members had spent three hours tidying the surrounds of the green. Today, members of affiliated bowls' clubs owning the right equipment may apply to play and the public may spectate. Extensive improvements to the club house were made in 1991 when members subscribed £6,050 for bonds to help pay for the improvements.

It was in 1971, that Clive South became Champion of Champions in The Chelmsford District Bowling Association. Andrew Squire, aged 15, played for the club in a match against Witham in May 1980. At the age of 20 he won the Chelmsford and District Bowling Association championship. This was the beginning of a successful competitive bowling career, culminating twenty-seven years later when he became the Men's English Bowling Association's Singles champion. In 1973, Mrs. Ruth Springett won her County badge after being selected to represent Essex in a match against Buckinghamshire - the first Maldon member to achieve this.

This successful club celebrated its centenary in 2008. Men and women enjoy a full programme of competitions and friendly matches. The larger clubhouse with a bar enables the club to entertain visitors more suitably and arrange more social activities for the members. Maldon Club has implemented latest government legislation and granted full club membership to ladies in 2011. Many local people play bowls in the summer on grass at Maldon Bowls Club. In winter, eight hundred from various local clubs go to the Jacks Bowling Club at Latchingdon for indoor bowls.

25.9 Fishing

The land around Heybridge and this part of Essex is sand and gravel bearing. The exhausted pits fill with water. Early worked out pits were not bound by 106 Agreements which detail the restoration that must take place after the gravel has been extracted; for example, Heybridge Hall was just left and the unwanted heavy equipment lies in the bottom of the lake.

Essex is the driest county in England; some farmers have created reservoirs, after extracting the sand and gravel, and stocked them with fish. Anglers need rod licences issued by the Environment Agency every year. Full licences cover two rods and, around 2009, cost annually £27, senior concessions and disabled £18, juniors 12-16 £5 and those under 12 free. One day rod licences cost £3.75 and eight day £10. There is a closed season for coarse fishing from 15th March to 15th June. Coarse fish that are caught must be thrown back but not trout. A few of the opportunities for angling are detailed below. They show what a popular hobby it is.

Chelmer and Blackwater Navigation Angling Association - Members of the Association fish the Navigation from Brown's Wharf in Chelmsford to Heybridge Basin as well as fifteen lakes. The club had 1,700 members in 2009 when the subscriptions were £64 for seniors (adult males), £44 for ladies, £25 for 12 to 15 years old and £42 for senior citizens. Night fishing is included in the subscription for members fishing in the Navigation. Day tickets are available. In addition, members must have a rod licence from the Environment Agency which permits them to fish with two rods. There is a close season from 14th March to 16th June on the Navigation.

Big shoals of bream, roach, tench, chub, perch, pike and carp to over 30lb flourish in the deep, slow moving waters of the canal. Species such as gudgeon, minnow, stickleback, and some crayfish are there. Fishermen, it is usually men, sit on the canal bank under their green umbrellas with their rod fishing lines in the water. Very serious competitions take place when the catches are weighed. Southend Waterworks Company re-stocks the waterways with indigenous coarse fish that die when the water is polluted. The company relies on the public to report when they see dead fish so that the cause can be traced and restocking begun. A bailiff polices the Navigation inspecting official rod licences of the various clubs and selling day tickets.

Maldon Angling Society: this society was established in 1895 and shares fifteen miles of the Navigation with the Chelmsford and Backwater Navigation Angling Association and has fifteen still waters; Members of Chelmsford Angling Association, Kelvedon District Angling Association and Dunmow all fish in the Chelmer and Blackwater Navigation.

Totham Pit: a sixty-five year old gravel pit with; large tench up to 9lb, bream up to 12lb and carp up to 30lb.

Howells Lake Langford: common to minor carp up to 30lb.

Bog Grove Great Totham: tench, crucian, rudd, carp.

Beckingham Hall Tolleshunt Major: a risen farm reservoir of 4 acres; common and mirror carp to upper doubles, tench, roach/bream hybrids.

Langford Little Park: a pair of small lakes stocked as Bog Grove.

River Blackwater Wickham Bishops to Langford: over one mile of untamed river; chub up to 5lb, roach, perch, dace, gudgeon and occasional barbel.

Ashmans Farm Little Braxted: the lake was opened to members in 2009. It closes from 1st October to 31st January for shooting parties; roach, rudd, bream, perch, carp up to 20lb and plenty of tench.

Whitehouse Farm Tolleshunt D'Arcy: this 1.6 acre farm reservoir was opened spring 2010; bream to 7lb, roach to $1^1/2$lb, hybrids to 4lb and carp to upper doubles.

Railway Pond, Heybridge: renowned for weed but has produced wonderful bags of fish; small tench, roach, crucian and ghost carp. Day tickets from 16th June to 14th March. Around 2009: adults £5, concessions £3, juniors £2. The ticket allows access to the nearby Navigation.

Slough House, Heybridge: covers 5 acres; carp approaching 30lb, perch, rudd, tench and big bream.

Little London Reservoir Goldhanger: covers $1^1/2$ acres; roach, perch, crucian. Silver fish, bream up to 8lb and carp to doubles.

Rook Hall (3 lakes): three very different waters.

New Hall Reservoir Purleigh:. this small water resembles a truncated section of canal; roach, bream and rudd. Some anglers have been surprised to catch large eels. Their membership fees range from £70 for an adult, £40 for a retired or disabled adult to £8 for an under 12 with an adult. There were 673 members from all classes in 2009.

Chigborough Lakes, Heybridge: Chigborough Fisheries cover 53 acres from which gravel was extracted in the 1970s. There are eight lakes; four coarse fishing lakes that cover 20 acres, three are open to £8 day tickets holders and a day season ticket cost £95 in 2009. One lake is for members only from which large carp and other fish including catfish are caught. There are four trout lakes. Tuition is possible and tackle for sale, boat and bank fishing is available. On the site there is a restaurant and smokehouse.

Fishing syndicates: like game shooting, there are syndicates that stock lakes and maintain them.

25.10 The Basin Oars

Jill Doubtfire, Marion Hobden, Patti Mead, Brenda Riches and Crys McPherson are sporting Basin ladies who, from 2008, carry on the tradition of raising thousands of pounds for the RNLI by dressing up and rowing in races on such days as Boxing Day and New Year's Day.

25.11 Maldon and Heybridge Swimming Club

The Penny Farthing, the Maldon and District Museum Association Newsletter, recounts the history of Maldon and Heybridge Swimming Club founded on 13th June 1906. At the Annual General Meeting in March 1907, there were seventy one members; sixty-three men and eight ladies and the annual subscription was five shillings.

Sir Claude de Crespigny and E. H. Bentall were among the nine vice-presidents. The club affiliated to the Southern Counties Amateur Swimming Association and the Royal Life Saving Society. Swimming and diving championships, attracting enormous crowds from long distances, were held annually in the Marine Lake. By 1914, membership had increased to one hundred and forty-eight, including fifty-two ladies, but during the last two years of W.W.1 the club's activities ceased. Membership reached one hundred and eleven by 1924 but enthusiasm varied and, despite the efforts of some members and vice-presidents, the club's fortunes wavered; their eleven cups were deposited in Barclays Bank in June 1940. Heybridge disappeared from the club's name and no activities were recorded until 1946 when it was decided that the club should amalgamate with Maldon Town Athletic Club and became known as Maldon Town Swimming Club. Apart from a successful water polo section that included Alan Plastow there followed a slow decline with the last minute dated 15th November 1966 which seemed to mark the end of a once great swimming club.

25.12 Maldon and Little Baddow Hockey Club

Joyce Binder was connected with Maldon Hockey Club after W.W.2; this club seems to have disappeared. It was revived by Roy and Merle Pipe in 1979. Sport England, then the Lottery Sport Fund, contributed £150,000 towards the pitch built in 1996; they regard it as a "key" club being the only hockey club in the area. In the last few years, the club has fielded two men's teams who play in the Eastern Region which includes London, Hertfordshire, Suffolk and even further afield; and two ladies teams (girls over 13 can play in adult teams) who play teams from Essex. Mini junior hockey is played by forty-six children between the ages of 6 and 12 and there is an academy team for young players. There are seventy members over 13. Mixed hockey used to be played on Sundays but fewer clubs now play it and there are only occasional mixed games. The club is twinned with Cuijk in Holland. Roy Pipe was a keen player but has umpired for the last 25 years. Over the years, the club owned two minibuses in which the teams went to matches. Travelling together helped to foster the team spirit but first one and then the second vehicle succumbed to old age and now members share cars or parents ferry players to matches.

25.13 Blackwater Judo Club

This club was started in 2000.

25.14 Maldon Croquet Club

This club was founded in April 2011, thirty-four people enrolled in the first summer. The club has two lawns on the out field of the cricket pitch at Draper's Farm.

26.0 Societies and Clubs

Heybridge is a legal entity separate from Maldon. However, since they adjoin, they have always shared many joint ventures. Heybridge residents belong to these societies; and some serve as committee members and officers. The manager of Maldon Tourist Information Centre says there is a club for every interest or activity in Maldon, suggesting sixty or seventy societies and clubs; for example interests include singing, art, gardening, amateur dramatics, history, bridge and so on. Apologies if your club is not mentioned.

26.1 1st and 2nd Essex Volunteer Engineering Corps

Mr. E. H. Bentall was a member of the Maldon Company of Volunteers in its early days. He raised the 1st Essex Volunteer Engineering Corps in Heybridge. He commanded one company himself, his son, E. E. Bentall, commanded the second company. He paid for the cost of the equipment and built the Drill Hall in 1861. This large building had a drill hall with armoury for the newly enrolled corps of the 1st Essex Engineers Volunteers, which is why it was known as the Headquarters. The Volunteer Companies came to an end in 1876.

26.2 Headquarters

Until the 1960s, the Headquarters was a venue for many social activities. Mr. and Mrs. Knowles held popular weekly Old Tyme Dance sessions assisted by Ted Wire. Quaff (Clifford) Gill (who cycled around Heybridge on a tall, old fashioned bicycle when he was over 90) and Min, his partner, were keen dancers. Ballroom dances were held on the famous sprung Canadian maple floor over which Ted Wire had already spread French chalk in preparation for the dances. Harry Davidson's Orchestra, a nationally popular dance band, was an attraction on one occasion. Refreshments were served in the canteen at the back of the hall and Miss Hepburn catered for the dances. On Saturday evenings, Ken Osborne drove a coach to bring in dancers from villages and the hall would be full. Ted Wire also organised weekly whist drives. Bentall's Badminton Club played matches in the hall in the Chelmsford Badminton League until the hall was demolished by Acrow. Various other organisations held functions there.

During W.W.2, and for several years after, Alf Bacon was the steward of the Bentall's Works' Club located at the end of the main hall above the canteen where snooker and darts were played. Bentall's provided a tea in January for all employees' children in the Headquarters; a conjuror was hired to entertain and Mrs. Bentall gave each child a bag containing goodies. Cakes and jellies were luxuries then, as was the orange they took home. During W.W.2 Ted Wire organised 'Workers' Playtime' for Bentall's workers. The show took place at lunchtime when artists such as Anne Shelton, Elsie and Doris Waters and Tommy Handley performed. Joy, Ted's daughter, was allowed to attend in school holidays and stood on a chair at the back.

The Headquarters was demolished in the 1960s by Acrow and the site became part of the ICS Triplex complex that manufactured highly technical oil rig equipment. When this firm was taken over and the main production was moved to their other factory part of the complex was still used as their offices and manufacturing. Other buildings on the site are let out to various firms and the old Ever Ready factory remained empty for many years other than for short term lets.

The first three of the following entries are listed in Fitch's Directory 1898.

26.3 Ancient Order of Foresters

Court House Queen's Head Inn Heybridge, Members 776. Forester Juvenile Court 'Pride of Youth' met at Going's Wharf, Heybridge Members 118.

26.4 The Band of Hope

Fitch records that sixty-eight members belonged to the Heybridge Basin Band of Hope. There are many references to Bank of Hope branches which started in 1847. In the nineteenth century, and way into the twentieth century, young people were warned of the dangers of drinking alcohol and the misery it caused and urged to sign the pledge never to drink alcohol. At a time of no TV or radio, their meetings and slide shows attracted young people. Licensing hours began to be restricted in public houses during W.W.1. Instead of 16 or 17 hours a day, 19 in London, by 1921 they were reduced to 8 or 9 hours on weekdays.

26.5 Maldon and Heybridge Horticultural Society

26.5a Exhibition of Fruit and Vegetables 1894

Ruth Davis and Vivienne Allan did some research on the history of this society; information was sparse but they did find a poster for the Maldon Society's show on Wednesday 14th November 1894.

Fitch lists a public hall with six hundred seats at 45 High Street that was erected by a public company in 1859. It was intended for public meetings, concerts, and lectures etc. and as a corn exchange. There was a series of fires in the nineteenth century between Market Hill and the Moot Hall. This hall was on the site of the former vacant post office between the then library and the Town Hall and within the fire torn area so that one may assume it was burned down.

26.5b The Society today

In 2011 this successful horticultural society had over two hundred members. It offers members monthly meetings with talks on a range of gardening topics including flower gardens, indoor gardens and allotments, and general interest. It organises spring, summer and autumn shows, a series of competitions at the monthly meetings and annual events for pumpkins and sunflowers. Generous discounts on horticultural supplies through bulk buying are secured for members and visits are organised to gardens and places connected with gardening topics.

26.5c Friary Garden

This garden is probably the site of the Carmelite Friary Garden founded in 1293. Following the dissolution of the monasteries in 1538, it became a site of a Tudor mansion. By the nineteenth century there were two Georgian houses there, then the garden was let to tenant gardeners who planted many fruit trees, vines and flowering shrubs. The last tenant was a keen plants man and the planting reflected his interests. The garden was neglected and shut up in the 1970s but in 1987, the offer of Maldon and Heybridge Horticultural Society to take over the fifth of an acre garden and restore it as a working garden was accepted, although Essex County Council retains ownership. Wynne John (nee Jones) led the volunteer work teams in 1987 until she moved to New Zealand when Arthur Cox took over and continued to guide and lead the team from 1988 until October 2010. When bottles, cans and the dense overgrowth was cleared, a network of narrow paths between box hedges and many interesting plants and masses of bulbs were revealed. Volunteer gardeners work on the garden on the first Sunday in the month when the public are welcome to view. Visits can be arranged at other times for parties, school groups and individuals. Volunteers carry out general work; some have small beds where they grow flowers or vegetables.

26.5d Allotments

Mr. Free had created allotments on the frontage of land he bought from the Milbanke Estate next to the entrance to the cemetery. It is recorded that, in January 1888, a strip of land containing allotments was purchased to provide a road entrance to the cemetery. There were allotments off what is now a cul-de-sac off Crescent Road where houses were built around 1970 by Mr. Mott. A large allotment site was bounded by Barnfield Cottages, Stock Terrace and Springfield Cottages where houses have now been built. The path through the allotments behind St Georges Church in Heybridge Basin was a short cut to the river until houses were built on the allotments and May and Butcher's yard.

Historically, the traditional size of an allotment has always been ten rods. A rod was the distance between the back of the plough and the front of the ox. Allotments were roughly the size of a tennis court; about 300 square yards or a plot 30ft. by 100ft. It was based on a calculation that this size was needed to feed a family of four for a year. In modern times, half a plot is thought to be enough for households.

The duty to provide allotments had been a controversial item in the Act of Parliament creating parish councils in 1894 when parish councils were granted the power to hire or buy land for them and were encouraged to do so. In 1987, when Heybridge Parish Council was revived, requests were made for the provision of allotments in Heybridge through the Maldon and Heybridge Horticultural Society allotment section. Heybridge Parish Council asked for names and addresses of Heybridge people who wanted allotments before committing the Council to the heavy expenditure for fencing, hard surfacing footpaths and water supplies but no reply came. The same request was made years later but no reply came. This was unfortunate because Heybridge Parish Council were being consulted about planning applications for large developments of housing and could have sought provision of allotments as planning gain from the plans submitted. Heybridge Parish Council, prompted by Councillor Mrs. Veronica Miller, did not have any luck in seeking allotment sites in 2010. Heybridge residents who have allotments in Maldon receive help and support from the Horticultural Society and all are entered for the competition held annually that selects the best kept allotment. Today, Heybridge residents do not receive favourable consideration for allotments in Maldon.

26.6 Heybridge Women's Institutes

There were two branches of the Women's Institute in Heybridge.

26.6a Heybridge and Langford Women's Institute

The Women's Institute movement was founded in Canada and came to the United Kingdom in 1915. Heybridge and Langford Women's Institute was one of five started in Essex in 1917 with Mrs. E. E. Bentall as president, an office she held for thirty years. Mrs. Bentall attended meetings regularly until September 1957 and died later that year. There have been ten presidents in eighty-eight years. The early records were tragically lost but ninety-five members were listed in 1951. At one time, there were one hundred and fifty members; there were about thirty members in 2005.

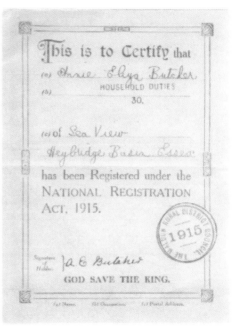

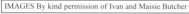

IMAGES By kind permission of Ivan and Maisie Butcher

The branch has always met in the Waring Room on the first Wednesday of the month. Yes, they do begin by singing Jerusalem and finish with the National Anthem. The main part of the meeting is taken up with a speaker or demonstrator on a wide variety of topics ranging, in 1925, from "The British Empire", a lantern lecture on "India", "Local Government in Village Life", "Best Home Made Labour Saver". The 2005 programme included "The Story of Glyndebourne", "The Good Life", "All about Beads" and "The Craft of the Potter". Members take turns to be tea hostesses and bring their favourite homemade cakes. The monthly competition judged during the tea interval is usually linked to the speaker's theme. Recent topics have included "Amusing Newspaper Cuttings", "Recycled Object", Flower Arrangement" and "Salt Dough Object". The afternoon concludes on a lighter note with a social half hour. Tradition can be comforting and the friendships made at meetings are valued.

Heybridge and Langford meet up with Purleigh, Maldon Centre, Wickham Bishops and Great Totham Women's Institutes for a Spring Group Meeting going to each village in turn. Essex

Women's Institutes belong to the Essex Federation, which arranges County meetings. A representative from the local groups attends the National Federation's Annual Meeting, which used to be held in the Royal Albert Hall regularly but now goes to venues around the England, for example Birmingham, Cardiff and Brighton have been used.

Heybridge and Langford W.I. Supper 1967. President Mrs. R. E. Claydon back row.
PHOTO by kind permission of the Maldon and Burnham Standard

Women's Institutes are non-party political as the Prime Minister Blair found out in 2000 when he began to extol the achievements of his government and received a slow handclap at the Wembley Arena Annual Meeting attended by Doreen Clarke from Heybridge. Resolutions to the Annual Meeting are discussed and voted upon at branch meetings attended by county advisers. Those passed do influence government ministers and public bodies, possibly because branches have no party affiliation. The 90th conference took place in the Royal Albert Hall in 2005 attended by Jeanette Lovely from Heybridge who said that the speaker, Jane Fonda, the American actress, held the audience spellbound. These are just two examples of the wide range of speakers at the National Annual Meetings.

County advisers attend branch Annual Meetings to keep members informed about Women's Institute affairs nationally and in Essex and help them follow correct procedures. The knowledge gained of committee procedure has resulted in some Women's Institute members going on to undertake public service in other spheres.

Heybridge and Langford Women's Institute members often visit other parts of Essex to attend events organised by the County Federation or to visit places of interest. They have visited Ely, Kew Gardens, Syon Park, The Royal Hospital Chelsea, Southwold and Bury St Edmunds recently. In earlier times, Dennis Fenn remembers his mother not returning to Heybridge until 9pm after a visit to Bourneville. In Mrs. Bentall's time, garden meetings were held at the Towers. A recent year's president, Linda Hawkins, welcomed members to her garden. There is a tradition of providing hospitality teas to groups visiting the area. Forty-two members of the Post Office Retirement Club from Kent and forty-eight members of the Clacton on Sea Women's Institute were entertained in 2005. This has proved to be a useful way of raising funds and visitors know they will have a real, old-fashioned afternoon tea.

26.6b Freshwater Women's Institute

Dorene Carr writes that Heybridge had its share of young women from the new estates in 1969. They were kept busy during the day with the usual chores of baby rearing, shopping, delivering older children to and from school and cooking evening meals. The thriving afternoon W.I. was not for them so when a suggestion was made at the baby clinic that an evening institute be formed, there was lots of enthusiasm among those present. A meeting was arranged at the Waring Room in November 1969, chaired by Dot Norburn of Happy Days Holiday Camp and attended by twenty-three women all eager to proceed but twenty-five were required to start a new institute. They were on the point of leaving when the door opened and two more women arrived to a hearty cheer and a round of applause. The formalities complete, all they now needed was a name for the new institute and, after several suggestions, it was agreed to use the name Freshwater who had been tenants of Heybridge Hall for over one hundred years and remembered by a memorial in Heybridge Church.

Most of the activities of the Institute in the early years seem to have involved Happy Days Caravan Park; parties, pantomimes, rummage sales and barn dances in 1977. Freshwater moved from the Waring Room to Plantation Hall because it was a larger and warmer venue. The membership increased to almost seventy. By the mid-1980s however, things were starting to go downhill. A lot of members left when groups of young people began gathering around the hall and causing deliberate disruption to meetings.

26.6c Heybridge Women's Institute

Freshwater W.I. had lasted thirty-nine years; it merged with Heybridge and Langford W.I. in January 2009 to form the new Heybridge W.I.

26.7 Scouts, Cubs and Beavers

Mrs. Easter was a stalwart leader of the Brownies for many years. Dennis Fenn recalls Mr. Mugglestone, scoutmaster in the 1930s when the troop met in various places including the Waring Room and camped in Langford Park in the summer.

The 1st Heybridge Scout group was reformed by the Rev. A. Godsell on 24th February 1965; it was sponsored by St Andrew's Church and met in the Waring Room. The group moved to the new Rowan Drive Heybridge Primary School in 1990. This group had to leave Heybridge Primary School in 2010 and now meets at Prances in Wickham Bishops but hopes it will not be too long before they find a home in Heybridge. Mrs. Frost, who lived at Heybridge Mill, bequeathed a field behind Holloway Road to St Andrew's Church who allow Heybridge Group to use for outdoor activities and practice camps. Clive Searle is the present leader of the group (2011). There are one hundred and eighty members, boys and girls aged 6 to 18 years, in the Scouts, Cubs and Beavers' sections.

26.8 Maldon Choral Society

When unemployed Welsh miners came to Maldon in the mid-1920s to look for work, they founded a male voice choir with sixty members. A separate ladies' choir was amalgamated in 1948. This choir was known as the SX Choir until 1984 when some singers from Great Baddow joined them. Since 2003, the musical director has been Dr. Gillian Ward Russell. In 2011, there were forty members who regularly give concerts in the town.

26.9 Dramatic societies

Maldon with Heybridge members has had various dramatic groups.

26.9a The Maldon Amateur Operatic Society was active in the late 1930s. They performed operettas: The Pirates of Penzance, My Lady Molly and Ivor Novello's popular works to the accompaniment of a piano, violin and cello.

26.9b Maldon Dramatic Society was active in the 1940s. Beth Grigsby acted and produced and Clara and Norah Bate were founder members. Arthur Knowles, deputy head of Maldon Grammar School acted and produced while Phyl Nicholson, Connie Towler and Mary Knightbridge appeared in many plays. Two productions a year were undertaken in March and October. The club folded in 1952.

26.9c Blackwater Players - Joan Mansfield performed many roles in this group; she acted, produced and was secretary and treasurer. The society met in the Friends' Meeting House and prominent members were Denny Griffiths, Frank Cruess, Ted Creeson, Ian Edmunds, George Crisp and Phyl Nicolson. These were busy people holding demanding jobs who had to drop out and the club folded in 1992.

26.9d Maldon Pantomime Society attracted some members from the Blackwater Players when they finished.

26.9e The Promenaders began in 1981 as part of the Plume Parent Teachers' Association when they were called the Plume Players. Later, when few members had connections with the Plume School, their name was changed to The Promenaders. Their shows raise money for good causes. The thirtieth anniversary concert had four members of the original cast: Leonie Mott, Jill Light, Marg Ashworth and Jackie Tosic.

26.9f All Saints' Drama Guild was founded in 1952 as a church group. Their productions took place in the Parish Hall near the Moot Hall until Wallace Binder gave them land on the corner of Wellington Road when a modern building replaced the original hall. Alfred Knightbridge has been a long standing member who attended his first performance sixty years ago. He has undertaken many roles and still acts, prompts and helps in various ways and is now president. Mr. Jelly, Head of All Saints Primary School, was a very important member as producer and actor; he was a sad loss when he died young. His daughter was a good actress too. Joyce Binder, a strong character in the All Saints' group, left to perform with the Mundon Society and then returned to play important roles in All Saints' group. Some will remember performances by Jeanette Lovely, Connie Towler and Norah Gray. In 2002, the links with the church were much less strong and the group became the Maldon Drama Group. Productions had taken place in the church hall in London Road until 2003; they now take place in the Town Hall.

26.9g Harambee - This group attached to the Methodist Church performs musicals with a religious connection such as Godspell.

26.9h MAC, The Maldon Actors' Company - This is a non-profit making company providing "Arts events and drama for the community and by the community of the District of Maldon" It was formed in 1995 by Barrie Jaimeson and Nicola Essen, two professional actors who live locally. In the summer of 1996, Barrie Jaimeson was asked to go to local primary schools and organise workshops on the Promenade Park involving art and drama. This resulted in a video-filmed Viking soap opera. In 1997, a professional cast of six toured local villages to support the Plume School's bid to be a Performing Arts College. The first outdoor performance of a Shakespeare play in the Promenade Park took place in 2003; this has become an annual event in the amphitheatre that was built in 2006. In the productions, there are some professional actors but local people are invited to audition whether or not they have acting experience and some come from local drama groups. They rehearse from January and put on three or four performances in the summer. Back stage work is also carried out by volunteers.

26.9i Maldon Players - For several years past, Maldon District has a Heritage Weekend in September when interesting historic buildings are open to the public. Alison Woolard writes about the history of the area and her work has been used by Vicky Trotman to write a play on a topic that is performed by the Maldon Players at an historic location. In 2011, St Giles Leper Hospital in Spital Road was chosen as the venue and the play's title was 'A day in the life of the leper hospital in 1482'. Alfred Knightbridge played the part of a monk.

26.9j The Gimson Trophy - This trophy was inaugurated in memory of Brigadier Gimson. Various local dramatic societies: Great Totham, Wickham Bishops, Bocking, Braintree, Kelvedon, and All Saints Maldon perform one act plays. The adjudicators' comments are eagerly awaited and the winners receive a trophy.

26.10 Heybridge Darby and Joan Club

The inaugural meeting of this club took place on 20th February 1975 in Heybridge Community Centre under the auspices of the WRVS when Mrs. Hill became chairman and Mr. and Mrs. Kettle and Mrs. Cannon took leading roles. About fourteen other names were mentioned as being present. Mrs. Ivy Churchill was chairman in the 1900s and around that time Joan Mansfield became secretary and treasurer. In 2011 Mrs. Janet Logan, assisted by a committee, runs the club.

Maldon WRVS persuaded the Heybridge Club to accept members from Maldon when Maldon lunch clubs had no vacancies. Originally, transport was provided for those who needed it by a rota of WRVS controlled drivers using their own car but now the club books and pays for Viking transport for a mileage charge of £1 per mile. Passengers arrive between 10.15am and 10.30am, tea and coffee is served and members enjoy social time when they do what they want - read newspapers or magazines, play cards (whist, sevens, WHOT, chinese patience) or chat.

A very important event of the day is the two course lunch served around 12.15pm. In the early days, the WRVS was able to provide a rota: four teams of volunteer lady cooks who shopped, cooked and used their own transport. Today, only Mrs. Titheridge and Mrs. Ivy George are the volunteer cooks. Mrs. Titheridge shops for the food; great care must be taken as to the choice of menu since demanding cooking regulations must be followed, and then she and Mrs. George cook and serve the food. Some new younger retirees help with laying tables, serving the food and washing up. Unfortunately, there has always been a shortage of Derbies, none lately.

On the rare occasions when Mrs. Titheridge and Mrs. George are not available, fish and chips are collected from the shop. Vegetarians and diabetics are catered for.

Ivy George received the MBE in 2001 when she had given over 30 years' service to Maldon lunch clubs, to Heybridge Darby and Joan Club and to Meals on Wheels and she has received the WRVS Service Medal and Clasp. There are many members of Heybridge Darby and Joan Club who are younger than their cooks.

After lunch four or five more members arrive. Occasionally there is a talk; recently a sailmaker spoke about his life and craft, the Plume School Performing Arts Department gave a programme of songs and dance, the NHS directed seated exercises monthly that were very popular until funds ran out, and there was a demonstration by Canine Partners.

There is a weekly raffle and competitions. The club's birthday and Harvest Festival are celebrated; at Christmas there is a buffet lunch to which the cooks, Viking drivers and others who helped the club are welcomed.

The club organises some visits to garden centres where plants can be viewed, shops visited and tea is available.

26.11 Maldon Society

This society was founded in 1957 to stimulate interest in the history of Maldon, to study planning applications in Heybridge and Maldon and to help to preserve the best in architecture, the appearance and the character of the area. The society has installed blue plaques in Heybridge and meets monthly for interesting lectures.

The Maldon Museum collection of photographs was given to the Maldon Society. John and June Prime founded the photographic archive in Maeldune Heritage Centre in 1991. Originally there were 2,250 glass plates, negatives, black and white paper photographs and postcards from 1861 to 1972. Digitisation began in the 1997 and there are now 11,700 photographs and more continue to be received. They may be viewed at the Maeldune Centre. Lloyd Blackburn has now joined John Prime to continue the work.

26.12 Latchingdon Arts and Drama Society

This society was founded in 1958. Peter Jones has produced every play since the first production in January 1958. Whilst LADS is a big team effort, their real success is due to Peter Jones' charismatic leadership. In addition to a core of members who travel in from a wide area including Heybridge, talented amateur actors coming to live in Essex are attracted to this adventurous, bold society. Youngsters are encouraged, especially in the annual Show Hits productions that raise money for charity, to enjoy the rehearsals and benefit from the stage training. Many progress to perform in the main productions. The 100th production was Cavalcade in 1995 in the village hall. The society last performed in Latchingdon Village Hall in January 1998. Amazing feats were accomplished on the 15ft. wide stage.

Peter Jones is a farmer who inherited London Heyes Farm from his father; LADS is his hobby and he had a dream of building a theatre. He designed a dual purpose building that could house and repair the farm machinery and also be a theatre with a raised roof at one end so that scenery could be 'flown' in. Planning permission for the dual use was initially granted for five years to see whether the performances would cause traffic problems. There was one condition; there were to be only four productions a year. His farm workers built the large shed which now houses vintage tractors. These tractors were no longer required when the farm reverted to grass that had been ploughed up during the wartime food campaigns. Beef cattle are now reared on the pastures.

Kathy Lang remembers accompanying Peter Jones and two other members to Severalls Hospital Colchester when the vast theatre of this mental hospital was being dismantled. They toured the theatre and selected things they knew the society could use; curtains, chairs, props, back stage rigging lighting, gantry and exit signs. A team of five LADS members took five years to create today's amazing theatre - the Tractor Shed. The 'theatre' has a spacious stage, elegant curtains, a central block of seating on either side of which are the old tractors. The computer controlled lighting system and professional sound systems at the back of the auditorium were bought. A small team of four builds the scenery. The first performance in the Tractor Shed was Cinderella in February 1998. The Green Room below the wardrobe where the society's extensive collection of costumes are stored is on the side of the auditorium. The car park adjoins the Tractor Shed but groups come by coach to the performances that average four a year.

Kathy first attended a performance of Fantastic Fairground at Latchingdon Village Hall in 1984 as a member of the audience. She helped with costumes for the first time in 1991 when she made a costume for her daughter, Emma, in the Canterbury Tales. Since the departure of the then wardrobe mistress, she has made most of the costumes for large and small productions. She devises and makes costumes for period plays, modern plays and plays in foreign settings, now having a fine collection of clothes. She and her daughter performed in Under Milk Wood in 1992 and Kathy has since performed in around fifteen productions. The society continues to thrive and give polished performances of adventurous plays.

26.13 British Motorcycle Owners' Club

This club was started in 1984 in the Ship Public House in Maldon. They moved to Draper's Farm two years later. All of the members, numbering around eighty-five, own British motorcycles. The club meets twice a month and members go on rides and they fund raise for the Air Ambulance as well as having barbecues and other social events.

26.14 Camera Club

This is a thriving friendly club for traditional and digital photographers. There is a separate portrait group which photographed Heybridge Parish Council in the 1990s. The club meets on Thursdays from September to May for lectures and practical sessions.

26.15 Heybridge Bridge Club

Thirty members were present in the Waring Room in December 1986 at the inaugural meeting with students from Mrs. Yvonne Dagwell's Friary Maldon bridge class. The club moved to the new Plantation Hall in October 1992. In 2011, Bill West was the director; in his absence various members fulfil the role. The club meets at 1.15pm on Monday afternoons and enjoys a friendly reputation. There were around seventy members in 2011 and they come from places as far afield as Burnham on Crouch, Terling, Witham, Chelmsford, Tiptree and Tollesbury, there can be as many as twelve tables or as few as seven.

26.16 Maldon All Saints' Handbell Ringers

The team's bells were cast at Whitechapel foundry in 1842.

26.17 Maldon Film Club

Vanessa Cooper was instrumental in starting this club in 2005. Nineteen films are shown each year. The committee of six draws up a list of forty international films from all over the world, including South America and most European countries and the members vote for ten of them. Some of them have not been shown in the big cinemas, the rest are chosen by the committee. In addition, there are two social evenings annually.

26.18 Heybridge U3A (University of the Third Age)

The newest society in Heybridge is the Heybridge University of the Third Age (U3A). When the two branches in Maldon were full, the Heybridge branch was inaugurated in Plantation Hall in Heybridge in March 2009. Two years later, there were one hundred and fifty-eight members; few more members can be accepted since the capacity of the hall is nearly reached. Membership is open to people who are in the third age and no longer in full employment. There is a monthly meeting with a speaker. It is a self help organisation where members share and exchange educational, creative and leisure activities during the day time. Heybridge had twenty-two active groups in 2011 who meet regularly and whose activities range from bird watching to local history, to luncheons, marine and coastal, to Scrabble, to painting and photography. In 2012 a fourth U3A has started in Maldon.

Perhaps those people who complain that there is nothing going on in Heybridge could get ideas from this list.

The author playing bridge at U3A

Aerial view showing the location of three caravan parks

PHOTO By kind permission of the family ofPadge Wakelin

A   Barrow Marsh Caravan Park

B   Mill Beach Caravan Park

C   Three pounds into which water flowed on rising tides. Sluices diverted water
    as the tide went out to drive the water wheel

D   Saltcote Mill

E   Happy Days Caravan Park

F   Mill Beach Hotel

27.0 Caravan Parks in Goldhanger Road, Heybridge

There are two caravan parks westward from Decoy Point built on the site of The Round Tree; a large prominent tree marked on maps as long ago as 1900. Along this section of the shore there is a small natural beach known as Mill Beach which runs along the foot of the sea wall. Suzanne Benbow remembers her mother joining Hilda Butcher, Arthur's wife, and Joan Lappage, Hilda's daughter, to swim at Mill Beach and visiting Butcher's café there. I have been told that many ladies of that generation and their children swam regularly in the river. It is sad that today there is no public right of way onto the sea wall between Goldhanger and Heybridge Basin.

The four serviced caravan parks in Heybridge: Osea Road, Mill Beach, Happy Days and Barrow Marsh are situated in the Flood Risk Zone where the risk of flooding is acute, particularly during the winter months. Present day policies prohibit further permanent accommodation in these areas as well as restricting access to caravans in the winter. Mill Beach opens from April to October; the other three parks open from March to November. In the 1960s, 70s, 80s and 90s each caravan park had their own sailing club and bar. At one time, all four caravan sites had shops selling groceries, vegetables and sweets - none do now.

Campers enjoyed fetes and other village fun. Locals welcomed them and good causes, including the church fete, benefited. It is sad that Maldon Carnival no longer attracts the crowds of the past and the massive firework display, staged on the Marine Lake, a natural arena, can no longer take place because there are too few helpers and the insurance premiums are prohibitively high. Let us hope they will be revived.

27.1 Osea Leisure Park

Diversification in farming is not new. In 1931, at a time of farming depression, Osea Leisure Park was established by Leslie and Mabel (nee Bunting) Speakman who farmed Vaulty Manor Farm. They established a camp site on marsh land where sheep grazed and mussels were found when there was no sea wall to protect the site, merely a hump of soil with a ditch on the camp side crossed by wooden bridges with steps up the hump. The sea wall has been raised and strengthened many times but especially after the heavy flooding in 1953.

Visitors used to arrive on motorcycles and side cars from as far afield as London bringing palliasses, ridge and bell tents or they bivouacked. Receipts from 1935 show that a bicycle paid 1d., a bivouac was 6d., a bell tent £35 for a season, a ridge tent 4s.6d. and a motorcycle 9d. for three nights. Campers bought straw to stuff the palliasses from Speakman's farm and everyone had a big bonfire with the straw at the end of the season. Mrs. Speakman sold eggs, beans, potatoes and milk to the campers. A newspaper seller came round the site on his bike and a man in a wheelchair sold stamps. A mobile fish and chip van stopped outside Wakelin's Farm once a week.

Pat Yates' parents had camped before W.W.2 and travelled on a motorbike from Chadwell Heath. After the war, Pat Yates (nee Ellis) remembers they had a ridge tent, cooked on a primus stove, had a biscuit tin for an oven and cooked the fish which fishermen landed on the beach. One night, eels escaped from an enamel bowl and wriggled all over their tent. They were next door to the Turner family who had a bell tent. In 1947, her father and friends built a basic chalet which came in sections on a lorry. They had an oil lamp, a calor gas cooker and, in a hut behind the chalet, an Elsan toilet which was emptied at night by Charlie Upson who worked on the Speakman's Farm and lived at Aerodrome Bungalow on the Goldhanger Road. They were joined by others and the camp, which began on two fields, gradually expanded to cover six. Tents, chalets and caravans were sited around the edges leaving a big open space in the centre of the site. Children enjoyed making nests out of the newly cut hay in May or June. Communal shower blocks were built and more Elsan disposable points installed. When the early chalets were demolished, it was found that some had been built around charabancs.

Marilyn Green, nee Clark, remembers her mother and father, two brothers and her twin sister making the 'long' journey from Chelmsford to Osea Road in the early 1950s in Fowler and Hewitt's builders' lorry which belonged to the firm where Mr. Clark was employed. Later, he owned a car during the time when there was a massive increase in car ownership. (There were 2.3 million cars and vans on the roads in Britain in 1951, the number had quadrupled by 1964 to 8 million. The first car to sell one million was the Morris Minor designed by Alec Issigonis in 1948. He produced the Mini in 1959 and 5 million were sold. The first Minis cost £350). Pat's family was not alone in going down to the camp nearly every weekend from Easter onwards and often stayed for six weeks in the summer.

Marilyn Green's family took part in the camp site fancy dress competitions each year. She remembers her twin sister being dressed as a hula hula girl while she was a snowdrop. They joined in sports and rounders. Marilyn remembers falling off a plank that bridged the dyke crossing from the field to the sea wall and having to sit in a round tin bath afterwards to wash off the mud.

In the 1940s and 50s, Tom Lewis moved from Mill Beach shop to a wooden hut built on stilts over the sea wall on Osea Road site. The shop was open fronted with a roofed area at the front. He had a fridge and sold ice cream, bottles of fizzy drinks as well as milk, bread, coffee, snacks, sausages, fruit and vegetables; inside there were a few slot machines including 1d. games machines for children. He was helped by his daughter, Sheila, and later by his three grand daughters. As the shop was seasonal, during the winter months he delivered logs.

At one time, there were five hundred caravans, tents and chalets on the Osea Road Park sited around the edges of the fields. In the 1970s, the whole site was redeveloped; the park owners said this was to satisfy the changing needs of clients. Existing tenants had to remove their caravans, tents, and railway carriages! Some like Mr. Ellis who had built his chalet with a veranda had to demolish them. Today, the caravans are luxuriously fitted out; all have internal facilities and are linked up to electricity, mains water supply and the sewer. Owners pay an annual licence fee for their site. Some retired people make this their only home and go to Spain during the months of December, January and February when overnight stays are not permitted. To preserve the family atmosphere, no sub-letting is permitted. Tenants come from all over England; from as far apart as Bristol and Newcastle-upon-Tyne but even local people from Tiptree and Heybridge have caravans on the site. The attraction of the site is evident from the fact that some of the original tenants still come. Today, there are four hundred static caravans that are protected by CCTV cameras and automatic barriers. The standard plots are sited at right angles to the made-up roads with strips of grass between them where some people plant flowers and shrubs. The arrangement seems spacious. At one end, caravans are in a circle around a landscape feature on larger plots. Caravans from various manufacturers are for sale and boast double glazing and central heating. A recent innovation is attractively wooden clad lodges that arrive on the site in two sections and are put together to form three bedroom accommodation with living rooms, kitchens and balconies. The lodges have to be moveable on wheels and are in a line parallel with Osea Road; land is being cleared for more lodges. Some people remember it nostalgically from their childhood; the simple lifestyle and a bit of roughing it so that you knew you had been on holiday. Mrs. Margaret Emberton, who has been coming for fourteen years, showed the author around her caravan. It was a revelation; a sitting room at the front, a kitchen with a big bottle of gas, cooker and kitchen sink next to what she called a single bedroom but it contained twin beds and then a shower, toilet and wash basin. Passing by this there was a double bedroom with its own wash basin and toilet. A visitor, Bill Murphy, was resting in her attractive garden. He had been coming for thirty years and remembers when there were garden competitions.

Margaret and Bill chronicled the changes that have taken place on the site. They remembered the communal shower blocks and the Elsan disposal points, known as 'bucket and chuck it', and feel, that in some ways, the old arrangement fostered a camaraderie that has been lost. There used to be sports days around a big, open marquee where the ladies served refreshments and soldiers from Colchester barracks helped to organise the day. There were discos, raft races for 'children' of all ages and raffles that raised hundreds of pounds; for example, £12,000 was raised for thalidomide victims. Pat Yates and Marilyn Green recalled times when they went down Osea Road for winkles or, armed with buckets and rakes, walked across toward Northey for cockles at low tide. The winkles were carried back to the tent to be boiled - when they screamed. A pin was used to extract the flesh. There was a spinney where they climbed trees and everyone went on the beach at high tide. Children, as well as adults, played outdoors; swam in the river, had canoes, and picked teams for games such as rounders. In the evening, many walked along the sea wall or along the road to Millbeach Hotel and were dive bombed by bats. A sailing club was founded by campers around 1958; it met on the beach, next they had a beach hut as the club house and then a purpose built club house with a slip way that burned down mysteriously in the late 1980s. The club was never reformed.

Today, the park is often strangely quiet, although many residents have bicycles and go for bike rides. The private members' clubhouse 'The Osea Barge', built overlooking the estuary, has a licensed bar, family room, pool room, catering and entertainment at weekends by professional performers, karaoke and horse racing games. The shop on the sea wall has now closed.

Mrs. Speakman used to raise turkeys and let them wander round the fields to fatten up as Christmas approached; often they used to roost on Pat Yates' chalet veranda. The turkeys were taken to Maldon station for trains to London. During W.W.2 Mabel Speakman's daughter, Pamela, drove ambulances and milked cows. The Speakman family continue to farm the land of Vaulty Manor. They bought many of their farm implements from Bentall's but Vaulty Manor Farm House has been sold and is licensed for civil wedding ceremonies and caters for weddings and other functions and there are chalets in the former farmyard. The grand daughter of the founder, Mrs. Boutflour, and her daughter, Janie Robinson, actively concern themselves with the day-to-day running of the Osea Road Leisure Park. Alf Foakes began work on the farm sixty-six years ago, in 1988 he moved over to the park as groundsman. He was still going strong at 80 teaching the ropes to new staff.

27.2 Mill Beach Caravan Park

The land currently belonging to Mill Beach Park Caravan Park and Barrow Marsh Caravan and Chalet Park was one unit in the nineteenth and early twentieth centuries and known as Barrow Marsh or Barrow Hills. They came under separate ownership after W.W.1; Barrow Marsh was owned by the Rev. Ling and farmed by Douglas Wakelin who was able to buy it in December 1918. Mr. C. R. B. Barrett sketched Mill Beach in 1891 when only two of the wind sails were left. When he visited a year later, the windmill had gone and in its place was a restaurant. Arthur Butcher bought the foreshore adjoining Mill Beach Hotel in 1930 and the field behind on which people camped in bell tents. Towing caravans began to come just before W.W.2. During W.W.2, Jack Rayner remembers he and his friends were playing on the site when soldiers were based there with their tanks training to invade France. Petrol was rationed; the boys found cans of petrol in the pig shed in the middle of the field where May and Butcher dumped sawdust to burn. Soldiers had removed the petrol from ships and were selling it.

Dan Kingston owned two public houses in the East End of London; the Adam and Eve, where he and his wife lived, and the William IV that his father managed. When looking for a house outside London before W.W.2, he found that agricultural land values were so low that he could buy a farm for the same price as a house. Advertisements at the time quoted £5 per acre. Dan was certain war was coming and thought, quite rightly, that a farm would be a good idea. He bought Honeypot Farm at Weeley in about 1938. Later, he moved to another farm nearer to Clacton-on-Sea. Noticing that the caravan park on Valley Farm was doing well after the war, he contacted the owner, an elderly widow, and secured first refusal should she decide to sell. The time came and the transaction seemed to be settled when Dan went away for a week's holiday and returned to find the vendor's solicitor had assembled a group of financial backers who bought the caravan park. However, in conversation with a relation, George Chaplin, an estate agent, Dan learned that he was auctioning Mill Beach for the Butcher family. There were chalets and a café on this land that were not profitable. Dan paid £4,500 for it; a large sum in 1947. He knew that East Enders were not savers and liked to spend their money and he was proved right as caravans were brought to the site. Some tenants planted gardens and had roses on pergolas that hid the separate earth closet. Holidaymakers and day trippers patronised the general shop and café on the seawall. Mr. Rowe, a Kelvedon barber, hired one of the ten beach huts before Mr. Kingston acquired the site. The author remembers spending the days there in the 1940s. The hut was built on stilts and their son-in-law said the family would crawl under it when enemy aircraft flew over. When the first hut disintegrated, Mr. Rowe moved to another one that his grandson was still renting in 2012. There were ten beach huts when Dan Kingston acquired the site, only two remain.

Millbeach was flourishing before cheap package foreign holidays began in the 1950s. Now, Londoners use their caravans at weekends and many retired people stay for longer visits in the summer. Dan agreed to sell Mill Beach in the early 1950s, but the sale was never completed on his wife's advice and he managed to rescind the contract for a price. The site's handyman, John, cycled from Latchingdon to work and Dan gave him a new bicycle. Dan Kingston managed the site from 1947 for 25 years. He was a man of vision; he saw opportunities and had the courage to take them. His son, Rupert, took over and now his son, Matthew, manages the park.

Robert Pleace, who rents the shop premises, remembers when there were four toilet blocks with showers. Now every caravan is linked up to the sewer and electricity. Here too the 'bucket and chuck it' regime fostered a friendly atmosphere that seems to have been lost. Now luxury caravans are sited on plots and have sitting areas and many have small metal sheds for the storage of garden furniture etc. It is very quiet. Mr. Pleace remembers when he sold smokeless fuel in 28lb sacks for the fires that used to heat the caravans and the cupboards built around the chimneys to air washing. He sold 5cwt of smokeless fuel each week. Cookers and gas mantles for lighting were fuelled by calor gas cylinders that stood outside the caravans. Families stayed for the six week school holidays and Ford's workers came when the whole factory closed for two weeks.

By the mid 1970s, it was apparent that holidaymakers did not want non-serviced caravans so the site was re-modelled in 1986. Facilities were improved and hard surfaced roads constructed and henceforth the type of caravan was strictly controlled. The site fee in 2006 was £1,200 per year and included rates, VAT, and electricity. It had been seven guineas in 1948. All caravans have full main services connected; water, electricity and drainage. Some even have central heating and double glazing. Originally, the site was licensed for three hundred and fifty caravans, now there are two hundred and ninety five. Day visits are allowed during the winter closure. In 1960, the Rivers Board repaired and raised Mill Beach sea wall and the Environment Agency carried out more work in 1999.

Mill Beach Sailing Club, with the club house next to the boundary with Osea Road Leisure Park, was owned by Dan Kingston. It burned down in 1993, a year after the shop.

Mill Beach Caravan Park Shop

David Cannon, sometime Mayor of Colchester, remembers cycling to Mill Beach from his home in Tiptree. When his friend had drunk a bottle of Daniels' mineral water, he threw the bottle into the bushes behind the kiosk. David went to look and found many empty bottles. He made about seven trips to the site, collected bottles, took them home washed them and took them to a nearby shop to claim 1d. for small bottles and 2d. for large ones.

Tom Lewis ran a shop on the sea wall until he moved to Osea Road Park. The author remembers that the floor of the first shop at Mill Beach was level with the sea wall and adjacent to it; the building was a timber structure covered with chicken wire and plaster and painted white. Holiday makers bought their groceries and supplies from the shop before the days of local supermarkets. Now, it is only a convenience store for the things they have forgotten. The space below the first shop was used for storage including tractors. This building burned down two weeks before the site closed for winter in 1993 and the new brick building was ready the next year. It had to be sited 6 metres behind the sea wall. The ground floor was used as the shop and for light refreshments and a launderette. Upstairs in the club room there are two massive television screens, a pool table and bar. Sunday lunches are served here and holiday makers from the other caravan parks come to enjoy the food. Richard Pleace and his wife came to run the shop in 1966 and, later, the club. Their son, Robert and his wife, Margaret, run the shop and club now, assisted by their son, Robert 2 and his wife, Caroline.

27.3 Barrow Marsh Caravan Park

Douglas Wakelin had to give up farming in 1929 as a result of the depression; the farmland was sold to his brother, Richard Wakelin, and his brother-in-law, George Bunting. Douglas's family stayed in Barrow Marsh Farm House. Chickens were kept in the large field to the north of the site in 1930; this field was known as chalet field. In the late 1930s chalet field became available to campers. Campers with their bell tents came on the front field north of Goldhanger Road. Visitors stayed in their tents while they built chalets on the chalet field. A tenant placed three railway carriages close to the entrance to chalet field and used it as a holiday base.

In 1940, when the war was going badly, all use and development was stopped at Barrow Marsh and Mill Beach. The three fields where the caravans and chalets are now were too wet to be ploughed up. This is still a problem today. The chalets surround a large 'village' green where there is adventure equipment. Suzanne Benbow remembers visiting Mrs. Uniack from Brentwood who had an old railway carriage in the front field - she visited in a small car.

Peter Wakelin was cycling home from Maldon Grammar School in July 1944 when an ARP warden stopped him and told him that a doodle bug had destroyed Barrow Marsh Farm House and stack but that his parents were fine. Men on the stack threshing had been blown off. John Wakelin remembers he, his wife and two sons moved into one of the railway carriages in chalet field for six months until a small bungalow near the road, known as Magrath, became empty. Mrs. Douglas Wakelin's niece Suzanne Benbow remembers visiting Magrath with her friends and having great fun; her aunt organised activities and joined in with them - she was not interested in housework!

After 1945, some Londoners discovered Mill Beach chalets and asked to build their own chalets on Barrow Marsh, others brought caravans for the other non-arable fields. In the early 1950s, Mr. and Mrs. Wakelin ran a shop selling mainly local fruit and vegetables and free range eggs. Their customers came from Mill Beach as well as Barrow Marsh and there were long queues in the summer months. Peter Wakelin remembers that Arthur and Hilda Butcher ran a café opposite the caravan site on the other side of the road selling teas, soft drinks and ice creams with a shell fish stall nearby where the windmill used to be. The site and caravans suffered badly during the 1953 floods. A breach in the sea wall led to the front field and the low field being under water. Mr. Wakelin toured the site in a boat viewing the caravans floating in the water. Fortunately, everything was in order for the summer.

Today, the caravan site is on three of the farm fields near the road. It is owned now by the sons of Douglas Wakelin; John Wakelin, a retired headmaster, who resides in Cambridge but who lives in the bungalow on the site for the six summer months and his brother, Peter, who farms in Little Totham. The site of the old farm was developed in the late 1980s. The ages and design of the caravans situated in two fields adjacent to the road vary. They have well established gardens with flowers and roses and even vegetables but the design of fences is different and plots vary in size and shape. The ground rents depend on the length of the caravan. Mrs. Hillman, the manager, told the author that until electricity came, in 1988, caravans were lit with mantles in gas lamps that had to be lit and heating and cooking was carried out with gas from calor gas cylinders. Some caravan owners had electric generators. Caravans that were connected to the electricity supply when it became available were metered.

A new building containing lavatories, wash basins, showers and washing machines was erected in 1983. More caravans and chalets were connected to the water supply. In 1988 electricity was provided for the whole site for any tenant who wished to be connected and a sewerage system was introduced gradually to be available by the end of 1990. There is provision for the internet.

It was in 1963 when Grace Gosling and her docker husband from Poplar visited two of her husband's work mates in their caravans in Barrow Marsh. When they saw a small, low caravan for sale at £75, they courageously bought it and paid the ground rent of £12 a year. They tidied up the site that year. In 1964, they bought a caravan that had been a builder's office in London and towed it down to Barrow Marsh. Since then, and always on the same site, they have bought a series of second-hand caravans but their last one was new. They were joined by their friends, Kathleen Waller and her husband from Stepney. They were very poor in early times. Grace and her three daughters and a son and Kathleen and her two sons and a daughter lived like gypsies during the six weeks' school holidays. They used to walk across fields to Heybridge Basin to buy meat at Leonard's, the butcher, and remember one shopkeeper who gave them carrots to go with the meat. Kathleen's husband was a butcher and when he brought meat on his visits it was welcome because money was tight.

Mr. Wakelin had a shed on the site where he sold basic groceries, sweets and chickens he had reared. Before electricity came to the site, Grace remembers that they powered their television sets with six volt batteries; the picture got smaller as the batteries ran down and viewing had to be carefully selected so that there would be power for 'Coronation Street'. She and her husband are grateful to Mrs. Thatcher for enabling them to buy their council home and they are amazed at the price they have reached in the open market in the early years of 2000. Kathleen would like to sell up on Barrow Marsh site and move into the Maldon area.

Kathleen and Grace remembered Mrs. Andrews, a teacher, who welcomed children some thirty years ago to her caravan and planned activities for them; she was strict and demanded high standards. Today, during the long school holidays, the popular manager, Mrs. Margaret Hillman, hires a leader who may be a student to organise games (cricket, volley ball, football, rounders etc.) for a small fee per session from 2pm to 4pm and 6pm to 8pm. Grace and Kathleen enjoyed 'tanner' bingo sessions at Mill Beach but they never left their children alone in the evenings. Today, Grace's three daughters have caravans nearby as have Kathleen's two daughters; she gave her son a caravan but he had to sell it to help buy a house at Rayleigh. The children enjoy playing outside because 'playing out' is unsafe in London. Caravaners celebrated the Queen's Jubilee in 2002 with a big sports day followed by a disco in a marquee. This now happens every year.

In 2009, there are one hundred and sixty-six caravans and chalets on Barrow Marsh, of these fifteen were not on the sewer and only two had no piped water or electricity supply. However, these numbers are likely to be reduced shortly. Shower blocks with washing machines are available and are spotlessly clean. The advertisement in Taylor's, the estate agents in Maldon in September 2007, for "an early two bedroom chalet style (wooden) detached holiday home" with en-suite w.c, shower room and smart furnishings on the original chalet field, for £65,000, would astonish the first owner.

27.4 Happy Days Caravan Park

Reginald and Doris Norburne parked their Blue Bird caravan on Mill Beach Park after W.W.2. They lived in Collier Row and believed it was good for the health of their son and two daughters to come to Mill Beach whenever possible. Their caravan was flooded with two inches of water during the 1953 floods. They learned that the field next to Saltcote Mill was for sale and were able to buy it for £1,750 on 3rd September 1953 through George Ernest Reed, one of a group of relations who had inherited it from a spinster aunt. The large shed on the frontage that was full of tents was not included in the transaction and they were not able to buy it until some years later. They named the field Happy Days. Grass on the field was waist high and had to be burned in big bonfires. Their son Peter, aged 8, received a reward for the hundreds of milk bottles that were taken away in a milk float that he had collected from all over the field. Two or three bell tents were up permanently and two or three tiny little caravans were parked on the site. In order to get a licence, Mr. Norburne had to build a toilet block and install water closets; cess pits were installed so that the effluent was piped straight into the River Blackwater. Mr. Hallet, Borough Sanitary Inspector, came and pulled the chain and then granted a licence for fifty static caravans. Sites for caravans are rented for a year; in 1954 the charge was £11.0s.0d. per annum.

Early visitors used to come by bus and train. Caravan owners are a varied group of people; one customer surprised Peter Norburne - he came to buy a caravan in a Ford Fiesta and then visited in a Rolls Royce, leaving his telephones at home; one owner sold his home and built a granny annexe on to his daughter's house where he and his wife go in the closed season; another has family in New Zealand where they go in winter; another has a home in Spain and comes in July and August when Spain is too hot and others go abroad during the winter. There are shop keepers who live over their shop while 10% regard the caravan as their main home.

To prepare for the closed season, electricity is turned off; all pipes are drained and anti-freeze put in w.c. pans. Owners do not usually visit in winter because they know their caravans are safe.

Improvements seem to be being made all the time; only one road remains to be paved with brick blocks. When a contractor made a bad job of one of the roads, Mrs. Norburne took up all the bricks so they could be laid properly. Again, the personal management of the park is reflected in the quiet friendly atmosphere. Happy Days is on a convenient bus route and the opening of Tesco halved the sales overnight in the site's shop making it no longer viable. There was a licensed club which was so successful that a marquee used to be needed over the August Bank Holiday. Now drink driving laws deter local people from joining the club. Foreign holidays have replaced a stay in a caravan as a summer holiday goal and caravans are used as a week-end retreat.

Peter Norburne is planning for his retirement. He has recruited a warden to free him and his wife from the seven days a week, 24 hour tie and his children have made successful careers elsewhere. He plans to demolish the shop, the club house and his own home to build a new house for himself. There used to be three chalets on the sea wall that were let out in the season by the week. They became dilapidated and he is refurbishing two of them, the third must be demolished as a planning condition for the new house. The two chalets will be sold on a thirty year lease.

All caravans were on concrete bases when Peter Norburne took over in 1979 and all caravans were connected to electricity in the early 1980s when the supply was put underground. A new caravan cost £515 in 1966 but in 2008 they cost an average of £30,000. Since caravans have become much larger; two are placed where three used to be sited. All caravans are now serviced with their own sanitation and showers. Again, older residents miss the camaraderie of the toilet blocks, they used to walk down to the bath in their dressing gowns and curlers to shower or bath and chat with neighbours on the way.

27.5 Touring Caravan Sites

Members of the Caravan Club can find pitches for their stays from this organisation. They list certified locations that accommodate up to five caravans. Currently sites are listed at Saltcote Hall in Heybridge, in Goldhanger at Pear Tree Farm Hatfield Peverel, and Burnham on Crouch.

MILL BEACH CAMP FROM SEA WALL

Two beach huts remain out of the ten original. SOURCE Ellen Hedley collection

Pat Yates dressed in Junion Jack with friends celebrating Festival of Britain 1951 in Osea Leisure Park

28.0 Recreation Areas

In addition to some small informal play areas, the village has four major recreational areas:

(a) King George V Playing Field

(b) Saint George's Playing Field Heybridge Basin

(c) Oak Tree Meadow

(d) Elizabeth Way Play Area

In 2009, Heybridge Parish Council and Maldon District Council invested £20,000 to upgrade Elizabeth Way Play Area especially for children under 5 years of age. They raised the footpath from Abbotsmead for easier access and to combat flooding.

Heybridge Girls' School pre W.W.1. No names but the faces may be known to existing family members.

Afterword

It is hoped that readers will have glimpsed what life was like in the past in this factory 'town'. For older readers, it may have revived happy memories and outsiders will now know that Heybridge is more than Colchester Road, The Street and Heybridge Basin.

A report of Bentall's Office v Works cricket match in 1871 shows many names still familiar in Heybridge today.

References and acknowledgements

Information has been culled from books, magazines and newspapers and from conversations with people over many years. Unfortunately, many of the sources were not recorded at the time.

Every effort has been made to discover the source of illustrations; please let me know if I have inadvertently published one that is in copyright. Over the years photographs and images have been given or loaned to me - if those who contributed contact me, I will be pleased to return them.

100 Years of the Fisher Family in Essex (1893-1993) *Rodney Bass*
A barge on the Blocks Clifford *J Cook*
  [copyright by Mrs J M Cook Western House Tenterfield Rd (J Coker)]
A Hidden Countryside *Helen Pitchforth*
A History of the Company of Proprietors of the Chelmer & Blackwater Navigation *Peter Came*
A History of Witham *Janet Gyford*
A Prospect of Maldon 1500-1689 *W J Petchey*
Around Maldon *John Marriage*
Barges *John Leather*
Booklet celebrating Maldon Bowling Club's centenary
Branch lines to Maldon *D L Swindale 1978 edition*
Brick in Essex *Pat Ryan*
Britain in old photographs
British Military Powerboat Trust
Broad Street Green 1879-1948 *Ev Last memoir (unpublished)*
Broad Street Green Church a brief history *Sylvia Tappin*
Canada Works and the Crimea War *Bridget Geoghegan*
Changing Chelmsford J*ohn Marriage (Phillimore)*
Chelmer & Blackwater Navigation Company
Chelmsford A Pictorial History *John Marriage (Phillimore)*
Church History Exhibition *C M & J D Griffiths*
Circular walks in & around Heybridge (1) the Industrial Heritage of Heybridge *B A Claydon*
Coates Cuttings *various editions*
David Williams
Deeds for the bankruptcy sale of the Hoy 1829
Deeds of 17 Goldhanger Road *P Gill*
Deeds of 3 Lime Terrace Mrs. Ken Smith
Deeds of Heybridge Cemetery *Maldon District Council*
Deeds of Pleasant Cottage *H Lewis*
Diary 1870-May 1930 *Frederick Mott*
Dissertation on the Chelmer & Blackwater Navigation *Peter Came*
ECC Historic Buildings Records Officer *Adam Garwood*
English History from Essex Sources 1750-1900 *A F J Brown*
English Social History *G M Trevelyan*
Essex and the Industrial Revolution *John Booker*
Essex Countryside April 1959 *Reginald Clarke on Sir Claude de Crespigny*

Essex Countryside *various editions*

Essex Farming 1900-2000 *Peter Wormell*

Essex Place Names *James Kemble*

Essex Police website Sir Claude de Crespigny

Essex Record Office

Essex Record Office catalogue

Essex Sail Volume 1 Port of Maldon

Football and other sports in Heybridge *E V Last 1949*

Gentlemen Cricketers of Maldon *Richard Cooper*

Goldhanger *Maura Benham*

Heinkels over Heybridge *Stephen P Nunn & A Wyatt*

Here's Good Luck to the Pint Pot *Ken Stubbings*

Heybridge Basin 1796-2002 *Denys Harrison*

Heybridge Heritage Walk *B A Claydon*

Hidden Heybridge ECC Elms Farm excavation booklet

Historical Publications

History Gazetteer & Directory of the County of Essex *William White 1848*
  (borrowed from Barry Pearce)

History of football in Heybridge *Ev Last*

History of Mill Beach Caravan Park *Rupert Kingston*

History of St Andrews Church Heybridge *C M & J D Griffiths & L & P Wood*

History of the Bentall families from Shropshire, Essex and elsewhere *compiled by Ann Turner*

Imperial War Museum Duxford

In & About Maldon Maldon Museum useful photos

In and around Maldon *R S Brazier*

Inland Waterways - map of the Navigation

Inland Waterways Journal February 2006-03-10

Islands of Essex *Ian Yearsley*

Ivan & Maisie Butcher

Langford Cross *Dr Waseem Ahmed*

Last Stronghold of Sail *Hervey Benham*

Little Totham - The story of a small village

Maldon & Heybridge in old picture postcards *P Came*

Maldon & Heybridge the Archive Photograph Series *P Lacey*

Maldon & the Blackwater Estuary *John Marriage (Phillimore)*

Maldon & the Dengie Hundred Images of England *P Lacey (Tempus Publishing Stroud)*

Maldon and Burnham Standard

Maldon and the Dengie Hundred *Patrick Lacey*

Maldon and the River Blackwater *E A Fitch 1898*

Maldon District Council

Maldon High Street West Square to Jacob's Cross 2nd Ed *George Ginn Private publication*

Maldon Society

Maldon Then & Now *Maldon & Burnham Standard*

Memoirs of Sir Claude de Crespigny *edited by G A B Dewar*

Merchant Sailing Ship Registration details 1796-1996 *Richard H Perkes*

REFERENCES AND ACKNOWLEDGEMENTS

Multi Map Birds Eye View of Heybridge

My life smilingly unravelled *Ariel Crittall*

Navigation walks - along and around the Chelmer & Blackwater *Essex County Council*

Ninety Years of Family Farming *Sir William Gavin*

Notes on the history of Marconi Sailing Club *Ron Greygoose*

Once upon a tide *Hervey Benham*

Osborne's Buses from Tollesbury *Geoff R Mill*

Osea Island on the Blackwater Estuary *Paul Fletcher, Cyril Wisbey, Albert Chaplin*

Penny Farthing Maldon Museum's magazines

Practical Ways of Flying a Carpet *John Folkard (History of L A D S)*

Report of the appeal to the House of Lords by Arthur Butcher in the matter of government sale of surplus tentage 1922 (In the House of Lords an appeal from His Majesty's Court of Appeal (England) between May & Butcher's appellant & His Majesty the King's Respondent)

Rochester Sailing Barges *Bob Childs*

Rural Britain Then And Now *Roger Hunt*

Seedtime the History of Essex Seeds *Elinor M C Roper*

Sir John Crofton obituary *Daily Telegraph 02 12 09*

St Paul's The Cathedral Church of London 604-2004
  edited by D Keene, A Burns, A Saint (Yale University Press)

Sunshine and Flowers *Ralph Newman Sadler*

Tales of the Chelmer & Blackwater Navigation e*dited D Courtman & J Marriage*

The Automobile August 1987

The Bentall Story *P K Kemp*

The Changes in the Structure of Heybridge Basin since the 19th century *Jamie Swann*

The Changing Face of Maldon & Heybridge *C G C Tait*

The Chelmer & Blackwater Navigation Cruising Guide for boaters & walkers

The Continuing Years Sadds *P K Kemp*

The development of the Friary Garden his account on the internet *Arthur Cox*

The Essex Coastline - then and now *Matthew Fautley & James Garon*

The Great Tide *Hilda Grieve*

The Industrial Archaeology of Heybridge a dissertation *Lynda Harris*

The Maldonians *David Hughes*

The Railway Barons *David Mountfield*

The Rev. John Wade Articles including Records of Victorian School Life in Heybridge

The Salty Shore *John Leather*

The Story of Ernest Doe & Sons A century of service *Alan Doe*

The Story of Moore Bros *Bryan Everitt*

The Story of the Blackwater Sailing Club *Jan Wise (Blackwater Sailing Club)*

The Story of the Chelmer & Blackwater Navigation through 200 years *J F & A M St J Cramphorn*

The Witham to Maldon Railway *Len Wilkinson*

Thomas Brassey 1805-1870 *Jack Gould*

Thomas Brassey 1805-70 the Greatest Railway Builder in the World *Tom Stacey*

Tollesbury to the Year 2000

Tollesbury Past *Keith Lovell*

Yesterday's Heroes The lives of Working Men & Women Told by Essex People